Mark H

ONE JUMP AHEAD
AHEAD

CW00693330

THE TOP NH HORSES
TO FOLLOW FOR **2019/2020**

THE AUTHOR

Mark Howard is 44 and graduated from Manchester University with a BA Honours Degree in History. For the last 26 years, he has written the National Hunt horses to follow book *One Jump Ahead*. He also writes the Flat racing equivalent, *Ahead On The Flat*. In addition, he appears as a pundit on *Racing TV* (Sky Channel 426) and, prior to that, Attheraces. He has also written for *The Irish Field*, *Sports Advisor* and *Racing & Football Outlook* (*Borderer* & *Trainer File*) and is Ambassador for the successful syndicate ValueRacingClub.co.uk

FRONT COVER: *Top 40 Prospects* entry, **TOPOFTHEGAME** (Harry Cobden) wins the RSA Chase by half a length from Santini at Cheltenham in March.

BACK COVER: Another *Top 40 Prospects* entry, **ENVOI ALLEN** wins the Cheltenham Festival bumper under Jamie Codd. The Gordon Elliott trained five year old won all four of his starts last season.

Front & Back cover photographs supplied by GROSSICK RACING PHOTOGRAPHY. The Steadings, Rockhallhead, Collin, Dumfries. DG1 4JW. Telephone: 01387 750 512.

Published by *Mark Howard Publications Ltd*. 69, Fairgarth Drive, Kirkby Lonsdale, Carnforth, Lancashire. LA6 2FB. Telephone: 015242 71826 Email: mark.howard@mhpublications.co.uk Website: www.mhpublications.co.uk

(Please note: If you are currently NOT on the *Mark Howard Publications* mailing list and you would like to be, and therefore receive all information about future publications then please post / email / phone your name and address to the above).

Printed by H&H REEDS. Southend Road, Penrith, Cumbria. CA11 8JH. Telephone: 01768 864214. www.hhreeds.co.uk

All information correct at the time of going to press. Every care is taken with compilation of *One Jump Ahead*, but no responsibility is accepted by the publishers, for error or omissions or their consequences.

All rights reserved. Unauthorised duplication contravenes applicable laws.

ISBN: 978-0-9929224-8-1

CONTENTS

INTRODUCTION 4

FOREWORD by NICK LUCK 6

TYPE OF TRACK 7

The TOP 40 PROSPECTS 9

OWNERS' ENCLOSURE

    RICH & SUSANNAH RICCI 50

    JARED SULLIVAN 52

    VALUE RACING CLUB 55

TALKING TRAINERS

    Kim BAILEY 58

    Harry FRY 63

    Warren GREATREX 68

    Philip HOBBS 74

    Alan KING 82

    Tom LACEY 89

    Donald McCAIN 93

    Olly MURPHY 99

    Paul NICHOLLS 105

    Jonjo O'NEILL 117

    David PIPE 124

    Nicky RICHARDS 129

BROMLEY'S BEST BUYS 135

CHANGING CODES 140

ENGLISH POINTERS 142

FRENCH REVOLUTION 145

HANDICAP SNIPS 151

IRISH POINTERS 155

STABLE GOSSIP 173

APPENDIX 176

INDEX 182

ONE JUMP AHEAD UPDATES 2019/2020 187

AHEAD ON THE FLAT 2020 195

INTRODUCTION

There are some things in National Hunt racing which never change. Paul Nicholls was crowned champion trainer for the eleventh time following a magnificent campaign and became only the third trainer to send out over 3000 winners, while Richard Johnson won his fourth consective jockeys' title. Over in Ireland, Willie Mullins claimed his thirteenth championship sending out 11 winners from 80 runners at the Punchestown Festival in the process, while his son Patrick won the amateur championship for an eleventh time. Just for good measure, the Closutton outfit won the French Champion Hurdle for a fifth time courtesy of the top-class mare Benie Des Dieux.

However, there are two things which will be different this winter. Firstly, there will be no R.Walsh appearing on our racecards or in the racing press. The 40 year old announced his retirement immediately after partnering Kemboy to his sixth win in the Grade 1 Punchestown Gold Cup on Wednesday 1st May. Born in Kill, County Kildare, he rode 2,756 winners, 1,050 of those were for Willie Mullins and 679 for Paul Nicholls. Siren Song provided him with his first winner in a bumper at Gowran Park on the 15th July 1995. His first Cheltenham Festival winner came aboard Alexander Banquet in the bumper in 1998 and his 59th and final one on Klassical Dream in the *Skybet* Supreme Novices' Hurdle in March. In total, he partnered 213 Grade 1 winners and was champion jockey in Ireland on twelve occasions. His CV included 2 Grand Nationals, 2 Cheltenham Gold Cups and 4 Champion Hurdles. Walsh was associated with some brilliant horses such as Big Buck's, Denman, Faugheen, Hurricane Fly, Kauto Star and, my personal favourite, Vautour. I have been fortunate enough to work with him on *Racing TV* and he is a class act in and out of the saddle.

Secondly, compatriot Noel Fehily called time on his riding career on Saturday 23rd March after steering Get In The Queue to victory at Newbury. The 43 year old rode seven Cheltenham Festival winners, including Eglantine Du Seuil for his good friend Jared Sullivan nine days before he hung up his boots. From County Cork in Ireland, he partnered 1,352 winners in total, including 27 Grade 1 victories. His first win under Rules came aboard Desertmore in a hunter chase at Clonmel on the 5th February 1998. The pair will be sorely missed.

One young weighing room member whose career is starting to gather momentum at a rate of knots is Jonjo O'Neill junior. Ever since watching him win on his father's The Tailgater at Doncaster in December 2017, I have been a big fan. Sidelined for eight months with a damaged back in 2018, he enjoyed a terrific season with 30 domestic winners last winter. Palmers Hill provided him with his first winner at Cheltenham in November, Big Time Dancer won the valuable Lanzarote Hurdle in January and the 21 year old steered the J.P.McManus owned Early Doors to

Cheltenham Festival winner number one – his father Jonjo rode his first in 1976 – in the Martin Pipe Conditional Jockeys' Handicap Hurdle. There were other momentous days to follow during the spring with his first double at Newbury on the 23rd March, including aboard Annie Mc in the mares' final, and then on Saturday 13th April, Jonjo junior clocked up his first treble. Plus, he has ridden two winners at the Punchestown Festival thanks to Dead Right (2017) and Musical Slave (2019). Granted luck, he looks champion jockey material.

Jonjo O'Neill senior has trained 26 Cheltenham Festival winners and the head of Jackdaws Castle has bolstered his team substantially during the spring/summer with a number of expensive recruits. His purchases include horses costing £62,000, £150,000, £78,000, £105,000, £160,000, £440,000, £82,000, £40,000, £20,000, £30,000 and £72,000. I am therefore delighted to include the Irishman in the *Talking Trainers* section of *OJA* for the first time since the 2005/2006 season.

Also back this year is one of Jonjo's former neighbours when he trained near Penrith in Cumbria. Nicky Richards tasted more Grade 1 glory last winter thanks to Simply Ned in Ireland, while Takingrisks won the Scottish National at Ayr. The Greystoke handler has assembled a fine team of youngsters and I spent an enjoyable afternoon at Rectory Farm in July.

Leading owners Rich Ricci and Jared Sullivan have also kindly run through their teams of exciting horses for the season ahead, while former French champion jockey James Reveley has offered his views on some of the key horses which have been snapped up to race in the UK and Ireland this campaign. James comments are included in the *French Revolution* section.

Ante-Post betting isn't everyones cup of tea but the likes of Envoi Allen (33/1) and Vautour (40/1) have certainly done me a couple of good turns in recent years, plus Min (50/1) was unlucky to bump into a certain Altior in the *Skybet* Supreme Novices' Hurdle in 2016. I suggest readers have a look at the some of the new recruits from France and Ireland which are featured in the *Top 40 Prospects*. There is some value to be found, in terms of next spring's Cheltenham Festival.

Finally, thank you to all those who have helped with the production of *One Jump Ahead* – from owners, trainers, jockeys, bloodstock agents, secretaries, photographers, proof readers etc – and subscribers for your continued support, it is much appreciated.

Enjoy the winter.

Mark Howard

FOREWORD
by Nick Luck

Broadcaster of the Year 2007, 2008, 2009, 2011, 2013 & 2014, 2016

A funny thing happened recently. I was working with Mark Howard on *Racing TV* and it wasn't raining. Far from it, in fact: the sun beat down on the Knavesmire on the fourth and final day of the Ebor Festival in August. During a brief interlude between races, our producer decided that a quiz would be the order of the day to see which member of the team could recall some of the events of the mesmerising few days that had gone before.

As widely predicted, Mark turned away the combined brain power of Hislop, Hannity and Dixon with consummate ease. I had sensibly opted for the role of question master, knowing that I had scant chance of bettering the analyst whose grip on the finer detail of the game has always been vice-like.

As predictable as his mini victory that afternoon was Mark's annual gentle chivvying to deliver the Foreword to *One Jump Ahead*, a task that is always a pleasure, but which seems so out of kilter when it's cracking the flags and you're busy going through tomorrow evening's card at Salisbury. Suddenly, those August shop-window Christmas displays seem to make sense.

In truth, the hiatus between what you might call the traditional winter jumps season is contracting all the while. Sparked up by the extensive reporting of the trainers' Open Days, you start beating the drum for the return of your favourites well before the leaves have started to fall. And that fervour is only intensified by racing's vibrant social media community, already fully engaged in whether Altior or Cyrname will emerge victorious if and when they ever should meet.

What the Twitter jousting and peacocking won't give you, however, is the objectivity and depth of knowledge that you are about to find between the covers of this book. I've said it before, but Mark is just as much about predicting the sport's power bases as he is reflecting them. His inclusion of Jonjo O'Neill in the *Talking Trainers* section, for example, is founded on the realisation (long before it was made public) that Jonjo's yard is restocked with some serious potential talent from the sales and a raft of fresh owners.

It is equally good to see the ever consistent Warren Greatrex merit a full stable tour this time: his handling of La Bague Au Roi last season was a magnificent training feat. Other personal highlights from the 18/19 season included the finishes of the RSA Chase and the Liverpool Hurdle, won respectively by Topofthegame and If the Cap Fits, both of whom unsurprisingly featured among Mark's *Top 40 Prospects* twelve months ago.

The horses mentioned, plus Tiger Roll's barnstorming second National and that fabulous and frenetic 'golden hour' at Cheltenham featuring Bryony Frost and Paisley Park, only serve to make you wish away these early autumn days that bit quicker.

I hope you enjoy *One Jump Ahead* one more time. This is the goldmine for the price of a goldfish: the book that proves that - year in, year out - Mark gets more of the answers right than most of us.

TYPE OF TRACK

AINTREE	National Course	Left-Handed, Galloping
	Mildmay Course	Left-Handed, Tight
ASCOT		Right-Handed, Galloping
AYR		Left-Handed, Galloping
BANGOR-ON-DEE		Left-Handed, Tight
CARLISLE		Right-Handed, Stiff / Undulating
CARTMEL		Left-Handed, Tight
CATTERICK BRIDGE		Left-Handed, Tight / Undulating
CHELTENHAM		Left-Handed, Stiff / Undulating
CHEPSTOW		Left-Handed, Stiff / Undulating
DONCASTER		Left-Handed, Galloping
EXETER		Right-Handed, Stiff / Undulating
FAKENHAM		Left-Handed, Tight / Undulating
FFOS LAS		Left-Handed, Galloping
FONTWELL PARK	Chase Course	Figure of Eight, Tight
	Hurdle Course	Left-Handed, Tight
HAYDOCK PARK	Chase Course	Left-Handed, Galloping
	Hurdle Course	Left-Handed, Tight
HEREFORD		Right-Handed, Tight
HEXHAM		Left-Handed, Stiff / Undulating
HUNTINGDON		Right-Handed, Galloping
KELSO		Left-Handed, Tight / Undulating
KEMPTON PARK		Right-Handed, Tight
LEICESTER		Right-Handed, Stiff / Undulating
LINGFIELD PARK		Left-Handed, Tight / Undulating
LUDLOW		Right-Handed, Tight
MARKET RASEN		Right-Handed, Tight /Undulating
MUSSELBURGH		Right-Handed, Tight
NEWBURY		Left-Handed, Galloping
NEWCASTLE		Left-Handed, Galloping
NEWTON ABBOT		Left-Handed, Tight
PERTH		Right-Handed, Tight
PLUMPTON		Left-Handed, Tight / Undulating
SANDOWN PARK		Right-Handed, Galloping
SEDGEFIELD		Left-Handed, Tight / Undulating
SOUTHWELL		Left-Handed, Tight
STRATFORD-UPON-AVON		Left-Handed, Tight
TAUNTON		Right-Handed, Tight
TOWCESTER		Right-Handed, Stiff / Undulating
UTTOXETER		Left-Handed, Tight / Undulating
WARWICK		Left-Handed, Tight / Undulating
WETHERBY		Left-Handed, Galloping
WINCANTON		Right-Handed, Galloping
WORCESTER		Left-Handed, Galloping

IRELAND

BALLINROBE	Right-Handed, Tight
BELLEWSTOWN	Left-Handed, Tight / Undulating
CLONMEL	Right-Handed, Tight / Undulating
CORK	Right-Handed, Galloping
DOWNPATRICK	Right-Handed, Tight / Undulating
DOWN ROYAL	Right-Handed, Tight / Undulating
FAIRYHOUSE	Right-Handed, Galloping
GALWAY	Right-Handed, Tight / Undulating
GOWRAN PARK	Right-Handed, Tight / Undulating
KILBEGGAN	Right-Handed, Tight / Undulating
KILLARNEY	Left-Handed, Tight
LEOPARDSTOWN	Left-Handed, Galloping
LIMERICK	Right-Handed, Galloping
LISTOWEL	Left-Handed, Tight
NAAS	Left-Handed, Galloping
NAVAN	Left-Handed, Galloping
PUNCHESTOWN	Right-Handed, Galloping
ROSCOMMON	Right-Handed, Tight
SLIGO	Right-Handed, Tight / Undulating
THURLES	Right-Handed, Tight / Undulating
TIPPERARY	Left-Handed, Tight
TRAMORE	Right-Handed, Tight
WEXFORD	Left-Handed, Tight

ACKNOWLEDGEMENTS

I would like to thank all the following Trainers who have given up their time, during the summer, to answer my inquiries:

Talking Trainers: Kim Bailey, Harry Fry, Warren Greatrex, Philip Hobbs, Alan King, Tom Lacey, Donald McCain, Olly Murphy, Paul Nicholls, Jonjo O'Neill, David Pipe, Nicky Richards, plus Colin Tizzard. Thank you also to the following secretaries for organising the appointments/answering queries: Sarah (Paul Nicholls), James (David Pipe), Carolyn Harty (Nicky Henderson), Teresa (Olly Murphy), Antonia Reid (Nicky Richards), Nicole (Henry De Bromhead), Victoria Bewley (George Bewley).

Thank you also to Anthony Bromley, David Minton & Bernice Emanuel (Highflyer Bloodstock), Nick Luck (Foreword), Declan Phelan (Ireland), Jared Sullivan, James Reveley, William Haggas, Mags O'Toole, Bobby O'Ryan, Rich Ricci, Joe Chambers (Racing Manager), Chris Richardson (Managing Director Cheveley Park Stud), Dan Downie (Axom), Joe Foley (Ballyhane Stud), Michael Shinners & Oliver Gray (*Skybet*), Fran Berry, Niall Hannity, Kate Harrington & Jonathan Neesom (*Racing TV*), Bruce Jeffryes, Ian Robinson, Scott Salkeld, James Couldwell (valueracingclub.co.uk).

The TOP 40 PROSPECTS FOR 2019/2020

ALLAHO (FR)

5 b g No Risk At All (FR) – Idaho Falls (FR) (Turgeon (USA))
OWNER: CHEVELEY PARK STUD
TRAINER: W.P.MULLINS. Bagenalstown, Co.Carlow.
CAREER FORM FIGURES: 2 - 4132
CAREER WIN: 2019: Feb CLONMEL Good/Yielding Grade 3 NH 3m

Willie Mullins has won the RSA Chase at the Cheltenham Festival on four occasions (Florida Pearl (1998), Rule Supreme (2004), Cooldine (2009), Don Poli (2015)) and there is a strong belief at Closutton that the ex-French trained Allaho will emerge as a live contender for the 2020 version.

Runner-up in a Listed hurdle at Auteuil in March last year when handled by Guy Cherel, he was bought soon afterwards on behalf of Cheveley Park Stud and joined Mullins last summer. A half-brother to three times winning stablemate Shanning, he was all the rage for the bumper at Leopardstown on St Stephen's day but could only finish fourth. Sent off 11/8 favourite in a race his stable won in 1996 with Florida Pearl, he was beaten around five lengths by Jessica Harrington's Exit Poll. Subsequent winners Sempo and Fury Road finished third and fifth respectively. Switched to hurdles and stepped up to three miles in a Grade 3 event at Clonmel in February, Allaho produced an excellent performance to beat Minella Indo by four lengths. His trainer remarked afterwards: **"He is a nice horse who disappointed me hugely in a bumper at Christmas, compared to the work he had been doing at home. He looks a real chaser in the making."** The Henry De Bromhead trained runner-up turned the tables in the Grade 1 Albert Bartlett Novices' Hurdle at the Cheltenham Festival. Ruby Walsh's mount was travelling well jumping the second last and held every chance between the final two hurdles but was ultimately outstayed having raced keenly early on. It was a similar story in the Grade 1 staying novice hurdle at the Punchestown Festival, although the winning margin between the pair was reduced to a couple of lengths. Attempting to make all, Allaho was headed on the approach to the final flight before keeping on after the last.

"He is a real chaser and I was delighted with his run when he finished third in the Albert Bartlett. I can't wait to go chasing with him next season. He is a horse that shows us plenty at home. He's a fine big chasing type," remarked Ireland's champion trainer in March. Inclined to race keenly in his races, it is possible the five year old will drop back to two and a half miles initially once sent chasing. A good jumper over hurdles, the No Risk At All gelding has the make and shape of a chaser and can take high rank over fences this winter. Rated 147 over timber, he promises to make an even better chaser.

POINTS TO NOTE:
Probable Best Distance   -   2m 4f - 3 miles
Preferred Going   -   Good/Soft
Connection's Comments: **"We were travelling really well, but Allaho just didn't have the hardness when he got a bit empty and got close to the last. He stayed on again and was running on again in the last fifty yards, but he doesn't have much experience. He's a gorgeous horse with a huge future." Ruby WALSH at Cheltenham (15/3/19)**

GOING:	R	W	P	TRACK:	R	W	P
Very Soft	1	0	1	Left Handed	3	0	2
Yielding	1	0	1	Right	2	1	1
Good/Yielding	2	1	0	Galloping	3	0	2
Good/Soft	1	0	1	Stiff/Undul.	1	0	1
				Tight/Undul.	1	1	0

TRIP:	R	W	P	JOCKEY:	R	W	P
2m	1	0	0	R.Walsh	3	1	2
2m 2f	1	0	1	Mr P.Mullins	1	0	0
3m	3	1	2	G.Re	1	0	1

AL DANCER (FR)

6 gr g Al Namix (FR) – Steel Dancer (FR) (Kaldounevees (FR))
OWNER: WALTERS PLANT HIRE Ltd
TRAINER: N.A.TWISTON-DAVIES. Naunton, Gloucestershire.
CAREER FORM FIGURES: 2314 - 11110
CAREER WINS: 2018: Mar BANGOR Soft NHF 2m; Oct CARLISLE Good/Soft NH 2m 1f;
Nov FFOS LAS Soft NH 2m; Dec CHELTENHAM Good HH 2m 1f: 2019: Feb ASCOT Good/
Soft Grade 3 HH 2m

Nigel Twiston-Davies trained 63 winners during the 2018/2019 season with his total prize-money reaching £1,257,830. Stable star Bristol De Mai won the Grade 1 *Betfair* Chase at Haydock for a second time, while novice Al Dancer provided his stable with their third win in the *Betfair* Hurdle in the last six years.

Indeed, Al Dancer is one of three exciting recruits to fences this season for the Twiston-Davies team. A grey gelding by Al Namix who cost €60,000 as a yearling, he began his career with rookie handler Christian Williams being placed in a couple of bumpers at Ffos Las during the Autumn of 2017. Transferred to Grange Hill Farm later the same season, he won at Bangor before finishing a highly creditable fourth in the Grade 2 championship bumper at Aintree's Grand National meeting.

Sent hurdling last season, he developed into one of the UK's best novices winning four of his five races and earning an official rating of 151. Successful at Carlisle and Ffos Las in October and November respectively, he then made a mockery of an opening mark of 129 when trouncing eight rivals on his handicap debut at Cheltenham's December meeting. An eleven lengths scorer, he was raised twelve pounds as a result. Nigel Twiston-Davies immediately nominated the valuable *Betfair* Hurdle as his next target and, while the race was abandoned at Newbury in February due to inclement weather, it was rescheduled at Ascot a week later. Despite racing keenly early on, the grey held too many aces for his rivals and wasn't hard pressed to win by nearly three lengths. Sent off 9/2 joint favourite for the *Skybet* Supreme Novices' Hurdle, Sam Twiston-Davies' mount was in trouble soon after the third last before finishing a disappointing tenth behind Klassical Dream. His trainer commented afterwards: **"Nothing has come to light since the race. It wasn't long (24 days) after the Ascot race – maybe Cheltenham came too soon for him."**

I like the fact Al Dancer skipped Aintree and Punchestown and was allowed to fill his ample frame during the summer. In terms of his future, it is interesting to note his trainer's comments at Cheltenham last December: **"He's a beautiful mover, a lovely, proper racehorse. I'm sure he's a stayer in the future but as you saw he's quite buzzy in his races. As long as he learns to settle, he'll be going two and a half to three miles in the future."** Despite those comments, one would expect the six year old to reappear over the minimum trip before being possibly stepped up in trip later on. Although connections may be tempted to stay over hurdles and aim him at something like the Grade 3 Greatwood Hurdle at Cheltenham (17th November), it is hoped Al Dancer goes chasing.

Nigel Twiston-Davies has had 9 winners from only 25 runners (36% strike-rate) at Carlisle during the last five seasons and he invariably runs some of his best novices at the track. Don't be surprised if some of his leading novice chasers make the journey up the M5 and M6 during the Autumn. There is a two miles beginners' chase on Thursday 24th October at the Cumbria track, which looks ideal for Al Dancer's chasing debut.

POINTS TO NOTE:

Probable Best Distance	-	**2 miles**
Preferred Going	-	**Good/Soft**

Connection's Comments: "In terms of raw ability, he's superb. Look at the scope of him – he's such a good jumper and you'd imagine he'd find fences even easier." Nigel TWISTON-DAVIES at Ascot (16/2/19)

GOING:	R	W	P		TRACK:	R	W	P
Heavy	1	0	1		Left Handed	7	3	2
Soft	5	2	1		Right	2	2	0
Good/Soft	2	2	0		Galloping	4	2	2
Good	1	1	0		Stiff/Undul.	3	2	0
					Tight	2	1	0

TRIP:	R	W	P		JOCKEY:	R	W	P
2m	6	3	2		S.Twiston-Davies	5	4	0
2m 1f	3	2	0		Mr J.Savage	1	1	0
					J.Bargary	1	0	0
					C.Deutsch	1	0	1
					R.Johnson	1	0	1

CAP DU MATHAN (FR)
4 b g Kapgarde (FR) – Nounjya Du Mathan (FR) (Antarctique (IRE))
OWNER: The STEWART FAMILY
TRAINER: P.F.NICHOLLS. Ditcheat, Somerset.
CAREER FORM FIGURES: 42

Leading bloodstock agent Anthony Bromley has bought some wonderful horses for owner Andy Stewart over the years. Ten times Grade 1 winner Big Buck's tops the list but his familiar red, black and white silks have also been carried with distinction by Celestial Halo, Cenkos, Le Roi Miguel, Napolitain, Saphir Du Rheu and Tataniano, who all scored at the highest level, too. Grade 2 winners Hoo La Baloo, Le Duc, My Will, Tatenen and Turko weren't bad either.

Following a few 'quiet' years, Stewart has once again called upon the Newmarket based agent and arguably his most interesting purchase is the twice raced Cap Du Mathan. A four year old by Kapgarde, he raced a couple of times over hurdles at Auteuil under the guidance of Arnaud Chaille-Chaille. Making his debut in a conditions event for unraced colts and gelding in October, he finished a creditable fourth behind the Guillaume Macaire trained St Romain Du Derby (the third, fifth and seventh have won since). He returned to the Parisian track three weeks later and was two and a half lengths runner-up behind Arverne. The winner was subsequently sold to J.P.McManus and finished third behind Quel Destin in the Grade 1 Finale Hurdle at Chepstow over Christmas.

I spoke to former French champion jockey James Reveley in August and he feels Cap Du Mathan is a promising sort on the basis that Arnaud Chaille-Chaille's horses aren't gunned first time out and invariably improve with experience. Therefore it appears Andy Stewart and Paul Nicholls have another exciting recruit from France on their hands.

POINTS TO NOTE:

Probable Best Distance	-	2m 4f	
Preferred Going	-	Soft	

GOING:	R	W	P	TRACK:	R	W	P
Heavy	1	0	1	Left Handed	2	0	1
Very Soft	1	0	0	Galloping	2	0	1

TRIP:	R	W	P	JOCKEY:	R	W	P
2m 1f	1	0	1	P.Dubourg	2	0	1
2m 2f	1	0	0				

CHANTRY HOUSE (IRE)
5 br g Yeats (IRE) – The Last Bank (IRE) (Phardante FR))
OWNER: J.P.McMANUS
TRAINER: N.J.HENDERSON. Lambourn, Berkshire.
CAREER FORM FIGURES: U11
CAREER WINS: 2018: Dec TATTERSALLS FARM Yielding/Soft 4YO Mdn PTP 3m: 2019: Mar WARWICK Soft NHF 2m

Former champion trainer Nicky Henderson and leading owner J.P.McManus had an enviable team of novice hurdlers last season with the dual Grade 1 winner Champ, Grade 2 winner Birchdale, plus the likes of Champagne Platinum, Dickie Diver, Epatante and Rathhill. Expect more of the same during the 2019/2020 campaign and there are few more potentially exciting than ex-Irish pointer Chantry House.

A gelded son of Yeats, he was acquired for £295,000 at the Cheltenham December Sale having run in two points for Cian Hughes. Expert Declan Phelan explains: **"Given that he was originally prepared for his point debut in the spring of 2018 by the late Willie Codd, there is a sense of melancholy attached to this tall bay gelding. After Wille passed away, he moved to Cian Hughes who then raced him at Stowlin (Yielding) in April 2018: that day he made a big move from sixth to first heading to fifth last: one sensed he may have used too much gas: he was just coming off the bridle when unseating his jockey at the third last. Returning to action at Tattersalls (Yielding) in December and this time partnered by Jamie Codd (brother of the late Willie): patient tactics were employed and he came with a sustained effort from three out to conquer a decent rival, Envol Pierji, in the final hundred yards. He jumped cleanly and galloped resolutely at the climax. He changed hands when Nicky Henderson/JP McManus paid £295,000 as the sales topper at Cheltenham Tattersalls auction in December. He was a late withdrawal from two bumpers before he made light work of scoring at Warwick (Soft) in March. Signs are that Henderson fancies this horse needs some cut in the ground for optimum returns. He is a half-brother to the 128 rated The Last Day, and I think he can transform into a 140+ novice hurdler this season: he will operate at two and a half miles and a mid-term target like the Challow Hurdle at Newbury could be a Grade 1 that holds distinct possibilities for him. The Cheltenham Festival novice hurdles will also loom on his horizon, provided he gets the chance to race on rain cushioned ground, it could make him a player in the novice hurdle championship race of his choice (Ballymore?)."** A three and a half lengths winner at Warwick during the spring, Chantry House beat the Alan King trained Edwardstone who had also finished runner-up in his previous two starts.

Nicky Henderson invariably unleashes his leading novice hurdlers at either Ascot, Kempton or Newbury so don't be surprised to see the Yeats gelding reappearing at one of those venues in the Autumn. Declan Phelan nominated the Grade 1 Challow Hurdle at Newbury (28th December) as a realistic mid winter target and it is a race Henderson and McManus have won with Captain Cutter (2013) and Champ (2018). Chantry House looks a high-class novice hurdler in the making.

POINTS TO NOTE:
Probable Best Distance   -   2m 4f
Preferred Going   -   Good/Soft
Connection's Comments: "Chantry House is a nice horse. We didn't run him at Kempton because it was too quick, while Newbury just dried out last week, but he doesn't want a bog - just safe ground. He has to come on for that, but he's nice for the future and you'd dream he'd be a three-mile chaser." Barry GERAGHTY at Warwick (10/3/19)

GOING:	R	W	P	TRACK:	R	W	P
Soft	1	1	0	Left-Handed	1	1	0
Yielding	2	1	0	Right	2	1	0
				Tight/Undul.	1	1	0

TRIP:	R	W	P	JOCKEY:	R	W	P
2m	1	1	0	B.Geraghty	1	1	0
3m	2	1	0	J.Codd	1	1	0
				A.J.Fox	1	0	0

DICKIE DIVER (IRE)
6 b g Gold Well – Merry Excuse (IRE) (Flemensfirth (USA))
OWNER: J.P.McMANUS
TRAINER: N.J.HENDERSON. Lambourn, Berkshire.
CAREER FORM FIGURES: 1 - 214
CAREER WINS: 2017: Dec TEMPLENACARRIGA Heavy 4YO Mdn PTP 3m: 2019: Feb CHEPSTOW Good/Soft Mdn Hdle 2m 3f

Nicky Henderson appears to be blessed with a whole raft of promising novice chasers for this season. Angels Breath, Birchdale, Champ, Mister Fisher, Precious Cargo and Rathhill are all set to embark on fencing careers this winter. Dickie Diver, who was featured in last year's *Top 40 Prospects*, is another name to add to the list and there is every reason to believe he will develop into Grade 1 winning chaser in the future.

A twenty lengths winner of his only Irish point when handled by Michael Goff, the Gold Well gelding was acquired by J.P.McManus for £210,000 at the Goffs UK January Sale at Doncaster last year. Dickie Diver didn't make his Rules debut until January 2019 and, following an absence of 383 days, he ran a cracker at Chepstow and was unlucky not to maintain his unbeaten record. Staying on strongly after the last, he failed to reel in subsequent Grade 2 winner Lisnagar Oscar by a head. Barry Geraghty's mount had previous winners Truckin Away and Down The Highway behind him in third and fourth respectively. Returning to the same course and distance a month later, Nicky Henderson's charge made short work of his thirteen opponents. Aidan Coleman took over in the saddle and, despite a mistake at the last, he won hard held by two and a quarter lengths. That win booked his place at the Cheltenham Festival with the head of Seven Barrows commenting: **"Dickie Diver is a lovely horse, a fine chaser in the making, but he has the raw ability to run a big race in the Albert Bartlett Novices' Hurdle. He's very professional and the step up to three miles will suit him."** The six year old acquitted himself well at the Festival finishing a highly creditable fourth, faring best of the home contingent behind the Irish trio Minella Indo, Commander of Fleet and Allaho. Beaten less than eleven lengths, he held every chance at the second last before keeping on in the closing stages. Given the fact he only made his Rules and hurdling debut two months earlier, he achieved plenty in a short space of time earning an official rating of 141.

Given a break since, the decision to skip Aintree and Punchestown looks a sensible one and that patience is likely to be rewarded now Dickie Diver turns his attentions to his real vocation. He is a tremendous chasing prospect and one who could provide Nicky Henderson with his fourth win in the RSA Chase at Cheltenham next March. Remember what point expert Declan Phelan wrote in last year's *OJA*: **"Tall bay gelding with a physical presence: handled by Mick Goff for his point win at Templenacarriga (Heavy) in late December. Confidently ridden from the front, he easily outclassed his rivals as he drew right away on the uphill finish, to record a twenty lengths win in the fastest time of the day. Dare I say it, there was a touch of the racing exuberance associated with the likes of Carvills Hill and Denman, in his performance. You find some class acts in his family tree, including Merry Gale and Racing Demon. He could be one of the most exciting pointers that McManus has bought in some time. With big feet, the heavy ground was to his taste at Templenacarriga, a sounder surface for now represents an unknown factor. He could mature into a fine 140+ staying chaser."**

POINTS TO NOTE:
Probable Best Distance   -   2m 4f – 3 miles
Preferred Going   -   Soft
Connection's Comments: "He's a very nice horse and was entitled to win like he did. He can only go on from here." Aidan COLEMAN at Chepstow (23/2/19)

GOING:	R	W	P	TRACK:	R	W	P
Heavy	1	1	0	Left Handed	3	1	1
Good/Soft	3	1	1	Right	1	1	0
				Stiff/Undul.	3	1	1

TRIP:	R	W	P	JOCKEY:	R	W	P
2m 3f	2	1	1	A.Coleman	2	1	0
3m	2	1	0	B.Geraghty	1	0	1
				S.Fitzgerald	1	1	0

DOLCITA (FR)
4 b f Saint Des Saints (FR) – Orcantara (FR) (Villez (USA))
OWNER: SULLIVAN BLOODSTOCK Limited
TRAINER: W.P.MULLINS. Bagenalstown, Co.Carlow
CAREER FORM FIGURES: 32

There have been four runnings of the Grade 2 Dawn Run Mares' Novices' Hurdle at the Cheltenham Festival and Ireland's champion trainer Willie Mullins has enjoyed a clean sweep thanks to Limini (2016), Let's Dance (2017), Laurina (2018) and Eglantine Du Seuil (2019). The last two named were owned by Jared Sullivan and the same patron may have acquired another major contender for the 2020 version in the twice raced Dolcita.

From the same source in France as Let's Dance and Laurina, namely Guillaume Macaire, the Saint Des Saints filly made her debut in an eighteen runners conditions hurdle at Pau (2m 1f : Very Soft) in December. Hampered early on, she made good headway approaching the hometurn before challenging on the outside. Having run down the final hurdle – she may be better racing left-handed – Dolcita stayed on well under Bertrand Lestrade to fill third position, nearly four lengths behind the winner Montroty. The runner-up Baiser Interdit was subsequently bought by Simon Munir and Isaac Souede and won on her UK debut for Nicky Henderson at Sedgefield before disappointing next time (reportedly bled).

Reappearing at Auteuil (2m 2f : Very Soft) towards the end of February, she was denied by a nose in the Prix Marise, another conditions hurdle confined to four year old fillies. The winner Femme De Tete has been beaten in her next three outings but the fourth (Peggy) has won since. Acquired soon afterwards, Dolcita spent the summer with Noel Fehily, who looks after a number of Jared Sullivan's horses, before going into training with Mullins at the start of September. Her previous trainer was reportedly keen to hold on to her and it will be interesting to see how far she can progress for her next connections. Typically, for one who learned their trade under Macaire, she is a very accurate jumper.

POINTS TO NOTE:

Probable Best Distance			-	**2m – 2m 4f**			
Preferred Going			-	**Soft**			

GOING:	R	W	P	TRACK:	R	W	P
Very Soft	2	0	2	Left Handed	1	0	1
				Right	1	0	1
				Galloping	2	0	2

TRIP:	R	W	P	JOCKEY:	R	W	P
2m 1f	1	0	1	B.Lestrade	2	0	2
2m 2f	1	0	1				

EMITOM (IRE)

5 b g Gold Well – Avenging Angel (IRE) (Heron Island (IRE))
OWNER: The SPERO PARTNERSHIP Ltd
TRAINER: W.GREATREX. Upper Lambourn, Berkshire.
CAREER FORM FIGURES: 1 - 11112
CAREER WINS: 2018: Apr WARWICK Good/Soft NHF 2m; Nov ASCOT Good NHF 2m, FFOS LAS Soft NH 2m 4f: 2019: Jan LINGFIELD Good/Soft NH 2m; Mar NEWBURY Good/Soft NH 2m 4f

Cole Harden (World Hurdle in 2015) and One Track Mind (Champion Stayers Hurdle 2016) have provided Warren Greatrex with Grade 1 success at the Cheltenham and Punchestown Festivals respectively in recent years and the head of Uplands feels he has another potentially top notch staying hurdler on his hands in Emitom.

A gelded son of Gold Well, he was well bought for £30,000 at the Doncaster Spring Sales as a three year old. A dual bumper at Warwick and Ascot, he made a mighty impressive hurdling debut at Ffos Las in November when trouncing subsequent Grade 2 winner Lisnagar Oscar by five lengths. Stepping up to two and a half miles, Gavin Sheehan sat motionless for much of the contest before taking over at the penultimate flight. He then overcame a mistake at the first hurdle at Lingfield in January before running out a facile winner by a handful of lengths. **"He's got pretty much everything you'd want. He's seriously good and I think he's right up there** with the best I've trained. He's so talented – a bit special," enthused Greatrex afterwards. The five year old completed his hat-trick over hurdles when winning by three parts of a length from winning English pointer Interconnected (sold since for £620,000) conceding ten pounds. Having purposely swerved the Cheltenham Festival, Emitom headed to Aintree for the Grade 1 Sefton Novices' Hurdle and ran a cracker. Beaten three lengths by Nicky Henderson's Champ, he was held up early on before finishing well. **"He's run a great race. I just thought the winner got first run on us. We tracked Champ all the way and our horse has run all the way to the line. He could be a Stayers' Hurdle horse next season and is going to do very well,"** remarked his trainer afterwards. Ironically, the aforementioned Cole Harden finished runner-up behind another Seven Barrows inmate (Beat That) in the same race five years earlier.

The Grade 2 West Yorkshire Hurdle at Wetherby (2nd November) has been earmarked for Emitom's return to action. Cole Harden landed the three miles prize in 2014 en route to World Hurdle glory the following March. Fingers crossed this progressive gelding can do likewise.

POINTS TO NOTE:
Probable Best Distance   -   3 miles
Preferred Going   -   Good/Soft
Connection's Comments: **"We've always loved him at home and it's been clear from the start that he has serious ability – his two bumper wins were really impressive. I must thank Henrietta Knight who has taken him on two separate occasions to work on his jumping. She has done a fabulous job with him. He's got a long way to go but is hugely exciting and it's great to have a horse in the yard who potentially has what it takes to go all the way to the top." Warren GREATREX at Ffos Las (23/11/18)**

GOING:	R	W	P	TRACK:	R	W	P
Soft	2	1	1	Left Handed	5	4	1
Good/Soft	3	3	0	Right	1	1	0
Good	1	1	0	Galloping	3	3	0
				Tight	1	0	1
				Tight/Undul.	2	2	0

TRIP:	R	W	P	JOCKEY:	R	W	P
2m	3	3	0	G.Sheehan	4	3	1
2m 4f	2	2	0	H.Teal	1	1	0
3m	1	0	1	A.Tinkler	1	1	0

ENVOI ALLEN (FR)
5 b g Muhtathir – Reaction (FR) (Saint Des Saints (FR))
OWNER: CHEVELEY PARK STUD
TRAINER: G.ELLIOTT. Longwood, Co.Meath.
CAREER FORM FIGURES: 1 - 1111
CAREER WIN: 2018: Feb BALLINABOOLA Yielding/Soft 4YO Mdn PTP 2m 4f; Dec FAIRYHOUSE Good NHF 2m, NAVAN Yielding Lstd NHF 2m: 2019: Feb LEOPARDSTOWN Good/Yielding Grade 2 NHF 2m; Mar CHELTENHAM Soft Grade 1 NHF 2m

Two of the success stories of last season's *Top 40 Prospects* were the unbeaten bumper pair Envoi Allen and Malone Road. The former pointers won six out of six between them for Cheveley Park Stud, Gordon Elliott and Jamie Codd. The former was acquired for £400,000 at the Cheltenham February Sale last year having won his point by ten lengths at Ballinaboola eleven days earlier under the tutelage of Colin Bowe – Samcro (£335,000), another of Elliott's 25 Cheltenham Festival winners, also started his career with County Wexford handler.

A four lengths winner on his Rules debut in a bumper at Fairyhouse in early December, Gordon Elliott commented afterwards: **"He's a serious horse and a really nice prospect for the future. He ran very green and had been on grass only once this season."** Significantly, Envoi Allen then headed to Navan for a Listed contest, which the triple Grand National winning trainer has won with the likes of Don Cossack (2011), Death Duty (2015) and Samcro (2016), and the Muhtathir gelding didn't disappoint with a comprehensive four and three quarters of a length defeat of Midnight Run (won since). **"He's very good. We knew we'd get to see how good he is today and he's showed he's very good,"** enthused Jamie Codd afterwards. His third win of the season came in the Grade 2 Matheson Flat race at the Dublin Racing Festival at Leopardstown in early February. Taken wide by Codd, he stayed on strongly to beat Meticulous by a length and a quarter. His rider remarked: **"He's a beautiful specimen. He won his point-to-point this time last year at Ballinaboola. He's 17 hands and is just a monster of a horse. What you're going to see from him in the next couple of years is going to be incredible. He is a lovely jumper and is very exciting."** Envoi Allen crowned a superb season with a hard fought three parts of a length win in the Grade 1 Cheltenham Festival bumper. Leading three out, he fended off the strong challenge of Blue Sari, who was in receipt of eight pounds, to maintain his unbeaten record. His trainer said afterwards: **"He's a three mile chaser down the line – all I know is that he's a real racehorse. The most important thing about this horse is that he knows how to win, and he certainly wants to win. We have a lot to look forward to."**

It is fair to say at times that you get what you pay for and, while Envoi Allen wasn't cheap, he is an outstanding prospect for hurdles and fences. In an ideal world, Malone Road will head down the two mile route, while this five year old will be steered towards the Ballymore Novices' Hurdle at Cheltenham next spring

POINTS TO NOTE:
Probable Best Distance   -   2m 4f – 3 miles
Preferred Going   -   Good/Soft
Connection's Comments: "Envoi Allen is an incredible horse and still a big baby really. The plan is to continue to educate him for a future over hurdles. It's great to be associated with such a horse." Jamie CODD at Cheltenham (13/3/19)

GOING:	R	W	P	TRACK	R	W	P
Soft	1	1	0	Left Handed	4	4	0
Yield/Soft	1	1	0	Right	1	1	0
Yielding	1	1	0	Galloping	3	3	0
Good/Yielding	1	1	0	Stiff/Undul.	1	1	0
Good	1	1	0				

TRIP:	R	W	P	JOCKEY:	R	W	P
2m	4	4	0	J.J.Codd	4	4	0
2m 4f	1	1	0	B.O'Neill	1	1	0

FAROUK D'ALENE (FR)

4 b g Racinger (FR) – Mascotte D'Alene (FR) (Ragmar (FR))
OWNER: GIGGINSTOWN HOUSE STUD
TRAINER: G.ELLIOTT. Longwood, Co.Meath.
CAREER FORM FIGURES: 1
CAREER WIN: 2018: Mar BELCLARE Soft 4YO Mdn PTP 3m

"Bulky bay French bred gelding with a white blaze on his face. He dominated the five runner maiden at Belclare (Soft) in March, jumping boldly and proving too classy for his rivals, posting an emphatic eighteen lengths win. He appears to possess a high cruising speed. Because he was in a different league to his rivals, it is tricky to classify this horse. The Belclare track in three of the four previous annual fixtures produced above average winners from the four year old maiden. All now rated 140+ on the track: in 2015, Ballyoisin won in 6:07, in 2016 Topofthegame clocked 6:44, and in 2017 First Assignment 6:04. In a solo run in 2019 Farouk D'Alene posted a time of 6:13, which contrasted with his predecessors is respectable. He does have a light pedigree, yet the class on display encouraged Gigginstown/Gordon Elliott to pay £200,000 at Cheltenham March Sales for his future services. He is one of the more exciting prospects to emerge from the spring 2019 crop of four year olds. Aspirations for Graded success over hurdles and fences are justifiable in his case and he can be viewed as future Cheltenham Festival material. His strong galloping style leads one to regard him as likely to excel when racing at two and a half miles and upwards rather than shorter trips, though he should initially collect a two mile bumper as a starting point to his track career," believes expert Declan Phelan.

He was bought four days after his victory at the Cheltenham Festival Sale in March. Gigginstown House Stud, who have owned 91 Grade 1 winners, including two Cheltenham Gold Cups (and three Grand Nationals), are set to scale down their operation over the next few years with Farouk D'Alene being one of their last major 'signings.' Only four, the gelded son of Racinger is likely to be campaigned in bumpers this winter.

POINTS TO NOTE:
Probable Best Distance   -   2 miles
Preferred Going   -   Soft
Connection's Comments: "We thought a lot of him coming here today and thankfully he did the job." Donnchadh DOYLE at Belclare (10/3/19)

GOING:	R	W	P	TRACK	R	W	P
Soft	1	1	0	Right	1	1	0

TRIP:	R	W	P	JOCKEY:	R	W	P
3m	1	1	0	J.P.O'Rourke	1	1	0

FAUSTINOVICK

5 b g Black Sam Bellamy (IRE) – Cormorant Cove (Fair Mix (IRE))
OWNER: TAYLOR & O'DWYER
TRAINER: C.TIZZARD. Milborne Port, Dorset.
CAREER FORM FIGURES: 2 - 2

Owners Paul Taylor and Richard O'Dwyer were responsible for one of the leading novice chasers last winter. Lostintranslation won the Grade 2 Dipper Novices' Chase at Cheltenham on New Year's Day and the Grade 1 Mildmay Novices' Chase at Aintree in April, in addition to finishing runner-up behind his old rival Defi Du Seuil in the JLT Novices' Chase at the Cheltenham Festival. Colin Tizzard's seven year old is set to head down the Gold Cup route this season and, with an official rating of 161, he doesn't have to improve too much to emerge as a leading contender.

The Flemensfirth gelding isn't the only exciting prospect who carries the Taylor and O'Dwyer silks because they are also responsible for the twice raced Faustinovick. Like his more illustrious stablemate, the five year old began his career in Irish points finishing runner-up behind the potentially top-class Andy Dufresne at Borris House in March 2018. Featured in the *Irish Pointers* section of *One Jump Ahead* last year, expert Declan Phelan wrote: **"A really attractive bay gelding with a distinctive grey tail and prominent rear white sock and white star on his face. A beautiful walker, he posted an excellent debut second at Borris (Yielding/Soft) in March. Nursed around out the back for two miles by Derek O'Connor, he gradually improved his position and entered the picture as a close third jumping the third last. He was unable to match Andy Dufresne when that rival kicked on between the last two fences, and Derek elected to coast home to finish a clear second. He travelled very smoothly for much of the journey and could be a horse as comfortable at two and a half miles as three miles. Ellie Marie Holden purchased him at a cost of €26,000 at the 2017 Land Rover Sale and garnered an excellent profit by selling for £170,000 at Aintree Sales. Colin Tizzard has already demonstrated that he can upgrade a promising Irish point maiden into a top class track horse (Native River for example), and I would be very positive on the prospects of Faustinovick making a proper impact on the track in high end races. I have him amongst a select band of "very exciting" recruits from the 2018 spring campaign."**

Faustinovick made his Rules debut in a thirteen runner bumper at Newbury in early March. Sent off 4/1, Robbie Power's mount ran well in second finishing six lengths behind subsequent Grade 2 winner McFabulous. Considering it was his first run for 358 days and Paul Nicholls' victor scored in three of his four bumpers last season, it was a most encouraging run. Expected to go straight over hurdles, the Black Sam Bellamy gelding is one to follow this season and beyond.

POINTS TO NOTE:

Probable Best Distance	-	2m – 2m 4f
Preferred Going	-	Good/Soft

GOING:	R	W	P	TRACK:	R	W	P
Yielding/Soft	1	0	1	Left Handed	2	0	2
Good/Soft	1	0	1	Galloping	1	0	1

TRIP:	R	W	P	JOCKEY:	R	W	P
2m	1	0	1	R.M.Power	1	0	1
3m	1	0	1	D.O'Connor	1	0	1

FERNY HOLLOW (IRE)

4 bb g Westerner – Mirazur (IRE) (Good Thyne (USA))
OWNER: CHEVELEY PARK STUD
TRAINER: W.P.MULLINS. Bagenalstown, Co.Carlow.
CAREER FORM FIGURES: 1
CAREER WIN: 2019: Feb KNOCKANARD Soft 4YO Mdn PTP 2m 4f

As predicted in last year's edition of *One Jump Ahead*, Cheveley Park Stud made a significant splash on the National Hunt scene last season with Cheltenham Festival victories for Envoi Allen (bumper) and A Plus Tard (novices' handicap chase). Their familiar red, white and blue silks were carried to victory on thirteen occasions in Ireland and a handful of times in the UK during the 2018/2019 campaign. With the likes of Allaho, A Plus Tard, Envoi Allen and Malone Road amongst their ranks, more big race successes look assured this term, too. Their squad of jumpers has been bolstered still further with the addition of two more former Irish pointers, namely Deploy The Getaway (£200,000) and Ferny Hollow.

The latter was purchased for £300,000 at the Cheltenham February Sale. Irish expert Declan Phelan reports: **"Colin Bowe's cousin paid €38,000 for this powerfully build bay gelding at the 2018 Derby Sale. It was for the Bowe yard that he debuted at Knockanard (Soft) in February in a two and a half miles maiden. He forced the pace from the beginning: in the last mile he gradually upped the tempo: kicking on from three out, he pushed his rivals out of their comfort zones: the only minor blemish was getting in tight to the second last: this fence at the bottom of a punishing climb can be an expensive one to get wrong: to his credit Ferny Hollow filled up quickly after the blunder and maintained a brisk gallop to the final fence before sprinting up the run in to record a spectacular fifteen lengths win over Bloodstone. A half-brother to four other track winners, back in his pedigree we find the Champion Hurdle winners Morley Street and Granville Again: those two champions were bred by Ken Parkhill, as was Ferny Hollow. It was little wonder that he commanded much attention at the Cheltenham February Sales, with Willie Mullins launching the successful bid of £300,000 on behalf of Cheveley Park Stud. Ferny Hollow could be top class and, if tracing the bumper route this season will be a leading player in that division. One of a handful of four year olds from the 2019 academy who I predict will have little trouble winning Graded track races, even to Grade 1 rank in time."**

Willie Mullins has won the Cheltenham Festival bumper on no less than nine occasions and, both he and Cheveley Park Stud, may have a serious contender for the 2020 version.

POINTS TO NOTE:

Probable Best Distance	-	2 miles
Preferred Going	-	Good/Soft

GOING:	R	W	P	TRACK:	R	W	P
Soft	1	1	0	Right	1	1	0

TRIP:	R	W	P	JOCKEY:	R	W	P
2m 4f	1	1	0	J.P.O'Rourke	1	1	0

FLY SMART (FR)
4 b g Day Flight – Abacab (FR) (Boris De Deauville (IRE))
OWNER: Mrs S.RICCI
TRAINER: W.P.MULLINS. Bagenalstown, Co.Carlow
CAREER FORM FIGURES: 2

It is early days to be thinking about the Cheltenham Festival opener, namely the *Skybet* Supreme Novices' Hurdle, but Willie Mullins has been very much the trainer to follow in recent years. Ireland's champion trainer has won the Grade 1 event no less than six times and three of those winners (Champagne Fever (2013), Vautour (2014) & Douvan (2015)) have been owned by Rich and Susannah Ricci. The brilliant but ill-fated Vautour started his career in France under the tutelage of Guillaume Macaire and the once raced Fly Smart did likewise.

A four lengths winner on the Flat at Niort (1m 3f : Soft) in September last year, he then finished two lengths runner-up on his hurdles debut in the Prix Isopani at Auteuil (2m 2f : Very Soft) the following month. The form of his race has worked out exceptionally well – the third, fifth, sixth, seventh, eighth (three times, including a Listed chase) and ninth (three times) have all won since. Bought soon afterwards on behalf of the Ricci's, he has been given plenty of time to settle in at Closutton and is held in the highest regard by his new connections.

I asked James Reveley about the four year old: **"Previously owned by Pierre Pilarski, I am surprised he was sold because he is a nice horse who ran well on his hurdles debut and the form looks decent."** Rich and Susannah Ricci have around seventeen novice hurdlers for this season and Fly Smart could prove one of, if not, the best. He is a hugely exciting prospect.

POINTS TO NOTE:

| Probable Best Distance | - | 2m – 2m 4f |
| Preferred Going | - | Soft |

GOING:	R	W	P	TRACK:	R	W	P
Very Soft	1	0	1	Left Handed	1	0	1
				Galloping	1	0	1

TRIP:	R	W	P	JOCKEY:	R	W	P
2m 2f	1	0	1	B.Lestrade	1	0	1

GENERATION TEXT (IRE)
4 b g Getaway (GER) – Maid In Glenavy (IRE) (King's Theatre (IRE))
OWNER: HIGHCLERE THOROUGHBRED RACING
TRAINER: D.SKELTON. Shelfield Green, Warwickshire.
CAREER FORM FIGURES: 2

The legendary fifteen times champion Martin Pipe trained over 200 winners on eight occasions with a personal best 243 winners during the 1999/2000 campaign for the Pond House team. Dan Skelton became only the second trainer to reach the milestone when sending out a six timer on Easter Sunday with Montego Grey providing winner number 200 at Market Rasen. The 34 year old former assistant to Paul Nicholls has trained 27, 73, 104, 118, 156 and 205 winners during the last five seasons. It is a monumental rise through the training ranks.

Never one to rest on his laurels, Skelton has further strengthened his already formidable team of equine talent with a number of recruits from point-to-point ranks. Watch out for the former Tom Lacey trained Cadzand, who has joined the Warwickshire based outfit, and also ex-Irish pointer Generation Text, who will sport the familiar Highclere Thoroughbred silks this winter and beyond. **"Fine strong lengthy bay gelding with a white nose and four white socks: appeared once in points racing for the Denis Murphy team. Partnered by Jamie Codd, he participated in what has turned out to be one of the hottest maidens of the spring of 2019. At Borris (Soft) in early March in an eleven runner field, he received a near copybook ride. He settled nicely and was positioned to challenge at the third last. Easing to the lead on the approach to the second last, he was alongside another travelling strongly, Sporting John. Generation Text landed awkwardly over the last fence, lost momentum and this allowed the pendulum to swing to Sporting John who kicked on to win by over two lengths. Apart from the slip on landing over the last fence, Generation Text posted a most pleasing debut and, although silver was his lot, the performance was rich in future promise. Andy Dufresne won the corresponding race in 2018, the time he recorded was near identical to the 2019 edition: that fact, plus the third, fourth and fifth from the race all winning their next point starts, certainly gave real substance to the standard of race being amongst the higher echelons. Generation Text does have a light pedigree and it looks like he alone will boost the page: Denis Murphy paid €30,000 for him at the 2018 Derby Sale: he travelled with this gelding to the Cheltenham March sales: he failed to sell at £95,000 under the hammer, but I gather Dan Skelton agreed a deal in that ballpark in a private transaction on behalf of Highclere Thoroughbred Racing. I like this horse and think he will be a worthwhile addition to the Skelton string. He will be a force in the better class two and a half miles plus novice hurdles in the UK this winter and should be capable of competing at the Festival,"** believes point expert Declan Phelan.

Speaking to my contact in the Skelton yard, Generation Text has reportedly settled in well and his regular work rider has been very impressed. It remains to be seen whether the Getaway gelding makes his Rules debut in a bumper or goes straight over hurdles.

POINTS TO NOTE:

Probable Best Distance	-	2 miles	
Preferred Going	-	Soft	

GOING:	R	W	P	TRACK	R	W	P
Soft	1	0	1	Left-Handed	1	0	1

TRIP:	R	W	P	JOCKEY:	R	W	P
3m	1	0	1	J.Codd	1	0	1

GIANTS TABLE
4 br g Great Pretender (IRE) – Bold Fire (Bold Edge)
OWNER: LADY BAMFORD
TRAINER: N.J.HENDERSON. Lambourn, Berkshire.
CAREER FORM FIGURES: 1
CAREER WIN: 2018: Mar BALLYCAHANE Soft 4YO Mdn PTP 3m

"This middle-sized bay is the offspring of a five time jumps winning French dam and cost Colin Bowe €60,000 at the 2018 Derby Sale. He won his one point, the four year old geldings maiden at Ballycahane (Soft): fourth four from home, he improved to lead leaving the backstraight and drew three lengths clear away from the second last, he was in command when his nearest challenger exited at the final fence and he was allowed

to ease down to score by three lengths. This four year old geldings maiden clocked a time some thirteen seconds slower than the mares' one, which preceded it (won by My Whirlwind): rarely do we get such an outcome between the sexes, as mostly the geldings are faster: the weather may have played a role in the time differential: Giants Table race was run during a heavy snowstorm and conditions were deteriorating ground wise by the minute, consequently I would not get hung up on the time aspect. To have won in horrible conditions does suggest this four year old has a hardy constitution and excellent racing attitude, and he will be a potent force in testing terrain. Possibly a horse for the depths of winter and there is a fair chance he can become at least a Grade 3 hurdler/chaser or higher over staying trips," believes Declan Phelan.

Eleven days after his point win, Jamie Codd paid £160,000 for the Great Pretender gelding on behalf of owner Lady Bamford at the Cheltenham Festival Sale in March. The four year old has subsequently joined Nicky Henderson and is another exciting recruit for Seven Barrows.

POINTS TO NOTE:
Probable Best Distance		-		**2m 4f**
Preferred Going		-		**Soft**

Connection's Comments: "This is a lovely type of horse, that we fancied coming down here." Colin BOWE at Ballycahane (3/3/19)

GOING:	R	W	P	TRACK	R	W	P
Soft	1	1	0	Left-Handed	1	1	0
TRIP:	R	W	P	JOCKEY:	R	W	P
3m	1	1	0	B.O'Neill	1	1	0

GIN ON LIME (FR)
3 b f Doctor Dino (FR) – Quiche Lorraine (FR) (Bateau Rouge)
OWNER: ROBCOUR
TRAINER: Mrs J.HARRINGTON. Moone, Co.Kildare.
CAREER FORM FIGURES: 1
CAREER WIN: 2019: July CLAIREFONTAINE Very Soft NH 2m 1f

Jessica Harrington has trained eleven Cheltenham Festival winners, including Jezki in the Champion Hurdle in 2014. It was announced in August that the son of Milan has been retired at the age of eleven. Successful in two of his three bumpers, he won 14 of his 35 races over hurdles and earned £968,358 in prize-money. An eight times Grade 1 winner over trips ranging from two to three miles, he appeared five times at the Cheltenham Festival (83148) enjoying his finest hour when beating the same owner's My Tent Or Yours in hurdling's Blue Riband over five years ago.

The County Kildare handler has taken charge of a potentially very smart juvenile hurdler from France in Gin On Lime. A three year old daughter of Doctor Dino, she was an impressive nine lengths winner of her only start over hurdles for Guillaume Macaire in France. Partnered by Felix De Giles, she jumped well before quickening clear after the last at Clairefontaine in July. The runner-up Stamina Chope has finished fifth and second again since. It was the manner of her victory which was most striking and the visual evidence was backed up by the comments of former French champion jockey James Reveley when I spoke to him in late August. **"Highly regarded by the Macaire team, she was very impressive at Clairefontaine. It is difficult to say what the form amounts to but she looks one of the best three year old fillies seen out in France this year."**

Owners Robcour, who are building up a strong team of jumpers, bought her soon afterwards and Jessica Harrington may have another top-class jumper on her hands. The same patrons have been very active in the French market in recent months acquiring three more youngsters who are featured in the *French Revolution* section of *OJA*.

POINTS TO NOTE:

Probable Best Distance	-	2 miles
Preferred Going	-	Soft

GOING:	R	W	P	TRACK:	R	W	P
Very Soft	1	1	0	Right	1	1	0
				Tight	1	1	0

TRIP:	R	W	P	JOCKEY:	R	W	P
2m 1f	1	1	0	Felix De Giles	1	1	0

GOOD BOY BOBBY (IRE)

6 b g Flemensfirth (USA) – Princess Gaia (IRE) (King's Theatre (IRE)
OWNER: PAUL & CLARE ROONEY
TRAINER: N.A.TWISTON-DAVIES. Naunton, Gloucestershire.
CAREER FORM FIGURES: 1131 - 1311
CAREER WINS: 2017: Nov CHEPSTOW Soft NHF 2m: 2018: Jan CHEPSTOW Heavy NHF 2m; Mar WETHERBY Heavy NHF 2m; Oct CARLISLE Good/Soft NH 2m 1f: 2019: Mar SOUTHWELL Good NH 2m; Apr FFOS LAS Soft NH 2m 4f

It was revealed in August that leading owners Paul and Clare Rooney intend cutting down their string to concentrate on quality rather than quantity. Good Boy Bobby certainly fits the former description having won six of his eight career starts and is officially rated 139 over hurdles. A free going sort who is learning to relax, the six year old is improving with every race and is set to take high rank amongst this season's novice chasers.

A gelded son of Flemensfirth, who cost €80,000 as a three year old when purchased at the Tattersalls Derby Sale in June 2016, he is related to Grade 1 winning mare Voler La Vedette. A three times bumper winner during the 2017/2018 season, his only defeat came in a Listed contest at Newbury when third behind Acey Milan. Sporting a hood in two of his four bumpers races, the headgear was refitted for his hurdles debut (and all four of his runs over jumps) at Carlisle last Autumn. Despite racing keenly, he proved too strong for the opposition and wasn't hard pressed to beat subsequent winner Weather Front by a couple of lengths. His sole defeat over hurdles came at Ffos Las next time when Nigel Twiston-Davies charge could only finish third behind Remastered and Smiths Cross. Good Boy Bobby wasn't seen again until early March (off 113 days) but he regained the winning thread with a forty four lengths victory, making all under Sam Twiston-Davies. He completed his education over timber with a third win when beating the 127 rated Quoi De Neuf by seven lengths at Ffos Las in April, conceding six pounds to Evan Williams' runner-up. That was his first run over two and a half miles with his owner's racing manager Jason Maguire saying afterwards: **"Good Boy Bobby can sometimes be his own worse enemy as he can be a bit too free, but he has got into a nice rhythm in front on his first try at this trip."**

Good Boy Bobby has reportedly thrived during the summer and his connections are very much looking forward to sending him chasing. Described as much more settled compared to his younger days, he has purposely been steered away from the major spring Festivals during the last two seasons because his trainer didn't feel he was ready mentally for such occasions. That may well be about to change.

POINTS TO NOTE:

Probable Best Distance — 2m 4f
Preferred Going — Soft

Connection's Comments: "He could be very special. I can't tell you how disappointed I was that he was beaten on his previous start at Ffos Las. He'll jump fences next season, which is something to really look forward to over the summer." Sam TWISTON-DAVIES speaking shortly after his win at Southwell in March.

GOING:	R	W	P		TRACK:	R	W	P
Heavy	3	2	1		Left Handed	7	5	2
Soft	3	2	1		Right	1	1	0
Good/Soft	1	1	0		Galloping	4	2	2
Good	1	1	0		Stiff/Undul.	3	3	0
					Tight	1	1	0

TRIP:	R	W	P		JOCKEY:	R	W	P
2m	6	4	2		S.Twiston-Davies	8	6	2
2m 1f	1	1	0					
2m 4f	1	1	0					

ISRAEL CHAMP (IRE)

4 b g Milan – La Dariska (FR) (Take Risks (FR))
OWNER: JOHN WHITE & ANNE UNDERHILL
TRAINER: D.E.PIPE. Nicholashayne, Somerset.
CAREER FORM FIGURES: 1
CAREER WIN: 2019: Mar MONKSGRANGE Good/Yielding 4YO Mdn PTP 3m

David Pipe announced in the spring that the curtain had come down on the careers of two of his fifteen Cheltenham Festival winners. Moon Racer was purchased for £225,000 in April 2014 having won a bumper at Fairyhouse's Easter Festival five days earlier. The Saffron Walden gelding subsequently won five races for his owners Professor Caroline Tisdall and Bryan Drew, including the Grade 1 Festival bumper the following year, and a Grade 2 novice hurdle at the same track in November 2016. Stablemate Un Temps Pour Tout was acquired for £450,000 at the DBS Hennessy Sale at Newbury in November 2013 having won three times over hurdles for Francois Nicolle in France. The Robin Des Champs gelding won the Ultima Handicap Chase twice (2016 & 2017) for his new connections but his biggest success came in the Grade 1 Grande Course de Haies d'Auteuil (the French Champion Hurdle) when he beat Thousand Stars by ten lengths under James Reveley in June 2015.

The Pond House team have therefore started the search for a new star and hopes are high that former Irish pointer Israel Champ will fill the void in years to come. Purchased privately on behalf of owners John White and Anne Underhill, who have enjoyed plenty of success courtesy of the likes of Dynaste, Ramses De Teillee and Umbrigado, he made a big impression on his only start at Monksgrange last March. Point expert Declan Phelan explains: **"Amateur jockey Harley Dunne signed for this strapping bay gelding at the 2018 Derby Sale for €32,000, and he shared ownership of the horse with trainer James Doyle and a bloodstock agent. To date, his dam has produced no track winners from six foals, but looking back through the pedigree one will locate plenty of Graded winners from France (dam was French). Israel Champ lined up at Monksgrange (Good/Yielding) on the last day of March and proceeded to deliver one of the smartest four year old performances of the spring. Charging to the lead at the start, he set a proper gallop and the tempo burned off his rivals as he left them in his midst entering the homestraight and powered to the line to win by** twelve lengths, clocking the fastest time of the day. He has a very high cruising speed and such a characteristic will lend itself to plenty of track success. One could imagine this gelding becoming a 130+ track horse without much hassle, whether he can make the step to Graded level, depends on how he will cope with competition when properly tested. In the old days of the Martin Pipe dominance, such front runners virtually guaranteed multiple successes: inmates of David Pipe's yard less frequently front run, I wonder if they would be prepared to revert to the past tactics with this gelding. He won on good ground, given his pedigree and size he shouldn't be troubled by rain softened conditions. He changed hands for a very large six figure price and is the most expensive ex-Irish pointer purchased by David Pipe." It is worth noting the runner-up at Monksgrange, namely On The Bandwagon, was bought by Jonjo O'Neill for £160,000 and is held in high regard at Jackdaws Castle. Israel Champ hails from the same source as his new stablemate and unbeaten Listed bumper winner Eden Du Houx, who also won his only point at Monksgrange. His former trainer James Doyle commented in early March, prior to his win: **"We think a lot of this lad and he is a proper staying chaser for the future."**

POINTS TO NOTE:

Probable Best Distance	-	2m 4f	
Preferred Going	-	Good/Soft	

Connection's Comments: "He was very impressive there in what looked a good contest. We were confident we had a nice horse but everyone else thought the same." James DOYLE at Monksgrange (31/3/19)

GOING:	R	W	P	TRACK:	R	W	P
Good/Yielding	1	1	0	Left Handed	1	1	0

TRIP:	R	W	P	JOCKEY:	R	W	P
3m	1	1	0	H.Dunne	1	1	0

JON SNOW (FR)

4 br g Le Havre (IRE) – Saroushka (FR) (Westerner)
OWNER: Mrs S.RICCI
TRAINER: W.P.MULLINS. Bagenalstown, Co.Carlow
FLAT CAREER FORM FIGURES: 841
CAREER WIN: 2018: May MAISONS-LAFFITTE Good Mdn 1m 4f

Despite the fact he has yet to jump a flight of hurdles in public, the ex-French trained Jon Snow has already been touted as a live contender for the *Skybet* Supreme Novices' Hurdle at the Cheltenham Festival next March. Along with the aforementioned Fly Smart, he will be sporting the pink and green silks of Susannah and Rich Ricci.

The Le Havre gelding was mooted a possible Triumph Hurdle horse last winter but never saw a racecourse. He raced three times on the Flat in France for Fabrice Chappet before being purchased by Mullins during the summer of last year. Unraced as a juvenile, he finished eighth on his debut at Chantilly (1m 2f : Heavy) before appreciating the step up to a mile and a half at Compiegne (Good/Soft) in April 2018. Beaten two and a half lengths in fourth behind the Godolphin owned Lindberg, he then scored at the third time of asking at Maisons-Laffitte the following month. A length and a quarter winner under Tony Piccone, he was bought soon afterwards with a view to going hurdling.

Jon Snow has reportedly impressed in his work since arriving at Closutton and, given the fact he has only raced three times, is open to significant improvement.

POINTS TO NOTE:

Probable Best Distance	-	2 miles		
Preferred Going	-	Good/Soft		

GOING:	R	W	P	TRACK:	R	W	P
Heavy	1	0	0	Left Handed	1	0	0
Good/Soft	1	0	0	Right	2	1	0
Good	1	1	0	Galloping	3	1	0

TRIP:	R	W	P	JOCKEY:	R	W	P
1m 2f	1	0	0	T.Piccone	3	1	0
1m 4f	2	1	0				

KING ROLAND (IRE)
5 br g Stowaway – Kiltiernan Robin (IRE) (Robin Des Champs (FR))
OWNER: MASTERSON HOLDINGS Limited
TRAINER: H.FRY. Seaborough, Dorset.
CAREER FORM FIGURES: 1 - 11
CAREER WIN: 2018: Mar LARKHILL Good/Soft Mdn PTP 3m; Dec UTTOXETER Heavy NHF 2m: 2019: Feb FFOS LAS Good/Soft NHF 2m

The unbeaten Get In The Queue will forever be remembered for providing Noel Fehily with his final winner on his final ride at Newbury on Saturday 23rd March. Unfortunately, the Mount Nelson gelding sustained an injury at the Berkshire track and therefore won't be in action until the second half of this season. However, he is not the only unbeaten five year old trained by Harry Fry who is set to go novice hurdling this winter. King Roland produced one of the best performances seen by a bumper horse last winter when annihilating eight rivals by upwards of twenty two lengths at Uttoxeter in December. Ironically, Paul Nicholls' former assistant had won the corresponding event two years earlier with another Masterson Holdings Limited owned ex-pointer, namely the ill-fated Neon Wolf.

The Stowaway gelding was originally bought as a three year old for €40,000 at the Derby Sales in Ireland by Tom Lacey and was a ten lengths winner of his point-to-point at Larkhill in the spring of last year when handled by his wife Sophie. Tom commented in *One Jump Ahead* last season: **"I think he is exceptional. He jumps beautifully, stays and gallops. He was very raw and still up behind when he made his debut. With another summer under his belt, he could be anything and possesses the ability to win a bumper."**

Bought privately to join Fry, King Roland was heavily supported on his Rules debut at the Midlands track and he didn't disappoint with an awesome performance (fitted with a hood). Still on the bridle when hitting the front with half a mile to run, he was sent clear by Fehily and pulverized the opposition. Reappearing 67 days later, he defied a penalty at Ffos Las towards the end of February. While he wasn't as impressive as on his Rules debut, the five year old beat previous winner Stick With Bill by a length conceding five pounds to Harry Whittington's runner-up with the pair over three lengths clear of the third. Connections contemplated a trip to Ireland in the spring for the Punchestown Festival but decided to let him off for the summer.

King Roland reportedly jumps brilliantly, according to his trainer and he looks tailormade for two and two and a half miles novice hurdles on soft/heavy ground this winter, provided he learns to settle.

Probable Best Distance - 2m 4f – 3 miles
Preferred Going - Soft
Connection's Comments: "He's a lovely horse who was very impressive in his point-to-point and Harry (Fry) has loved him since the day he got him." Noel FEHILY at Uttoxeter (21/12/18)

GOING:	R	W	P	TRACK:	R	W	P
Heavy	1	1	0	Left Handed	2	2	0
Good/Soft	2	2	0	Right	1	1	0
				Galloping	2	2	0
				Tight/Undul.	1	1	0

TRIP:	R	W	P	JOCKEY:	R	W	P
2m	2	2	0	N.Fehily	2	2	0
3m	1	1	0	Tommie O'Brien	1	1	0

L'AIR DU VENT (FR)
5 b g Coastal Path – Bleu Perle (FR) (Pistolet Bleu (IRE))
OWNER: BROCADE RACING
TRAINER: C.TIZZARD. Milborne Port, Dorset.
CAREER FORM FIGURES: F1
CAREER WIN: 2019: Apr BANGOR Good NHF 2m

Brocade Racing have enjoyed a tremendous amount of success courtesy of their 2018 Cheltenham Gold Cup winner Native River. The Indian River gelding started his career in an Irish point when trained by Denis Ahern before being bought privately. The nine year old won three times over hurdles before developing into a top-class chaser. Rated 167, he is a dual Grade 1 winner and also has the Hennessy Gold Cup and Welsh National on his CV with his current earnings standing at £946,697.

The same owners have two potentially smart novice hurdlers for this season, including this former Irish pointer. "Tall bay with a broad white face: French bred, a €70,000 store from the 2017 Derby Sale, a half-brother to Si C'Etait Vrai. Housed with Denis Murphy, he appeared in one point, at Lingstown (Good) in November. Himself and the eventual winner (Shishkin) moved in unison, cruising to the third last fence: sadly, L'Air Du Vent failed to get his landing gear working and fell at the third last, denying spectators what may have been an enlightening conclusion. Bought privately by Brocade Racing, he debuted at Bangor in April for Colin Tizzard and won a bumper apologising, oozing class. This is the smartest pointer the owners have acquired since Native River and I think his main vocation will rest as a classy 2m 4f hurdler/chaser. Both runs to date have been on good ground and his family seem to prefer such conditions," believes Irish point expert Declan Phelan.

Sent off 10/11 favourite at Bangor during the spring, he quickened up well off a slow gallop to win by a hard held four and a half lengths. Jonjo O'Neill jnr partnered him and was reportedly very impressed. Conceding eleven pounds to the runner-up, L'Air Du Vent looked a classy sort at the Welsh track and is a horse with a bright future.

POINTS TO NOTE:

Probable Best Distance	-	2m – 2m 4f
Preferred Going	-	Good

GOING:	R	W	P	TRACK:	R	W	P
Good	2	1	0	Left Handed	1	1	0
				Right	1	0	0
				Tight	1	1	0

TRIP:	R	W	P	JOCKEY:	R	W	P
2m	1	1	0	J.J.O.Neill Jnr	1	1	0
3m	1	0	0	J.Codd	1	0	0

LE CAMELEON

4 bb g Great Pretender (IRE) – Countess Camilla (Bob's Return (IRE))
OWNER: The PRETENDERS
TRAINER: N.WILLIAMS. South Molton, Devon.
CAREER FORM FIGURES: 6

Both Jane and Nick Williams have plenty of young horses to look forward to this season. Erik Le Rouge, Monsieur Lecoq and Moonlighter ought to make above average novice chasers for the former, while the latter must be excited by the prospect of Cheltenham Festival winner Siruh Du Lac running in Graded company this winter.

Nick Williams is also responsible for a couple of interesting novice hurdle prospects. Prudhomme, who is a half-brother to Grade 1 winner Pont Alexandre, won a bumper in convincing fashion at Ffos Las in April, while the once raced Le Cameleon looks a promising type for the future as well.

Le Cameleon is from a family his trainer knows well being out of Kim Bailey's five times winner Countess Camilla. A half-brother to George Nympton (3 wins), Horatio Hornblower (5) and the aforementioned Moonlighter (2), who are/were trained by the Williams family, he shaped most encouragingly in a steadily run bumper at Newbury in early March. Sent off 6/1, he finished sixth, around eight lengths behind the subsequent Grade 2 Aintree bumper winner McFabulous. The highly regarded pair Faustinovick and Silver Hallmark finished runner-up and third. The Great Pretender gelding fared best of the three four year olds in the line-up. Capable of winning a bumper, Le Cameleon will appreciate two and a half miles over hurdles and is an interesting dark horse to keep an eye on. It appeared a strong bumper in which he made his debut.

POINTS TO NOTE:

Probable Best Distance	-	2m 4f
Preferred Going	-	Soft

GOING:	R	W	P	TRACK:	R	W	P
Good/Soft	1	0	0	Left Handed	1	0	0
				Galloping	1	0	0

TRIP:	R	W	P	JOCKEY:	R	W	P
2m	1	0	0	C.Williams	1	0	0

LINELEE KING (IRE)

4 gr g Martaline – Queen Lee (FR) (Lone Bid (FR)
OWNER: Mrs D.L.WHATELEY
TRAINER: OLLY MURPHY. Wilmcote, Warwickshire.
CAREER FORM FIGURES: 1
CAREER WIN: 2019: Feb TINAHELY Good/Yielding 4YO Mdn PTP 3m

It is hardly surprising given the fact he learned his trade under Gordon Elliott's tutelage, but Olly Murphy has undoubtedly been one of the success stories amongst the training ranks in recent seasons. The three times Grand National winning trainer's former assistant sent out 47 winners during his first season with a license followed by another 82 last winter. Thomas Darby provided Murphy with his first Cheltenham winner last Autumn, while Hunters Call was his first significant success in the Grade 3 Racing Welfare Handicap Hurdle at Ascot in December 2017.

Warren Chase Stables looks particularly strong in the novice chase department this term with Brewin'upastorm, Itchy Feet and Thomas Darby all set to jump fences for the first time. Not one to rest on his laurels, the 28 year old has been active at the various sales during the last twelve months with his new purchases including Dundrum Wood (£270,000), Grandads Cottage (£200,000), Kerrkenny Gold (£60,000), Overthetop (£150,000) and Presence of Mind (£70,000). Linelee King was acquired for £160,000 at the Cheltenham Festival Sale in March on behalf of Diana Whateley having won his only point-to-point in Ireland for Colin Bowe. Declan Phelan reports: **"Solidly built French bred grey gelding with many continental jumps winners in his family. Bought at a cost of €38,000 at the 2018 Land Rover sale by Colin Bowe, he was put to the test once between the flags, at Tinahely (Good/Yielding) in late February. Only four runners in this race and it was one of those affairs with a steady pace and quickening up last half mile. Linelee King relaxed through the race for jockey Barry O'Neill and, in the wind up, he supplied an armchair ride, as O'Neill merely had to nudge him out for a smooth eight lengths win. Impossible to say if there was much merit in beating three ordinary rivals, in terms of style Linelee King would have scored highly. Olly Murphy elected to pay £160,000 for this talented youngster at Cheltenham March Sales and at that price he now has a genuine aspirant for Graded success as a hurdler and chaser and an inmate who may become a flagship for an upwardly mobile yard."**

Speaking to Olly during the summer, Linelee King is likely to be kept to bumpers this season. It is a policy which has paid off handsomely in the past for his former boss – Grade 1 Cheltenham Festival winners Don Cossack, Envoi Allen and Samcro spent a whole season in bumpers as four/five year olds.

POINTS TO NOTE:
Probable Best Distance	-	2 miles		
Preferred Going	-	Good/Soft		

GOING:	R	W	P	TRACK:	R	W	P
Good/Yielding	1	1	0	Right	1	1	0

TRIP:	R	W	P	JOCKEY:	R	W	P
3m	1	1	0	B.O'Neill	1	1	0

LONGHOUSE POET (IRE)

5 b g Yeats (IRE) – Moscow Madame (IRE) (Moscow Society (USA))
OWNER: SEAN & BERNARDINE MULRYAN
TRAINER: M.BRASSIL. Dunmurray, Co.Kildare.
CAREER FORM FIGURES: 1 - 1
CAREER WIN: 2019: Jan BOULTA Yielding 5YO Mdn PTP 3m; May PUNCHESTOWN Good/
Yielding NHF 2m 2f

Owner Sean Mulryan has been associated with some top-class horses over the years both in Ireland and France. Grade 1 winners Cyrlight, In Compliance, Mid Dancer and Zaiyad all sported his familiar black and yellow silks. The 65 year old Irish property developer, and founder and chairman and CEO of the Ballymore Group, tasted Cheltenham Festival glory last March when City Island won his own sponsored race, the Ballymore Novices' Hurdle.

The Court Cave gelding is all set to go chasing this winter but he is not Mulryan's only exciting prospect in training with Brassil. French recruit Gaspard Du Seuil could be very smart in novice hurdles and that comment also applies to the unbeaten Longhouse Poet. Expert Declan Phelan describes the Yeats gelding: **"Strong big boned bay gelding: recorded a very impressive debut win at Boulta (Yielding) in January as Derek O'Connor enjoyed an armchair ride en route to a four lengths win. I can recall Derek saying to the then owner John Duggan in the post-race chat that, if he wanted to keep a star chaser then this gelding would fit the bill, or alternatively he could cash in for big bucks. Owner Duggan chose the latter option, as he struck a private deal with Sean Mulryan and the horse moved from Sam Curling (point trainer) to Martin Brassil. The deep financial investment looked justified when Longhouse Poet landed a bumper at the Punchestown Festival in some style. Although his half-sister, Longhousesignora is a modest hurdler in the UK, this gelding will be the flagbearer for his equine family into the future. Likely to contest the top two and a half miles and upwards novice hurdles this season, with wins on yielding and good ground, he has versatility and I think he will prove good enough to book a ticket to the Cheltenham Festival, and may represent his owner in the Ballymore (a race he sponsors)."**

It is interesting to note crack amateur Derek O'Connor retained the ride at the Punchestown Festival when beating another former pointer Monkfish by two and a half lengths (the ninth Bentham has won twice since). Longhouse Poet could be another Grade 1 winner in the making for Sean Mulryan.

POINTS TO NOTE:
Probable Best Distance   -   2m 4f +
Preferred Going   -   Good/Soft
Connection's Comments: "He has thrived since we've got him. He won his point well and jumps great. He's a real winter horse and we will go jumping with him in the autumn."
Martin BRASSIL at Punchestown (3/5/19)

GOING:	R	W	P	TRACK:	R	W	P
Yielding	1	1	0	Left Handed	1	1	0
Good/Yielding	1	1	0	Right	1	1	0
				Galloping	1	1	0

TRIP:	R	W	P	JOCKEY:	R	W	P
2m 2f	1	1	0	D.O'Connor	2	2	0
3m	1	1	0				

LOSSIEMOUTH

4 b g Makfi – First Bloom (USA) (Fusaichi Pegasus (USA))
OWNER: LADY COBHAM
TRAINER: T.LACEY. Woolhope, Herefordshire.
CAREER FORM FIGURES: O11
CAREER WIN: 2018: Dec NEWCASTLE Soft NHF 1m 6f: 2019: Feb CARLISLE Good/Soft
NHF 2m 1f

Herefordshire based Tom Lacey continues to impress amongst the training ranks with 38 winners last season, including Listed successes for Glory And Fortune (4yo bumper at Cheltenham on New Year's Day) and Jester Jet (mares' hurdle at Warwick in February). He has also made his name in recent seasons by selling on high quality jumpers, namely Grade 2 winners Blackbow (£150,000) and the ill-fated North Hill Harvey (£100,000), plus the promising and unbeaten trio King Roland, Energueme and Ramillies (£215,000). The last two named are now under the guidance of Willie Mullins. Lacey also trained the record breaking Interconnected to win his point-to-point before being sold to owners Grech and Parkin for £220,000. The five year old has been acquired since for a huge £620,000 following one run under Rules for Nicky Henderson, and joined Dan Skelton this summer.

Tom Lacey therefore knows what a good horse is and he believes the dual bumper winner Lossiemouth could be one of the best he has handled. A homebred owned by Lady Cobham, he had the misfortune to run out on his debut in a junior bumper at Huntingdon in mid November. Sent off 6/1, he was travelling well under Tommie O'Brien when veering left through the wings of what normally would be the second last hurdle. However, the Makfi gelding put the record straight over a month later when winning a similar event at Newcastle before Christmas. Alan Johns took the ride and, having been held up early on, he led entering the final furlong before being pushed clear to win by two and half lengths. The runner-up Alright Sunshine, who was conceding seven pounds to Lossiemouth, won his next two bumpers and has scored three times on the Flat this summer and is rated 93 on the level. To add further substance to the form, the sixth and seventh won subsequently. Returning from an eight weeks break, the four year old defied a penalty under champion jockey Richard Johnson at Carlisle (inner track) in February. Responding to pressure three out, he led with a furlong to run before powering clear to win by four and a half lengths. He was then due to contest the Grade 2 Aintree bumper but a minor setback ruled him out. Described as a slower learner by this trainer, he is improving with every run.

Despite being Flat bred, Lossiemouth appears to have plenty of stamina and shouldn't have any trouble staying two and a half miles over timber. He is an exciting prospect for his upwardly mobile trainer.

POINTS TO NOTE:
Probable Best Distance   -   2m 4f
Preferred Going   -   Good/Soft
Connection's Comments: "Lossiemouth is a super horse and, apart from the unfortunate incident at Huntingdon, he's been pretty straightforward." Tom LACEY at Carlisle (18/2/19)

GOING:	R	W	P	TRACK:	R	W	P
Soft	1	1	0	Left Handed	1	1	0
Good/Soft	1	1	0	Right	2	1	0
Good	1	0	0	Galloping	2	1	0
				Stiff/Undul.	1	1	0

TRIP:	R	W	P	JOCKEY:	R	W	P
1m 5f	1	0	0	R.Johnson	1	1	0
1m 6f	1	1	0	A.Johns	1	1	0
2m 1f	1	1	0	Tommie O'Brien	1	0	0

MALONE ROAD (IRE)

5 b g Kalanisi (IRE) – Zaffarella (IRE) (Zaffaran (USA))
OWNER: CHEVELEY PARK STUD
TRAINER: G.ELLIOTT. Longwood, Co.Meath.
CAREER FORM FIGURES: 1 - 11
CAREER WIN: 2018: Mar LOUGHANMORE Yielding/Soft 4YO Mdn PTP 3m; Nov DOWN
ROYAL Good/Yielding NHF 2m, PUNCHESTOWN Good NHF 2m

Despite the fact Cheveley Park Stud and Gordon Elliott captured the Cheltenham Festival bumper with the aforementioned Envoi Allen, one of the most disappointing aspects of last season was the fact we never got the chance to see the unbeaten Malone Road during the second half of the campaign following two mighty impressive victories in November.

Purchased for £325,000 at the Goffs UK Aintree Sale in April 2018 having won his only point-to-point for Stuart Crawford twelve days earlier, the half-brother to Ravenhill Road (joined Sue Smith during the summer) and Windsor Avenue made his Rules debut in a bumper at Down Royal in early November. Gordon Elliott's new recruit was sent off 2/5 favourite under Jamie Codd and never gave his supporters an anxious moment. Making all, he quickened clear approaching the final furlong to beat Valdieu (won twice since) by seven and a half lengths. Reappearing fifteen days later, he was arguably even more impressive when beating the highly regarded Mt Leinster by eight and a half lengths at Punchestown. Held up on this occasion, he sprinted clear from the two marker in the manner of a potentially top-class horse. **"Jamie (Codd) thinks he'll learn plenty as he was half green through the race and behind the bridle. He's a horse that does everything easily and probably it's the first time being in around horses. I thought he was very impressive,"** enthused Gordon Elliott afterwards.

Unfortunately, it was announced it early December that Malone Road had suffered a knee injury and he had undergone surgery with a screw inserted. Absent since, I spoke to Cheveley Park Stud managing director Chris Richardson at York's Ebor Festival in August and he confirmed that the five year old is back to full fitness. I also had it confirmed from a different source during the same month that the Kalanisi gelding was back in work. Both Envoi Allen and Malone Road are two terrific novice hurdle prospects and one suspects the latter will develop into a *Skybet* Supreme Novices' Hurdle contender because he is evidently blessed with an abundance of speed.

POINTS TO NOTE:
Probable Best Distance - 2m – 2m 4f
Preferred Going - Good/Soft
Connection's Comments: "He was good at Down Royal and we thought he had improved. He was very impressive here, beating a good horse of Willie's (Mullins) and I loved the way he picked up and quickened clear." Gordon ELLIOTT at Punchestown (18/11/18)

GOING:	R	W	P	TRACK	R	W	P
Yield/Soft	1	1	0	Left Handed	1	1	0
Good/Yielding	1	1	0	Right	2	2	0
Good	1	1	0	Galloping	1	1	0
				Tight/Undul.	1	1	0

TRIP:	R	W	P	JOCKEY:	R	W	P
2m	2	2	0	J.J.Codd	2	2	0
3m	1	1	0	B.Crawford	1	1	0

MICK PASTOR (FR)
3 b g Meshaheer (USA) – Mick Oceane (FR) (Urban Ocean (FR))
OWNER: J.P.McMANUS
TRAINER: P.F.NICHOLLS. Ditcheat, Somerset.
CAREER FORM FIGURES: 1
CAREER WIN: 2019: May AUTEUIL Heavy Hdle 2m 1f

Champion trainer Paul Nicholls has won the Triumph Hurdle twice (Celestial Halo (2008) & Zarkandar (2011)) and the head of Team Ditcheat may have a prime contender in the impressive Auteuil winner Mick Pastor.

Handled in France by Mikael Mescam, the son of Meshaheer only cost €7,000 as a two year old and he finished thirteenth of seventeen on his sole run on the Flat at Fontainebleau (1m 1f: Soft) in November last year. Switched to hurdles, he was an emphatic six lengths winner of the Prix De Pouilly, a conditions event, at the Parisian track in May. I watched a replay of the race on *Equidia* and, having taken control jumping the fifth last, Mick Pastor stayed on strongly to win easily. The form received a boost, too, with the runner-up Nirvana Du Berlais winning a Grade 3 hurdle over the same course and distance in June. Snapped up by legendary owner J.P.McManus soon afterwards, he reportedly cost a small fortune and arrived in Somerset in August with a lofty reputation.

A quick and accurate jumper, I asked James Reveley about his prospects and he said: **"He was an impressive winner at Auteuil beating a nice horse who has boosted the form since. He comes from a small yard in France but Mikael Mescam is a promising young trainer."** Mick Pastor's UK debut is eagerly anticipated.

POINTS TO NOTE:

Probable Best Distance	-	2 miles
Preferred Going	-	Soft

GOING:	R	W	P	TRACK:	R	W	P
Heavy	1	1	0	Left Handed	1	1	0
				Galloping	1	1	0

TRIP:	R	W	P	JOCKEY:	R	W	P
2m 1f	1	1	0	D.Mescam	1	1	0

MIDNIGHT SHADOW

6 b g Midnight Legend – Holy Smoke (Statoblest)
OWNER: Mrs AAFKE CLARKE
TRAINER: Mrs SUE SMITH. High Eldwick, West Yorkshire.
CAREER FORM FIGURES: 127 – 1222U71 - 20110
CAREER WINS: 2016: Dec NEWCASTLE Soft NHF 1m 6f: 2017: Oct UTTOXETER Soft NH
2m: 2018: Apr AYR Good Grade 2 Hdle 2m; Dec AINTREE Soft HH 2m 4f: 2019: Jan
CHELTENHAM Good/Soft Grade 2 Hdle 2m 4f

Midnight Shadow justified his inclusion in last year's *Top 40 Prospects* with two victories, including the Grade 2 Relkeel Hurdle at Cheltenham on New Year's Day. The six year old appreciated the step up to two and a half miles last winter winning a valuable handicap hurdle at Aintree three weeks earlier before producing a career best effort at Prestbury Park at the start of 2019. Officially rated 155, the Midnight Legend gelding is set to embark on what will hopefully prove an even more successful career over fences following one more run over hurdles.

Beaten a neck by Innocent Touch on his reappearance at Wetherby off 140 in October, the former Scottish Champion Hurdle winner failed to fire in the Greatwood Hurdle at Cheltenham the following month. The drying ground may not have played to his strengths and the fact three hurdles were omitted due to low sun wasn't ideal either. Stepped up in distance at Aintree's Becher chase meeting in early December, Danny Cook's mount travelled powerfully before fending off the challenge of subsequent County Hurdle winner Ch'tibello to score by half a length. Returning to Graded company at Cheltenham on New Year's Day, he beat Wholestone, who was attempting to win the Relkeel Hurdle for a second successive year, by two and a quarter lengths. Midnight Shadow tracked Nigel Twiston-Davies' triple Grade 2 winner before accelerating away after the last to win decisively. Sue Smith's stable star was then stepped up to three miles in the Grade 2 Cleeve Hurdle at Cheltenham's Trials meeting but failed to get home. He held every chance at the second last but was a spent force by the time he was badly hampered at the final flight. A minor fracture ruled him out of the rest of the season but that may prove a blessing in disguise as he missed the spring Festivals.

Reportedly back to full fitness, Midnight Shadow is likely to reappear in the Grade 2 West Yorkshire Hurdle at Wetherby (2nd November) before going chasing. He should develop into one of the north's leading novice chasers over two and a half miles plus this winter.

POINTS TO NOTE:

Probable Best Distance	-	**2m 4f**
Preferred Going	-	**Good/Soft**

Connection's Comments: "I think he's very smart. He's got a touch of class and he's got a very big engine." Sue SMITH at Cheltenham (1/1/19)

GOING:	R	W	P		TRACK:	R	W	P
Heavy	3	0	2		Left Handed	15	5	3
Soft	6	3	0		Galloping	5	2	1
Good/Soft	3	1	0		Stiff/Undul.	3	1	0
Good	3	1	1		Tight	6	1	2
					Tight/Undul.	1	1	0

TRIP:	R	W	P		JOCKEY:	R	W	P
1m 6f	1	1	0		D.Cook	12	4	3
2m	10	2	3		R.Hogg	3	1	0
2m 1f	1	0	0					
2m 4f	2	2	0					
3m	1	0	0					

MR GREY SKY (IRE)

5 gr g Fame And Glory – Lakil Princess (IRE) (Bering)
OWNER: P.J.ANDREWS
TRAINER: K.C.BAILEY. Andoversford, Gloucestershire.
CAREER FORM FIGURES: 11
CAREER WIN: 2018: Dec HAYDOCK Heavy NHF 2m, HAYDOCK Soft NHF 2m

Numerically, Kim Bailey enjoyed his second best season since the 1996/1997 campaign with 51 winners last term and total prize-money of £601,872. The stable had four Grade 2 winners, including Charbel's victory in the Peterborough Chase at Huntingdon in December and, in recent years, it has built up a strong team of youngsters. Based at Andoversford in Gloucestershire, the Grand National, Cheltenham Gold Cup and Champion Hurdle winning trainer has two Grade 1 wins on his CV thanks to Alderbrook and Master Oats but it may not be long before that tally is added to.

Mr Grey Sky is a promising young horse who is unbeaten following two wins in bumpers at Haydock in December. Purchased by agent Aiden Murphy for €92,000 at the Tattersalls Derby Sale in June 2017, the gelded son of Fame And Glory is a half-brother to three miles winners Lastbutnotleast and Danny Whizzbang. Making his debut in a 'newcomers' event at the Merseyside track, he raced keenly early on under Mikey Hamill but responded well to pressure to win going away by two and a half lengths from Ebony Jewel. The runner-up was subsequently sold for £70,000 and won next time for Nick Alexander before finishing sixth in the Grade 2 championship bumper at Aintree. Mr Grey Sky returned to the same track later that month and defied a penalty with another gutsy display. David Bass did the steering on this occasion and, having headway two out, he led soon afterwards and was pushed clear for a length success. The runner-up, Highway Companion, is well regarded by Keith Dalgleish even though he disappointed next time, while the third (Some Detail) won on his next start before finishing seventh in the Cheltenham Festival bumper. I spoke to Kim Bailey afterwards and he described his five year old as 'a proper horse.' Given plenty of time since, he was purposely put away for the spring/summer with his education in bumpers complete.

While Mr Grey Sky is expected to start his hurdling career over two and a half miles, he is likely to come into his own over further. A physically imposing individual, his long-term future lies over fences but it will be disappointing if he doesn't develop into a smart staying novice hurdler this winter. He has yet to encounter ground quicker than soft.

POINTS TO NOTE:
Probable Best Distance   -   2m 4f – 3 miles
Preferred Going   -   Soft
Connection's Comments: "Mr Grey Sky is a very nice horse. He was a bit too free today but he has done well carrying a penalty." Kim BAILEY at Haydock (30/12/18)

GOING:	R	W	P	TRACK:	R	W	P
Heavy	1	1	0	Left Handed	2	2	0
Soft	1	1	0	Tight	2	2	0
TRIP:	R	W	P	JOCKEY:	R	W	P
2m	2	2	0	D.Bass	1	1	0
				M.Hamill	1	1	0

MY WHIRLWIND (IRE)
4 b f Stowaway – Garranlea Maree (IRE) (Presenting)
OWNER: J.P.McMANUS
TRAINER: N.J.HENDERSON. Lambourn, Berkshire.
CAREER FORM FIGURES: 1
CAREER WINS: 2019: Mar BALLYCAHANE Soft 4YO Mdn PTP 3m

Legendary owner J.P.McManus is currently responsible for some high-class mares. The Peter Fahey trained Gypsy Island was unbeaten in four bumpers last season, Elimay won at the Punchestown Festival in the spring and Sancta Simona is a Grade 3 winner. His team of mares has been bolstered still further during the spring/summer with the addition of the unbeaten pair Gin On Lime and My Whirlwind. The latter became the most expensive point-to-point mare bought at public auction when acquired for £400,000 at the Cheltenham Festival Sale in March and has subsequently joined Nicky Henderson.

Point expert Declan Phelan believes: **"Tall rangy bay mare: a €42,000 2018 Derby Sale purchase by County Down handler Pat Turley, plenty of familiar jumping names on her page, including the likes of Mister Morose, Sizing Coal and Albertas Run. She has already gained her own fame, because she sold for the record fee of £400,000 at Cheltenham March Sales, becoming the most expensive pointing mare in history. That transaction occurred due to her debut win at Ballycahane (Soft): prominent all the way and bold jumping, having stacked the pack behind her three out, by the second last she had injected further pace and decimated the field: she was in complete control when her nearest rival fell at the last and she could ease down to win by four lengths from Madam De Luxe. The previous big money pointing mare which Nicky Henderson located was Theatre Territory, one who has been frustrating on the track. My Whirlwind has more class and based with a handler who excels in novice/Graded races for the fairer sex, My Whirlwind could be gifted enough to climb towards the top of the ratings ladder as a mares' novice hurdler and win Graded hurdles. Progeny by Stowaway tend to enjoy good ground, as a winner on deep tacky ground, this lady may be versatile in terms of ground and trip (she has natural speed). You can expect her to make her presence felt at the big Festivals next spring."**

Only four, it will be interesting to see if the daughter of Stowaway heads down the bumper route or she goes straight over hurdles. If her new connections pursue the latter option, then the Grade 2 Dawn Run Mares' Novices' Hurdle is likely to be her number one target this season. Nicky Henderson has trained some top-class mares over the years and he may have been sent another one.

POINTS TO NOTE:
Probable Best Distance	-	2m – 2m 4f	
Preferred Going	-	Good/Soft	

GOING:	R	W	P	TRACK:	R	W	P
Soft	1	1	0	Left Handed	1	1	0

TRIP:	R	W	P	JOCKEY:	R	W	P
3m	1	1	0	D.Lavery	1	1	0

NO REGRETS (IRE)

5 b g Presenting – E Mac (IRE) (Old Vic)
OWNER: STRAIGHTLINE BLOODSTOCK
TRAINER: N.G.RICHARDS. Greystoke, Cumbria.
CAREER FORM FIGURES: 4

On Tuesday 20th November last year, one of most popular National Hunt horses of recent years, Monet's Garden, passed away at the age of 20. The grey son of Roselier was bought as a three year old at the Derby Sale in Ireland in June 2001 for 35,000gns and he won 17 of his 32 races, earning £683,265 in prize-money. Rated 166 over fences and 157 over hurdles, he was a triple Grade 1 winner and won the Grade 2 Old Roan Chase at Aintree no less than three times. The two and a half miles event is now named in his honour. Nicky Richards' charge claimed some notable scalps along the way, including the brilliant Kauto Star and five times Grade 1 winner Mid Dancer. Seven different jockeys rode him with Tony Dobbin partnering him to 13 victories and his form figures at his beloved Aintree were 211147131. He was the north's version of Desert Orchid and provided a lot of people with a lot of pleasure.

Another Greystoke stalwart Simply Ned won the Grade 1 Paddy's Rewards Club Chase at Leopardstown over Christmas for the second consecutive year, while Takingrisks provided the stable with Scottish National glory in April. The late Gordon Richards won the event in 1969 (Playlord) and 1990 (Four Trix) and twenty nine years later his son's name was added to the roll of honour after Sean Quinlan had steered the ten year old to a four lengths victory. With 42 domestic winners and prize-money of £680,690 last season, it is excting times at Rectory Farm.

I was fortunate enough to interview Nicky during the summer and the stable is blessed with a host of promising young horses. The once raced No Regrets is a case in point having shaped with plenty of encouragement in the concluding bumper at Ayr on Scottish National day. From the family of the useful middle distance hurdler Blue Buttons, the Presenting gelding was purchased for €42,000 at the Tattersalls August Sale in Ireland as a three year old. Sent off 11/4 favourite on his debut, he was held up early on and, having made headway turning for home, the five year old was tapped for speed before finishing well in fourth. Beaten eight lengths by Phil Kirby's December Second, the winner subsequently finished sixth in the Grade 1 bumper at the Punchestown Festival before winning next time. He has also developed into a 92 rated Flat racer winning by five lengths at Haydock in August. It is traditionally a strong bumper, which was won by Sprinter Sacre in 2010 and has been contested by some high-class horses over the years. Reported to have come out of the race well, No Regrets will go straight over hurdles this Autumn and it will be disappointing if he doesn't develop into an above average northern novice.

POINTS TO NOTE:

Probable Best Distance	-	2m 4f	
Preferred Going	-	Good/Soft	

GOING:	R	W	P	TRACK:	R	W	P
Good	1	0	0	Left Handed	1	0	0
				Galloping	1	0	0
TRIP:	R	W	P	**JOCKEY:**	R	W	P
2m	1	0	0	C.Nichol	1	0	0

ONE FOR ROSIE

6 gr g Getaway (GER) – Whisky Rose (IRE) (Old Vic)
OWNER: PAUL & CLARE ROONEY
TRAINER: N.A.TWISTON-DAVIES. Naunton, Gloucestershire.
CAREER FORM FIGURES: 1 - 13123
CAREER WINS: 2017: Oct BANGOR Good NHF 2m: 2018: Nov CARLISLE Good NH 2m 4f:
2019: Feb WARWICK Good NH 2m 3f

The second potentially high-class novice chaser owned by Paul and Clare Rooney and trained by Nigel Twiston-Davies, One For Rosie was a dual winner over timber last winter but arguably produced his best two performances in defeat during the spring. Rated 145 over hurdles, he was Grade 1 placed last season and could take even higher rank over the larger obstacles.

A fine, big strapping son of Getaway, he was acquired for €48,000 as a three year old at the Goffs Landrover Sale in June 2016 and is a half-brother to Air Horse One and Listed winning bumper mare Misty Whisky. A bumper winner at Bangor on his racecourse debut during the Autumn of 2017, One For Rosie was then absent for 369 days until returning over hurdles at Carlisle in November last year. A five lengths winner, he beat subsequent Grade 2 winning novice chaser and leading Arkle Trophy contender Glen Forsa, with another future winner Hill Sixteen back in third. Surprisingly beaten at the same track six weeks later, One For Rosie didn't appear to enjoy the testing conditions at the Cumbrian venue finding Captain Zebo eighteen and a half lengths too good. Given a break of 68 days, he was back to his best with a smooth five lengths win from Falco Blitz at Warwick in February. Given a rating of 138, he then carried top weight on his handicap debut in the EBF Final at Sandown (Soft) and ran a cracker to finish second. Beaten a short head by Hughie Morrison's Third Wind, conceding seven pounds, Sam Twiston-Davies' mount led at the last only to get headed on the line. One For Rosie rounded off his hurdles campaign by trying his hand in Grade 1 company at Aintree in April. Dead-heating for third in the Mersey Novices' Hurdle, he held every chance at the second last but couldn't match the pace of Colin Tizzard's Reserve Tank. However, he was only beaten five and a half lengths.

Unbeaten first time out, One For Rosie will be hard to beat on his chasing debut and it will be a surprise if he doesn't develop into a Graded novice this winter, although he may not want bottomless ground.

POINTS TO NOTE:
Probable Best Distance   -   2m 4f
Preferred Going   -   Good
Connection's Comments: "He's a proper horse. We've not been able to get much schooling into him as he hits the ground quite hard. He's nowhere near the finished article." Sam TWISTON-DAVIES at Carlisle (4/11/18)

GOING:	R	W	P	TRACK:	R	W	P
Soft	2	0	1	Left Handed	3	2	1
Good	4	3	1	Right	3	1	1
				Galloping	1	0	1
				Stiff/Undul.	2	1	0
				Tight	2	1	1
				Tight/Undul.	1	1	0

TRIP:	R	W	P	JOCKEY:	R	W	P
2m	1	1	0	S.Twiston-Davies	5	2	2
2m 3f	2	1	0	J.J.Burke	1	1	0
2m 4f	3	1	2				

PHOENIX WAY (IRE)

6 b g Stowaway – Arcuate (Arch (USA))
OWNER: J.P.McMANUS
TRAINER: H.FRY. Seaborough, Dorset.
CAREER FORM FIGURES: 1 - 521
CAREER WIN: 2018: Jan KILLEAGH Soft 5YO Mdn PTP 3m: 2019: Jan PLUMPTON Good/ Soft NH 2m 4f

This former Irish winning pointer retains his place in the *Top 40 Prospects* with the strong belief that Harry Fry has barely scratched the surface with this potentially well handicapped six year old. Phoenix Way was denied the opportunity to show what he is capable of during the second half of last season, due to a minor injury. However, the J.P.McManus owned gelding is back in work and lined up for some of the valuable staying handicap hurdles this winter off his opening mark of 133.

A twelve lengths winner of his point at Killeagh in January 2018, his previous handler Donnchadh Doyle remarked afterwards: **"He's a smart horse that does everything very easily in his work at home. He jumped very well out there today."** Subsequently sold for £270,000 seventeen days later at the Goffs UK January Sale at Doncaster, he raced three times over hurdles last season for his new connections. Despite being strong in the market on his Rules debut in a two mile maiden hurdle at Bangor in November, he could only finish fifth behind Donald McCain's The Some Dance Kid (won twice more since and rated 133). Phoenix Way shaped much more encouragingly next time though when five lengths runner-up behind the well regarded I Can't Explain in a similar event at Sandown less than a month later. Subsequent winners Hold The Note (3rd), Baddesley Knight (5th) and Greaneteen (6th) were in behind. Stepped up to two and a half miles for the first time at Plumpton early in the New Year, Harry Fry's charge made no mistake at the Sussex track. Partnered by Aidan Coleman, he was always going well and quickened up smartly on the run-in to win by a length from Hughie Morrison's Third Wind. The runner-up won his next two starts, including the EBF Final at Sandown in March. The third home (Commanche Red) also won next time.

Unfortunately, that was the last we saw of Phoenix Way, who returned to his owner's stud in Ireland for recuperation during the spring/summer following a minor setback. However, the Stowaway gelding is all set to make up for lost time with the £100,000 Grade 3 *Betfair* Exchange Stayers' Handicap Hurdle at Haydock Park (23rd November) pencilled in as a possible starting point. The step up to three miles is expected to bring about further improvement and it is worth recalling Irish point expert Declan Phelan's comments in last year's *OJA*: **"A powerful bay unit: running for the Monbeg stable, he coasted to the lead at the third last and thereafter dominated an above average maiden at Killeagh (Soft) in January. It was a race run at a proper lick and clocked the day's fastest time by over ten seconds. Plenty of point winners have since emerged from the "also rans" to give solid foundations to the form. This five year old may be the ideal mix of possessing gears added to his obvious athleticism for jumping fences, allied to reserves of stamina. I would rate him the best five year old that Monbeg had through their hands last season, and quite possibly their smartest pointer in any age group. A career as a Grade 1 or 2 chaser is on the horizon and, based on Killeagh, Phoenix Way can win races from two miles to three miles and will be comfortable on most terrains."**

POINTS TO NOTE:
Probable Best Distance	-	2m 4f – 3 miles
Preferred Going	-	Soft

Connection's Comments: "He's a nice horse who jumps very well." Aidan COLEMAN at Plumpton (6/1/19)

GOING:	R	W	P	TRACK:	R	W	P
Heavy	1	0	1	Left Handed	3	2	0
Soft	1	1	0	Right	1	0	1
Good/Soft	2	1	0	Galloping	1	0	1
				Tight	1	0	0
				Tight/Undul.	1	1	0

TRIP:	R	W	P	JOCKEY:	R	W	P
2m	2	0	1	A.Coleman	2	1	0
2m 4f	1	1	0	B.Geraghty	1	0	1
3m	1	1	0	R.James	1	1	0

RATHHILL (IRE)

6 b g Getaway (GER) – Bella Venezia (IRE) (Milan)
OWNER: J.P.McMANUS
TRAINER: N.J.HENDERSON. Lambourn, Berkshire.
CAREER FORM FIGURES: 2 - 14
CAREER WINS: 2018: Dec NEWBURY Soft Mdn Hdle 2m

As discussed, Nicky Henderson has a formidable team of novice chasers for this season, many of which belong to J.P.McManus. Birchdale, Champ and Dickie Diver look set to take high rank over two and a half miles plus this winter, while the lightly raced Rathhill could emerge as one of Seven Barrows' leading two milers in the same division.

Trained by Colin McKeever and owned by Wilson Dennison, who have been responsible for so many good horses over the years, the Getaway gelding finished runner-up in his only point-to-point at Loughbrickland in November 2017. It is worth recalling what expert Declan Phelan wrote in last year's *OJA*: **"Derek O'Connor has for several years had a retainer to ride for leading Northern point owner Wilson Dennison. In the last two years, he has added a retainer to ride for J.P. McManus in amateur races as well as guiding said owner regarding pointing talent. Rathhill raced in the Dennison silks once during the autumn, at Loughbrickland (Heavy) in November. He moved best for the majority of the race, until he began to struggle on the climb to the final fence and was eased to finish a twelve lengths second to Derby. Viewing the race, I think the horse gave Derek a very good feel, and he looked after him when the horse found the testing conditions too taxing in that last quarter mile. Derek encouraged J.P. McManus to buy the horse and he has dispatched the five year old to Nicky Henderson. In 2016/17, O'Connor advised McManus to purchase the talented Jerrysback from the same pointing source, so the top amateur's judgement may be that Rathhill has a bright future and has shown him enough to recommend that he is a young horse of 120 + track potential."**

The Getaway gelding made a winning start to his Rules career when winning a twenty runner maiden hurdle over two miles at Newbury in December. Leading on the run-in, Rathhill sprinted clear to win by a hard held one and a half lengths. Subsequent winners Pistol Whipped (3rd), Dashel Drasher (4th) and Umndeni (5th) were in behind. **"I think he's got a big future but he's only a baby,"** commented Nicky Henderson. Sent off 6/5 favourite for the Grade 1 Tolworth Novices' Hurdle at Sandown in early January, he failed to give his running having come under pressure leaving the back straight. Beaten nearly twelve lengths in fourth behind Elixir De Nutz, the race may have come too soon (only seventeen days after his reappearance). Not seen since, his trainer issued a positive bulletin during the summer with novice chasing on the six year old's agenda this season.

Rathhill has only raced on testing ground and, even though he is related to five times Grade 1 winner Bellshill (same source), he didn't look slow at Newbury and is expected to be kept to trips around two miles.

POINTS TO NOTE:

Probable Best Distance	-	2m – 2m 4f	
Preferred Going	-	Soft	

Connection's Comments: **"He's got a great temperament and attitude to life. He's a very burly horse who has taken a lot of work, but he's done it well and handled the ground. He's a point-to-pointer but he's got plenty of gears so two miles is fine." Nicky HENDERSON at Newbury (19/12/18)**

GOING:	R	W	P	TRACK:	R	W	P
Heavy	1	0	1	Left Handed	2	1	1
Soft	2	1	0	Right	1	0	0
				Galloping	2	1	0

TRIP:	R	W	P	JOCKEY:	R	W	P
2m	2	1	0	B.Geraghty	2	1	0
3m	1	0	1	D.O'Connor	1	0	1

SHISHKIN (IRE)

5 b g Sholokhov (IRE) – Labarynth (IRE) (Exit To Nowhere (USA))
OWNER: Mrs J.DONNELLY
TRAINER: N.J.HENDERSON. Lambourn, Berkshire.
CAREER FORM FIGURES: 3 - 11
CAREER WINS: 2018: Nov LINGSTOWN Good 4YO Mdn PTP 3m: 2019: Mar KEMPTON Good/Soft NHF 2m

Bookmaker turned investor Joe Donnelly sold his business for around €27m in the 1990s and has traded commercial buildings since then, including one on the Champs Elysee in Paris. His yellow and black silks have become increasingly common on Irish and UK racecourses in recent seasons with Al Boum Photo winning the Magners Cheltenham Gold Cup in March. Melon has finished runner-up three times at the Festival, including twice in the Champion Hurdle and Donnelly had his first horse in training with Nicky Henderson last season, namely ex-pointer Shishkin.

Bought at the Tattersalls Derby Sales as a three year old for €28,000, the Sholokhov gelding raced twice in Irish points for Virginia Considine. An eight lengths winner at Lingstown in November on his second start, his trainer said afterwards: **"We have always liked him and we were confident coming here today."** Subsequently sold at the Cheltenham December Sale for £170,000, Shishkin was an impressive eight lengths winner of a bumper at Kempton in March. Making all under Nico De Boinville, he quickened away from his eight opponents two furlongs from home, looking a high-class prospect in the making. From the family of Grade 1 winning mare Voler La Vedette, the five year old is all speed and is set to develop into a major contender for the leading two mile novice hurdles this season.

Irish point expert Declan Phelan believes: **"A tall elegant bay gelding: housed with Virginia Considine, he ran in two points: indicated a minor degree of promise when a fair third in a four year old maiden at Inch (Yielding/Soft) in March 2018. The summer break had a telling impact, because he was a more powerful unit when reappearing at Lingstown (Good) in November: that race was setting up as a grand shootout between him and L'Air**

Du Vent when that rival fell three out and Shishkin strode home majestically for an emphatic eight lengths win. A £170,000 sale at Cheltenham in December resulted in a move to Nicky Henderson. He added to his reputation with a smooth bumper win at Kempton in March. I note all three of his runs have been on flat right-handed tracks: this is a pointer blessed with raw speed and one who could conceivably operate to a very high level over two and two and a half miles. He has a full brother called Marcle Ridge, a one-time Irish pointer, now pointing/hunter chasing in the UK: this sibling is a bridle horse, and it remains to be seen how Shishkin will fare on a stiff track or when put under pressure. If kept to tracks like Kempton, Haydock etc, he can win over hurdles at Graded level: he may be more of an Aintree Festival horse than a Cheltenham operator.

POINTS TO NOTE:
Probable Best Distance   -   2m – 2m 4f
Preferred Going   -   Good/Soft
Connection's Comments: "Shishkin is a wonderful big horse, still very raw with plenty of growing and filling out to do. He has showed raw pure ability and we're over the moon to see that today. He will need a good summer break to mature and Nico [de Boinville] was suitably impressed. We were hoping to take a lead but there was no pace so he let him bowl." Toby LAWES, assistant trainer, at Kempton (16/3/19)

GOING:	R	W	P	TRACK:	R	W	P
Yielding/Soft	1	0	0	Right	3	2	0
Good/Soft	1	1	0	Tight	1	1	0
Good	1	1	0				

TRIP:	R	W	P	JOCKEY:	R	W	P
2m	1	1	0	N.De Boinville	1	1	0
3m	2	1	0	R.James	2	1	0

SPORTING JOHN (IRE)
4 bb g Getaway (GER) – Wild Spell (IRE) (Oscar (IRE))
OWNER: J.P.McMANUS
TRAINER: P.J.HOBBS. Minehead, Somerset.
CAREER FORM FIGURES: 1
CAREER WIN: 2019: Mar BORRIS HOUSE Soft 4YO Mdn PTP 3m

Owner J.P.McManus and trainer Philip Hobbs enjoyed further Grade 1 success last winter courtesy of former Triumph Hurdle winner Defi Du Seuil. The ex-French gelding gained the fourth and fifth Grade 1 victories of his career in the Scilly Isles and JLT Novice Chases at Sandown and Cheltenham respectively. Rated 162 over fences, the son of Voix Du Nord has been a tremendous horse for his connections. The pair also successfully combined at the Punchestown Festival in May with Musical Slave winning the Adare Manor Opportunity Series Final Handicap Hurdle under budding star Jonjo O'Neill junior.

The multiple winning champion owner has sent the unbeaten Irish pointer Sporting John to Hobbs having purchased the Getaway gelding for £160,000 at the Cheltenham Festival sale in March. One of fifteen horses in training with Ballingaggin, County Wexford based Matt O'Connor, he was a two and a half lengths winner of his sole start eleven days earlier. Irish expert Declan Phelan comments: **"This is a tall elegant brown gelding, a half-brother to current UK hunter chaser Kalabaloo, former jump jockey Matt O'Connor secured him at the 2018 Land Rover sale for €33,000 and prepared him for his one point outing at Borris (Soft): this track in County Carlow is getting a reputation for staging a quality four year old** maiden at the March fixture and the 2019 renewal was one of the smartest maidens of the spring. Sporting John sat towards the rear, until his jockey, Jimmy O'Rourke, moved him closer three out: from there to the finish he locked horns with Generation Text and finished the stronger to win by two and a half lengths. He was bought by J.P. McManus for £160,000 at Cheltenham March sales. Andy Dufresne, who McManus also picked up in 2018 when winning the corresponding maiden, clocked a time of 6:33 in similar ground: we know that Andy Dufresne looks like a Grade 1 standard jumps horse: Sporting John clocked 6:32 in 2019 and the third, fourth and fifth from this Borris race have all won since, giving the form a tremendous boost. From a family containing Oscar Whisky and Seeyouatmidnight, I would describe Sporting John as a rock solid stayer with a touch of quality: the decision to send this gelding to Philip Hobbs may result in a Graded class novice hurdler/chaser emerging. I think he will always prefer some element of cut in the ground." It is also worth noting that the 142 rated hurdler Sinoria won the five year old mares' maiden on the same card in 2018 in a time of 7m 4.00s. Philip Hobbs may have inherited a smart prospect.

POINTS TO NOTE:
Probable Best Distance	-	2m 4f – 3 miles	
Preferred Going	-	Soft	

Connection's Comments: "He did that very well. We bought him in the Land Rover off Dick Frisby and, ever since getting him home, I have loved everything about him. I was a small bit afraid coming here that I hadn't got him fit enough because he does things so easily at home. He jumped like a buck the whole way and all of his work has been 110%." Matt O'CONNOR at Borris House (3/3/19)

GOING:	R	W	P	TRACK:	R	W	P
Soft	1	1	0	Left Handed	1	1	0

TRIP:	R	W	P	JOCKEY:	R	W	P
3m	1	1	0	J.P.O'Rourke	1	1	0

THE BIG BREAKAWAY (IRE)
4 ch g Getaway (GER) – Princess Mairead (IRE) (Blueprint (IRE))
OWNER: ERIC JONES, GEOFF NICHOLAS, JOHN ROMANS
TRAINER: C.TIZZARD. Milborne Port, Dorset.
CAREER FORM FIGURES: 1
CAREER WIN: 2019: Apr QUAKERSTOWN Good/Yielding 4YO Mdn PTP 3m

Colin Tizzard finished fourth in the trainer's championship during 2018/2019 with 77 winners and total prize-money of £1,888,757. Elixir De Nutz (Tolworth Hurdle), Lostintranslation (Mildmay Novices' Chase) and Reserve Tank (Mersey Novices' Hurdle & Champion Novices' Hurdle) provided the stable with Grade 1 victories, while Elegant Escape won the Welsh National in December. Tizzard, who has trained seven Cheltenham Festival winners during his career, was busy recruiting new stock during the spring/summer purchasing Bold Conduct (£150,000), Fiddlerontheroof (£200,000), Ofalltheginjoints (€75,000) and Royal Crown (£110,000) amongst others. His most expensive 'signing' though was the former Irish pointer The Big Breakaway, who was bought for €360,000 at the Goffs Punchestown Horses in Training Sale in early May.

Expert Declan Phelan comments: "The name drops a clue that this chestnut is one massive unit and, in physique, he is not far removed from another previous Monbeg/Don Doyle winning pointer, Topofthegame. With a choice pedigree, half-brother to Kildisart and his Granny bred 2019 Grand National runner-up Rathvinden, he cost €55,000 as a store at the

2018 Derby Sale. One run later the Monbeg lads cashed in handsomely. That run occurred at Quakerstown (Good/Yielding) on Easter Sunday, and in a nutshell, he took the race by the scruff of the neck at the third last and galloped away from the rest of the field, posting a ten lengths win. This four year old maiden at Quakerstown is another with a proven record of unearthing special talents. For a time comparison (albeit on various ground conditions), in 2011 Champagne Fever won this race in 5:59, in 2016 Next Destination in 6:42, in 2017 Brewin'upastorm in 5:51, in 2018 Champagne Platinum clocked 6:34..... so the time of The Big Breakaway in 2019 of 6:01 reads as more than respectable, if the calibre of opponent he defeated is suspect. He became the sales topper at Punchestown Goffs auction, reaching a price of €360,000 and knocked down to Colin Tizzard. Leaving aside the hefty price tag, this is one case of the ideal horse for the perfect trainer. As a long striding galloper, the future for The Big Breakaway most likely will be concentrated on staying hurdles and chases: Tizzard is excellent at conditioning and campaigning such stayers, and The Big Breakaway could repeat the exploits of Elegant Escape (another Tizzard trained ex-Irish pointer) and win at the top level as a staying chaser. In the short term, he can make a mark as a staying novice hurdler this winter and a date with the three mile Albert Bartlett Novices' Hurdle at the Cheltenham Festival could feature on his itinerary."

POINTS TO NOTE:

Probable Best Distance	-	2m 4f – 3 miles	
Preferred Going	-	Good/Soft	

Connection's Comments: "He's very smart. Rob (James) felt he was green early on but when he got there he quickened up very well. He could be anything." Donnchadh DOYLE at Quakerstown (21/4/19)

GOING:	R	W	P	TRACK:	R	W	P
Good/Yielding	1	1	0	Left Handed	1	1	0
TRIP:	R	W	P	JOCKEY:	R	W	P
3m	1	1	0	R.James	1	1	0

THE OLYMPIAN (IRE)
3 ch g Olympic Glory (IRE) – Basira (FR) (Azamour (IRE))
OWNER: J.P.McMANUS
TRAINER: A.KING. Wroughton, Wiltshire.
FLAT CAREER FORM FIGURES: 221
CAREER WIN: 2018: Oct NEWMARKET Good Mdn 1m 2f

Alan King sent out 91 winners last season and earned £1,259,316 in prize-money. Alsa Mix, Sceau Royal and The Glancing Queen supplied the Barbury Castle team with Grade 2 victories, while Talkischeap provided the icing on the cake to an excellent campaign with a stunning ten lengths win in the Bet365 Gold Cup at Sandown on the final day of the season.

David Nicholson's former assistant feels the stable are particularly strong in the novice hurdle department with bumper winners Heart of A Lion, Major Dundee, San Rumoldo, Sheshoon Sonny, The Glancing Queen and Wynn House. Add to that a potentially strong team of juvenile hurdlers and all the ingredients are there for a formidable squad of youngsters.

The Olympian was featured in the *Top 40 Prospects* of *Ahead On The Flat* but, at the time of writing, hasn't reappeared on the level as a three year old. However, that has been by design having been purchased during the winter by J.P.McManus with a view to go hurdling this season. From the family of Group 1 Grand Prix de Paris winner and Breeders' Cup Turf placed Behkabad, he raced three times as a two year old earning an official rating of 86. Runner-up on his first two starts at Windsor and Goodwood, he was beaten three parts of a length behind Pablo Escobarr at the latter venue. The William Haggas trained winner has subsequently finished runner-up behind Epsom Derby winner Anthony Van Dyck in the Listed Lingfield Derby Trial and is rated 103. The Olympian got off the mark at the third time of asking when scoring by a neck at Newmarket over ten furlongs in late October. Mind The Crack, who is rated 91, was three lengths back in third.

Originally owned by King, Anthony Bromley and Jamie Magee, the Olympic Glory gelding stays well and handles easy ground and is therefore tailormade for jumping hurdles. His stable have unearthed some top-class juvenile hurdlers over the years, including Triumph Hurdle winners Penzance (2005) and Katchit (2007), and they may have another smart one on their hands in The Olympian, who may be picking up a gold medal himself on the Cheltenham podium next March.

POINTS TO NOTE:

Probable Best Distance	-	2 miles	
Preferred Going	-	Good/Soft	

Connection's Comments: "The Olympian could be very exciting with a winter on his back. We will see what the handicapper does, but I think he'll be a decent three-year-old, he's got a decent attitude and gets the trip." Alan KING at Newmarket (24/10/18)

GOING:	R	W	P		TRACK:	R	W	P
Good/Soft	1	0	1		Right	3	1	2
Good	1	1	0		Galloping	1	1	0
Good/Firm	1	0	1		Tight	1	0	1
					Tight/Undul.	1	0	1
TRIP:	R	W	P		JOCKEY:	R	W	P
1m	1	0	1		M.Harley	3	1	2
1m 2f	2	1	1					

TOPOFTHEGAME (IRE)
7 ch g Flemensfirth (USA) – Derry Vale (IRE) (Mister Lord (USA))
OWNER: CHRIS GILES & Mr & Mrs P.K.BARBER
TRAINER: P.F.NICHOLLS. Ditcheat, Somerset.
CAREER FORM FIGURES: 1 – 142 – F412 - 2212
CAREER WINS: 2016: Mar BELCLARE Yielding/Soft Mdn PTP 3m; Dec ASCOT Good/Soft MH 2m 5f: 2018: Feb SANDOWN Soft Grade 3 HH 2m 7f; Mar CHELTENHAM Soft Grade 1 NC 3m

The giant chestnut features in the *Top 40 Prospects* for the fourth consecutive season in the belief that he could provide champion trainer Paul Nicholls with his fifth win in the Cheltenham Gold Cup next March. Team Ditcheat is currently blessed with six Grade 1 winning two and a half miles plus chasers, namely Black Corton, Clan Des Obeaux, Cyrname, Frodon, Politilogue and Topofthegame. The last named though looks set to develop into the stable's leading hope for steeplechasing's Blue Riband in the spring.

Runner-up in the Coral Cup at Cheltenham in March 2018, the Flemensfirth gelding had fallen on his chasing bow at Newbury earlier the same season before a decision was made to revert back to the smaller obstacles. Back over fences at Exeter (2m 3f) in December, Topofthegame ran a remarkable race. Having whipped around at the start and forfeited twenty lengths, he got back in contention and was only beaten three and a half lengths by subsequent dual Grade 1 winning novice chaser Defi Du Seuil. His luckless run continued at Kempton in the Grade 1 Kauto Star Novice Chase on Boxing Day. Paul Nicholls was seeking his fifth win in the race and, having taken charge at the third last, the seven year old looked set to prevail comfortably. However, he was worried out of it after the last by the top-class mare La Bague Au Roi and was beaten a length and a half. Incidentally, the winning time was only a second slower than the King George. Harry Cobden may have hit the front too soon at the Sunbury track but he was brilliant aboard Topofthegame in the RSA Chase at the Cheltenham Festival. Delivering him to perfection, he stayed on strongly on the run-in to beat Santini and Delta Work (won a Grade 1 since) by upwards of half a length. He jumped and travelled beautifully throughout and looked every inch a future Gold Cup horse in the making. His rider said afterwards: **"He's a big raw horse who is progressing a lot and will be even better next year."** While he was unable to follow up at Aintree, he ran well in second but looked flat and didn't race with his usual enthusiasm. Six lengths in arrears of Lostintranslation, he remains a novice until the end of October, which means Nicholls may give him more chasing experience before tackling open company.

The Ladbrokes Trophy at Newbury (30th November) is likely to be his first main target. Officially rated 164, Paul Nicholls has won the race three times (Strong Flow (2003) off 140) & Denman (2007) off 161 and (2009) off 174). Still lightly raced over fences, there is every chance we still haven't seen the best of Topofthegame.

POINTS TO NOTE:

Probable Best Distance	-	3 miles +
Preferred Going	-	Good/Soft

Connection's Comments: **"He's not unlike Denman and, God willing, will be in the Gold Cup next year. He's got plenty of boot and this is the only race we've been training him for. The next one will be next year's Gold Cup." Paul NICHOLLS at Cheltenham (13/3/19)**

GOING:	R	W	P	TRACK:	R	W	P
Soft	8	2	5	Left Handed	5	1	2
Yield/Soft	1	1	0	Right	7	3	4
Good/Soft	3	1	1	Galloping	4	2	1
				Stiff/Undul.	4	1	2
				Tight	3	0	3

TRIP:	R	W	P	JOCKEY:	R	W	P
2m 3f	2	0	2	H.Cobden	4	1	3
2m 4f	1	0	0	S.T-Davies	5	2	2
2m 5f	3	1	2	S.Bowen	1	0	1
2m 6f	1	0	0	N.Fehily	1	0	0
2m 7f	1	1	0	R.James	1	1	0
3m	3	2	1				
3m 1f	1	0	1				

TRUCKERS PASS (IRE)

5 br g Kalanisi (IRE) – Lady Knightess (IRE) (Presenting)
OWNER: BROCADE RACING
TRAINER: P.J.HOBBS. Minehead, Somerset.
CAREER FORM FIGURES: 2

In addition to the aforementioned L'Air Du Vent, Brocade Racing are also responsible for another ex-pointer, Truckers Pass, having paid £175,000 at the Cheltenham December Sale for the once raced gelded son of Kalanisi. Declan Phelan remarks: **"Tall bay gelding with scope when he fills out his frame: raced once for Cork handler Batty O'Connell: at Ballindenisk (Yielding/Sofy) in December, having moved readily to challenge on the approach to the second last, he inherited a three lengths advantage when the leader, Rookie Trainer, clouted that fence and lost momentum. Heading to the last with a few lengths lead, supporters of Truckers Pass were counting their potential winnings: they did not reckon on a dogged Rookie Trainer fighting back and Truckers Pass wilting and succumbing right on the line, as he lost out by a head in a photo finish. The race was run in a smart time, sixteen seconds faster than the preceding division (won by Overthetop). His dam won a Wexford bumper and it could turn out that three miles stretches his stamina. He changed hands for a mighty £175,000 at Cheltenham December sales."**

Sent into training with Philip Hobbs, Truckers Pass was due to run last spring but a bout of coughing meant his Rules debut was put on hold. However, the Minehead based handler informed me during the summer that the five year old did some 'fantastic' pieces of work last season. I have been fortunate enough to interview Philip Hobbs on numerous occasions during the last twenty years and rarely have I heard him speak so enthusiastically about a horse. If reproducing his homework, Brocade Racing may have acquired another exciting prospect from the Irish pointing scene.

POINTS TO NOTE:
| Probable Best Distance | - | 2m – 2m 4f |
| Preferred Going | - | Good/Soft |

GOING:	R	W	P	TRACK:	R	W	P
Yielding/Soft	1	0	1	Right	1	0	1

TRIP:	R	W	P	JOCKEY:	R	W	P
3m	1	0	1	S.Baragry	1	0	1

WIDE RECEIVER (IRE)

4 b g Sholokhov (IRE) – Sagarich (FR) (Sagamix (FR))
OWNER: GIGGINSTOWN HOUSE STUD
TRAINER: G.ELLIOTT. Longwood, Co.Meath.
CAREER FORM FIGURES: 1
CAREER WIN: 2019: Feb CRAGMORE Yielding/Soft 4YO Mdn PTP 2m 4f

"Cormac Farrell is a new addition to the pointers training ranks and the Wexford based handler made an instant impact in 2019: having bought Wide Receiver for €25,000 at the 2018 Derby Store Sale, he struck gold because one run and win later and inside the space of nine months, his next date with an auction produced a sales topping price of £410,000 at Cheltenham February Sales. Wide Receiver is by a sire of a Gold Cup winner (Don Cossack), his dam was a moderate dual purpose mare: she won a twelve furlongs maiden at Wexford when with Charlie Swan and then, having moved to England, she won a low key novice hurdle over two miles at Market Rasen for Mick Quinlan. The dam side of the family does contain many Flat and jumps winners on the continent, mainly in France and Germany. Wide Receiver did supply a visually impressive success on his only start: that win was at Cragmore in February: the land over which this fixture is staged is owned by the exors of the late Tom Costello, a pointing legend. They have raced since 2015 and the four year old maiden has been run over the two and a half miles distance. In the five editions of this race, previous winners include Death Duty, The Big Lense and Sams Profile: the race tends to favour four year olds with some toe. In 2019 just a handful runners lined up, from three out Wide Receiver hit top gear and sprinted up on the climb to the finish, scoring by eight lengths: the form has not been advertised, the runner up has been parked up injured and none of the other three runners have done anything of note. Timewise, at 5:04, he clocked a winning time in line with Death Duty (2015). This horse should supply Gordon Elliott with a sure-fire bumper winner, though I am not convinced he has the stellar quality to contend for a Cheltenham Festival bumper: his career peak may be as a two and a half miles chaser," believes Declan Phelan.

As discussed, Gordon Elliott invariably keeps his four year old ex-pointers to bumpers in their first season under Rules. Expect him to do likewise this winter with this potentially high-class recruit.

POINTS TO NOTE:
Probable Best Distance	-	2 miles
Preferred Going	-	Good/Soft

Connection's Comments: "We came here for a bit of nice ground and the trip was perfect for him as he has a nice bit of boot and class about him. This horse has been so straightforward from the start, we feel he's one that has a huge future." Cormac FARRELL at Cragmore (10/2/19)

GOING:	R	W	P	TRACK:	R	W	P
Yielding/Soft	1	1	0	Left Handed	1	1	0
TRIP:	R	W	P	JOCKEY:	R	W	P
2m 4f	1	1	0	S.Cavanagh	1	1	0

OWNERS' ENCLOSURE
RICH & SUSANNAH RICCI

Novice Hurdlers

EL BARRA has yet to run for us having picked up a minor injury during the second half of last season. Runner-up in his only Irish point-to-point, he was an expensive purchase at the Cheltenham May Sale last year. He was going well at home last season and due to run in a bumper until he had a hiccup. Back in work now and, given the fact he is five already, we are keen to crack on with him over hurdles. He is a nice type. We have bought a lot of new horses from France, including the unbeaten **EDEN FLIGHT**. A five year old by Great Pretender, he won his only Flat race by three lengths in October 2017 and has been given plenty of time. **FEU DU BRESIL** is a young horse I am really looking forward to seeing run. Runner-up on his only start at Auteuil in the Autumn last year, he is a four year old by Blue Bresil and the form of his race has worked out well with the third, fifth and seventh winning since. We like him a lot. **FIGAROC** is a nice four year old by Masterstroke who finished second at Compiegne in the spring on his only start over hurdles. **FIVE O'CLOCK** raced three times over hurdles at Auteuil, finishing third and second on his latest two starts. A four year old by Cokoriko, he is a chaser in the making but we are hoping he will do well in novice hurdles this season. The form of **FLY SMART**'s only run at Auteuil has worked out incredibly well. A gelding by Day Flight, he won on the Flat before going hurdling for Guillaume Macaire. Beaten a couple of lengths, the third, fifth, sixth, seventh, eighth and ninth have all won subsequently. I am excited about him. We have also bought a couple of juvenile hurdlers for this season, including **GRAND BORNAND**. A three year old by Montmartre, he won an APQS Flat race at Senonnes in June, while **HOOK UP** is a nice filly by No Risk At All. She raced four times on the Flat winning at Compiegne in March. **JON SNOW** is another one to look forward to having shown progressive form on the Flat in France. A winner over a mile and a half, he is by Le Havre and we purposely kept him off the track last season. Willie (Mullins) invariably buys the French horses as three year olds and keeps them back for the following season. He is a lovely big horse. **MONKFISH** is a winning pointer by Stowaway and we were delighted with his run in a bumper at the Punchestown Festival finishing second. Very much a chaser in the making, he may have another run in a bumper but it won't be long before he goes novice hurdling. He is a big strong horse. **N'GOLO** is an interesting horse we bought at the Arqana Sale in France last October. Nearly white in colour, he is a four year old by Galileo who raced four times on the Flat for Nicolas Clement. Placed in his first three starts, he then won over a mile and six at Clairefontaine. **REBELLITO** has not raced for a couple of years and has yet to run for us. A dual winner on the Flat in France, he scored over a mile and ten furlongs and is a five year old by Montmartre. He is ready to go novice hurdling. Despite the fact he remains a maiden, **TIGER TAP TAP** showed a good level of form contesting two Grade 1s last season, including the Triumph Hurdle. Given time to strengthen up, I think he will have benefited from another summer and he reminds me of Let's Dance, who improved in her second season over hurdles.

Novice Chasers

ANNAMIX has been something of a talking horse for the last couple of years and we were disappointed with him last season. However, he won over hurdles at Clonmel last time and we feel he will make a better chaser. Still maturing, he jumps well and we think he will make a decent novice chaser. **ANTEY** didn't run last season but is back in training and ready to go over fences. He won twice over hurdles, including at the Punchestown Festival, and I think he will deveop into a nice chaser. Only six, he remains lightly raced. **BAPAUME** won the Grade 2 Prix

La Barka at Auteuil last year and finished runner-up in the same race in June having been fourth in both the Stayers' Hurdle at Cheltenham and the French Champion Hurdle. It is possible he doesn't fully see out the three miles trip at the top level but is a lovely horse who has earned a lot of prize-money. There is every chance he could go novice chasing as he has a very sound jumping technique and plenty of experience, but it will be a few months before we decide that. **BRAHMA BULL** has done very well for us and has a great strike-rate with six wins from nine starts. He came back this spring/summer and has won two out of three over fences. Despite doing his winning on good ground during the summer, we think he will appreciate softer ground and should stay well now that he is putting it together mentally. **DEAL D'ESTRUVAL** is another who is back having missed the whole of last season. Progressive over hurdles, I like him and I think he is going to stay well this year. **SALSARETTA** is a lovely mare who won twice over hurdles last season. She is a fine big filly and I think she will do well in staying mares' novice chases. There is such a good programme for novice chasing mares in Ireland nowadays.

Hurdlers

BENIE DES DIEUX is a brilliant mare and, having won the Grade 1 Annie Power Mares' Champion Hurdle at Punchestown in May, she then won the Grande Course de Haies d'Auteuil – the French champion Hurdle – which was a great thrill. She got the trip well and, while it is tempting to go back over fences, she is more likely to stay hurdling. She is in great nick and there are plenty of options for her. There is the mares' hurdle at Cheltenham, in which she was so unlucky last season, and also the Stayers' Hurdle because we know she stays. **FAUGHEEN** has been an incredible horse for us winning nine Grade 1 races. Third in the Stayers' Hurdle at Cheltenham in March, he has had a good break during the summer but no decision has been made regarding future plans. He loves racing but we want to make sure he is 100%. **SALDIER** is a very interesting horse. A Grade 1 winning juvenile hurdler a couple of seasons ago, he broke his nose when falling at the last in a Grade 3 hurdle at Naas last November. I thought he was going better than the subsequent Champion Hurdle winner Espoir D'Allen when he fell. He was getting to his feet when another horse bumped into him hence his broken nose. Given plenty of time since, I am very excited about him because he could be a real force in the two miles division, if recapturing his best form. **SHARJAH** is a lovely horse who had a great season winning the Galway Hurdle and then the Grade 1 Morgiana and Ryanair Hurdles at Punchestown and Leopardstown respectively. Brought down early on in the Champion Hurdle in March, he doesn't want heavy ground and I would expect him to follow a similar programme this season.

Chasers

BURROWS SAINT provided us and Willie (Mullins) with our first Irish National when winning at Fairyhouse over Easter. Ruby (Walsh) mentioned Aintree afterwards but we feel he could improve again and may even develop into a Gold Cup horse. Rated 156, he was fifth in the Grand Steeple-Chase de Paris at Auteuil last time and Paul (Townend) thought it was his best performance to date. It is a tough race to win and I thought he ran a great race. I love him. **CHACUN POUR SOI** came back from a long absence (1089 days) to win both his novice chases at Naas and Punchestown. A very talented horse, he beat the Arkle and JLT winners at Punchestown and we have plenty of options for him. Despite the fact both his wins came over two miles, we could experiment and try him over further because we think he will stay, even though he has a lot of speed. No decision has been made regarding future targets. **DOUVAN** has won eight Grade 1s for us and, having missed last season, he came back into training earlier than usual this summer. We haven't made any plans because it is all about keeping him right. **GETABIRD** remains lightly raced over fences having only raced three times last season.

A winner on his chasing debut at Punchestown, he was then narrowly beaten in a Grade 2 at Limerick on Boxing Day following a mistake at the last. He needs to go right-handed. **MIN** was a triple Grade 1 winner last season and I thought he was spectacular at Aintree when winning the Melling Chase. Runner-up at Punchestown last time, he is a brilliant horse on his day. His only disappointing run came in the Queen Mother Champion Chase when we changed the tactics and I don't think it suited him. He is likely to follow a similar programme.

RICH'S HORSES TO FOLLOW: FLY SMART & JON SNOW
RACING MANAGER JOE CHAMBERS' HORSE TO FOLLOW: HOOK UP

JARED SULLIVAN

Nicky HENDERSON

DIESE DES BIEFFES (FR) 6 gr g Martaline – Chanel Du Berlais (FR)
He is back in work having missed the whole of last season and the plan is to send him novice chasing. A useful novice hurdler, he won three times and was fifth in both the Lanzarote Hurdle at Kempton and the Martin Pipe Conditional Jockeys' Handicap Hurdle at the Cheltenham Festival. Good ground is ideal.

SON OF CAMAS (FR) 4 ch g Creachadoir (IRE) – Camas (FR)
Bought as a three year old at the Goffs Landrover Sale, he made his debut in a bumper at the Punchestown Festival last spring but was disappointing. Found to be clinically abnormal afterwards, Nicky (Henderson) has always liked him and we hope he is a lot better than he showed that day. He will go novice hurdling.

Willie MULLINS

CHEF DES OBEAUX (FR) 7 b g Saddler Maker (IRE) – O Dame De Gene (FR)
A Grade 2 winning novice hurdler a couple of seasons ago, he won over fences at Chepstow last season before pulling up in the National Hunt Chase at the Cheltenham Festival. The key to him is soft ground and, with that in mind, he was transferred to Willie Mullins during the summer. Rated 149, we will be aiming him at some of the good staying handicap chases in Ireland in testing ground.

DOLCITA (FR) 4 b f Saint Des Saints (FR) – Orcantara
She is a potentially exciting filly who raced twice over hurdles in France. Third on her debut at Pau in December, she was then beaten a nose at Auteuil in late February. Her previous trainer Guillaume Macaire was desperate to keep hold of her and we will campaign her in mares' novice hurdles.

DONT HESITATE (FR) 6 b m Diamond Boy (FR) – Quibble (FR)
She has only raced twice for us having had her problems but I like her. A ten lengths winner on her hurdles debut at Ballinrobe in September last year, she then jumped poorly in a Grade 3 mares' hurdle at Down Royal next time. Absent since, she has got an engine and we think she will stay further than two miles.

DORRELLS PIERJI (FR) 6 br g Coastal Path – Playa Pierji (FR)
He had a busy campaign last season winning a couple of bumpers and then he won twice over

hurdles at Listowel and Galway. I thought he ran very well at the Punchestown Festival finishing third in a valuable handicap hurdle behind stablemate Mr Adjudicator, who has subsequently won a Grade 2 at Auteuil and a twelve furlongs handicap on the Flat at the Galway Festival. Daryl Jacob rode him that day and liked him and felt he had the speed to drop back to two miles. He has had a good break since and will go novice chasing.

DUC DES GENIEVRES (FR) 6 gr g Buck's Boum (FR) – Lobelie (FR)
Did very well over fences last season winning twice, including the Arkle Trophy at the Cheltenham Festival. I thought he was very good that day even though the race fell apart to an extent. Third last time in the Grade 1 Ryanair Novice Chase at the Punchestown Festival, the ground wasn't soft enough for him. I am keen to aim him at the Tingle Creek Chase at Sandown (7th December) because I think the uphill finish will suit him. His long-term target is the Queen Mother Champion Chase, provided the ground is soft enough.

EGLANTINE DU SEUIL (FR) 5 b m Saddler Maker (IRE) – Rixia Du Seuil (FR)
She is a high-class mare who won the Grade 2 mares' novice hurdle at the Cheltenham Festival before finishing third in Grade 1 novices at Fairyhouse and Punchestown. Only beaten two and a quarter lengths against the geldings at the latter track, the first two got first run on her because she was trapped on the rails before staying on. She is very tough and had some good form earlier in the season, too. Third behind the subsequent Grade 1 winner Aramon at Listowel over two miles in September, she is suited by two and a half miles and will remain over hurdles this season. She is a very good mare.

ESTELLE MA BELLE (FR) 5 ch m Air Chief Marshall (IRE) – Ozalid (FR)
A big mare, she was a dual winner on the Flat in France but didn't make her hurdles debut until August. Considering she hadn't raced for 762 days and met a useful race fit rival at Galway, I thought she ran well in second. Beaten four lengths, she was keen early on. Unfortunately, she threw a splint afterwards but hopefully it won't be too long before she is running again in mares' novice hurdles. Willie (Mullins) feels she will benefit from racing left-handed and we are hoping she will be good enough to contest the mares' novice hurdle at Cheltenham in March.

FABULOUS SAGA (FR) 7 b g Saint Des Saints (FR) – Fabalina (FR)
Missed the whole of last season but is back now and will go novice chasing. A former winning pointer, he had a busy campaign the previous season winning a bumper and four times over hurdles, including Grade 2 and 3 events at Cork and Limerick. He stays well with three miles being his trip.

FAST BUCK (FR) 5 b g Kendargent (FR) – Juvenil Delinquent (USA)
Bought at the Newmarket Horses in Training Sale in the Autumn of 2017, he didn't make his hurdles debut until January this year. Placed on her first two runs at Cork and Naas, he then had a wind operation, which made a huge difference. Returning in the summer, he won easily at Listowel and followed up in a Listed novices' hurdle at the Galway Festival. Ruby Walsh was impressed with him and, even though he has been winning over two miles, he will stay two and a half miles. We like him.

GETAREASON (IRE) 6 ch g Getaway (GER) – Simple Reason (IRE)
Kept busy last season, he won twice over hurdles at Galway and Tramore and was placed in a Grade 1 at Naas in January. Prior to that, he was runner-up in the Grade 2 Navan Hurdle. We thought he would run well in the Martin Pipe Conditional Jockeys' Handicap Hurdle at the Cheltenham Festival but he weakened after the second last. I think he had had enough by that stage of the season having been on the go for a long time. Two and a half miles is his trip and he will go novice chasing.

LAURINA (FR) 6 b m Spanish Moon (USA) – Lamboghina (GER)
She won her first two races last season, Listed mares' hurdles at Sandown and Punchestown, before finishing fourth in the Champion Hurdle at Cheltenham. Ruby (Walsh) said she was never travelling even though she looked as though she was full of running coming down the hill. She went out like a light after the second last. She didn't run again because they couldn't get her right. Despite the fact it was a two runner race, I was impressed with her at Sandown because she tanked through it. I don't think she was at her best at Punchestown next time even though she won. She has had a good summer break and we are going to keep her over hurdles, although I don't know what her best trip will prove to be. She deserves another crack at the top hurdle races before we think about going chasing.

LUCKY ONE (FR) 4 bl g Authorized (IRE) – Lady Anouchka (IRE)
Runner-up in two starts over hurdles at Fontainebleau for Guillaume Macaire, we bought him last winter and have given him plenty of time. A big scopey, good looking four year old, he spent the summer with Noel Fehily before going into training with Willie in early September. Noel likes him a lot and he is one to look forward to in novice hurdles this season.

LUXY LOU is a three year old by Nathaniel with a very good pedigree. I bought him as a yearling and Noel (Fehily) likes him a lot. He will start off in a bumper and is potentially useful.

REAL STEEL (FR) 6 b g Loup Breton (IRE) – Kalimina (FR)
He developed into a very good novice chaser winning three times, including a valuable novices' handicap chase at the Punchestown Festival. Sixth in the JLT Novices' Chase at Cheltenham, he was also runner-up in the Grade 1 Ryanair Gold Cup at Fairyhouse over Easter. His latest win was over two miles five but I think he will stay three miles this year. He pleasantly surprised us last season because, although we have always liked him, he had fallen at the last in a Grade 1 novice hurdle at Leopardstown the previous season and it took him a long time to get over that. Indeed, he fell on his chasing debut at the same track, too, but he hasn't looked back since. We feel he is a better horse going right-handed.

RIO VIVAS (FR) 7 b g Voix Du Nord (FR) – Rio Amata (GER)
Placed in his two Irish points, he was quite a useful bumper horse for us a couple of seasons ago, winning at Navan before finishing fourth at the Punchestown Festival. Forced to miss last season due to a back injury, he is 100% now and will go novice hurdling over two and a half miles plus.

ROCHESTON (FR) 4 b g Kapgarde (FR) – Ravna (FR)
Third on his only run over hurdles at Bordeaux in September last year when trained by Guillaume Macaire, he spent the summer with Noel (Fehily) and has gone into training with Willie (Mullins). Noel likes him and he will hopefully develop into a smart novice hurdler.

STORMY IRELAND (FR) 5 b m Motivator – Like A Storm (IRE)
A Listed winner over hurdles at Punchestown on her reappearance, she finished runner-up in her next four races, including Grade 1 mares' hurdles at Cheltenham and Punchestown. She is only small, so I am keen for her to stay over hurdles and she deserves to win a big one, with two and a half miles being her trip. She will follow a similar programme.

Olly MURPHY

ETOILE REBELLE (FR) 4 b g Walk In The Park (IRE) – Line Mexia (FR)
Unraced, he was an expensive foal who was bought at the Goffs December Sale. He will start off in a bumper.

MONBEG ZENA (IRE) 7 ch m Flemensfirth (USA) – Mandys Gold (IRE)
Despite the fact she is a seven year old, she has only raced once for us winning over hurdles at Southwell last season. A former Irish pointer, she then had a problem with her pelvis, hence she didn't run again. Noel (Fehily) feels she is a Graded mare and she will jump fences eventually.

Paul NICHOLLS

CHANTE NEIGE (FR) 5 b m Martaline (FR) – Russian Taiga (FR)
She finished third at Auteuil on her only start over hurdles in March 2017. Stormy Ireland finished runner-up in the same race. She has been in training with Willie Mullins but had problems hence she hasn't run for us yet. A big mare measuring 16.2hh, she spent the summer with Noel and has gone into training with Paul (Nicholls). I hope she will be running this season because Willie always thought she was very good.

SENDING LOVE (IRE) 6 b g Scorpion (IRE) – Dato Vic (IRE)
Another who has yet to run for us, he won his only Irish point-to-point by five lengths in February 2017, before being bought the same month. In training with Willie Mullins since, he has had his problems. I decided to send him to Paul Nicholls with a view to going novice hurdling and hopefully he can start making up for lost time.

> **JARED'S HORSE TO FOLLOW: LUCKY ONE**

VALUE RACING CLUB

Leading syndicate ValueRacingClub.co.uk already have an Imperial Cup, Durham National and Listed Summer Hurdle on their burgeoning CV. A number of years ago, I was asked to become the Club's Ambassador and was delighted to accept the role. With horses in training with Phil Kirby, Dr Richard Newland, David Pipe, Alastair Ralph and Jamie Snowden, their racing manager is **James Couldwell** and he has kindly run through the pick of their string for the winter ahead.

ARTISTIC LANGUAGE 3 b g Archipenko (USA) – Kiswahili
Trainer: Alastair RALPH
We've had plenty of success with our juvenile hurdlers over the years and this gelded son of Archipenko ticks every box. He showed a good level of form on the Flat for Brian Meehan earning a mark of 73. Bought privately, he stays well and handles heavy ground and is related to a couple of jump winners. Given a break of six weeks after his purchase, he's done well but is still immature and has plenty of growth left in him. Provided he takes to jumping, we are hoping he will develop into a Fred Winter Juvenile Hurdle contender next spring.

BROUGHTONS ADMIRAL 5 b g Born To Sea (IRE) - Chanter
Trainer: Alastair RALPH
One of the toughest horses we've ever owned. Despite the fact he isn't very big and won't jump a fence, he's an excellent syndicate horse. Winning at Doncaster in March before giving his owners a day out at the Cheltenham April meeting on his first try over three miles was a big thrill. He travelled strongly in the Safran Landing Handicap Hurdle, jumping the last three lengths in front. Frustratingly, the Pertemps Final runner-up, Tobefair caught us on the run to the line. On his final start, although he ran well in third, he was over the top by then but remains unexposed over three miles. The plan this season is to run into a big field handicap off near

bottom weight. If everything goes right, don't be surprised if he runs well. Given the fact he takes a fair amount of work to get fit, he is one to look out for after a couple of runs.

FLASH DE CLERVAL (FR) 4 b g Maresca Sorrento (FR) – Nonita De Clerval (FR)
Trainer: Dr Richard NEWLAND
He was purchased privately for £30,000 from Ireland and is a well related French bred by the same sire as Pineau De Re, who Dr Newland trained to win the Grand National. He raced four times over hurdles in Ireland showing useful form in the process and gave the impression he is crying out for a step up in trip. Based on his breeding – he is a half-brother to a couple of two miles five winners, we expect him to improve as he goes up in distance. Still a shell of a horse when he first arrived, he's blossomed over the summer and grown more than any other horse we've purchased before. Still a maiden, I would like to think he will shed that tag sooner rather than later and develop into a smart Novice hurdler. We like him.

HUGO 'N TAZ 8 b g Kayf Tara – Ryde To Arms
Trainer: David PIPE
We tried to buy him during the Summer of 2018 and came close to agreeing a deal but his owner changed his mind at the last minute. Just over a year later, I was pleased to see him entered in the Goffs UK August sale at Doncaster and we managed to secure him for £19,000. A big horse who measures 16.2h, he is built like a tank and has benefited from a break, having been on the go for nearly sixteen months. Despite the fact the majority of his races have been on decent ground, his best form is in much more testing conditions. The fact he remains a maiden over fences is a bonus, too. We think he is crying out for a trip on heavy ground, having finished sixth in the Cork Grand National in last November. Since arriving, his training regime has changed completely and his first main target is the Lincolnshire National at Market Rasen on Boxing Day. Given his optimum conditions, we're confident he can land a nice prize off his current mark of 111.

LEONCAVALLO (IRE) 7 br g Cape Cross (IRE) – Nafura
Trainer: Dr Richard NEWLAND
A horse that needs little introduction having won his first five starts over hurdles for John Ferguson, including the Listed Wensleydale Juvenile hurdle at Wetherby, before finishing fifth in the Triumph Hurdle in 2016. After seeing him entered in the Goffs UK sales in January 2018, we were keen to buy him. Surprisingly, he was friendless at the sale and we secured him for £21,000. We gave him a break and immediately dropped him back in trip after his previous connections had been running him over longer distances. He has always worked like a class horse and won hard held at Ludlow in May 2018. He provided us with one of our best days when third in one of the most valuable handicaps run all year, namely the Galway Hurdle. Fifth in the Scottish Champion Hurdle and eighth in the Swinton Hurdle, he was struggling with his feet at the time (he is flat footed). Work has continued on his feet throughout the summer and everything looks good. While we don't have any specific targets, he'll continue to run in all the valuable two mile races but he doesn't want heavy ground. He's got a big race in him.

QUIET PENNY 5 b m Sholokhov (IRE) – Pennys Pride (IRE)
Trainer: Dr Richard NEWLAND
Yet to race for us, we're hoping Quiet Penny could be one of the nicest horses we've owned. A stunning looking mare, she is a class act in person and on pedigree and we loved her at the sales. A big strong mare, we purchased her for £32,000 at the Goffs UK Spring Sale at Doncaster in May. A home bred from the Reveley's and trained by Gillian Boanas, she is from a very good family and was handled with kid gloves during the early part of her career. Stepped up to three miles for the first time at Newcastle in April, she won hard held by seventeen lengths. Visually, it was very impressive. Turned out for three months since arriving, she's done very well during the summer and we are delighted with her. I'm not sure where we'll start, but she's

National Hunt MOPS qualified, so we will be looking for a £10,000 mares' bonus race. I think she's hugely exciting and feel she can take high rank in mares' chasers over the next few years.

PISGAH PIKE (IRE) 4 b g Famous Name – Music On D Waters (IRE)
Trainer: Dr Richard NEWLAND
Another yet to run for us, he is an interesting recruit. He was bought cheaply in a private deal having finished sixth of eighteen in a bumper at Cork. The race has worked out well, too. In both bumper starts, he has travelled well moving into contention on the bridle before fading late on. Interestingly, he wore a tongue tie and has come from a very small yard in Ireland, who have had less than ten runners under Rules in the last five years. Since acquiring him, both the fourth and fifth at Cork have won subsequently. A nice looking horse, he stands at 16.1h and is a flashy type. We'll get his wind checked and, with the assistance of Dr Newland, we are hoping he is open to plenty of improvement. He'll start in a bumper and we will go from there.

VELVET REVOLUTION 6 ch g Pivotal – Gino's Spirits
Trainer: Alastair RALPH
A lovely looking horse who was above average on the Flat for Marco Botti (rated 84). Purchased for 22,000gns at the Newmarket Horses in Training Sale last Autumn, he made an encouraging start for us finishing runner-up twice over hurdles at Ffos Las and Newton Abbot and the form has worked out well. However, on each occasion, the jockeys have reported an issue with his wind. Hobdayed since his last run, we are hoping he will handle easier ground during the Autumn/winter. I will be disappointed if we can't get his head in front sooner rather than later, before hopefully progressing into a candidate for some of those valuable handicap hurdles in the spring.

VALUE RACING CLUB'S HORSE TO FOLLOW: QUIET PENNY

Please see pages 187-194
for details of the
One Jump Ahead Updates

Don't forget to read my Diary @
www.mhpublications.couk

TALKING TRAINERS
Kim BAILEY
Stables: Thorndale Farm, Withington Road, Andoversford, Cheltenham, Gloucestershire.
2018/2019: 51 Winners / 263 Runners 19% Prize-Money £601,872
www.kimbaileyracing.com

ADJOURNED 4 gr g Rip Van Winkle (IRE) – Bite Of The Cherry
He won a bumper for James Bethell at Southwell before we bought him at the Cheltenham November Sales. Fourth on his only run for us under a penalty at Wincanton in April, he had been on the go for a long time and I don't think he was at his best that day. We have schooled him over hurdles and he jumps very well. He will start off in a two miles novice hurdle.

BOBHOPEORNOHOPE (IRE) 4 b g Westerner – Bandelaro (IRE)
A nice looking four year old who won his only Irish point for Cormac Doyle in April. His form looks OK but we haven't done a lot with him since buying him at the Cheltenham April Sale. He could start off in a bumper before going hurdling.

CATCH ME NOT 4 b f Flemensfirth (USA) – Dorabelle (IRE)
Bought at the Derby Sales in Ireland last year, she is a nice filly by Flemensfirth who has worked well at home and we will start her off in a mares' bumper.

CHARBEL (IRE) 8 b g Iffraaj – Eoz (IRE)
Enjoyed a good first half of the season winning twice, including the Grade 2 Peterborough Chase at Huntingdon. He struggled with his breathing during the second half of the campaign and we have therefore operated on his wind since his last run at Sandown. The Peterborough Chase (8th December) is very much his target once again and I am keen to try him over three miles at some stage.

COMMODORE BARRY (IRE) 6 br g Presenting – Specifiedrisk (IRE)
A four times winner over hurdles last season at Worcester, Southwell (twice) and Doncaster, he finished second on his chasing debut at Ayr in May. I was disappointed he didn't win but he was only beaten narrowly and has enjoyed a good summer. I hope he will develop into a decent staying novice chaser this season.

CRESSWELL LEGEND 8 b g Midnight Legend – Cresswell Willow (IRE)
He won over fences at Ludlow in the spring but the ground was very quick and he came back jarred up. Disappointing at Perth last time, I think he was still feeling the effects and we have therefore given him a good break since. Three miles on decent ground on a right-handed track are his optimum conditions.

DANDY DAN (IRE) 6 b g Midnight Legend – Playing Around
He had a very good first year over fences winning at Bangor, Kelso and Ayr. I thought he ran well on his final start, too, at Ayr finishing second in a valuable novices' handicap chase on Scottish National day, on ground which was too fast for him. It won't be easy this time around off a mark of 145, but he is tough and we will aim him at the decent three miles plus handicap chases.

DIAMOND GAIT 6 b m Passing Glance – Milliegait
Twice a winner over hurdles at Ludlow and Doncaster, I think she is capable of winning a decent mares' handicap hurdle off her mark this season. I think she will stay further this year.

DOES HE KNOW 4 b g Alkaased (USA) – Diavoleria
An interesting horse we acquired at the Cheltenham April Sale, having won his only point-to-point in Yorkshire for Cherry Coward. Only four, I like him and we may start him off in a bumper before going hurdling.

DONNIE BRASCO (FR) 6 b g Buck's Boum (FR) – Parislatino (FR)
Another who won an English point-to-point, we bought him at the Cheltenham Sales in February. Previously trained by Tom Ellis, he won at Alnwick in January and both the second and third have won since. We nearly ran him last season but he wants soft ground and it started to dry up, so we put him away. A chaser in the making, he will go straight over hurdles.

DRUMREAGH (IRE) 5 b m Court Cave (IRE) – Mollyash (IRE)
A relatively cheap buy at the Cheltenham May Sale, she had two runs in Irish points for Stuart Crawford. Brought down on her debut in late April, she then finished runner-up three weeks later. We are still getting to know her but I would imagine mares' novice hurdles will be on her agenda.

DUKE OF EARL (FR) 3 b g Noroit (GER) – Visiorienne (FR)
Purchased at the Goffs UK Spring Stores Sale at Doncaster in May, he is a lovely young horse and very much one for the future. Only three, he may not even run this season.

EL PRESENTE 6 b g Presenting – Raitera (FR)
Absent since the spring of last year, he is back in work and I have always liked him. In fact, the time off won't have done him any harm. A winner over hurdles at Huntingdon a couple of seasons ago, he will go novice chasing.

FIRST FLOW (IRE) 7 b g Primary (USA) – Clonroche Wells (IRE)
Endured a frustrating season only running once. He ran a very good race in the Imperial Cup at Sandown finishing fifth, considering he had been off the track for a year. We tried to get a run into him beforehand, but he needs soft ground and never got his conditions. Earlier in the season, he was due to make his chasing debut at Hereford, but had a dirty trachea wash and therefore couldn't run. Then, it was such a dry winter, he didn't reappear until March and it was too late to go chasing by then. A Grade 2 winning novice hurdler the previous season, I have been pleased with him during the summer and he will go novice chasing.

FUBAR (IRE) 5 ch g Le Fou (IRE) – Petite Mielle (IRE)
Performed well in bumpers without winning, being placed at Market Rasen and Warwick and finishing fourth at Ascot. He made his hurdles debut at Wincanton in May but didn't jump as well as he can and it was clear he wasn't happy. We therefore had him x-rayed afterwards and it transpired he was suffering with a kissing spine. He has had an operation on his back since and I hope he will show what he is capable of over hurdles this season.

HAPPYGOLUCKY (IRE) 5 bb g Jeremy (USA) – Mydadabishop (IRE)
A nice type by a good stallion, he was runner-up in his only Irish point in November before we bought him the following month. We planned to run him last season but the ground changed, so we elected to give him a break. I like what I've seen at home and he will go novice hurdling in the Autumn.

HES NO TROUBLE (IRE) 6 b g Scorpion (IRE) She's No Trouble (IRE)
He's a nice horse who won a point-to-point before we bought him. An easy winner over hurdles at Huntingdon in February, he disappointed at Ludlow last time but the track didn't suit him and the ground was too quick. The plan is for him to go novice chasing and, while he has the speed for two miles, he will stay further. I think he will prove versatile, in terms of trip.

ILLUMINATED BEAUTY (IRE) 6 b m Flemensfirth (USA) – Native Beauty (IRE)
Still a novice over hurdles, she was runner-up at Stratford last time and is capable of winning a handicap off her mark. However, she is a winning pointer and will make a better chaser. Her jumping has always been very good.

IMPERIAL AURA (IRE) 6 b g Kalanisi (IRE) – Missindependence (IRE)
He is a very nice horse who I have always liked. Unbeaten in two starts over hurdles, he beat Sole Pretender at Carlisle who has won his next three races and finished fifth in the Galway Hurdle and is rated 148. He was then absent for four months, due to sore shins, but he won nicely under a penalty at Newcastle in February. Rated 133, he could go novice chasing but I think he is on a good mark and we are tempted to aim him at a decent handicap hurdle. I think he will be effective over any trip.

JAVA POINT (IRE) 4 b g Stowaway – Classic Sun (GER)
Trained in Ireland by Colin Bowe, he won his second point-to-point by fifteen lengths and we bought him four days later at the Cheltenham Festival Sale in March. He has only cantered and done some roadwork for us, so it is early days, but he looks a nice horse for the future.

LORD APPARELLI 4 ch g Schiaparelli (GER) – La Marette
Another very nice unraced four year old we bought at the Goffs UK Sale at Doncaster last year. He is a big horse and a full-brother to Prince Llywelyn, who we train and they are very similar. We will start him off in a bumper.

MINELLA WARRIOR (IRE) 7 b g King's Theatre (IRE) – Bobbi's Venture (IRE)
We were going to send him chasing last season but decided to keep him over hurdles. He had a good season, too, winning three times at Warwick, Uttoxeter and Wetherby and finishing a close second at Huntingdon. We have operated on his wind since his last run and I hope he will make a useful staying novice chaser. Three miles is his trip.

MR GREY SKY (IRE) 5 gr g Fame And Glory – Lakil Princess (IRE)
An exciting prospect who won both his starts in bumpers at Haydock last winter. Measuring over 17hh, there was no point running him again, so we decided to put him away and give him time. I have been very pleased with him during the summer and I think he will stay well over hurdles this season. Nico De Boinville, who rode against him on his debut, has been down to sit on him at home.

NEWTIDE (IRE) 6 br g Getaway (GER) – C'Est Fantastique (IRE)
He has taken a bit of time to come good but I was pleased with him last year winning twice over hurdles at Haydock and Ffos Las. Runner-up in a point-to-point, three miles is his trip and he enjoys soft ground. He will go novice chasing.

PARTY FUZZ 4 b g Great Pretender (IRE) – Very Special One (IRE)
We trained his mother, who was placed in the mares' final at Newbury. Bought at the Goffs Landover Sale in Ireland last year, we have a very nice bunch of four year old bumper horses and I only ran one last season. He is a lovely horse who I like and his owners are very patient.

PRINCE LLYWELYN 5 ch g Schiaparelli (GER) – La Marette
Another lovely young horse who performed well in bumpers last season. A winner at Wetherby on his second start, he finished runner-up in the other two and could easily have won all three. His form is good and I am looking forward to sending him novice hurdling. I think he will stay well.

RED RIVER (IRE) 6 ch g Beneficial – Socker Toppen (IRE)
A very good jumper, he was unlucky on his chasing debut at Ludlow in December. He had every chance when he did the splits at the fourth last and pulled some muscles, which ruled him out for the rest of the season. Back in work, he will resume in staying novice chases and I hope he will do well.

RHOSNEIGR (IRE) 4 ch g Iffraaj – Sadinga (IRE)
A three times winner on the Flat for Charlie Hills, he joined us earlier this year with a view to going hurdling. He schooled for the first time in July and jumped very well. I hope he will make his mark over jumps.

ROCKY'S TREASURE (IRE) 8 b g Westerner – Fiddlers Bar (IRE)
I was delighted with his first season over fences winning four times, including a Grade 2 contest at Doncaster in December. Rated 147, his first main target is the Becher Chase at Aintree (7th December) and then we will plan for the rest of the season after that.

SADLERMOR (IRE) 5 b g Morozov (USA) – Lucyjane (IRE)
He won a bumper at Huntingdon on his second start in March before disappointing at the same track under a penalty over a month later. Given a long break since, we haven't schooled him yet but he will go novice hurdling over two and a half miles.

SHANTOU EXPRESS (IRE) 4 ch g Shantou (USA) – Spanker
He is the only four year old I ran last season and, while he ran a very good race, I was disappointed when he finished second at Ludlow. However, the form has worked out well with the third winning his next three races. He is a very nice horse who will probably have another run in a bumper before going hurdling.

STATION MASTER (IRE) 8 b g Scorpion (IRE) – Gastounette (IRE)
Very consistent over fences last season, he won at Huntingdon and finished runner-up on four occasions, including at Cheltenham in November. Rated 135, he kept running well and won't be the easiest to place. There is every chance he will go back to Cheltenham in November for the amateur riders race once again (15th November).

SUBWAY SURF (IRE) 5 b m Milan – Dante Rouge (IRE)
She's a nice mare who did well in bumpers last season winning two out of three at Ludlow and Chepstow. A point-to-point winner, she stays well and will go novice hurdling and I hope she will have another good season in mares' only events.

TALK OF FAME 4 b g Fame And Glory – Princess Oriane (IRE)
Another nice unraced four year old who has pleased me at home. We nearly ran him last season but decided to give him more time and he has grown during the summer. He will go down the bumper route.

THE BULL MCCABE (IRE) 5 b g Yeats (IRE) – Twilight View (IRE)
Ran in three Irish points winning on his latest start in April and we purchased him the following month at the Goffs UK Spring Sale. By Yeats, whose stock we have done well with, we haven't done much with him but I hope he is another promising young horse to go hurdling with.

THE EDGAR WALLACE (IRE) 4 b g Flemensfirth (USA) – Annalecky (IRE)
An expensive purchase at the Goffs Landrover Sale in Ireland last year, he is a big horse measuring 17hh with an excellent pedigree. A half-brother to Cheltenham Festival winner Black Hercules, he was very forward last season and could have run in February. He is a very nice horse who will make his debut in a bumper.

THE MILAN GIRL (IRE) 5 b m Milan – En Vedette (FR)
She won one of her three bumpers but could very easily have won all three. Successful at Bangor on her second run, she jumps well and will run in mares' novice hurdles.

TWO FOR GOLD (IRE) 6 b g Gold Well – Two of Each (IRE)
A dual bumper winner, he had a good season over hurdles last winter winning at Wetherby and Bangor. He is a big horse though who wants to go chasing and I hope he will make a nice novice. Three miles is his trip.

VINNDICATION (IRE) 6 b g Vinnie Roe (IRE) – Pawnee Trail (IRE)
He has had a wind operation since his run at the Cheltenham Festival and remains a very progressive horse. Still only six, his first race is likely to be in the Grade 2 Charlie Hall Chase at Wetherby (2nd November), which we won with Harry Topper in 2013. A Grade 2 winner last season at Ascot, he didn't have the best of preparations for the JLT Novice Chase at the Festival, but wasn't disgraced in what turned out to be a very strong race. He finished behind the two horses, namely Defi Du Seuil and Lostintranslation, which he had chased home in the Grade 1 Scilly Isles Novices' Chase at Sandown on his previous start. He was still very green last year and I think he will improve this season, especially when stepped up to three miles for the first time.

WANDRIN STAR (IRE) 8 b g Flemensfirth (USA) – Keralba (USA)
He is owned by Mrs Perriss, who also has Station Master with us, and they are both rated 135 over fences. A wide margin winner on two occasions at Bangor last season, he has strengthened up again during the summer and will be aimed at three miles handicap chases.

WHAT A BALOO (IRE) 4 b g Jeremy (USA) – Luca Lite (IRE)
Still a baby last year, he was bought as a three year old and is a half-brother to Those Tiger Feet, who we also train. He is one of two horses by Jeremy we have in training and they are the first ones we have ever had. I have been pleased with him during the summer and he is another one for bumpers.

WINTER GLORY (IRE) 4 b g Fame And Glory – Winter Shadows (FR)
Purchased in Ireland as a three year old, he has filled out during the summer and I like him. He will run in a bumper in the Autumn and we will go from there.

YEAVERING BELLE 5 ch m Midnight Legend – Fruit Yoghurt
Placed in an English point-to-point, she is a tough mare who surprised us when winning a bumper at Warwick in February on her first run for us. She ran a corker in another bumper at Cheltenham in April and then she won on her hurdles debut at Newton Abbot at the end of May. Back in work, she will continue to run in mares' novice hurdles.

YOUNEVERCALL (IRE) 8 b g Yeats (IRE) – Afarka (IRE)
He is not the easiest horse to deal with and has a preference for going right-handed. However, he was progressive last season winning at Kempton in November and then a Grade 2 hurdle on the final day of the season at Sandown. Rated 157, he needs to improve again, but we are going to test the water going left-handed by running him in the Grade 2 West Yorkshire Hurdle at Wetherby (2nd November). Then, all being well, he will go for the Long Walk Hurdle at Ascot (21st December).

TRAINER'S HORSE TO FOLLOW: FUBAR

Harry FRY

Stables: Manor Farm, Seaborough, Beaminster, Dorset.
2018/2019: 47 Winners / 242 Runners 19% Prize-Money £823,437
www.harryfryracing.com

ACTING LASS (IRE) 8 b g King's Theatre (IRE) – Darrens Lass (IRE)
Things didn't go right for him last season only racing once and finding the ground too quick at the Punchestown Festival in the spring. Back in work, he was a useful novice chaser the previous campaign winning three times. Rated 143, he will be aimed at the decent three mile handicap chases on slow ground.

AIR HORSE ONE 8 gr g Mountain High (IRE) – Whisky Rose (IRE)
He hasn't won for a long time and has slipped down to a winnable mark, as a result. We tried him over three miles for the first time at the Punchestown Festival but he didn't stay. Runner-up at Taunton in January, that run proved he retains plenty of ability. He won't jump fences, so will continue in handicap hurdles.

ANY DRAMA (IRE) 8 b g Gamut (IRE) – Oak Lodge (IRE)
A faller on his chasing debut at Uttoxeter in December, he incurred a nasty injury in the process, which ruled him out for the remainder of the season. He hasn't been a natural over fences so he will revert back to hurdles and go handicapping over two and a half miles plus.

AS I SEE IT 7 b g King's Theatre (IRE) – Chomba Womba (IRE)
Missed the whole of last season, but he is back in work and will hopefully make up for lost time. A former winning pointer, he won a maiden hurdle at Huntingdon the previous season and is rated 125. He may start off in a handicap hurdle before going novice chasing later on. Two and a half to three miles is his trip.

BAGS GROOVE (IRE) 8 b g Oscar (IRE) – Golden Moment (IRE)
Enjoyed a very good first season over fences winning four times, including the Grade 2 Rising Stars and Pendil Novice Chases at Wincanton and Kempton respectively. We stepped him up to three miles for the first time at Huntingdon in December and he won nicely but his next run in the Grade 1 Kauto Star Novices' Chase at Kempton on Boxing Day came too soon. Back on track in the Pendil Novices' Chase over two and a half miles a couple of months later, we then let him take his chance in the Grade 1 novice at Aintree, but he ran flat and it was probably one run too many. We are looking forward to his second season over fences with two and a half miles or an easy three miles on flat tracks being ideal. Rated 151, he could reappear in the Grade 2 Old Roan Chase at Aintree (27th October) and then we will consider races such as the Grade 2 Peterborough Chase at Huntingdon (8th December).

BLACK MISCHIEF 7 b g Black Sam Bellamy (IRE) – Miss Mitch (IRE)
He won a decent prize over hurdles at Haydock's *Betfair* Chase meeting in November under an inspired ride by Richard Johnson. A non stayer over three miles in the Pertemps Final at the Cheltenham Festival, he made his chasing debut at Uttoxeter in May over two miles and it was good experience for him. He will be aimed at novice chases over two and a half to two miles six.

BULLIONAIRE (IRE) 6 b g Gold Well – Dontcallerthat (IRE)
A very promising bumper horse a couple of seasons ago winning the Goffs UK Spring Sales bumper at Newbury on his debut before finishing second in a Listed event at Ascot. He was then off for a long time before making his hurdles debut at Newton Abbot in May. He ran no sort of race though, but it wasn't a total surprise because he hadn't convinced us he was the horse he was in his work at home beforehand. Following some tests we found he was a Grade 2 (out of 5) wobbler, which has been treated since. We are hoping he can return to something like his best, but he has plenty to prove. Novice hurdles over two and two and a half miles are on his agenda.

CAPTAIN DRAKE (IRE) 6 b g Getaway (GER) – Julika (GER)
Progressive over hurdles last season, he won at Uttoxeter and Southwell before finishing runner-up in a decent handicap at Kelso in March. A former Irish pointer, he loves the mud and I think he will make a nice staying novice chaser this winter. Long-term, it wouldn't surprise me if he developed into a Welsh or Midlands National horse.

CARIBERT (FR) 6 b g Ballingarry (IRE) – Cardamine (FR)
Like Bullionaire, he hasn't had much luck since winning the Goffs UK Spring Sale Bumper at Newbury in 2018. Runner-up on his hurdles debut at Exeter on New Year's Day, he then ran at the Punchestown Festival. Having travelled well, he stopped quickly and we found he had bled. Unfortunately, he has suffered with a bout of colic since and therefore plans are on hold, although he is still a novice over hurdles.

DALILA DU SEUIL (FR) 6 gr m Bachir (IRE) – Misery (FR)
A dual Listed winner over hurdles in France, she won nicely on her chasing debut for us at Exeter but then fell early on next time at Warwick. She incurred an injury there, which ruled her out for the rest of the season. Back in work, she looks ideal for the mares' chases and we will hopefully have a clear run because we know her better now. Two or two and a half miles on soft ground are her optimum conditions.

DEADRINGERFORLOVE 5 b m Black Sam Bellamy (IRE) – La Perrotine (FR)
Despite winning over hurdles at Chepstow in March, she didn't progress as much as we had hoped. We threw her in at the deep end in a Listed mares' hurdle at the Punchestown Festival but she found the ground too quick. She likes slow ground and I think she will benefit from stepping up to two and a half miles this season. Still a novice over hurdles until the end of October, she could go chasing later on and, being a half-sister to Cheltenham Gold Cup winner Sizing Gold, I hope she will improve over fences.

DEFINITELYANOSCAR (IRE) 6 b m Oscar (IRE) – Bobs Article (IRE)
She won over hurdles at Warwick in November before finding the ground too soft at Cheltenham the following month. Third behind a subsequent Punchestown Festival winner (Musical Slave) at Ludlow, she was unlucky last time because she won at Newton Abbot in August but was later disqualified. That was her first run since a wind operation because she we felt she wasn't quite finishing off her races and it seemed to make a difference. We are going to send her novice chasing over two and two and a half miles on better ground.

FEHILY (IRE) 4 b g Asian Heights – Leahs Joy (IRE)
A lovely unraced four year old we bought at the Doncaster Spring Sales last year. From the family of Diamond Harry, he was in training last season but we purposely haven't rushed him. He has done everything nicely at home and we will aim him at a bumper in the Autumn.

GENTLEMAN KAP (FR) 3 b g Kapgarde (FR) – Sabubelle (FR)
Unraced, we bought him as a two year old at the Arqana Sale in France. A nice individual, he will start off in a bumper from January onwards.

GET BACK GET BACK (IRE) 4 b g Lord Shanakill (USA) – Bawaakeer (USA)
He has only recently joined us having scored on three occasions on the level for Clive Cox at up to a mile and a half on good ground. We are doing plenty of schooling with him in preparation for his hurdling debut this autumn.

GET IN THE QUEUE 5 b g Mount Nelson – Amarullah (FR)

He, unfortunately, won't be running until the second half of the season having picked up a slight injury following his win at Newbury in March. It is a shame because he was very progressive in bumpers last term winning all three starts, following in the hoofprints of Rock On Ruby and Bitofapuzzle, who also won three before developing into Grade 1 winners over hurdles. Impressive on his first two starts at Uttoxeter and Exeter, he provided Noel (Fehily) with a winner on his final ride at Newbury, but found the ground quick enough. He has already schooled well and will go novice hurdling in the New Year.

GREEN DOLPHIN (IRE) 5 b g Oscar (IRE) – Shamrock Miss (IRE)

A nice horse who shaped well on his debut in a bumper at Warwick and learned plenty from it. An eleven lengths winner at Wincanton next time, we ran him in the rescheduled Listed bumper at Newbury fifteen days later, but it came soon enough and he finished fifth. He has done well during the summer and will start off over two miles over hurdles on slow ground, but will stay further.

HELL'S KITCHEN 8 b g Robin Des Champs (FR) – Mille Et Une (FR)

Had a good season winning a nice prize at Ascot at Christmas before being highly tried in the spring running at the Cheltenham, Aintree and Punchestown Festivals. Fourth in the Queen Mother Champion Chase and Melling Chase, he is just below Grade 1 standard. A strongly run two miles or two miles two is ideal and, with that in mind, he is likely to start off in the Grade 2 Haldon Gold Cup at Exeter (5th November).

IF THE CAP FITS (IRE) 7 b g Milan – Derravaragh Sayra (IRE)

He had a very good season and has never run a bad race throughout his career. We started the campaign thinking he might be a Champion Hurdle horse and, having finished second in the Elite Hurdle at Wincanton on his reappearance, he stepped up to two miles three in the Grade 2 Ascot Hurdle and won in good style. Third in the Christmas Hurdle at Kempton, he found it too sharp. Stepped back up in distance in the National Spirit Hurdle at Fontwell, he had a flu jab a week before and that affected his performance. He didn't travel with his usual fluency and did well to finish as close as he did in second. Not entered at Cheltenham, we tried him over three miles for the first time in the Grade 1 Liverpool Hurdle at Aintree and he produced a tremendous performance to win narrowly. We therefore have a lot to look forward to with him over three miles this season. Very consistent, he has spent the summer with Jason Maguire (owners Claire and Paul Rooney's racing manager) and we will start him off in the Grade 2 Ascot Hurdle (23rd November). Then, he will return to Ascot over three miles for the Grade 1 Long Walk Hurdle (21st December) before the Cleeve Hurdle at Cheltenham in January and then, all being well, the Stayers' Hurdle at the Festival in March.

IMPERIAL ESPRIT (IRE) 5 b g Scorpion (IRE) – Shesourpresent (IRE)

Very much a chaser in the making, he had a couple of runs last season but isn't a bumper horse. Runner-up behind a good horse of Paul Nicholls (Ask For Glory) on his debut at Chepstow, he found the ground too quick on his next start at the same track. He will go hurdling and wants two and a half to three miles on slow ground.

ISHKHARA LADY 5 b m Scorpion (IRE) – Loxhill Lady

From a family we know well, she is a half-sister to Zulu Oscar who we used to train. She produced a very promising debut at Plumpton in December winning a bumper by fifteen lengths. Noel (Fehily) was very taken by her that day, but unfortunately she struggled with sore shins afterwards and hasn't run since. Back now, she has been given time to mature and we may aim her at the Listed mares' bumper at Cheltenham's November meeting (16th November). She looked a smart mare at Plumpton and we have high hopes for her.

JOLLY'S CRACKED IT (FR) 10 b g Astarabad (USA) – Jolly Harbour
Had been off the track for nearly two years when winning a decent handicap hurdle at Ascot in November. He is only a couple of pounds higher now and, given the fact he is best fresh, he will attempt to win the same race again (22nd November). He loves Ascot having won there four times, including when dead-heating in the Ladbroke Handicap Hurdle in 2015.

JUST A STING (IRE) 7 b g Scorpion (IRE) – Shanann Lady (IRE)
Made a good start to his chasing career winning his first two races at Uttoxeter and Exeter before finishing second at Kempton over Christmas. He appreciates better ground and found the conditions too slow in the Kim Muir at the Cheltenham Festival. Below par at Sandown on his final start, he has a bit to prove but I am hoping he will develop into a useful second season chaser. Three miles on good ground suits him and something like the Grade 3 Sodexo Gold Cup Handicap Chase at Ascot (2nd November) could be an ideal starting point.

KING ROLAND (IRE) 5 br g Stowaway – Kiltiernan Robin (IRE)
We are looking forward to seeing him run over hurdles this season. An English point winner, he blew us away on his debut in a bumper at Uttoxeter last December. He then followed up under a penalty at Ffos Las in a competitive race, despite doing everything wrong. He tanked through the race but still won. We were going to aim him at the Grade 1 bumper at Punchestown but decided to leave him off for the rest of the season because his run at Ffos Las lit him up. He has schooled brilliantly at home and, while we may start him off over two miles, he will be suited by two and a half miles on slow ground. He will continue to wear a hood and is an exciting prospect.

MANTOVANI (FR) 4 b g High Chaparral (IRE) – Ripley (GER)
Previously trained by James Fanshawe, he ran promisingly on his first start over hurdles for us at Exeter finishing third in November. Only fifth next time a month later at Taunton, we felt he would benefit from a long break and the plan is to bring him back in September/October. He has strengthened up since his last run and we hope he is ready to make up for lost time.

MILLBANK FLYER (IRE) 4 b g Milan – The Last Bank (IRE)
He is a lovely unraced four year old we purchased at the Goffs UK Doncaster Spring Sale last year. A half-brother to Chantry House and The Last Day, he has done everything right at home and enjoyed a good summer. He will make his debut in a bumper in the Autumn but is a chaser in the making.

MILLE SUSSURRI (IRE) 4 b g Milan – Silent Whisper
Another nice unraced four year old by Milan, I like him and he is one to look forward to in a bumper in the Autumn.

MISTY WHISKY 5 gr m Stowaway – Whisky Rose (IRE)
A half-sister to Air Horse One and One For Rosie, she is a lovely mare who progressed with every run in bumpers last season. She won on her second start at Ludlow and then produced a very good performance to win a Listed mares' bumper at Sandown in March. Over the top by the time she ran in the Grade 2 bumper at Aintree, we know the family well and she ought to make a very nice mares' novice hurdler. Already a Listed winner, she will start off over two miles but will stay further.

MOMELLA (IRE) 7 ch m Sholokhov (IRE) – Missing Link (IRE)
Joined us last season, she was in the process of running well when she fell after the second last in the Grade 2 Long Distance Hurdle at Newbury. She jumped the hurdle well but then appeared to trip herself up and she came down. That fall knocked her confidence and she was disappointing on her subsequent two starts at Kempton and Cheltenham. Given a break since, we have schooled her over fences and she jumps very well, so we are likely to aim her at mares' novice chases.

MR ONE MORE (IRE) 7 b g Asian Heights – Norah's Quay (IRE)
He is back having missed the whole of last season. A dual winner over hurdles, including when beating Summerville Boy at Stratford, he wants two and a half miles on soft ground. There is a possibility he will go novice chasing.

ONEFORTHEROADTOM 6 gr g Fair Mix (IRE) – Ifni Du Luc (FR)
Still a maiden over fences, he endured a frustrating season. His big target was the valuable three miles novices' handicap chase at Ayr's Scottish National meeting and he was going well when falling towards the end of the backstraight. He ran well at the Punchestown Festival last time finishing second. He will continue over fences with three miles on good ground being his optimum conditions.

OUTOFTHISWORLD (IRE) 6 bb m Shantou (USA) – Mystic Masie (IRE)
A full-sister to Grade 2 winner Angels Breath, she beat the subsequent Mares' Final winner Annie Mc by eight lengths at Market Rasen in November. Not disgraced when runner-up next time at Fontwell, she was never right thereafter. Pulled up at Ludlow, she was well held at Newbury last time and has had a break since. Good fresh, she could reappear in another handicap hurdle but we may try her over fences at some stage this season.

OVER TO SAM 8 b g Black Sam Bellamy (IRE) – Lady Brig
Off the track for over two years, he made his debut over fences at Newton Abbot in May and the ground was perfect for him. He jumped very well before finishing third. A winning English pointer, we will hopefully get a clear run with him this season. Three mile plus novice chases will be his target this year.

PHOENIX WAY (IRE) 6 b g Stowaway – Arcuate
Progressed with each start over hurdles winning at Plumpton in January last time. A former Irish point-to-point winner, he appreciated the step up in trip at Plumpton and the form has been boosted subsequently. Unfortunately, he suffered a setback afterwards and missed the remainder of the campaign. Still lightly raced, he will be running in two and a half miles plus handicap hurdles.

PURE BLISS 4 ch f Mount Nelson – Burton Ash
She is a nice filly we bought at the Punchestown Festival Sale in May having won her only Irish point for Denis Murphy. Flat bred, she is a big strong filly and by the same stallion as Get In The Queue. We will start her off in a mares' bumper and I think she will provide us with a lot of fun.

RUFIO 5 b g Schiaparelli (GER) – Mole End
He is not a bumper horse but he was by no means disgraced in two runs at Ffos Las and Exeter finishing third on both occasions. We won't see the best of him until he jumps fences but he'll go hurdling this season and will appreciate a step up in trip on slow ground.

SAMARQUAND 5 b g Malinas (GER) – Samandara (FR)
A horse with a lot of ability, but trying to channel it is the tricky bit. He won well on his hurdles debut at Ludlow and then should have followed up under a penalty at Exeter. He ran about between the final two flights and threw the race away, which was eventually won by Getaway Trump, who is now rated 155. Pulled up at Newbury last time, he bled and hasn't run since. The plan is for him to go novice chasing and, if he grows up, he could develop into a useful chaser. He wants two and a half miles plus.

SOUND WALL (IRE) 4 b g Milan – Wall of Silence (IRE)
Another nice unraced four year old by Milan who we bought at the Doncaster Spring Sales last year. From the family of Thomas Darby, he has a good pedigree and is one to look forward to in a bumper in the Autumn.

UNOWHATIMEANHARRY 11 b g Sir Harry Lewis (USA) – Red Nose Lady
He has been a horse of a lifetime and enjoyed another remarkable season winning the Grade 2 Long Distance Hurdle at Newbury for a second time before winning the Grade 1 Champion Stayers' Hurdle at the Punchestown Festival for a second time, too. That was one of the best days of my training career. I thought he was as well as we had ever had him in the Long Walk Hurdle at Ascot before Christmas and he was travelling strongly when he fell. Both he and Barry (Geraghty) were lucky to walk away that day. The Cleeve Hurdle came too soon and then he sulked at Aintree in the spring. Therefore when we took him to Punchestown, I was envisaging it being his last run before retirement. It was a fantastic performance at the age of eleven. It obviously won't be easy this season, but he will reappear at Newbury (29th November) in the Grade 2 Long Distance Hurdle and we will go from there. He owes us nothing though.

VALAJANI (GER) 4 rg c Jukebox Jury (IRE) – Ventiane (GER)
Formerly trained in Germany, where he was twice successful on the level before finishing runner up in the Italian St Leger last October. We are looking forward to seeing what he has to offer over hurdles this season.

WHITE HART LADY (IRE) 5 b m Doyen (IRE) – Hats And Heels (IRE)
She is a nice unraced mare who couldn't race last season due to a minor setback. Prior to that, she had been working better than Whitehotchillifili, who developed into a smart bumper mare. She will make her debut in a mares' bumper.

WHITEHOTCHILLIFILLI (IRE) 5 b m Milan – Mhuire Na Gale (IRE)
A well bred mare, she surprised us when winning by six lengths on her debut at Southwell. She was then due to run at Huntingdon but it was called off, due to the equine flu, and we needed to get another run into her before her main target the Listed mares' bumper at Sandown in March. Not disgraced under a penalty at Warwick in late February, the ground was quick enough for her. She ran well at Sandown finishing fourth considering her far from ideal preparation. Over the top at Aintree last time, I hope she will do well in mares' novice hurdles over two and two and a half miles.

WINNINGSEVERYTHING (IRE) 5 b g Flemensfirth (USA) – Baliya (IRE)
Overcame greenness to win in good style on his debut in a bumper at Market Rasen. Third and fourth on his next two outings under a penalty at Southwell and Ffos Las respectively, he wasn't disgraced. He will go hurdling now and will be suited by two and a half miles. The EBF Final at Sandown in March could be his long-term target.

> **TRAINER'S HORSE TO FOLLOW: KING ROLAND**

Warren GREATREX
Stables: Uplands, Upper Lambourn, Berkshire.
2018/2019: 38 Winners / 308 Runners 12% Prize-Money £563,701
www.wgreatrexracing.com

ANOTHER EMOTION (FR) 7 gr g Turgeon (USA) – Line Perle (FR)
A big strong horse who hasn't had a lot of racing since we bought him out of the Irish pointing field. Runner-up on his reappearance at Sandown on heavy ground in December, he took a lot out of himself that day and was never the same thereafter last season. Below par in both subsequent runs, he has had a good break and I think he will develop into a useful novice chaser. Three miles on soft ground is ideal and he has schooled well.

BAILARICO (IRE) 6 b g Dubawi (IRE) – Baila Me (GER)

Twice a winner over hurdles last season, including a walkover at Leicester, he has been running consistently on the Flat during the summer. Placed three times, he ran well in the Goodwood Stakes at the end of July. Being a former winning pointer, I am keen to try him over fences in the Autumn. He stays well with three miles being his trip.

BLUBERRY HIGH (IRE) 5 b m Getaway (GER) – Blu Louisiana (IRE)

We have sold her to Million In Mind and she will be their horse with us this season. She ran two good races in bumpers last season. Green first time out at Newton Abbot, she finished third but improved on that next time when runner-up at Bangor in the spring. The form has worked out well, too, and I think she will make a nice mares' novice hurdler. She is tough and has improved a lot. We will start her off over two miles but she will stay further.

BOB MAHLER (IRE) 7 b g Mahler – Cooladurragh (IRE)

He has his quirks and has been immature in the past but we think we may have found the key to him. He came good over fences at Newbury and Cheltenham during the spring enjoying the better ground. Over the top by the time he ran at Uttoxeter in May, he is a slow maturing horse who stays well. Rated 139, I would like to aim him at the Ladbrokes Trophy at Newbury (30th November) with one run beforehand. He jumps and stays and I think it would really suit him.

CALVARIO 4 g Falco

Owned by Andrew Brooks, he is a very nice unraced four year old. We did a bit of work with him last season and he went well. He has been schooled and jumps very well but we will give him a run in a bumper first. I really like him.

DON'T ASK (IRE) 6 b g Ask – Outback Ivy (IRE)

A well bred horse being a half-brother to Mick Channon's Grade 2 winning novice chaser Glen Forsa, he only raced twice last season. I thought he was unlucky not to win at Taunton last time when falling at the final flight. Unfortunately, he chipped a bone off his hock and hasn't run since. Back now, I have always been keen to send him chasing and I think he could be an exciting novice this season. He possesses a good cruising speed and, while two and a half miles suits him, he could drop back in trip.

DRUMLEE WATAR (IRE) 6 ch g Watar (IRE) – Dolly of Dublin (IRE)

A ten lengths winner of his Irish point, he has only raced twice for us. I thought he ran well on his hurdles debut at Chepstow finishing fourth but then found the ground too quick next time at Doncaster. He came back jarred up, so we have given him plenty of time since. Despite being a six year old, he has still been quite babyish and immature. However, he has done well during the summer and I am pleased with him. I think he will make a decent second season novice hurdler over two and a half miles.

ELLEON (FR) 4 b g Martaline – Ailette

I loved him last year and he made his debut in a warm looking bumper at Warwick in May. Only beaten three and a half lengths, we found he had a stress fracture the following day. Thankfully, that has healed and I would like to win a bumper with him in the Autumn before going hurdling. I have always thought the world of him.

EMITOM (IRE) 5 b g Gold Well – Avenging Angel (IRE)
We think he is a star in the making and are looking forward to going down the stayers' hurdle route with him. A dual bumper winner, he won his first three races over hurdles last season before finishing second in the Grade 1 Sefton Novices' Hurdle at Aintree in April. The winner (Champ) is obviously a very good horse but we rode our horse with restraint and he got first run on us, but he still ran an extremely good race and we pulled seven lengths clear of the third. A very laid back horse, he was still immature last year and his brain and his feet weren't always working together, hence he made a few mistakes on occasions. He had some intensive schooling sessions with Henrietta Knight and is learning all the time. He has had some sarcoids removed during the summer but it hasn't held him up and I am very pleased with him. We may start him off in the Grade 2 West Yorkshire Hurdle at Wetherby (2nd November). Alternatively, he could reappear over two and a half miles, if we decided we didn't want to go three miles first time out. In an ideal world, I would like to get four or five races into him before the Stayers' Hurdle at Cheltenham in March. Still weak last year, he is much stronger now and, while our previous World Hurdle winner Cole Harden was very good, this horse has more gears.

ENCORE CHAMPS (IRE) 5 b g Robin Des Champs (FR) – Dani California
Did well last season winning a bumper at Ffos Las in October before winning over hurdles at Wetherby and Kelso. He didn't go to grass early in the spring of last year and therefore was on the go a long time last season, and had enough by the time of his last couple of runs at Taunton and Sandown. I have always liked him and he is a horse who travels well and is a brilliant jumper. Inclined to do a bit too much during his races, he is learning to settle and we are looking forward to sending him novice chasing. Effective on any ground, we will start him off over two miles.

FRANKIE BABY (IRE) 4 b g Yeats (IRE) – Belsalsa (FR)
A half-brother to Mulcahys Hill and Penn Lane who we have trained, we bought him as a three year old at the Goffs Landrover Sale in Ireland last year. He was ready to run last spring but the ground dried out so we put him away. A nice horse, he shows plenty at home and I hope he will run well in a bumper in the Autumn before we decide whether to send him hurdling. He jumps well.

GANGSTER (FR) 9 ch g Green Tune (USA) – Dahlia's Krissy (USA)
A Grade 3 winning hurdler for Gigginstown House Stud, we bought him at the Goffs UK September Sale at Doncaster last year. Yet to run for us, we did a bit with him but the time off won't have done him any harm. We have sweetened him up and he looks well. I have been pleased with his schooling and the plan is for him to go down the hunter chase route.

JAMMIN MASTERS (IRE) 8 b g Sinndar (IRE) – Zara Million (ITY)
Still a novice over fences, he ran some good races in defeat last season. Runner-up on four occasions, including in a Listed chase at Ascot December, he won't be in action until the second half of the season, having had an issue with his knee. Below par at Uttoxeter last time, he wants soft ground and stays well.

JUST A SIP 4 b f Great Pretender (IRE) – One Gulp
She is a well bred filly out of a dual Listed hurdle winner. She has always gone well at home and ran well for a long way on her debut in a mares' bumper at Cheltenham in April, but tied up and didn't get home. Funnily enough, her mother also tied up. Daryl (Jacob) rode her at Cheltenham and loved her. Still weak last year, she wasn't strong enough to finish off her race. I am hoping she will be a different proposition this season because we have always liked her. She will run in another mares' bumper in October.

KEEPER HILL (IRE) 8 b g Westerner – You Take Care (IRE)
Having lost his confidence over fences, we switched him back to hurdles last season and he won a Pertemps qualifier at Warwick in January. I thought he ran very well at Aintree last time finishing third in a valuable handicap over three miles. We will send him back over fences this season because he is more mature this time. Plus, he had had a back issue, which required surgery, last time he went chasing. We have done plenty of schooling with him and he handles any ground.

KEMBLE'S CASCADE (IRE) 4 b g Kalanisi (IRE) – Beauty Star (IRE)
He is a very nice horse who made his debut in the same bumper at Warwick in April we won with Emitom the previous year. Only a four year old taking on older horses, he was beaten a length and a quarter and it looked a strong race. He has done very well during the summer and I am keen to win a bumper with him in the Autumn before we go hurdling. He may not want heavy ground and, while he will stay two and a half miles, he will start off over two miles when he goes jumping. He is right up there amongst the best of our bumper horses.

LA BAGUE AU ROI (FR) 8 b m Doctor Dino (FR) – Alliance Royale (FR)
She has come back in following her summer break looking amazing and I couldn't be happier with her. She had a brilliant season over fences last season winning four times, including the Grade 1 Kauto Star Novices' Chase at Kempton on Boxing Day and the Grade 1 Flogas Novice Chase at Leopardstown in February. Runner-up at Aintree over two and a half miles on her final start, she was staying on at the finish but Richard (Johnson) said she didn't have the same zip that day. The plan is for her to start off in the Grade 2 Charlie Hall Chase at Wetherby (2nd November) before a tilt at the King George on Boxing Day. We then have the option of going to Leopardstown for the Irish Hennessy in February followed by the Cheltenham Gold Cup. Alternatively, she could run in the Cotswold Chase at Cheltenham in January, if we feel she needs some course experience before the Gold Cup. We purposely haven't over raced her throughout her career and this could be her last season, depending on how she runs. She is rated 151 over fences and needs to improve but she doesn't have to improve that much to enter the Gold Cup picture. A big strong mare, it is very exciting to be training her.

LA HULPE (FR) 5 ch m No Risk At All (FR) – Belle Yepa (FR)
Dai Walters has sent her to us during the summer having had one run in a bumper at Southwell last April. Very well bred being a half-sister to Whisper, we haven't done much with her yet, but she looks nice and we will probably run her in another mares' bumper.

LOVENORMONEY (IRE) 8 br g Winged Love (IRE) – Dixies Gem (IRE)
Still a novice over fences, he wants heavy ground but rarely got his conditions last season hence he only raced a few times. Runner-up at Lingfield in January, he did well over hurdles the previous season and needs a wet winter this time around. He stays well with three miles plus being his trip.

MAHLERVOUS (IRE) 6 b g Mahler – Brook Style (IRE)
A cracking horse who has got a lot of talent, although he is lazy at home. He had a good season winning handicap hurdles at Kelso and Ayr's Scottish National meeting. Suited by decent ground, he is going novice chasing and, while three miles is his trip, we will start him off over two and a half miles. I think he will improve again over fences because chasing ought to suit him. One of his owners, Ray Green, is already eyeing the valuable three miles novices' handicap chase at Ayr's Scottish National meeting in April. That is his main target.

MAITREE EXPRESS 5 br g Malinas (GER) – Shatabdi (IRE)
A half-brother to Jameson and out of a Grade 2 winning mare, he had one run in a bumper at Warwick in late March but was disappointing. He is much better than he showed that day and I think he had had enough by then. We took him to work at Newbury earlier in the season and he went very well indeed. He has summered well at his owner Robert Waley-Cohen's stud and we will try and win a bumper in the Autumn before he goes hurdling.

MARTHA BRAE 4 b f Shirocco (GER) – Harringay
She is a well bred filly being out of a mares' hurdle final winner. Despite only finishing seventh on her debut at Sedgefield, Gavin (Sheehan) liked her but said everything happened too quickly for her. She then went to Bangor and surprised us by winning and Sean Bowen loved her. I was impressed with her that day and she has improved for another summer on her back. She will be aimed at mares' novice hurdles over two and a half miles.

MISS HONEY RYDER (IRE) 6 b m Stowaway – Seesea (IRE)
A half-sister to Western Ryder, she hasn't been as precocious as her brother but she did really well in bumpers last season. A tall filly, she has been weak and is only just starting to fill her frame. Twice a winner at Taunton, she ran a cracker in the Grade 3 mares' bumper at the Punchestown Festival finishing fourth. It was a very strong race. She has improved with each run and could be an exciting mares' novice hurdler this season. Effective on any ground, she will start over two miles but will stay two and a half miles.

MISSED APPROACH (IRE) 9 b g Golan (IRE) – Polly's Dream (IRE)
He won the Kim Muir Chase at the Cheltenham Festival in 2018 but only raced once last season, due to a niggling problem. I thought he ran well in the Becher Chase finishing sixth, especially having given the other runners a head start. His big target this season is the Grand National but we aren't going to rush him and he won't be in action before Christmas. Rated 145, he could reappear in something like the Welsh National (27th December).

MULCAHYS HILL (IRE) 7 b g Brian Boru – Belsalsa (FR)
Runner-up behind Jerrysback at Bangor in December, he ran well but then we put him in at the deep end in his subsequent two starts. Fourth of five in the Grade 1 Scilly Isles Novices' Chase at Sandown, he then fell at the second last in the National Hunt Chase at the Cheltenham Festival. Still a novice over fences, we are going to lower his sights and find some smaller races for him and build up his confidence. Two and a half to three miles is his trip.

PORTRUSH TED (IRE) 7 b g Shantou (USA) – Village Queen (IRE)
He has always been a smart horse and was a high-class bumper horse winning the Grade 2 championship event at Aintree in April last year. An easy winner on his hurdles debut at Perth last August, he had a touch of a leg afterwards and therefore missed the rest of his novice hurdle season. It isn't going to be easy this year having only raced once over hurdles, but we will try and get as much experience into him as we can. Rated 131, he loves soft ground with three miles being his trip. He has come back in looking stronger.

PRINTING DOLLARS (IRE) 6 br m Doyen (IRE) – Printing Polly (IRE)
A winning Irish pointer, she did well last season winning a bumper at Warwick and scoring twice over hurdles at Exeter. I thought she ran a very good race at Ayr on her final start, too. She wasn't over big last year, but has summered well and I think she will be very competitive in mares' handicap hurdles off her mark of 135. She doesn't have to improve too much before we start considering Listed and Graded hurdles and hopefully gain some black type. She handles any ground and stays three miles.

ROCCOWITHLOVE 5 b g Shirocco (GER) – Love Train (IRE)
He went to the sales at Doncaster in May as part of the Grech and Parkin dispersal and we decided to buy him back because he was a big raw horse last season. Rated 106 over hurdles, Richard (Johnson) rode him last time at Uttoxeter and was complimentary afterwards. A chaser in the making, he will reappear in a novices' handicap hurdle over two and a half miles, although he will stay three miles.

SANTA ADELIA (FR) 5 gr m Smadoun (FR) – New Delice (FR)
A well bred mare owned by Robert Waley-Cohen, she has joined us during the summer. She had some very good form in France for Guillaume Macaire winning twice over hurdles at Auteuil beating the subsequent Imperial Cup winner Malaya in the process. Runner-up at Listed level, she has had some time off but is back now and will go novice chasing. Only five, she is lightly raced and related to former Hennessy Gold Cup winner Smad Place.

SARIM (IRE) 4 b g Declaration of War (USA) – Silver Star
An interesting horse who had three runs on the Flat for Jamie Osborne last year, finishing runner-up at Bath over a mile and a half last time. He has had a touch of a leg since and we like him and he has schooled nicely. He has shown plenty of ability at home and, while we may give him another run on the Flat, he will be going novice hurdling.

SPEEDY CARGO (IRE) 6 b g Stowaway – Vics Miller (IRE)
Yet to run for us, he was never right last season having joined us from Harry Whittington's. Placed a couple of times in point-to-points and over hurdles, we are still learning about him but he looks well. A nice type of horse, he will start off in a novices' handicap hurdle off his mark of 109.

STAR OF LANKA (IRE) 5 b g Zoffany (IRE) – Indian Bounty
Despite still being immature last year, he had a good season over hurdles winning twice at Hereford. He wasn't at his best during the second half of the year, but he has come back in looking stronger having done well physically. Rated 128, he will continue handicap hurdling and it wouldn't surprise me if he ends up running in some of the better races.

SUNNY EXPRESS (IRE) 4 b g Jeremy (USA) – Golden Summer (IRE)
Still very raw last year, I love him and feel he is a very nice horse in the making. We struggled to keep condition on him, but he has always shown plenty of ability at home and we ran him in the bumper at Ayr's Scottish National meeting. He ran well in third and Gavin (Sheehan) said he gave him a great feel. We will run him in another bumper in the Autumn before going hurdling. His schooling has been very good and I think he will handle any ground. Two and a half miles will suit him over jumps.

SYMPHONY HALL (IRE) 4 b g Mahler – Coumhall (IRE)
Another nice young horse who shows plenty at home. He was green in both his races at Southwell and Ffos Las before finishing third and fourth respectively. I like him and we will try and win a bumper before he goes hurdling. He jumps well and is another who will appreciate a step up to two and a half miles over hurdles.

TALKTOMENOW 5 b g Shirocco (GER) – Sweet Stormy (IRE)
A point-to-point winner in the UK, he ran very well on his hurdles debut at Plumpton finishing second behind Getaway Trump. It was therefore frustrating that he was unable to reproduce such a performance on his subsequent starts. Owned by Tim Syder, we toyed with the idea of selling him but decided to keep him and I hope that decision is vindicated. The summer break has helped him and we will run him in a novices' handicap hurdle off his mark of 117.

TRIO FOR RIO (IRE) 6 bb g Getaway (GER) – Rio Trio (IRE)

Twice a winner over hurdles at Bangor and Wetherby, he is a horse I really like. Richard (Johnson) rode him on the latter occasion and was impressed. He went to the sales at Doncaster in May as part of the Million In Mind dispersal and Trevor Hemmings bought him and kindly kept him in training with us. A straightforward horse who won two Irish points before he joined us, he wants three miles plus and handles any ground. A good jumper, he will go novice chasing and it wouldn't surprise me if he ended up in something like the National Hunt Chase at Cheltenham in March.

WESTERN RYDER (IRE) 7 b g Westerner – Seesea (IRE)

Despite running some good races finishing third in the Grade 2 International Hurdle at Cheltenham and a valuable handicap hurdle at Ascot before Christmas, he endured a frustrating season. Having schooled very well, we are going to send him novice chasing and he could be exciting. We will start him off a low level because he is very much a confidence horse, but it would be nice to think he could develop into an Arkle Trophy contender next spring. Rated 147 over hurdles, he needs to improve and isn't over big, but he's athletic and his schooling has been good.

YOUNG LIEUTENANT (IRE) 5 b g Robin Des Champs (FR) – Be My Gesture (IRE)

A lovely horse who I really like. Runner-up in an Irish point for Denis Murphy, he ran twice for us in bumpers last season. Having shaped well at Wetherby first time, I thought he won in good style at Exeter on his second run. His work at home has always been good and he will go novice hurdling over two and a half miles. He enjoys some cut in the ground.

Unnamed 4 gr g Cloudings (IRE) – Exit Baby (IRE)

Trevor Hemmings has kindly sent us two very nice unraced four year olds who will be starting off in a bumper this season. This son of Cloudings was bought as a foal and is a lovely horse.

Unnamed 4 b g Jeremy (USA) – Ellen's Choice (IRE)

He is the other unraced four year old owned by Trevor Hemmings who joined us during the summer.

TRAINER'S HORSE TO FOLLOW: EMITOM

Philip HOBBS
Stables: Sandhill, Bilbrook, Minehead, Somerset.
2018/2019: 106 Winners / 561 Runners 19% Prize-Money £1,305,373
www.pjhobbs.com

AT ITS OWN EXPENSE (IRE) 5 ch g Arakan (USA) – Blow A Gasket (IRE)

Did well for the Taunton Racecourse Owners Club last season winning over hurdles there in February. Consistent in bumpers and hurdles, he now belongs to a new syndicate consisting of ten members. We will probably give him another run in a handicap hurdle over two and a half miles and then consider going chasing.

AWAKE AT MIDNIGHT 7 b g Midnight Legend – Wakeful

Enjoyed a good start to last season winning a novice hurdle at Worcester and then followed up on his chasing debut at Chepstow. Runner-up at Exeter last time, he will go handicap chasing over two and two and a half miles and, being lightly raced over fences, I hope he will continue to improve.

BALLOTIN (FR) 8 b g Enrique – Orphee De Vonnas (FR)
David Maxwell has a number of horses in training with us and the vast majority will go hunter chasing in the New Year. However, provided they don't win a class one or two race beforehand and therefore remain eligible for hunter chases, they will run in novice races or handicaps during the first half of the season. He is a grand horse who won two hunter chases last season at Leicester and Southwell, and I hope he will be competitive off his mark of 135 in handicap chases over two and a half miles.

BEAU DU BRIZAIS (FR) 7 gr g Kapgarde (FR) – Belle Du Brizais (FR)
Twice a winner at Ludlow during the winter, he produced another good performance to win at Kempton in May. Rated 135, he likes decent ground and will be aimed at staying handicap chases over three miles plus.

BIG SHARK (IRE) 5 b g Vinnie Roe (IRE) – Castlelost (IRE)
Runner-up in his only Irish point in April for Tom Keating, we bought him at the Goffs UK Spring Sale at Doncaster the following month. He is cantering at home at the moment and gives the impression he will be suited by a test of stamina. Novice hurdles will be on his agenda this season.

CAPE MILANO (IRE) 4 b g Milan – Shatani (IRE)
Owned by Mrs Judith Luff, we bought him at the Derby Sales in Ireland as a three year old. He has done everything right at home and we will start him off in a bumper in the Autumn.

CHEF D'EQUIPE (FR) 7 b g Presenting – Millesimme (FR)
He will run in two and a half miles handicap chases and ought to be competitive off 133. Then, in all likelihood, he will run in hunter chases from January onwards. A novice hurdle winner at Taunton last season, he also finished runner-up a couple of times over hurdles and fences.

COTSWOLD WAY (IRE) 6 b g Stowaway – Rosies All The Way
Had a very good season over hurdles winning four of his six races. The plan is to send him chasing and, having reached a mark of 140 over hurdles, I would like to think he will do well in level weights novice chases. Two and a half miles is his trip for the time being but I think he will want three miles eventually.

CROOKS PEAK 6 b g Arcadio (GER) – Ballcrina Girl (IRE)
A Listed bumper winner a couple of seasons ago, he scored three times over hurdles last term and looked good on occasions. He appears to be at his best when fresh with two miles being his trip at present. Rated 135, he will probably reappear in a handicap hurdle before going chasing later on. We haven't schooled him over fences but he jumps hurdles well.

DEFI DU SEUIL (FR) 6 b g Voix Du Nord (FR) – Quarvine Du Seuil (FR)
He spent the summer at Martinstown Stud in Ireland and arrived back looking magnificent at the beginning of August. I was very pleased with his first season over fences winning three times, including the Grade 1 Scilly Isles Novice Chase at Sandown before capturing the Grade 1 JLT Novice Chase at the Cheltenham Festival. He then dropped back to two miles at the Punchestown Festival and ran well in second, proving he has plenty of speed. Effective on any ground, he possibly wants soft ground to be at his best over two miles. We have a lot of options this year. With Altior stepping up in trip, the two miles division looks wide open. He has some very good form over two and a half miles and I think he will stay three miles, too. The very best horses are versatile tripwise. Desert Orchid had the speed to win top two miles chases but also had the stamina to win an Irish National. Kauto Star was the same. The Haldon Gold Cup at Exeter (5th November) or Shloer Chase at Cheltenham (17th November) are possible starting points followed by the Tingle Creek (7th December). Alternatively, he could reappear over two and a half miles and, in all likelihood, he will be given an entry in the King George at Kempton on Boxing Day. Either way, we have a lot to look forward to.

DEISE ABA (IRE) 6 b g Mahler – Kit Massini (IRE)

A big strong horse who won his only Irish point before joining us last season. He produced a good performance to win at Chepstow on his hurdles debut in November. Despite the fact he only finished fourth on his next two outings, he was quite a nervous horse last year and, having strengthened up during the summer, I think he will improve this season. Three miles novice chases will be his job this winter.

DIPLOMATE SIVOLA (FR) 6 ch g Noroit (GER) – None De Sivola (FR)

A lovely horse who improved out of all recognition last season winning a handicap chase at Lingfield in November and a novices' hunter chase at Catterick in the spring. He will revert back to handicap chases over three miles before going hunter chasing once again in the New Year.

DOLPHIN SQUARE (IRE) 5 b g Shantou (USA) – Carrig Eden Lass (IRE)

Tom Keating trained him in Ireland to win a point-to-point and he did well over hurdles for us last season. Twice a winner at Exeter and Newton Abbot, he will go novice chasing in the first half of the season and then probably go novice hunter chasing in the New Year. Only five, he ought to improve over fences and, while he has been winning over two and a half miles, he will stay further.

DOSTAL PHIL (FR) 6 b g Coastal Path – Quiphile (FR)

Runner-up a couple of times at Uttoxeter and Newbury, he produced a good performance to win at Exeter last time and I hope there is further improvement to come. His only disappointing run came at Cheltenham in November, where his lack of experience told. Successful over two and a quarter miles at Exeter, he will stay further. He will go handicap hurdling.

EBONY GALE 5 br g Shirocco (GER) – Glenora Gale (IRE)

He has looked a nice horse on occasions winning a bumper at Wincanton and over hurdles at Leicester last winter. However, he was disappointing on his final three runs. Rated 118, I hope he will improve over fences and we will start him off in a novices' handicap chase over two or two and a half miles.

ECU DE LA NOVERIE (FR) 5 b g Linda's Lad – Quat'Sous D'Or (FR)

Consistent over hurdles and fences last season, he produced a good performance to beat subsequent Grade 2 winner Mister Fisher in a two miles novice hurdle at Newbury in November. Placed in his next three starts, he was runner-up over fences at Ascot last time. I am not sure what is his optimum trip is but he is effective between two and two and a half miles. Another owned and ridden by David Maxwell, he will continue in handicap chases before going hunter chasing in the New Year.

FILOU DES ISSARDS (FR) 4 ch g Network (GER) – Rapiere (FR)

We bought him at the Goffs UK Spring Sale at Doncaster in May and I hope he is a nice horse. Third in his only Irish point for Timmy Hyde, he has a good pedigree and is a very likeable horse. He has been cantering at home and we will probably start him off in a bumper.

FLINCK (IRE) 5 b g Fame And Glory – Princess Supreme (IRE)

A half-brother to Casper King who we used to train, he had one run in an Irish point for Ian Ferguson before his owner Ronnie Bartlett sent him to us. Well beaten on his hurdles debut at Exeter, he ran much better at Taunton last time and was a bit unlucky not to win. I was pleased with the run though and he has shown enough to suggest he can win a novice hurdle before going chasing. Only five, he ought to keep on improving.

FOR LANGY (FR) 4 b g Day Flight – Jubilee II (FR)
Agent Guy Petit bought him on behalf of David Maxwell at the Arqana Sale in France during the summer. Unbeaten in two races, he won on the Flat in June and then followed up over hurdles twelve days later in the French Provinces. It is early days at the moment because he is only cantering and we don't know how good he is. He will go novice hurdling this season.

GALA BALL (IRE) 9 b g Flemensfirth (USA) – Nuit Des Chartreux (FR)
Very consistent throughout his career, he has won five races and being placed ten times from eighteen starts. Returning from a lengthy absence in the spring, he ran very well finishing second in the Grade 3 Greatwood Gold Cup Handicap Chase at Newbury in March. He then went one better at the same track three weeks later. Rated 148, he will continue to run in the decent two and a half miles handicap chases.

GARDE LA VICTOIRE (FR) 10 b g Kapgarde (FR) – Next Victory (FR)
Fourth at Chepstow in the Autumn on his reappearance, he picked up a leg problem and missed the rest of the season. He is a ten year old but the handicapper has dropped him a few pounds and we know he is a very decent horse on his day.

GOLDEN SOVEREIGN (IRE) 5 b g Gold Well – Fugal Maid (IRE)
A big horse who is very much a chaser in the making, he has yet to win but has been placed in a bumper and over hurdles. The sort to improve with time and experience, he will reappear in a novices' handicap hurdle and, being a half-brother to three miles winner Red Rising, he will benefit from a step up in trip.

GOSHEVEN (IRE) 6 b g Presenting – Fair Choice (IRE)
Still a novice, he ran encouragingly when finishing third in the Grade 2 Persian War Novices' Hurdle at Chepstow last Autumn but suffered a leginjury soon afterwards and hasn't raced since. He won't be in action until Christmas.

I'M A GAME CHANGER (IRE) 7 b g Arcadio (GER) – Drinadaly (IRE)
I am not sure what the plans are for him. Despite finishing second on his chasing debut at Exeter in November, he hasn't been the most natural of jumpers of fences both at home or on the track. We sent him back over hurdles and he won at Newbury in late December. He is a talented horse and we will probably start him over hurdles, but we will try him over fences again at some stage. Effective over two and two and a half miles, he is learning to settle better.

JATILUWIH (FR) 5 ch g Linda's Lad – Jaune De Beaufai (FR)
A winner over fences in France, he belongs to David Maxwell and won both his starts for us over hurdles at Ludlow and Chepstow in the spring. A novice over hurdles until the end of October, he will then go down the handicap hurdle route before going hunter chasing in the New Year. He is open to more improvement.

JERRYSBACK (IRE) 7 b g Jeremy (USA) – Get A Few Bob Back (IRE)
He is a lovely horse who developed into a useful novice chaser last season. A winner at Bangor on his second start, he was runner-up twice in Grade 2 company at Ascot and Haydock. Third in the National Hunt Chase at the Cheltenham Festival, I don't think four miles is his trip. Probably at his best racing right-handed, he will be aimed at the decent three mile handicap chases.

KALOOKI (GER) 5 b g Martaline – Karuma (GER)
A half-brother to Kruzhlinin who we used to train, he was placed in two of his four bumpers at Ascot and Exeter. I think he had had enough by the time of his last run, also at Exeter, in February. He will go novice hurdling over two and a half miles plus.

KAYF ADVENTURE 8 b g Kayf Tara – My Adventure (IRE)
Restricted to two runs last season, he had a few issues with his back. A faller at Sandown on his latest start, he wants bottomless ground but never really got his conditions last winter. Two and a half to two miles six is ideal.

KEEP ROLLING (IRE) 6 ch g Mahler – Kayles Castle (IRE)
Looked very promising when winning a bumper at Warwick in December in a race which has worked out well. He ran over hurdles at Haydock later the same month and was still in front when the race was declared void. We then decided to switch him back to bumpers because the season was getting on and we didn't want him to lose his novice status. Seventh at Newbury under a penalty, he is a big horse who should improve. He will go novice hurdling.

KEEP WONDERING (IRE) 5 b g Scorpion (IRE) – Supreme Touch (IRE)
Raced in three Irish points last season for Donnchadh Doyle winning by eight lengths on his latest start in March. He will spend this season in novice hurdles and looks a nice prospect.

LARKBARROW LAD 6 b g Kayf Tara – Follow My Leader (IRE)
Runner-up on his first three starts over hurdles, he won next time at Southwell and is going the right way. We operated on his wind before his last run and it obviously didn't do him any harm. He will go chasing and we will look for a novices' handicap off his mark of 126. Two and a half miles suit him but he will stay three miles eventually.

MASTER WORK (FR) 6 b g Network (GER) – Mascarpone (FR)
He has been a very weak horse but has strengthened and is getting better. Twice a winner over hurdles at Warwick and Leicester, he had a couple of runs over fences finishing third at Leicester and runner-up at Newbury. He looks well and will go novice handicap chasing over two miles.

MCNAMARAS BAND (IRE) 6 b g Getaway (GER) – Katies Pet (IRE)
A bumper winner a couple of years ago, he went hurdling last season but was still weak. He improved with each run though winning by ten lengths at Chepstow in the spring. Still a novice until the end of October, he should continue to progress and it won't be long before he goes chasing.

MELEKHOV (IRE) 5 b g Sholokhov (IRE) – Yorkshire Girl (IRE)
He is a dual bumper winner who looked good when winning over hurdles at Exeter in April. I was slightly disappointed he didn't win on his handicap debut at Plumpton, where he got behind early on but then looked like winning until making a mistake at the second last. Still a novice until the end of October, he will stay over hurdles this season with two and a half miles being his trip. Still only five, he should have more to offer.

MIDNIGHT GLORY 7 b m Midnight Legend – Land of Glory
She surprised us last season winning three times at Ludlow, Wetherby and Exeter. Rated 120, she will continue over hurdles for the time being but we will try her over fences at some stage even though she isn't over big. Three miles on good ground is ideal because she doesn't want it too soft.

MUSICAL SLAVE (IRE) 6 b g Getaway (GER) – Inghwung
A big strong horse who came good in the spring winning at Market Rasen, Ludlow and Punchestown. He stepped up to two miles five for the first time at the Punchestown Festival and improved again. The handicapper has put him up ten pounds since but he remains lightly raced and I hope there is more improvement to come. Long-term, he will jump fences but we will keep him over hurdles for the time being.

NO COMMENT 8 br g Kayf Tara – Dizzy Frizzy
Still a novice over fences, he looked good over hurdles earlier in his career but hasn't quite put it all together since sent chasing. Fifth in the Kim Muir Chase at the Cheltenham Festival, he came back with a nasty injury below his knee. The skin had been peeled off from his knee down to his fetlock joint and that would explain why he hung during the race. Thankfully, it has heeled and he will go for a staying novice chase in the Autumn and hopefully get a win over fences against his name.

OAKLEY (IRE) 6 b g Oscar (IRE) – Tirolean Dance (IRE)
Having shown promise in his first couple of runs over hurdles, he won twice at Ludlow and Kempton. Unfortunately, he suffered an injury to his fetlock joint at the latter venue and missed the rest of the season. Back in work, he will reappear in a handicap hurdle before we send him chasing later in the season. Two miles suits him, although I am sure he will stay further.

OFF THE PLANET (IRE) 4 ch g Presenting – Kings Diva (IRE)
A very nice unraced four year old owned by Claire and Paul Rooney. Bought at the Derby Sales in Ireland last year, we did a bit with him during the spring before he went for his summer break at Jason's Maguire's. He worked well and I like him. We will run him in a bumper in the Autumn.

ONE FOR YOU (IRE) 4 b g Yeats (IRE) – Tempest Belle (IRE)
A half-brother to Grade 1 winner Monalee, he is another lovely unraced four year old belonging to Claire and Paul Rooney, who was acquired at the Derby Sales in Ireland last year. He was nearly ready to run in a bumper last spring but we decided to give him time and put him away. He is another who will start off in a bumper.

PILEON (IRE) 5 b g Yeats (IRE) – Heath Heaven
Raced twice in Irish points finishing runner-up on his second start before we purchased him at the Cheltenham December Sale. He won very well on his first run for us in a bumper at Exeter in the spring and is a really likeable horse. His previous trainer Tom Keating didn't think he would win a bumper, but his work beforehand had been good and we were hopeful. He will go novice hurdling over two and a half miles.

POL CROCAN (IRE) 4 br g Shirocco (GER) – She's All That (IRE)
Unraced, we bought him as a three year old at the Goffs UK Spring Sale last year. He has had a minor issue with his withers, but he should be running in a bumper by Christmas. I think he is quite a nice horse.

POTTERS VENTURE (IRE) 5 b g Arcadio (GER) – Starventure (IRE)
Ran three times in Irish points finishing third on his latest start. We were going to run him last season but he suffered a bout of ringworm. Back in work, he will go novice hurdling.

RAGNAR 3 b g Toronado (IRE) – Inner Sea (USA)
An interesting horse who was bought at the Newmarket July Sales. Previously trained on the Flat by Dominic Ffrench-Davis and Roger Charlton, he is rated 82 and won twice, including over ten furlongs on soft ground at Sandown in June. We haven't schooled him yet but the plan is to send him juvenile hurdling.

RAVEN COURT (IRE) 5 b g Court Cave (IRE) – Lady Kate Ellen (IRE)
He ran well on his debut in a bumper at Aintree in a race which has worked out well. However, he was disappointing on his next two runs at Wincanton. Given a break since, I am hoping he will rediscover his form once switched to hurdles.

REIKERS ISLAND (IRE) 6 b g Yeats (IRE) – Moricana (GER)
Lightly raced over fences, he won at Wincanton in December but was still a bit weak last year. He must go right-handed and loves good ground. His owner has already earmarked a three miles handicap chase at Ludlow – 1.15 Kevin Mallon Celebrates 60th Handicap Chase (0-140) – on Wednesday 9th October. He will hopefully improve again this season.

ROCK THE KASBAH (IRE) 9 ch g Shirocco (GER) – Impudent (IRE)
We haven't made a plan but there must be every chance he will go back to Cheltenham in November for the Grade 3 handicap chase over three miles three (16th November), which he won last year. The ideal race for him is the Welsh National because he likes Chepstow but the problem is that he doesn't want the ground too soft and it is nearly always run on heavy ground. He was brought down in the Grand National last spring and, while we haven't ruled it out, I am not convinced he took to the fences.

ROLLING DYLAN (IRE) 8 ch g Indian River (FR) – Easter Saturday (IRE)
Ran some good races without winning last season, finishing third at Cheltenham in December and runner-up at Taunton in the spring. A very good jumper, the further he goes the better he is and I am hoping to run him in the cross country races at Cheltenham, but I need to convince his owner.

SAMBURU SHUJAA (FR) 6 b g Poliglote – Girelle (FR)
He has always been a scratchy mover but appreciated a step up in trip last season winning twice over three miles at Chepstow. The drying ground in the Pertemps Final at Cheltenham didn't suit him. We haven't schooled him yet, but we are going to send him novice chasing over three miles on soft ground.

SINGAPORE SAGA 4 b f Midnight Legend – Kim Tian Road (IRE)
I was very pleased with her debut run in a bumper at Cheltenham in April. Still green, I thought she performed really well. Only four, she will have another run in a mares' bumper in the Autumn.

SMARTY WILD 5 b g Fair Mix (IRE) – Blaeberry
Progressive over hurdles, he won at Ludlow in February and then followed up at Exeter and Taunton. Raised ten pounds for his last win, he is now rated 130 and we will aim him at another handicap hurdle. However, it won't be long before he goes chasing. He wants slow ground.

SPORTING JOHN (IRE) 4 bb g Getaway (GER) – Wild Spell (IRE)
Successful in his only Irish point in March, he was bought by J.P.McManus at the Cheltenham Festival Sale shortly afterwards and arrived here in the summer. We haven't made any plans regarding whether he starts off in a bumper or goes straight over hurdles, but he looks a very nice horse.

SPRINGTOWN LAKE (IRE) 7 b g Gamut (IRE) – Sprightly Gal (IRE)
A winner on his chasing debut at Sandown, he was runner-up at Haydock next time and wasn't disgraced at the Cheltenham Festival finishing fifth in the novices' handicap chase. Two and a half miles on soft ground is ideal and I think he is a better horse going right-handed. He is also very good fresh and has won first time out for the last two seasons.

STEELY ADDITION (IRE) 7 b g Craigsteel – Blond's Addition (IRE)
Despite being a seven year old, he hasn't had a lot of racing because he has struggled with his health. He is a useful horse though taking well to fences last season winning at Chepstow and Hereford. Indeed, he has won twice at Chepstow during his career and, with a rating of 150, we are going to aim him at the Welsh National (27th December). Three miles plus on soft or heavy ground is ideal and he gets on very well with Micheal Nolan.

STERNRUBIN (GER) 8 b g Authorized (IRE) – Sworn Mum (GER)
He has been a fantastic horse for us over the years and was twice a winner over fences last season. Reverting back to hurdles after Christmas, he ran well at Cheltenham and Aintree in the spring finishing sixth in the County Hurdle and fourth over two and a half miles in a Grade 3 handicap respectively. Rated 142 over hurdles and 138 over fences, he isn't the easiest horse to place, especially as he needs to go right handed over fences. We will mix and match between the two.

THYME HILL 5 b g Kayf Tara – Rosita Bay
He developed into a high-class bumper horse running a fantastic race at the Cheltenham Festival finishing third. We hoped he would go close on his debut at Worcester in October, but I must admit he surprised us how much he improved. Beaten a neck in a Listed event at Cheltenham in November, we then decided to shelve his hurdling career and wait for the Festival bumper in the spring. We have already schooled him over hurdles and we will start him off over two and a half miles.

TIDAL FLOW 6 b g Black Sam Bellamy (IRE) – Mrs Philip
Won his first two races over hurdles at Kempton and Newbury and looked an exciting prospect. Despite finishing runner-up at Exeter, he didn't progress as we had hoped but we are looking forward to sending him chasing this winter. I think two and a half miles on soft ground is ideal and I hope he will make a nice novice chaser.

TRUCKERS PASS (IRE) 5 br g Kalanisi (IRE) – Lady Knightess (IRE)
A very nice horse who was beaten a head in his only Irish point in December. Bought soon afterwards at the Cheltenham December Sale, he is owned by Brocade Racing. We were going to run him in the spring because his homework was fantastic, but he started coughing so we left him off. He is an exciting prospect for novice hurdles.

TRUCKIN AWAY (IRE) 6 br g Getaway (GER) – Simons Girl (IRE)
A really likeable horse who won impressively on his first run for us over hurdles at Ffos Las. Placed at Chepstow and Exeter since, he stays well and wants soft ground. A former Irish pointer, he will go novice chasing and I hope he will do well.

UMNDENI (FR) 5 bb g Balko (FR) – Marie Royale (FR)
I have always liked him and, despite winning a couple of times over hurdles at Fontwell and Wincanton, it took a while before the penny really dropped. I hope he is better than his mark of 130 and we will therefore start him off in a handicap hurdle and see how far he can progress before thinking about sending him over fences.

WESTEND STORY (IRE) 8 b g Westerner – Sarahall (IRE)
Fourth on his chasing debut at Exeter in December, it was a very good race won by Defi Du Seuil with Topofthegame in second. Absent since, he has had a few problems but is back now and will continue novice chasing.

WHO'S MY JOCKEY (IRE) 6 b g Yeats (IRE) – Scandisk (IRE)
He won over hurdles at Doncaster in March and then we decided to switch him to fences in early May. Fourth at Newton Abbot, he improved on that next time when leading close home at Hexham over three miles. Suited by long distances, he doesn't want it too soft and it wouldn't surprise me if he developed into a Scottish National contender.

WINTER GETAWAY (IRE) 6 b m Getaway (GER) – Galzig (IRE)
We bought her relatively cheaply at the Goffs UK Spring Sale at Doncaster in May having won two of her four races in Irish points for Michael Winters. She is a nice mare with a good attitude and I have been pleased with her. We will send her mares' novice hurdling.

ZAFAR (GER) 4 b g Kamsin (GER) – Zambuka (FR)
Placed in three of his four races over hurdles, he was below par last time but had an issue with a hind leg. Back in work, he has been gelded and looks capable of winning novice hurdles this season. I am expecting him to stay well this year.

ZANZA (IRE) 5 b g Arcadio (GER) – What A Bleu (IRE)
Had a good season over hurdles winning three times at Chepstow, Taunton and Newbury. He disappointed one day at Sandown, due to heavy ground, but I hope he will continue to improve and contest some decent handicap hurdles.

ZIZANEUR (FR) 4 b g Planteur (IRE) – Zitana (FR)
Arrived from France last season having won over hurdles. Runner-up at Ludlow and Newbury, he ran well for a long way in the Fred Winter Juvenile Hurdle at the Cheltenham Festival until tiring late on. Still in contention when losing his rider at the second last in a Listed hurdle at Auteuil in May, his rating of 130 looks OK and we will aim him at handicap hurdles. Still a bit keen, we will keep him over two miles for the time being.

> **TRAINER'S HORSE TO FOLLOW: TRUCKERS PASS**

Alan KING
Stables: Barbury Castle Stables, Wroughton, Wiltshire.
2018/2019: 91 Winners / 499 Runners 18% Prize-Money £1,259,718
www.alankingracing.co.uk

ALSA MIX (FR) 7 gr m Al Namix (FR) – Lady Tsana (FR)
She is a useful mare who won a bumper at Worcester in September before winning her first two starts over hurdles, including a Grade 2 novice at Sandown in December. That took a lot out of her and she wasn't quite the same in her subsequent two races. She has had a good break since and summered well. A big strong mare, she won her only Irish point and the plan is to send her novice chasing. We will start her off over two and a half miles and she likes some cut in the ground.

AZZERTI (FR) 7 b g Voix Du Nord (FR) – Zalgarry (FR)
Had a good season over fences winning at Ascot and Ludlow before finishing seventh at the Cheltenham Festival. Quite hot headed during the early part of his career, he is more relaxed now. He has strengthened up during the summer and we will campaign him in two and a half miles handicap chases, although I think he will stay three miles.

BALLYWOOD (FR) 5 b g Ballingarry (IRE) – Miss Hollywood (FR)
Developed into a useful novice chaser last season winning three times and appreciated better ground. Only five, he has grown during the summer and I hope he will continue to be competitive off his mark over fences. We tried him over two and a half miles at Ayr in the spring but he was too fresh and failed to settle. Although we will keep him to two miles for the time being, I think he will stay further in the future.

BURREN WALK 4 ch f Lucarno (USA) – Persian Walk (FR)
She ran well on her only start in a mares' bumper at Warwick finishing third. We intended running her again but she had a setback, which resulted in her having surgery on a kissing spine. She has got ability and we may run her in another bumper before going hurdling.

CANELO (IRE) 6 ch g Mahler – Nobody's Darling (IRE)
He had a minor problem last season and was never right, so we decided to give him the year off. Owned by J.P.McManus, he is back cantering and we are looking forward to sending him novice chasing. Twice a winner over hurdles the previous season, he has plenty of ability.

COLDITZ CASTLE (IRE) 5 ch g Getaway (GER) – Stowaway Sue (IRE)
Despite the fact he failed to win over hurdles, he looks progressive and I have been pleased with him during the summer. Still weak last year, he is capable of winning races and will continue over hurdles with two and a half miles being his trip.

DEYRANN DE CARJAC (FR) 6 b g Balko (FR) – Queyrann (FR)
Ran some good races over hurdles last season and was still in contention when falling at the second last in the Greatwood Hurdle at Cheltenham in November. We gave him one run over fences at Cartmel in May and I thought he was very good. I always thought he wanted better ground as a younger horse, but it was soft that day and he coped with it well. We purposely put him away after that and he remains a novice for this season. He has done well during the summer and is one to look forward to in two and a half miles novice chases.

DIDONATO (IRE) 4 b f Milan – Dream Lass (IRE)
A big backward filly last year, we managed to get a run into her in a bumper at Bangor during the spring and she ran well in fourth. We may give her another run or two in a bumper before going hurdling.

DINGO DOLLAR (IRE) 7 ch g Golden Lariat (USA) – Social Society (IRE)
A bit in and out last season, he ran a good race in the Ladbrokes Trophy at Newbury finishing third and was also runner-up in the Grimthorpe Handicap Chase at Doncaster. Rated 146, he will follow a similar programme but doesn't want the ground too soft. We will probably aim him at the Ladbrokes Trophy (30th November) once again with one run beforehand.

EDWARDSTONE 5 b g Kayf Tara – Nothingtoloose (IRE)
He is a fine big horse who finished runner-up in all three of his starts in bumpers. He ran well on each occasion but bumped into some smart horses. A huge horse, he has done very well during the summer and we will send him novice hurdling over two miles.

ELGIN 7 b g Duke of Marmalade (IRE) – China Tea (USA)
Missed the whole of last season but he is back in pre training and I am very happy with him. He won't be in action until around Christmas time but we know he is a high-class horse and, with a rating of 158, we will be aiming him at the top hurdle races.

ELYSEES (IRE) 4 ch g Champs Elysees – Queen of Tara (IRE)
A decent horse who won twice over hurdles at Warwick and Ludlow but is high enough off a mark of 134. He could go to Chepstow for a four year old limited handicap hurdle (11th October). A stiff two miles suits him but he may want further later on.

ESCAPABILITY (IRE) 4 b g Excelebration (IRE) – Brief Escapade (IRE)
We bought him at the horses in training sale at Newmarket last Autumn and he has run a few times for us on the Flat finishing third on a couple of occasions. Given a break since, I think that has benefited him. We have schooled him over hurdles and I will be disappointed if he doesn't win races.

EYES RIGHT 4 b f Passing Glance – Call Me A Star
From a family we know well, she is a lovely big mare who won well at Southwell in March before taking her chance in the Grade 2 mares' bumper at Aintree. She has schooled well over hurdles and we will start her off in a mares' novice over two miles.

FIDUX (FR) 6 b g Fine Grain (JPN) – Folle Tempete (FR)
He won twice over hurdles during the first half of the season, including a Listed event at Ascot in November. Despite the fact he is only small, we decided to school him over fences and he loved it. I was delighted with his wins at Hexham and Stratford in June and he remains a novice for this season. Life will be more difficult now but he is a grand horse with two and a half miles being his trip.

FRATERNEL (FR) 4 b g Kap Rock (FR) – Valence (FR)
A fine big horse who finished third on his only start over hurdles at Pau when trained in France. Owned by Tim Syder, he has never run on the Flat and is therefore eligible to run in National Hunt novice hurdles. We will start him off over two miles.

FUSEAU (FR) 4 b g Barastraight – Monopopee (FR)
Even though he didn't win last season, I like him. A tall weak horse last year, he ran very well on his debut at Doncaster finishing strongly in second. Fourth in a Listed bumper at Cheltenham on New Year's Day next time, I think he had had enough by the time he ran at Huntingdon on his latest start. He has done well during the summer and will go novice hurdling.

GALILEO SILVER (IRE) 4 gr g Galileo (IRE) – Famous (IRE)
The plan is to send him novice hurdling and I think he could be very good. He has run three times on the Flat this season winning over a mile and three at Kempton in July. Sent back to his owner Dai Walters for a break since, he will be suited by a step up to a mile and six on soft ground on the Flat in the Autumn. He is open to more improvement and then we will send him jumping.

GIVING GLANCES 4 b f Passing Glance – Giving
Twice a winner over hurdles at Hereford and Doncaster, she did well to win at the latter track in a Listed Juvenile Hurdle because she was passed her best by that stage. Having raced on the Flat the previous season, she hadn't had a break. She went back to her owner's stud during the spring/summer and I think she is better than her mark. We may give her a run on the Flat before aiming her at mares' handicap hurdles over two miles, although she doesn't want soft ground.

GLASHA'S PEAK 5 b m Flemensfirth (USA) – Peggies Run
A big scopey filly, she is a half-sister to Peggies Venture who we have trained to win four times. Fourth on her debut in a bumper at Taunton, she was fifth next time at Newbury but came back with sore shins. Still immature last year, she is back cantering and will go mares' novice hurdling over a stiff two miles to begin with.

GOOD MAN PAT (IRE) 6 b g Gold Well – Basically Supreme (IRE)
He looks very well having enjoyed a good summer. Despite winning over fences at Plumpton in February, he is another who struggled with sore shins last season but will grow out of it. I think there is more to come from him with two and a half miles or even three miles handicap chases on his agenda.

GROUP STAGE (GER) 3 b g Maxios – Good Hope (GER)
Runner-up at Nottingham and Newbury on the Flat this year, he has had a summer break since his last run at Windsor. We will give him another run or two on the Flat before going juvenile hurdling. He has been schooled and likes some dig in the ground.

HACKSAW RIDGE (IRE) 4 b g Stowaway – Erins Lass (IRE)
He is a lovely horse we bought at the Cheltenham May Sale having run in two Irish points. A winner on his second start, we did a bit of work with him when he arrived and I was very pleased with him. He is a very likeable horse who will go novice hurdling.

HARAMBE 6 br g Malinas (GER) – Crystal Princess (IRE)

He was a smart bumper horse a couple of seasons ago finishing third in the Grade 2 championship event at Aintree. Sent hurdling last year, he didn't have the best of luck early on, but it clicked in the second half of the season and he really got his act together. Twice a winner at Kempton and Market Rasen, he then finished runner-up behind Getaway Trump in a valuable novices' handicap hurdle at Sandown on the final day of the season. He will stay over hurdles because I think he is on a fair mark. We will consider races such as the Greatwood Hurdle at Cheltenham (17th November). A strong traveller, he will stay further, if necessary, and I think he is a proper horse.

HEART OF A LION (IRE) 4 b g Yeats (IRE) – Lady Secret (FR)

A lovely horse who won on his debut in a bumper at Southwell in July. He isn't a summer jumper but couldn't run during the winter having suffered a stress fracture. We managed to get one run into him and he won well. He has been exciting from day one and we will run him in another bumper and then consider the Listed bumper at Ascot (20th December). Owned by J.P.McManus, he is an exciting prospect.

HOSTILE 5 ch g Malinas (GER) – Skew

A half-brother to Valdez, it has taken him time for the penny to drop and he has been a bit of a playboy. However, he shaped well on his debut at Warwick and was getting the hang of things late on finishing strongly in second. We were going to run him again but the ground was too quick so we put him away. He has been schooled over hurdles but may have another run in a bumper beforehand.

HOTTER THAN HELL (FR) 5 ch m No Risk At All (FR) – Ombrelle (FR)

She is a funny mare who has ability but doesn't seem to handle the winter very well. A winner on her hurdles debut at Worcester in May, she is a novice for this season and will run under a penalty next time. She looks great at present and is suited by two and a half miles plus.

KINGS ROYAL HUSSAR (FR) 3 b g Zebedee – Ile Rouge

Despite finishing second at Nottingham and third a couple of times, he hasn't reproduced on that track what he shows us at home and remains a maiden on the Flat. I am not sure what his optimum trip is either, but we will school him over jumps with a view to going juvenile hurdling.

LABEL DES OBEAUX (FR) 8 b g Saddler Maker (IRE) – La Bessiere (FR)

Ran well in a Pertemps qualifier at Newbury finishing sixth but, unfortunately, got a leg afterwards and missed the rest of the season. Given plenty of time, he won't be running until later on and we may keep him over hurdles for the time being. He stays well but doesn't seem to like Cheltenham for some reason.

LISP (IRE) 5 ch g Poet's Voice – Hora

He is a grand horse who won at Fontwell before finishing runner-up in the Listed Gerry Feilden Hurdle at Newbury and another valuable Grade 3 handicap at Ascot before Christmas. Fifth in the County Hurdle at Cheltenham last time, we have schooled him over fences and he was brilliant. We might give him one more run over hurdles to take the freshness out of him before going novice chasing.

MADIBA PASSION (FR) 5 b g Al Namix (FR) – Birsheba (FR)

Purchased at the Cheltenham December Sale having won two of his three Irish points, I like him. I thought he ran well in a bumper at Kempton on his first run for us in February and then we let him take his chance in a Listed event at Newbury a month later. He scoped badly afterwards and we put him away. We will start him off at two miles over hurdles because he has plenty of speed.

MAJOR DUNDEE (IRE) 4 b g Scorpion (IRE) – Be My Granny
Another promising young horse who won his only bumper at Southwell in May in good style. Trevor Hemmings has bought him since and he is a horse I like. He will go hurdling and, while he will stay further, we will start him off over two miles.

MIDNIGHTREFERENDUM 6 b m Midnight Legend – Forget The Ref (IRE)
A useful mare, she had some very good form in bumpers finishing second in a Grade 2 mares' bumper at Aintree a couple of seasons ago. Sent hurdling, she won at Fontwell in December but was struggling with her breathing for much of last season. We therefore operated on her wind and she was hobdayed. Returning to action at Warwick in the spring, she won well and will continue handicap hurdling over two and a half to two miles six. She will jump fences one day, too.

MIDNIGHTS' GIFT 3 gr f Midnight Legend – Giving
A half-sister to Giveaway Glance and Giving Glances amongst others, she is a likeable filly who was placed in her two runs on the Flat this summer before winning her maiden over a mile and three at Lingfield in September. She will go juvenile hurdling.

MILLSTONE 5 b g Alkaased (USA) – Stoney Path
From a family we know well, he has been both mentally and physically backward. We gave him a couple of runs in bumpers last season and he improved a lot on his second start at Huntingdon finishing third. Still a frame of a horse last year, he could have another run in a bumper because I think it will help him. He will then go hurdling.

MR PUMBLECHOOK 5 b g Midnight Legend – Definitely Pip (IRE)
Started well over hurdles being placed a couple of times before winning easily at Plumpton in December. He looked a smart horse but didn't reproduce that form during the second half of the year and then got colic. Given a break, he has grown a lot during the summer and has done well. I think he is on a decent mark and we will aim him at two and a half miles handicap hurdles.

MYSTICAL CLOUDS (IRE) 6 gr g Cloudings (IRE) – Silent Valley
Despite winning on his reappearance at Bangor, he was unlucky thereafter. He was leading when falling at the second last at Uttoxeter next time and, on his latest start, he ran well enough at Kempton but got struck into and missed the rest of the season. Back now, he may have another run over hurdles but it won't be long before he goes chasing.

NEBUCHADNEZZAR (FR) 4 b g Planteur (IRE) – Trexana
A huge horse who still hasn't won a race but I think he has been weak physically. Runner-up on his hurdles debut at Bangor behind Nelson River, the winner subsequently finished fourth in the Triumph Hurdle. He had another couple of runs at Kempton and Warwick finishing fourth on each occasion. He will have another run on the Flat before going back over hurdles over two and two and a half miles.

NOTACHANCE (IRE) 5 b g Mahler – Ballybrowney Hall (IRE)
Runner-up in his only Irish point-to-point, he was consistent over hurdles last season. Having been placed three times, he won at Newbury and I think he will improve over fences. A real galloper, he stays well and will be going for a novices' handicap chase over three miles.

OUR POWER (IRE) 4 b g Power – Scripture (IRE)
Twice a winner at Market Rasen and Newbury, I thought he ran well in the Fred Winter Juvenile Hurdle at Cheltenham. He got behind early on but stayed on well. We may give him a run on the Flat but I am very happy with him and feel he has more to offer. He could run in the four year old limited handicap hurdle at Chepstow (11th October) and will stay further in time.

OUTONPATROL (IRE) 5 gr m Stowaway – Burnt Oil Babe (IRE)
She won an Irish point last season before we bought her and her work had been good prior to her running in a bumper at Uttoxeter in the spring. She didn't run her race though so we gave her time off afterwards. I have been pleased with her during the summer and we will send her novice hurdling over two and a half miles.

PERFECT PREDATOR 4 b g Passing Glance – Cosmea
A half-brother to Cosmeapolitan, Sula Island and William Hunter, he is straightforward and progressed in bumpers last season. A winner at Taunton, he was also second at Ludlow and Wincanton. He will go novice hurdling over two miles.

POTTERMAN 6 b g Sulamani (IRE) – Polly Potter
He has been doing well over fences during the summer winning three of his four starts, including over three miles at Worcester in August. He jumps well but the key to him is the ground because he wants its good. We will therefore keep him going during the Autumn until the ground changes and then give him a winter break before returning in the spring.

PRAECEPS (IRE) 4 b g Canford Cliffs (IRE) – Sliding Scale
Bought at the Newmarket Horses in Training Sale last Autumn, he enjoyed a good season over hurdles winning at Market Rasen and Plumpton and finishing sixth in the Fred Winter Juvenile Hurdle at Cheltenham in between. We have the option of running him on the Flat and he is another possible for the four year old limited handicap hurdle at Chepstow (11th October).

PRODUCTION 3 b g Oasis Dream – Pure Excellence
Owned by The Royal Ascot Racing Club, he won twice on the Flat for Richard Hannon, including over ten furlongs at Redcar this summer. We have schooled him over hurdles and he absolutely loves it. Rated 79 on the Flat, he will be running early on and I am very pleased with him.

SAN RUMOLDO 4 ch g Malinas (GER) – Ancora (IRE)
A horse I like a lot, he won on his debut in a bumper at Southwell in March and was subsequently bought by J.P.McManus. Having spent the summer in Ireland, he has come back looking magnificent. He has schooled well over hurdles but it's possible he will have another run in a bumper before going jumping.

SCARLET DRAGON 6 b g Sir Percy – Welsh Angel
A winner over hurdles at Huntingdon in January, he ran well at Sandown on the final day of the season finishing fourth in a £100,000 novices' handicap hurdle. I was very pleased with his run at Goodwood in August when fourth in another valuable handicap over a mile and six, although the trip stretched him. The ground was very quick at York last time and he will go back over hurdles. I think there is a good race in him.

SCEAU ROYAL (FR) 7 b g Doctor Dino (FR) – Sandside (FR)
He is in good form and the plan is for him to reappear once again in the Grade 2 Shloer Chase at Cheltenham (17th November), a race he won last year. Then, depending on the ground, he could run in the Tingle Creek at Sandown (7th December) but he doesn't want it too soft. If not, the Grade 2 Peterborough Chase at Huntingdon the following day is an option because we are keen to try him over two and a half miles at some stage. Third in the Queen Mother Champion Chase last season, he has been a very good horse for us.

SENIOR CITIZEN 6 b g Tobougg (IRE) – Mothers Help
Despite winning on his hurdles debut at Chepstow, he was still quite a weak horse last year hence he didn't progress as much as we had hoped. However, he has done well during the summer and I think he could be the real deal over fences. We haven't schooled him yet but he was runner-up in an Irish point and his jumping has never been an issue. He doesn't want the ground too soft with two and a half miles plus being his trip.

SHESHOON SONNY (FR) 4 b g Youmzain (IRE) – Minnie's Mystery (FR)
A progressive horse in bumpers last season, I like him a lot. Runner-up at Exeter on his second start, he then won well at Wetherby and we were going to run him again in the bumper at Ayr's Scottish National meeting, but the ground was too quick. He has a knee action and loves soft ground and is a very tough horse. We will send him hurdling over two miles and I think he is a smart horse.

TALKISCHEAP (IRE) 7 b g Getaway (GER) – Carrigmoorna Oak (IRE)
Did us proud last season winning twice over fences, including when producing a tremendous performance in the Bet365 Gold Cup at Sandown. I was hoping he would run well beforehand but it was such an impressive win scoring by ten lengths. He is now rated 157 and we will consider the Ladbrokes Trophy at Newbury (30th November) with the likelihood of one run beforehand. He is ground dependent because he wants good ground and, long term, his owner is keen to go to Aintree. The Scottish National is another option later on, too. I think he is possibly better racing right-handed though.

THE CULL BANK (IRE) 5 b m Yeats (IRE) – Crème D'Arblay (IRE)
A winning Irish pointer, we bought her at the Cheltenham December Sale and she did well over hurdles winning two out of three. Having won at Fontwell and Plumpton, she finished runner-up in a Listed novice at Cheltenham last time but found the ground too quick. She is a soft ground mare who will run in mares' handicap hurdles.

THE GLANCING QUEEN (IRE) 5 b m Jeremy (USA) – Glancing (IRE)
She is a lovely mare who I adore. Successful in her only Irish point-to-point before we bought her, she had a very good season in bumpers winning a Listed mares' event at Cheltenham in November and the Grade 2 mares' bumper at Aintree's Grand National meeting. She was very impressive that day and we are looking forward to sending her hurdling. We will probably start her off in a mares' novice hurdle but she ran very well against the geldings last season finishing third in a Listed race at Ascot before Christmas and fifth in the Champion bumper at the Cheltenham Festival. She possesses plenty of speed and we will start her off over two miles on good or slower ground.

THE OLYMPIAN (IRE) 3 ch g Olympic Glory (IRE) – Basira (FR)
He had some good form on the Flat as a two year old finishing second twice before winning over ten furlongs at Newmarket last Autumn. Subsequently bought by J.P.McManus, he didn't arrive back here until late summer because he wants cut in the ground. It was always the plan to leave him off until later in the year with a view to having a run on the Flat in the Autumn before going juvenile hurdling. He could be very good.

TIMOTEO (FR) 6 b g Diamond Green (FR) – Goldnella (FR)
We bought him back at the Doncaster May Sales because we still don't know how good he is having won both his starts over fences in March. Impressive at Stratford and Kempton, we were keen to run him again but the ground dried out and we didn't want to risk him. Rated 134, I am hoping he will develop into a Saturday horse with two and two and a half miles being his trip.

TRUESHAN (FR) 3 b g Planteur (IRE) – Shao Line (FR)

He will go juvenile hurdling and I think he could be very good. Sixth on his only start at Nottingham as a two year old last season, he won over a mile and a half at Wolverhampton in August and I loved the way he finished off. He then defied a penalty at Ffos Las nearly a month later before finishing second in a valuable three year old handicap at Haydock over a mile and six in September. He likes cut in the ground and is open to even more improvement on the Flat before going jumping.

VALDEZ 12 ch g Doyen (IRE) – Skew

Despite the fact he is twelve, he is still relatively lightly raced and I was very pleased with his run at Newbury last March when finishing third in the Grade 3 Greatwood Gold Cup. Hopefully, we can have a clear run with him this season and he can win another race.

WALTER WHITE (FR) 4 b g Maxios – Antique Rose (GER)

A winner on the Flat in France last year, he hasn't been the easiest horse to keep healthy. Sixth at Kempton in July, he then finished fifth at Newbury. He stays well and loves soft ground and will go hurdling.

WYNN HOUSE 4 ch f Presenting – Glorious Twelfth (IRE)

She is a lovely filly who I like a lot but we don't know how good she is. A winner on her debut at Uttoxeter in March, she was green that day but still won. Nothing can get her off the bridle at home. The plan is for to stay in bumpers for the time being.

TRAINER'S HORSE TO FOLLOW: SHESHOON SONNY

Tom LACEY

Stables: Cottage Field Stables Ltd., Sapness Farm, Woolhope, Herefordshire.
2018/2019: 38 Winners / 178 Runners 21% Prize-Money £377,918
www.cottagefield.co.uk

ADRIMEL (FR) 4 bb g Tirwanako (FR) – Irise De Gene (FR)

He is a fine big athletic horse who won his only Irish point-to-point by eight lengths in March. Bought at the Aintree April Sale, it is possible we will run him in a soft ground bumper to begin with. It would be nice to think he would start off at one of the bigger tracks.

CAPAC (IRE) 4 ch g Aizavoski (IRE) – Wigwam Mam (IRE)

A half-brother to Brave Inca, he has always pleased us and we thought he would run well on his debut in a bumper at Taunton in April. He will go novice hurdling and, while he will stay further, we will start him off over two miles because he isn't slow.

CHRISTOPHER ROBIN (IRE) 4 b g Camelot – Iowa Falls

We bought him at the Goffs UK Spring Sale at Doncaster in May having been recommended. A winner over hurdles in testing ground at Wexford for Joseph O'Brien, he finished runner-up at Fairyhouse's Easter Festival last time. Versatile in terms of ground, we are still getting to know him but we will be aiming him at handicap hurdles and I hope he will provide his new syndicate with plenty of fun.

CONINGSBY 6 ch g Midnight Legend – Motcombe (IRE)

He came good over fences at Exeter on his final start winning in convincing fashion. Raised nine pounds, he is probably high enough in the weights but is still lightly raced and has strengthened up during the summer. While he didn't run badly at Wetherby earlier in his career, we have always thought he is a better horse racing right-handed. He likes soft ground and staying chases are on his agenda.

DORKING BOY 5 ch g Schiaparelli (GER) – Megasue
He was very disappointing last season so we turned him away early and gave him a long break. Sore behind after his run in the Grade 2 Persian War Novices' Hurdle at Chepstow in October, he returned at Ludlow in February but raced too keenly. He has come back in looking a much happier horse so I hope he can leave last season's form behind. We will probably fit him with a hood in future and hopefully he will settle better. He will stay further but we will keep him over two miles until he learns to settle.

DORKING COCK (IRE) 5 b g Winged Love (IRE) – Kiss Jolie (FR)
Had a good season over hurdles winning at Sandown and Carlisle in the space of three days in February before finishing runner-up at the latter track on his final run. He has been schooled over fences and will go novice chasing. His jumping has been very good and I think he will be a big improver over fences. He has summered well and I am very pleased with him. While he wasn't the easiest horse to break, he hasn't put a foot wrong on the racecourse. Both his wins last season were over two miles, but I think he wants further.

EQUUS AMADEUS (IRE) 6 b g Beat Hollow – Charade (IRE)
He had plenty of racing last year winning twice at Wincanton and Doncaster and running some very good races in defeat. Third in the Scottish Champion Hurdle at Ayr, I think he would have finished second, if he had been ridden handier. We tried him once over fences last season and he will go back chasing this Autumn. He loves fast ground.

FAIR KATE 5 b m Fair Mix (IRE) – Silver Kate (IRE)
A half-sister to Kateson, she looks well following her summer break. Placed a couple of times over hurdles at Chepstow, she is will go for a novices' handicap hurdle off her mark of 112. She will benefit from stepping up in trip.

FIGHTER CASSUEL (FR) 4 b g Blue Bresil (FR) – Lady Tsana (FR)
Owned by Claire and Paul Rooney, he is a very nice unraced four year old who was bought at the Goffs Landrover Sale last year. A half-brother to Alan King's Grade 2 novice hurdle winner Alsa Mix, he will run in a bumper in the Autumn and is a lovely horse.

FLASHING GLANCE 6 b g Passing Glance – Don And Gerry (IRE)
A winner over hurdles at Ludlow in February, he is rated 130. We tried him over fences last season and he remains a novice, so we will go back down that route at some stage. However, we may run him in the Silver Trophy at Chepstow (12th October) beforehand. His career wins have been gained over two miles but he is settling better now and I think he will stay two and a half miles. He has summered well and developed into a stronger horse.

FLOATING ROCK (GER) 4 b g It's Gino (GER) – Fly Osoria (GER)
He won on his debut in a bumper at Catterick under Richard Johnson in February. We thought he would run well but his task was made easier when Keith Dalgleish's horse (L'Air Du Vent) was withdrawn. The plan is for him to go straight over hurdles with two miles being his trip to begin with.

GLORY AND FORTUNE (IRE) 4 b g Fame And Glory – Night Heron (IRE)
We bought him at the Derby Sale in Ireland as a three year old and it wasn't a surprise when he won a Listed bumper at Cheltenham on New Year's Day on his debut. We planned to run him in the Grade 2 championship bumper at Aintree but he did a piece of work and I wasn't happy with him so we put him away for the summer. He is a big horse who needs time and it is probably the best thing that could have happened. He will go hurdling in the Autumn and I would like to start him off low key over a stiff two miles at somewhere like Carlisle, Chepstow or Exeter. Good to soft or soft ground is ideal.

JOHNBB (IRE) 5 b g Stowaway – Flemins Evening (IRE)
A nice young horse who did nothing wrong over hurdles last season winning at Ayr and running well behind Birchdale at Warwick, prior to that. He got bogged down on the inside at Sandown, where the ground was its most testing on his latest start. We are going to send him chasing this Autumn and I think he will improve for a switch to fences. Two and a half miles suits him.

KATESON 6 gr g Black Sam Bellamy (IRE) – Silver Kate (IRE)
He has summered really well and, in all likelihood, he will go novice chasing. Rated 141, he won't be the easiest horse to place over hurdles and every jockey who has ridden him has said he is a horse to look forward to over fences. Twice a winner at Chepstow and Newbury, he also ran well finishing third in the Grade 1 Challow Hurdle at the latter track in a steadily run race. It was the correct decision not to take him to the Cheltenham Festival. He was badly hampered at Haydock and then had had enough by the time he ran at Aintree. We haven't schooled him over fences yet but I don't envisage any problems. Good to soft or soft ground is ideal, although his owner has always been keen to run him on better ground. Although his dam stayed well, his best form is over two and a half miles.

KIMBERLITE CANDY (IRE) 7 b g Flemensfirth (USA) – Mandys Native (IRE)
A winner on his reappearance at Ayr in November, he finished third at Sandown in February before failing to stay in the Eider Chase at Newcastle. He finished very tired and endured a hard race that day. Pulled up in the Irish National, he has built up a good rapport with Richie McLernon and he is keen to try him over the National fences. Therefore he could run in either the Grand Sefton (if soft) or the Becher Chase on Saturday 7th December. Given the fact he invariably runs well fresh, he could reappear at Aintree.

LAMANVER STORM 4 b g Geordieland (FR) – Lamanver Homerun
An unraced half-brother to Lamanver Odyssey, he is from a family who love soft ground. He has shown enough at home to suggest he can win races. He jumps well, although his owner may be keen to go for a bumper before going novice hurdling. Trips around two miles or two miles two will suit him to begin with.

L'INCORRIGIBLE (FR) 4 b g No Risk At All (FR) – Incorrigible (FR)
He is a very nice horse who won a junior bumper on his debut at Warwick in November. His homework had been good beforehand and therefore his performance didn't surprise us. We purposely left him off after that to give him time to mature. Still not back at the yard, he spent the summer with his owner and I hope he will develop into a lovely novice hurdler.

LOSSIEMOUTH 4 b g Makfi – First Bloom (USA)
A homebred belonging to Lady Cobham, I adore him and I think he is very good. We were training him for the Grade 2 championship bumper at Aintree and I thought he would have an outstanding chance, but he had some puss in one of his feet and we ran out of time. He ran out on his debut at Huntingdon but it is not the first time that has happened there. Something caught his eye and he swerved and went through the wing. He made amends at Newcastle next time and then followed up under a penalty at Carlisle. Strong at the finish that day, he has been quite a slow learner but is getting the hang of things and his jumping at home has been good. Suited by some ease in the ground, he could start in the same two miles three maiden hurdle at Ascot (22nd November), which we won with Kimberlite Candy in 2016.

MEEP MEEP (IRE) 6 ch m Flemensfirth (USA) – Charming Leader (IRE)
She has done well during the summer and looks well handicapped on her bumper form. We threw her in at the deep end over hurdles, although she was disappointing in the mares' final at Newbury on her final run. Given a break since, two and a half miles is her trip.

NEVILLE'S CROSS (IRE) 4 b g Stowaway – Dancing Bird (IRE)
Acquired at the Derby Sales in Ireland last year, he slipped up on the bend after the third last in his only point-to-point at Tabley in April. I think he would have won that day and we will start him off in a bumper. He is a nice horse who we have always liked.

POLYDORA (IRE) 7 b g Milan – Mandysway (IRE)
Third on his chasing debut at Aintree, he then won at Newcastle beating a 117 rated opponent. The handicapper raised him eleven pounds to a mark of 142, which was ridiculous. He struggled thereafter and has subsequently dropped to 135. Three miles on soft ground are his optimum conditions and I am hoping things will fall his way.

RED NIKA (FR) 4 br g Denham Red (FR) – Nika Glitters (FR)
Purchased at the Derby Sales in Ireland last year, he was slow to come to hand hence he didn't make his debut in a point-to-point until late April. Left clear at the last, he won by eighteen lengths at Woodford. He is a horse we like and his work has always been good. Subsequently sold to Mr Kellett, who has Thomas Patrick with us, he could make his hurdles debut at Hereford (15th October) over two miles three, as the owner is sponsoring the race.

SAINT ARVANS 4 b g Motivator - Castellina
A very nice unraced gelding by Motivator who is a full brother to Via Delle Volte, whom we trained to win over hurdles at Doncaster and finish third in a Grade 3 mares' hurdle at Cheltenham last spring. I like him and he will start off in a bumper.

SEBASTOPOL (IRE) 5 b g Fame And Glory – Knockcroghery (IRE)
Last season proved very frustrating having won a point-to-point and a bumper at Ayr the previous campaign. Fourth on his hurdles debut at Cheltenham behind Thomas Darby and Elixir Du Nutz, he returned with a very nasty wound on the point of his off hind joint. Back in action at Ayr early in the New Year, he finished third flying at the death. We then found he was suffering with a kissing spine which required surgery. Rated 127, I think he is well handicapped, although he is still a novice. He will appreciate a step up to two and a half miles.

SNAPDRAGON FIRE (IRE) 6 b g Getaway (GER) – Global Diamond (IRE)
A good fun horse who enjoyed a productive season winning three times over hurdles. Successful at Huntingdon (twice) and Ludlow, he likes fast ground and was runner-up on his chasing debut at Southwell in early September.

TEA CLIPPER (IRE) 4 b g Stowaway – A Plus Ma Puce (FR)
Bought as a three year old at the Goffs Landrover Sale in Ireland, he is a lovely horse who won a Restricted point-to-point at Larkhill in February on his debut by six lengths. He bolted up and has been subsequently bought by Jerry Hinds and Ashley Head. A horse with plenty of speed, he will go straight over hurdles and is an exciting prospect.

THAIS TOIR (FR) 4 b g Diamond Boy (FR) – Scotland Act (FR)
A nice unraced four year old we purchased at the Derby Sale over a year ago. He is a big horse who was too backward to race last season. He has summered well and I like him. We have schooled him but he may start off in a bumper before going hurdling.

THOMAS PATRICK (IRE) 7 b g Winged Love (IRE) – Huncheon Siss (IRE)
Runner-up in a Listed chase behind Elegant Escape at Sandown on his reappearance, he lost his way thereafter and struggled in his four subsequent starts. Following his run in the rearranged Denman Chase at Ascot, he underwent a full MOT and we discovered he was suffering from a bone pain in his pastern, similar to Presenting Percy. Hopefully that explains why he performed the way he did for most of last season. He has dropped to a mark of 140 and, if he can rediscover his best form, we could have some fun again.

VADO FORTE (FR) 6 b g Walk In The Park (IRE) – Gloire (FR)

Having done well the previous year, including winning the Sussex Champion Hurdle at Plumpton, he had a tough season last time around running only three times. The intention is to send him chasing and, while he is effective over two miles, he will stay further.

Unnamed 4 b g Kayf Tara – Megalex

Back in work, he was too backward to run last season. Well bred being a full brother to Ballyandy and Megastar, it is a fragile family hence we have given him time. I hope he will make his mark in a bumper before going hurdling.

Unnamed 3 gr g Martaline – Shahwarda (FR)

Owned by Jerry Hinds and Ashley Head, he is a lovely horse we bought during the summer (€85,000) at the Derby Sales. We have already schooled him over hurdles but he will start off in a bumper. He is a very nice horse.

Below are two promising youngsters Tom sold during the spring/summer and are worth looking out for this winter.

CADZAND (IRE) 4 b g Stowaway – Queens Mark (IRE)

"I think he is a very nice horse who won his only point-to-point at Charlton Horethorne in March by fifteen lengths. His victory wasn't a surprise because we have always liked him since we bought him at the Derby Sales as a three year old. We have sold him to **Dan Skelton** since and I would say he is capable of winning a bumper, if they decide to go down that route. Reports have it, he is held in high regard by his new stable."

RAMILLIES (IRE) 4 gr g Shantou (USA) – Mrs Wallensky (IRE)

"Another we bought at the Derby Sales in Ireland as a three year old, I loved him. He showed us plenty of raw ability and we hardly had to train him before he won by six lengths on his only start in a point-to-point at Bishops Court in the spring. He looked very good indeed. Like Blackbow and Energumene, who we trained to win their point, he was bought by **Willie Mullins** for £215,000 at the Cheltenham Festival Sale less than a fortnight later. He is a big horse with size and scope."

TRAINER'S HORSE TO FOLLOW: TEA CLIPPER

Donald McCAIN

Stables: Bankhouse, Cholmondeley, Cheshire.
2018/2019: 63 Winners / 558 Runners 11% Prize-Money £627,919
www.donaldmccain.co.uk

ARAB MOON 5 b g Elnadim (USA) – Albeed

A five times winner on the all-weather on the Flat for William Knight, we purchased him at the Newmarket Horses In Training Sale in October. Having had a busy spell on the Flat, we decided to give him a break with a view to going hurdling this Autumn.

BALLASALLA (IRE) 7 br g Presenting – Papoose (IRE)

A full-brother to Ballabriggs, he was a bit frustrating last season because he ran some good races over fences but didn't get his head in front. Runner-up three times, he was unlucky not to win at Doncaster having made a mistake at the last. Still a big immature horse, if he improves again then he ought to win races over fences this season. He is bred to stay three miles plus, but I have kept him to shorter trips. Rated 110, we will find a suitable novices' handicap chase.

BIRD ON THE WIRE (FR) 4 ch g Martaline – Titi Jolie (FR)
He won twice for Philip Rowley before we bought him at Goffs Aintree Sale in April. Eligible for a point-to-point bumper at the same track the following month, he did too much early on and ran no sort of race. Given a break since, he is a staying type and we will aim him at two and a half miles plus novice hurdles.

BRIGHT SIDE OFLIFE (IRE) 6 ch m Doyen (IRE) – Lough Lein Leader (IRE)
A point-to-point winner for Denis Murphy in Ireland, we bought her at the Ascot Sales in March last year. She took a long time to come right and we ran out of time. Although she ran OK in a bumper at Hexham in May, the track didn't really suit her. She will go novice hurdling over two and a half miles plus.

CHTI BALKO (FR) 7 br g Balko (FR) – Ina Scoop (FR)
Ran a couple of good races at Ayr and Haydock during the first half of last season but never really got his ground thereafter. He loves soft/heavy ground and is a different horse at Haydock compared to anywhere else. The handicapper has given him a chance so hopefully he will get his conditions this winter.

CHUVELO (IRE) 4 b g Milan – Bargante (IRE)
A nice horse we bought at the Cheltenham April Sale having run well in his only bumper for Sam Curling in Ireland. Beaten three parts of a length in second in the Tattersalls Ireland George Mernagh Memorial Sales Bumper at the Fairyhouse Easter Festival, there was a fair bit of carnage during the race but it was a very good run. He seems straightforward and has settled in well. There is every chance he could have another run in a bumper.

DEAR SIRE (FR) 7 gr g Al Namix (FR) – Polismith (FR)
Despite winning twice over fences at Cartmel and Sedgefield, he was unfortunate last season because he was cantering when falling at the second last at Cheltenham in October. He sprained his hock and it caused a fracture, which meant he missed the rest of his novice season. Back in work, he looks well and his run at Cheltenham suggests he is every bit as good over fences as he was over hurdles. Two or two and a half miles is ideal.

DOUBLE ESPRIT 3 b g Invincible Spirit (IRE) – Natural Spirits (FR)
Owners Simon Munir and Isaac Souede have kindly sent me three horses, including this unraced three year old. An expensive yearling, he has been schooled over hurdles with a view to going juvenile hurdling, but I need to get some experience into him on the Flat beforehand. Alternatively, he could start off in a junior bumper.

EMTARA 4 b f Kayf Tara – Miss Ballantyne
A two lengths winner of her only point-to-point for Colin Bowe, I thought she would make more than she did at the Punchestown Festival Sale. She isn't over big but has plenty of options, including starting off in a mares' only bumper. She looks a nice filly.

FINGAL D'ARTHEL (FR) 4 b g Cokoriko (FR) – La Fee D'Arthel (FR)
Arrived in the summer, we are still getting to know him having run in three bumpers in France. Runner-up behind Fix Sun, who has won over hurdles for Nicky Henderson since, at Paray-Le-Monial over twelve furlongs in March, he won by two and a half lengths on his next start a month later at Machecoul. Owned by Simon Munir and Isaac Souede, he will go novice hurdling.

FINISK RIVER 6 gr g Red Rocks (IRE) – Scopa D'Assi (IRE)
Despite being a six year old, he was a tall immature horse when we bought him at the Doncaster January Sale. He ran in two Irish points falling on his debut at the second last before finishing runner-up on his latest start. A strong traveller, who may not want heavy ground, he has done well during the summer and could run in a bumper before going hurdling.

FIRST ACCOUNT 5 bb g Malinas (GER) – Kind Nell
A six lengths winner of his only Irish point for Colin Bowe the previous season, he ran very well on his first start for us over hurdles at Carlisle in October finishing third behind Al Dancer and Windsor Avenue. Runner-up at the same venue a couple of months later, he wasn't suited by the inner track on that occasion. They are two completely different courses. Our horses weren't right in the early part of the New Year, so we decided to keep him as a novice for this year hence he hasn't raced since. He doesn't want extremes of ground and, given the fact he has been granted a mark of 114, we may send him straight over fences and aim him at a novices' handicap chase.

GABRIEL OAK 3 b g Sir Percy – Maleficent
A big horse we bought as a yearling, he finished fourth at Haydock on his debut on the Flat in June but the race wasn't run to suit him. Fifth at the same track in early September, we need to get more experience into him before he goes juvenile hurdling.

GAELIK COAST (FR) 5 br g Coastal Path – Gaelika (IRE)
Another ex-pointer, he ran very well first time out in a bumper at Bangor in December finishing second. Indeed, I thought he was unlucky not to win. He then came back a sick horse having finished fifth at Haydock and we decided to give him the rest of the season off. A strong traveller, he has schooled well and will go novice hurdling. We will start him off over two miles because he isn't slow.

GET IN ROBIN (IRE) 4 ch f Robin Des Champs (FR) – Get In There (IRE)
A racy filly who fell in her first Irish point before winning next time. Recommended to us by Donnchadh Doyle, we bought her at the Goffs UK Spring Sale at Doncaster in May. She may run in a mares' bumper before going hurdling. She is a nice filly.

GOOBINATOR (USA) 3 ch g Noble Mission – Lilac Lilly (USA)
We bought him as a yearling at the Tattersalls October Book 2 Sale. We have taken our time with him because he was quite keen to begin with. I was pleased with his debut run on the Flat at Carlisle in August finishing third over nine furlongs. Still green, he has schooled nicely over hurdles.

HEARTBREAK KID (IRE) 4 b g Getaway (GER) – Bella's Bury
A half-brother to Sonic, Derek O'Connor and I bought him as a store horse at the Goffs Landrover Sale last year and sent him to Colin Bowe to run in a point-to-point. He ran in an Auction maiden point and jumped like a buck and won by thirty lengths. A straightforward horse who loves soft ground, he is now owned by Tim (Leslie) and could run in a bumper in the Autumn. He is a staying type.

KHAMSIN MOOR (IRE) 3 b g Mastercraftsman (IRE) – Stroke of Six (IRE)
Like Goobinator, he was bought as a yearling at the Tattersalls October Book 2 Sale. Given time to mature, he is a huge horse measuring 17hh. Owned by Tim (Leslie), we will aim him at a junior bumper.

LADY TREMAINE (IRE) 4 b f Kalanisi (IRE) – Lough Lein Leader (IRE)
She is another filly who Donnchadh Doyle recommended to us having won her final start in three Irish points. We bought her at the Cheltenham May Sale and she looks a nice solid filly with plenty of speed.

LORD SPRINGFIELD (IRE) 6 ch g Well Chosen – Super Thyne (IRE)
We bought him at the Punchestown Festival Sale last year and he had three runs over hurdles last season. Rated 115, he is a big strong horse who could go straight over fences and run in a novices' handicap over two and a half or three miles.

LOUGH DERG JEWEL (IRE) 8 b g Oscar (IRE) – River Valley Lady (IRE)
He won at Doncaster in December before finishing second at Kelso the following month. Unfortunately, he suffered a suspensory injury and therefore hasn't raced since. Suited by small fields, he will be running in staying handicap chases but I don't think he wants extremes of ground.

MACKENBERG (GER) 4 b g Jukebox Jury (IRE) – Mountain Melody (GER)
Despite failing to complete in his two Irish points for Donnchadh Doyle, he came highly recommended and we purchased him at the Cheltenham April Sale. He is a full-brother to Mark Johnston's progressive three year old Mind The Crack and is a grand horse. Owned by Tim Leslie, he could have a run in a bumper before going jumping.

MINELLA TRUMP (IRE) 5 b g Shantou (USA) – One Theatre (IRE)
Bought at the Aintree April Sale, he is another grand horse who won his only point-to-point for John Nallen. A six lengths winner, he likes soft ground and is a staying type. I love his sire and he is very much my type of horse. He will go novice hurdling.

MOUNT MEWS (IRE) 8 b g Presenting – Kneeland Lass (IRE)
He ran OK on his first run for us at Kelso in January finishing second but I am not convinced he enjoys jumping fences. He was then due to contest the Martin Pipe Conditional Jockeys' Handicap Hurdle at the Cheltenham Festival but, having left the paddock, he got worked up going out on to the track and lost the plot. Then, there was a standing start and he didn't jump off. Too free at Aintree last time, I am keen for him to remain over hurdles with three miles being his trip.

MR MCGO (IRE) 8 b g Touch of Land (FR) – La Principal (IRE)
Restricted to four runs last season, he wants soft ground but didn't get many opportunities to experience such conditions last season. Still in contention when falling at the second last at Haydock in December, he ran OK at Sandown next time. Still a novice over fences, I think he wants two and a half miles on soft/heavy ground.

NAVAJO PASS 3 b g Nathaniel (IRE) – Navajo Charm
A very nice horse we bought as a yearling at the Tattersalls October Book 3 sale. He has raced four times on the Flat finishing third over seven furlongs at Redcar last Autumn and a close second over a mile and a half at Haydock on heavy ground in June on his reappearance. Runner-up again behind the useful hurdler Beyond The Clouds at Ripon, he then stayed on well to lead close home over a mile and six at Carlisle in August. Rated 85, his performances haven't surprised me because we have always liked him. I want to give him more experience on the Flat before going jumping. He has schooled well and I am looking forward to running him in juvenile hurdles in the Autumn.

NAYATI (FR) 5 b g Spirit One (FR) – Smadouce (FR)
Bought cheaply at the Goffs UK December Sale at Doncaster, he has been a star for us winning handicap hurdles at Bangor, Aintree and Perth. Third at Cartmel in July, he likes a strongly run race but things didn't work out for him at Market Rasen next time. However, he bounced back at Perth in August winning a good prize in the process. Rated 130 over hurdles, we have schooled him over fences and the intention is to send him chasing in the Autumn.

NOAH AND THE ARK (IRE) 5 ch g Vinnie Roe (IRE) – Well Water (IRE)
He has been doing well during the summer winning over hurdles at Ffos Las and Worcester in July. A strongly run two miles on fast ground is ideal and, being a former winning pointer, he will jump a fence, too. He gets on well with Harry Beswick, who isn't riding him any different to when we got pulled in before the stewards at Bangor last year.

O'HANRAHAN BRIDGE (IRE) 7 b g Gold Well – Greenacre Mandalay (IRE)
Yet to run for us, he hasn't raced for nearly two years having arrived with an injury. He ran in a couple of Irish points (disqualified having crossed the line in front on his second start) before finishing fourth in a bumper for Rebecca Curtis. That form looks OK, but it is a long time ago. I would imagine he will go novice hurdling.

ONTHEFRONTFOOT (IRE) 5 b g Shantou (USA) – On The Backfoot (IRE)
A point winner, he is a really likeable sort who won a bumper in the spring and twice over hurdles at Ayr and Cartmel in May. A strong traveller and slick jumper, he will stay two and a half miles. He reminds me of Son of Flicka, who won the Coral Cup for us at the Cheltenham Festival.

OTTONIAN 5 ch g Dubawi (IRE) – Evil Empire (GER)
Ex-Godolphin, he won both his starts on the Flat for Charlie Appleby a couple of years ago and we bought him cheaply at the end of last season knowing he had a problem. He is obviously fragile but has plenty of ability and loves soft ground. We have scanned him and he seems in good form at home. The plan is to send him hurdling.

PICHELOT (FR) 6 bl g Konig Turf (GER) – Haute Chartreuse (FR)
Trained in France by Guy Cherel, he belongs to Simon Munir and Isaac Souede and was a regular at Auteuil winning over fences a couple of years ago. A fine big horse, he remains a novice over hurdles and that is the plan this winter.

POGUE (IRE) 6 gr g Stowaway – Night Palm (IRE)
A winning pointer, he ran well on his first two starts over hurdles at Bangor and Kelso. However, he didn't handle the inner track at Carlisle last time and came back jarred up. He is a big horse measuring 17hh and, in all likelihood, we will send him straight over fences and aim him at a novices' handicap chase over two miles off his mark of 115.

POUGNE BOBBI (FR) 8 bb g Protektor (GER) – Amicus
Yet to run for us, we bought him out of Nicky Henderson's yard at the Doncaster Spring Sales last year, but he had a setback and was unable to race last season. He is 100% now and will be running in two and a half miles handicap chases on soft ground.

PRESENTANDCOUNTING (IRE) 5 b g Presenting – Count On Me (IRE)
Arrived with a big reputation having won the second of his two Irish points for Philip Dempsey. Derek O'Connor rode him that day and said he is one of only a handful of horses he has ridden with so much ability, but fragile mentally. A fine big horse, we bought him at the Goffs UK January Sale at Doncaster. He is an intriguing horse with size and presence and is quite a free going sort.

PULL GREEN (IRE) 4 b g Califet (FR) – Clogher Valley (IRE)
I am hoping he will prove good value having been acquired at the Cheltenham April Sale. He ought to have won his second start but fiddled the last and lost his momentum. He is a good size and may have a run in a bumper before going hurdling.

SHANTALUZE (IRE) 7 b g Shantou (USA) – Nut Touluze (IRE)
A bit delicate, he won twice over hurdles at Bangor last season and, when he's on a going day, he is a good horse. Quite hot and buzzy, two miles is his trip and we are going to send him novice chasing.

STEINKRAUS (IRE) 4 b g Jeremy (USA) – Red Fern (IRE)
By a popular sire, he was purchased at the Doncaster Spring Sale having finished runner-up on his second start in Irish points. The winner was subsequently sold for £110,000. Only four, I hope he will do a job in bumpers and over hurdles this season.

TESTIFY (IRE) 8 b g Witness Box (USA) – Tanya Thyne (IRE)
A Grade 2 winning novice chaser a couple of seasons ago, he needs soft or heavy ground but rarely got it last winter. The handicapper has dropped him a few pounds, which will help and hopefully he will show what he is capable of in handicap chases at the likes of Haydock.

THE CON MAN (IRE) 6 b g Oscar (IRE) – Phillis Hill
An easy winner of his only Irish point for Colin Bowe, we bought him at the Doncaster August Sales last year. He was impressive at Carlisle on his hurdles debut in December winning by five lengths but, unfortunately, he banged his knee in the process and didn't run again. We haven't made a plan for him because he obviously lacks experience and hasn't been given a mark yet. Colin Bowe maintains he wants soft ground with three miles being his trip eventually. Either way, he looked a nice horse at Carlisle.

THE SOME DANCE KID (IRE) 6 b g Shantou (USA) – River Rouge (IRE)
A very likeable horse who knows how to win. Successful in three of his four races over hurdles last season, we were training him for the EBF Final at Sandown in March but he had an abscess on his foot and we ran out of time. I wasn't surprised by how well he did last year because I have always liked him. Rated 133, he will jump fences in time but I don't think he is badly handicapped over hurdles. He wants two and a half miles but will stay three eventually.

TOTALLY REJECTED (IRE) 4 b g Mustameet (USA) – Boro Katie (IRE)
Raced twice in Irish points and, having fallen on his debut, he was runner-up next time. Purchased at the Goffs UK Spring Sale, he is a plain light framed horse by an unfashionable sire. However, his form looks OK and the horse who beat him last time (Face The Odds) was subsequently sold for £165,000. He is likely to run in a bumper.

WHITEOAK FLEUR 6 b m Black Sam Bellamy (IRE) – Harringay
She ran well in bumpers at Sedgefield and Kelso but has her own ideas and has needed a few runs over hurdles to put some manners on her. She has gained experience now and was placed at Kelso and Sedgefield. Her mark of 108 looks fair.

WHITEOAK MOLLY 5 b m Flemensfirth (USA) – Whiteoak (IRE)
Out of our Cheltenham Festival winning mare, she is as fragile as her mother and we haven't been able to run her since her debut in a bumper at Bangor in the spring of last year. She has been immature, plus a niggle held her up last season. It is possible she will have another run in a bumper before going hurdling, although we haven't schooled her yet.

WORD HAS IT (IRE) 5 b g Jeremy (USA) – Rathfeigh (IRE)
Acquired at the Doncaster January Sales, he was placed in his two Irish points and was recommended to us by Derek O'Connor. He has done very well during the summer and I am pleased with him. I think he's a nice horse.

YES NO MAYBE SO (IRE) 5 br g Stowaway – Godlylady (IRE)
He won a bumper at Musselburgh in December, despite the fact the track didn't play to his strengths. Below par at Kelso last time, I think he is crying out for soft ground but hasn't had his conditions yet. Two miles over hurdles will be OK to start with, but he will be suited by two and a half miles in time and I think he will develop into an above average northern novice hurdler this season.

TRAINER'S HORSE TO FOLLOW: FIRST ACCOUNT

Olly MURPHY

Stables: Warren Chase Stables, Wilmcote, Stratford Upon Avon.
2018/2019: 82 Winners / 431 Runners 19% Prize-Money £662,548
www.ollymurphyracing.com

ALPHA CARINAE (IRE) 4 ch f Robin Des Champs (FR) – Annas Present (IRE)
She's a nice mare who won her only Irish point-to-point impressively in May when trained by Denis Murphy. We bought her later the same month at the Cheltenham Sales. She has a good pedigree and is one to look forward to in mares' bumpers this season.

A PERFECT GIFT (IRE) 5 br m Presenting – Keyras Choice (IRE)
Made a winning start to her career in a mares' bumper at Uttoxeter on New Year's Eve. I then ran her back too quickly at Market Rasen less than three weeks later, but it was a Listed event and we were keen to get some black type. She finished fourth and we then decided to give her a break. I have been pleased with her during the summer and we will aim her at mares' novice hurdles starting over two miles before stepping up in trip later on.

ASTROLOGIST (IRE) 4 b g Sea The Stars (IRE) – Jumooh
A full-brother to Group 3 winner Raheen House, he had four runs on the Flat for Clive Cox before joining us. I was pleased with his run at Chelmsford in February finishing third but he has had a niggly time since. Back in work now though, we have schooled him over hurdles and, following another run on the Flat, the plan is to send him jumping in the Autumn and I will be disappointed if he can't win races.

BLAZER'S MILL (IRE) 5 b g Westerner – Creation (IRE)
Runner-up behind subsequent Grade 2 winner Birchdale in his only Irish point before we bought him at the Aintree Sale in the spring of last year, he had a minor setback last season hence he only raced once. However, he won a bumper at Fontwell in February and the form looks good with the runner-up winning his next two starts. He is one to look forward to other hurdles in the Autumn/winter. We will start him off over two miles.

BON CALVADOS (FR) 5 b g Bonbon Rose (FR) – Lamorrese (FR)
A half-brother to Grade 2 winning chaser Saint Calvados, his homework is second to none. Only sixth on his debut in a bumper at Newcastle in December, he came back sick. We operated on his wind and he ran much better at Market Rasen in the spring finishing second. He has been an immature horse who can only improve and, if he ever translates his homework to the track, he could be a very nice horse.

BREWIN'UPASTORM (IRE) 6 b g Milan – Daraheen Diamond (IRE)
He is a very smart horse who has summered well and we are looking forward to sending him novice chasing. A high-class novice hurdler last season, he only won once but ran some very good races in defeat, including at Cheltenham and Aintree in the spring. Coming down the hill at the Festival in March, I thought he was going to win the Grade 1 Ballymore Novices' Hurdle but he didn't quite finish off his race in fourth. Runner-up at Aintree last time in another Grade 1 novice hurdle, we have operated on his wind since and we are going to drop him back to two miles. I don't know if the reason why he wasn't finishing his races off was due to his wind or his stamina ran out. Therefore we will start him over fences over the minimum trip and plan from there. We haven't schooled him yet, but he is a real athlete, plus he won an Irish point for Timmy Hyde at the beginning of his career. I hope we have got a strong team of novice chasers and he is an exciting prospect.

BUBBLES OF GOLD (IRE) 6 b g Gold Well – Bubble Bann (IRE)
Another winning Irish pointer, he is a proper stayer who won over hurdles at Warwick in April. He remains a novice until the end of October and we are going to try and win another hurdle race before sending him chasing. I think he will appreciate a step up to three miles and and we know he likes soft ground, but never really got it last season.

CALIPSO COLLONGES (FR) 7 b g Crossharbour – Ivresse Collonges (FR)
Despite winning over fences at Uttoxeter on New Year's Eve, he is another who never really got his ground last season. Rated 131, I think he is on a good mark and I could see him developing into a nice staying chaser and being ideal for races such as the Peter Marsh Chase at Haydock in January and the Eider Chase at Newcastle the following month. He loves soft ground, stays well and is a horse with plenty of ability.

CHAMPAGNESUPEROVER (IRE) 4 b g Jeremy (USA) – Meldrum Hall (IRE)
He is a very nice unraced four year old we bought off Sean Doyle in Ireland. Owned by the McNeill Family, his work at home has been good and we will run him in a bumper in the Autumn.

COLLOONEY (IRE) 5 b g Yeats (IRE) – Amber Trix (IRE)
He is a grand horse who has done well for us winning a bumper at Huntingdon and a novice hurdle at Bangor. Placed in his other three starts over hurdles, I thought he ran well last time at Market Rasen and is the sort to keep progressing. His mark looks fair and I think he is the type to win a nice handicap hurdle this season. Two and a half miles suits him at the moment but I think he will stay further.

DUNDRUM WOOD (IRE) 5 b g Flemensfirth (USA) – Ruby Isabel (IRE)
Having run in two Irish points for Sam Curling winning by three lengths in November, we bought him at the Cheltenham December Sales. We ran him in a bumper at Warwick in the spring and I was amazed he got beaten. I couldn't believe it when he only finished third. He had done everything so easily at home and shown a lot of ability. When it came to the race though he was green and still looked raw. He will go straight over hurdles and I think he is a smart horse. We will start him off over two miles, but he will appreciate two and a half miles later on.

ENDLESSLY (IRE) 4 b g Nathaniel (IRE) – What's Up Pussycat (IRE)
Purchased out of Martyn Meade's yard at the Newmarket Horses in Training Sale last Autumn, he bolted up twice at Lingfield and Wolverhampton during the winter. We have schooled him and I think he will make a nice novice hurdler.

FIESOLE 7 b g Montjeu (IRE) – Forgotten Dreams (IRE)
Joined us last season and produced a good performance to win the Sussex Champion Hurdle at Plumpton in April before finishing fourth in the Swinton Hurdle at Haydock. Good ground is the key to him because he doesn't want it soft. Rated 139, he will continue to be competitive in handicap hurdles before we try him over fences next spring.

FINAWN BAWN (IRE) 6 b g Robin Des Champs (FR) – Kayanti (IRE)
I really like him and feel he is going to develop into a smart three miles novice chaser this season. Despite winning two of his four races over hurdles and earning a mark of 133, he is an out and out chaser in the making and is crying out for a step up to three miles. Therefore to win twice over hurdles over two and a half miles at Bangor and Huntingdon is a bonus. We haven't schooled him over fences yet but I don't envisage there being any problems.

FITZROY (IRE) 5 b g Fame And Glory – Forces Of Destiny (IRE)
Fifth on his debut in a bumper at Warwick in December, the form looks good with the third and sixth winning since. We then ran him at Stratford in March and I was very surprised when he got beaten. Half a length runner-up, he still showed signs of greenness and ought to improve. He will go novice hurdling in the Autumn and will hopefully win plenty of races.

FLETCH (FR) 4 b g Kayf Tara – Oeuvre Vive (FR)
Bought at the Derby Sale in Ireland last year, he is a lovely unraced horse. Big and backward last season, he has shown a lot of raw ability at home and we will run him in a bumper around Christmas time. I think he is a very nice horse.

FUSIONICE (FR) 4 b g Coastal Path – Oasice (FR)
A full-brother to Willie Mullins' dual Grade 1 winner Bacardys, he was trained by Denis Murphy when finishing fourth in his only Irish point-to-point in May. He joined us during the summer and is a lovely horse who will probably run in a bumper in the Autumn.

GARRETTSTOWN (IRE) 6 b g Doyen (IRE) – Azur (IRE)
He had a good consistent season over hurdles winning at Market Rasen in January and finishing second on three other occasions. We are going to send him over fences and he looks ideal for a two and a half miles novices' handicap chase off his mark of 129. I think that trip suits him because I don't consider him as an out and out stayer.

GENERAL CUSTARD 6 b g Shirocco (GER) – Diamant Noir
Another who won twice over hurdles with victories at Warwick and Market Rasen. Forced to miss the second half of the season, due to a minor setback, he is back in work and we will probably go down the novice handicap chase route with him, too. He is open to more improvement.

GRANDADS COTTAGE (IRE) 4 ch g Shantou (USA) – Sarah's Cottage (IRE)
A full-brother to Cheltenham Festival runner-up Super Duty, he is a very nice horse who won his only Irish point-to-point by six lengths in late March. Highly recommended by his trainer Donnchadh Doyle, we bought him five days later at the Aintree April Sale on behalf of John Hales. He is a lovely horse who will run in a bumper in the Autumn. I wouldn't have thought he will be going hurdling this season. Very straightforward, he is the sort to keep on improving.

GUNSIGHT RIDGE 4 b g Midnight Legend – Grandma Griffiths
We bought him privately after he won his only point-to-point impressively in May. His trainer Donnchadh Doyle recommended him and he looks a very nice horse. He will go down the bumper route this season.

HERE COMES TRUBLE (IRE) 4 b g Flemensfirth (USA) – Old Moon (IRE)
Another lovely unraced four year old whose family I know well. He is a full-brother to Noble Endeavor who I was involved with when I was assistant to Gordon (Elliott). The two horses are very similar and he is one to look forward to in a bumper in the Autumn. I have some very nice young bumper horses and he is one of them.

HIGHATE HILL (IRE) 5 b g Presenting – Lisrenny Lady
He ran in four Irish points for Denis Murphy winning his final start in November and we acquired him later the same month at the Cheltenham Sales. He made his debut for us in a bumper at Musselburgh in February and it was at a time when my horses weren't running well. Last of four, he is much better than he showed that day and, judged on his homework, he is capable of winning a bumper before going hurdling.

I K BRUNEL 5 b g Midnight Legend – Somethinaboutmolly (IRE)
He is a lovely horse and I think he is a Graded horse in the making. A good winner at Carlisle in a bumper on his debut last November, he finished third behind subsequent Grade 1 winner Elixir De Nutz over hurdles at Cheltenham over two miles in December. We then decided to keep him as a novice over hurdles but gained more experience by running him in the Grade 2 Dovecote Novices' Hurdle at Kempton in February. We are going to step him up to two and a half miles in the Autumn, but I view him as a three miler. The plan is to win a maiden hurdle and then step him back up in class.

ITCHY FEET (FR) 5 b g Cima De Triomphe (IRE) – Maeva Candas (FR)
Did us proud last season winning a bumper and then twice over hurdles, including a Listed novice at Kempton in October. Runner-up behind Elixir De Nutz in a Grade 2 at Cheltenham in November, he produced a career best at the Festival in March finishing third in the *Skybet* Supreme Novices' Hurdle. The going that day was soft, but it was the first race of the meeting, and I think we got the best of the ground because he has always looked a better horse on better ground. Both he and Thomas Darby were the best two UK trained novice hurdlers last season, judged on those performances. The original plan was to stay over hurdles and aim him at the Welsh Champion Hurdle at Ffos Las off his mark of 150, but we have had a rethink and he will go novice chasing. A very athletic and scopey horse, it would be nice to think he will develop into an Arkle Trophy contender.

JETAWAY JOEY (IRE) 4 b g Getaway (GER) – Present Your Own (IRE)
Another nice unraced four year old who has shown enough to suggest he will be very competitive in bumpers this season. By a good sire, he is a full-brother to Getaway John, who has won three races for Gordon (Elliott).

KERRKENNY GOLD (IRE) 5 ch g Sans Frontieres (IRE) – Cailins Honour (IRE)
Purchased at the Cheltenham November Sale, he has yet to run for us but has some strong form to his name. Previously trained in Ireland by Mags Mullins, he was runner-up in two of his three bumpers, including at Galway in October. Beaten a short head by Abacadabras, the winner subsequently finished fourth and second in the Grade 1 championship bumpers at the Cheltenham and Punchestown Festivals respectively. We gave him a break and he will probably run in another bumper before going hurdling.

LINELEE KING (FR) 4 gr g Martaline – Queen Lee (FR)
Only a four year old, he is a lovely horse who won his point-to-point by eight lengths in February when trained by Colin Bowe. Purchased at the Cheltenham Festival Sale the following month, he is very straightforward but we aren't going to rush him. He will probably spend this season in bumpers and is one to look forward to.

MIGHTY MEG 5 b m Malinas (GER) – Harry's Bride
Green on her debut in an all-weather newcomers' bumper at Newcastle in January, I thought she ran well in third. Given a break since, she looks capable of winning a mares' bumper before going hurdling. She may not want it too soft though.

MONBEG ZENA (IRE) 7 ch m Flemensfirth (USA) – Mandys Gold (IRE)
She won a mares' maiden hurdle over three miles at Southwell on her first start for us but then had a niggle and missed the rest of the season. She will be back later on and she is a mare with plenty of ability. We will give her a run in a handicap hurdle because she lacks experience but she is a proper chaser in the making having won an Irish point for Sean Doyle.

NICKOLSON (FR) 5 b g No Risk At All (FR) – Incorrigible (FR)
I have always thought the world of him and he was the only one of ours to win when our horses weren't right at the end of February. A two and a quarter lengths winner of a bumper at Ayr, he will start off in a maiden hurdle over two miles and is an exciting prospect.

NOTRE PARI (IRE) 5 br g Jeremy (USA) – Glynn Approach (IRE)
Runner-up behind the aforementioned Dundrum Wood in his point-to-point in Ireland in November, we subsequently bought him at the Cheltenham December Sale. He shaped with a lot of promise on his hurdles debut at Warwick staying on strongly in third. We will keep him to two miles for the time being and he is a nice horse who has shown more on the track than at home.

OVERTHETOP (IRE) 5 br g Flemensfirth (USA) – Dawn Bid (IRE)
A point winner for Denis Murphy in Ireland in December, we purchased him shortly afterwards at the Cheltenham Sales. He ran in the first division of the Warwick bumper in late April, in which Dundrum Wood ran in the second division. Despite the fact he wouldn't be as good as him at home, he won his race by two and a half lengths. He has a very good attitude and I think he will develop into a really nice staying novice hurdler this season. A full-brother to On Raglan Road, who was fourth in the Albert Bartlett Novices' Hurdle at the Cheltenham Festival, he wants a trip.

PEACHEY (IRE) 5 b g Robin Des Champs (FR) – Zita Hall (IRE)
Very much a chaser in the making, he shaped well on his hurdles debut at Huntingdon in November finishing fourth. Unfortunately, he picked up a knock and hasn't run since. He is back in work though and I would like to think he is good enough to win over hurdles before going chasing eventually.

PRESENCE OF MIND (IRE) 4 b g Presenting – Alleygrove Lass (IRE)
A five lengths winner of his only UK point-to-point at Charlton Horethorne in March for Charlie Poste and Francesca Nimmo, we bought him at the Cheltenham Festival Sale. He has settled in well and looks a nice horse to start off in a bumper.

ROQUE IT (IRE) 5 b g Presenting – Roque De Cyborg (IRE)
Third on his debut in a bumper at Bangor in December, he produced a good performance to win at Huntingdon three months later. He picked up an injury that day though and won't be back in action until after Christmas. Provided it's not too late by the time he comes back, he will go novice hurdling and is a staying type.

SANGHA RIVER (IRE) 6 br g Arcadio (GER) – Hidden Reserve (IRE)
He is back in training and looks very well. A former pointer, he won a bumper on his first run for us at Doncaster and was then unlucky not to follow up under a penalty at Lingfield, having met trouble in running, the previous season. Forced to miss the whole of last season, due to injury, he is potentially the best horse in the yard, if we can keep him sound. However, he isn't the easiest to train and it's a case of fingers crossed. He will go for a maiden hurdle in the Autumn and we will take it from there. A horse with a lot of speed, he will start off over two miles.

SEEMINGLY SO (IRE) 6 br g Dubai Destination (USA) – Jane Hall (IRE)
Runner-up in his only point behind Dlauro, who has won a bumper for Joseph O'Brien since, he scored on his hurdles debut at Market Rasen in November. Below par at Ayr last time, he came back very sick and we have given him a good break since. Rated 118, he should be competitive in handicap hurdles before we send him chasing.

SKANDIBURG (FR) 5 b g Sageburg (IRE) – Skandia (FR)
A horse who loves to please you, he won a bumper and novice hurdle at Fakenham and also scored at Huntingdon on his final start. Rated 124, I think he will improve when stepped up to three miles for the first time and I am keen to get him qualified for the Pertemps Final at Cheltenham in March.

SMACKWATER JACK (IRE) 5 b g Flemensfirth (USA) – Malachy's Attic (IRE)
He is a grand horse who won over hurdles at Ludlow in January before finishing second at Taunton. We will aim him at handicap hurdles this season and he is capable of winning more races off his mark.

ST GALLEN (IRE) 6 b g Majestic Missile (IRE) – Fly With Me (IRE)
Bought out of John Murphy's yard at the Newmarket Horses in Training Sale, he won his first two races over hurdles for us at Market Rasen and Kelso in the spring. I really fancied him in the Listed Summer Handicap Hurdle at Market Rasen in July but he ran a horrendous race pulling a shoe off in the process. He was in need of a break in any case and probably his first for about three years, but I still think he is capable of winning a good handicap. A lovely horse who handles any ground, we will bring him back around Christmas time and he will jump a fence one day, too.

THE BUTCHER SAID (IRE) 6 b g Robin Des Champs (FR) – Georgina Valleya (IRE)
Has improved a lot since learning to switch off in his races winning his last four races. We have given him a break since his last win at Newton Abbot in June and we will bring him back either for the Grade 2 Persian War Novices' Hurdle at Chepstow (11th October) or go for another novice hurdle at Cheltenham's first meeting (25th October). His next run will tell whether to stay over hurdles or go novice chasing.

THOMAS DARBY (IRE) 6 b g Beneficial – Silaoce (FR)
I have always thought the world of him and he developed into a top-class novice hurdler last season winning twice and finishing second in the *Skybet* Supreme Novices' Hurdle at the Cheltenham Festival. He struck into himself that day hence he didn't run again but he's OK now. Indeed, he has summered well and we are looking forward to going novice chasing with him. I hope there will be some big days in him over fences and, while we will start him off over two miles, it wouldn't surprise me if he wanted two and a half miles this season. Like Itchy Feet, he is a better horse on better ground but handled the conditions at the Festival, where the runners got the best of the ground with it being the first race of the meeting.

TIMEFORASPIN 5 b g Librettist (USA) – Timeforagin
Bought cheaply out of Brian Eckley's yard at the Goffs UK Spring Sale at Doncaster in May, he was placed in two of his four bumpers. Runner-up at Bangor in December, he finished in front of Roque It that day, hence my interest in him at the sales. We will send him novice hurdling and hopefully he will win races.

VINNIES GETAWAY (IRE) 5 b g Getaway (GER) – Trixskin (IRE)
A half-brother to Cheltenham Festival champion bumper winner Cousin Vinny, he won his only Irish point for Denis Murphy in December. He has run in three bumpers at Stratford during the summer, since joining us. Runner-up first time, he then made all to win by a dozen lengths before running flat on his latest start. Given a break since, he will go hurdling when returning in the Autumn and looks a staying type.

WHISKEY IN THE JAR (IRE) 7 b g Oscar (IRE) – Baie Barbara (IRE)
A useful novice hurdler a couple of seasons ago, he missed last year due to injury. He is back now though and is a horse with loads of ability. The softer the ground the better, he needs to go left handed and we will start him off in a handicap hurdle before jumping fences later on. I think he is on a nice mark.

Unnamed 4 b g Getaway (GER) – Ut Love (FR)
A lovely four year old we bought at the Goffs Landrover Sale last year. Owned by Clive Boultbee Brooks, he is a sharp sort who looks capable of being very competitive in bumpers.

TRAINER'S HORSE TO FOLLOW: GUNSIGHT RIDGE

Champion Trainer 2005/2006, 2006/2007, 2007/2008, 2008/2009, 2009/2010, 2010/11, 2011/12, 2013/2014, 2014/2015, 2015/2016 & 2018/2019

Paul NICHOLLS
Stables: Manor Farm Stables, Ditcheat, Somerset.
2018/2019: 135 Winners / 589 Runners 23% Prize-Money £3,307,573
www.paulnichollsracing.com

ADRIEN DU PONT (FR) 7 b g Califet (FR) – Santariyka (FR)
Won a decent handicap chase at Kempton over Christmas before finishing third in the Grade 3 888Sport Handicap Chase over the same course and distance in February. He needs to be held up in his races and, as a result, he can get behind and stuck in behind horses, which is what happened on that day. We will continue to aim him at the good three miles handicap chases, starting with the Grade 3 Sodexo Gold Cup Handicap Chase at Ascot (2nd November), in which he finished fourth last season.

ASK FOR GLORY (IRE) 5 b g Fame And Glory – Ask Helen (IRE)
He is a lovely horse who won impressively on his first run for us in a bumper at Chepstow over Christmas. We let him take his chance in the Cheltenham Festival bumper but he probably wasn't ready for such a race. However, the experience won't have been lost on him and he is one to look forward to in novice hurdles this season. I think he will want a trip.

BARBADOS BUCK'S (IRE) 4 b g Getaway (GER) – Buck's Blue (FR)
Purchased at the Punchestown Festival Sale in May, he is a nice horse who finished second in his only point-to-point a few days earlier. We also bought the winner (Skatman) and they are both promising horses for the future. From the family of Big Buck's, he has a good pedigree and we will start him off in a bumper. We have a lot of four year olds who will run in bumpers and we won't be rushing them.

BATHSHEBA BAY (IRE) 4 b g Footstepsinthesand – Valamareha (IRE)
A dual winner on the Flat for Richard Hannon and rated 87, he wasn't quite right last season hence he hasn't run for us yet. We have gelded him and operated on his wind and he will be ready to go hurdling in the Autumn.

BIRDS OF PREY (IRE) 5 b g Sir Prancealot (IRE) – Cute
Useful on the Flat, he won twice over hurdles at Taunton in the spring and is still a novice until the end of October. He has had his first summer break for a long time and we will bring him back in the Autumn and he may run in a two miles handicap hurdle at Chepstow (12th October).

BLACK CORTON (FR) 8 br g Laverock (IRE) – Pour Le Meilleur (FR)
He ran an amazing race in the Galway Plate in late July finishing second off a mark of 158. A Grade 2 winner at Sandown on the final day of last season, he keeps on improving but I haven't decided where he will go next. Runner-up in the Charlie Hall Chase at Wetherby (2nd November) last season, he could reappear there.

BLACKJACK KENTUCKY (IRE) 6 b g Oscar (IRE) – My Name's Not Bin (IRE)
Third a couple of times at Chepstow and Exeter, I want to try and win a three miles novice hurdle with him before he goes novice chasing. He wants soft ground and is a former winning Irish pointer.

BOB AND CO (FR) 8 b g Dom Alco (FR) – Outre Mer (FR)
A useful horse in France, he won three times over fences and once over hurdles. He has been bought by David Maxwell and will be going hunter chasing in the New Year. His main target is the Foxhunters' at the Cheltenham Festival.

BRAVEMANSGAME (FR) 4 b g Brave Mansonnien (FR) – Genifique (FR)
He is a lovely big horse who won his only Irish point for Donnchadh Doyle by eight lengths in March. Bought on behalf of John Dance and Brian Drew four days later at the Cheltenham Festival Sale, he was the highest rated four year old pointer in Ireland last season. He looks a very nice horse who will run in a bumper.

BRELAN D'AS (FR) 8 b g Crillon (FR) – Las De La Croix (FR)
Had a good first season over fences winning at Haydock and Fakenham before finishing third in the Grand Annual Chase at Cheltenham in March. Rated 138, he will continue to run in two and two and a half miles handicap chases.

BREWERS PROJECT (IRE) 5 b g Aizavoski (IRE) – Shaylee Wilde (IRE)
An easy winner of his only Irish point for Donnchadh Doyle, we bought him at the Cheltenham Festival Sale last year, but he has yet to run for us. He schooled beautifully last season but picked up a small injury, which meant we couldn't run him. He is 100% now and will go novice hurdling. I think he is a bloody nice horse.

BRIO CONTI (FR) 8 gr g Dom Alco (FR) – Cadoulie Wood (FR)
He won a decent handicap hurdle at Ascot in February before running a cracking race in the Coral Cup finishing fourth. The plan is for him to go back over fences and, while he lacks experience having only run in one chase, his target is the BetVictor Gold Cup at Cheltenham (16th November). We will try and get a run into him beforehand.

BROKEN HALO 4 b g Kayf Tara – Miss Invincible
Successful in his only Irish point-to-point for Colin Bowe, we bought him at the Cheltenham April Sale. He will start off in a bumper and we will go from there.

CALVA D'AUGE (FR) 4 b c Air Chief Marshall (IRE) – Hill Ou Elle (FR)
He raced in Listed and Group 3 races on the Flat in France as a two year old and has had six runs over hurdles since. Runner-up on three occasions, he has plenty of experience and will go novice hurdling.

CAP DU MATHAN (FR) 4 b g Kapgarde (FR) – Nounjya Du Mathan (FR)
A lovely big horse who has arrived from France having been bought by Andy Stewart. Previously trained by Arnaud Chaille-Chaille, he raced twice at Auteuil finishing fourth and second last Autumn. He will go novice hurdling and I like him a lot.

CAPELAND (FR) 7 b g Poliglote – Neiland (FR)
He improved massively over fences last season winning three times at Wincanton (twice) and Ludlow. He was on the go for a long time but kept progressing and I think he has more to offer. Rated 143, he could go to Newton Abbot (13th October) for an intermediate chase or, alternatively, we could aim him at the Grade 2 Haldon Gold Cup at Exeter (5th November).

CAPITAINE (FR) 7 gr g Montmartre (FR) – Patte De Velour (FR)
Despite winning over hurdles at Taunton in February, he endured a slightly frustrating season. We have tweaked his wind since his last run. I think his mark of 134 over hurdles, compared to 146 over fences, is a gift and he is more than capable of winning races off such a rating. He wants two miles on a flat track on good ground.

CAPTAIN CATTISTOCK 6 b g Black Sam Bellamy (IRE) – Pearl Buttons
A nice staying chaser who won twice over fences at Exeter and Fontwell. Lightly raced, he is rated 140 and I think he will stay forever. We will be aiming him at the good staying handicap chases.

CARRY ON THE MAGIC (IRE) 5 bb g Jeremy (USA) – Bisoguet (IRE)
Runner-up in his sole Irish point in December, we purchased him at the Cheltenham Sales later the same month. We did a bit with him last season and he worked nicely. It is possible he will have a run in a bumper but it won't be long before he goes novice hurdling.

CASKO D'AIRY (FR) 7 b g Voix Du Nord (FR) – Quaska D'Airy (FR)
Off for two years, due to injury, he won in good style at Ascot in December and ran creditably at Sandown last time in a Grade 3 handicap hurdle. He wants soft ground and will go chasing this season. Rated 127, he will start off in a novices' handicap chase.

CAT TIGER (FR) 5 b g Diamond Boy (FR) – Miss Canon (FR)
An exciting horse who has joined us from France. David Maxwell bought him at the Arqana Sales last November and he is a four times winner over fences in France, including two Grade 3 wins at Auteuil. Fourth in a Grade 1 chase at the same track last Autumn, he is only five and is a novice over hurdles. I am hoping he will develop into a very nice novice and he could run in the Grade 2 Persian War Novices' Hurdle at Chepstow (11th October), a race we have won seven times.

CHANCE FINALE (FR) 5 br g Blue Bresil (FR) – Ballade Nordique (FR)
A narrow winner of his only Irish point in December, we have given him plenty of time since arriving. Being a five year old, he is likely to go straight over hurdles.

CHEZ HANS (GER) 3 b g Mamool (IRE) – Chandos Rose (IRE)
He has been bought to go juvenile hurdling having been trained on the Flat by Christian Von Der Recke. He only raced four times winning by three lengths at Compiegne in March.

CHRISTOPHER WOOD (IRE) 4 b g Fast Company (IRE) – Surf The Web (IRE)
Bought at the Newmarket Horses In Training Sale last Autumn, he did well over hurdles winning at Fontwell and Newbury before finishing third in the Grade 1 4YO hurdle at Aintree in April. We have operated on his wind since his last run at Haydock and I think he will do well in two miles handicap hurdles, although he will stay further, if necessary. I like him a lot.

CILL ANNA (IRE) 4 b f Imperial Monarch (IRE) – Technohead (IRE)
She won a mares' point-to-point for Colin Bowe at the end of March and we bought her at the Aintree April Sale five days later. She is very much in the same mould as Silver Forever, who also won a point-to-point before doing well for us in bumpers last season. We may start her off in a mares' bumper, too.

CLAN DES OBEAUX (FR) 7 b g Kapgarde (FR) – Nausicaa Des Obeaux (FR)
He looks fantastic having done very well during the summer and I think there is more improvement to come from him. Still only seven, he did extremely well last year winning the King George and running well in the Cheltenham Gold Cup. He has a slight preference racing right-handed and, with that in mind, we may start him off in the JNwine.com Champion Chase at Down Royal (2nd November), which we have won four times. Then, his next big target will be the King George at Kempton on Boxing Day once again. We will make a plan for the rest of the season after that. There are plenty of big races he could go for during the second half of the year, including a trip to Punchestown in the spring.

COUP DE PINCEAU (FR) 7 b g Buck's Boum (FR) – Castagnette III (FR)
We placed him well last season winning novice chases at Exeter and Ludlow. Fourth in the Grade 2 Reynoldstown Novices' Chase at Ascot, he was runner-up at Warwick last time. Good fresh, he likes decent ground and will be campaigned in staying handicap chases.

CYRNAME (FR) 7 b g Nickname (FR) – Narquille (FR)
He is in great form at home and I love him, although he hasn't been the easiest horse to train. Beaten at Carlisle and Ascot in the first half of last season, I think those two defeats were the making of him. He turned the corner thereafter and hasn't looked back since producing an awesome performance to win a handicap at Ascot in January by twenty one lengths off a mark of 150. He then won the Grade 1 Ascot Chase by sixteen lengths and is now the highest rated chaser in training. We toyed with the idea of running him again in the spring but decided to put him away for the summer. His first race will be in the Grade 2 Christy 1965 Chase at Ascot (23rd November) over two miles five and then I am keen to step him up to three miles in the King George at Kempton on Boxing Day. I have always thought he wanted a trip and I think he will stay. His performance there will determine his programme for the rest of the season. We will try him left-handed again at some stage, but he is so effective on right-handed tracks.

DAN MCGRUE (IRE) 7 b g Dansant – Aahsaypasty (IRE)
A three times winning pointer, he wants soft ground and will go novice chasing. We have operated on his wind since his last run in the spring.

DANNY KIRWAN (IRE) 6 b g Scorpion (IRE) – Sainte Baronne (FR)
Runner-up in both his starts over hurdles, he sustained an injury after finishing second in a Grade 2 novice at Ascot before Christmas. Therefore he won't come back into work until September with a view to running in a novice hurdle early in the New Year. We also have the option of running in handicaps off his mark of 120, which is very tempting. He will go novice chasing next season.

DANNY WHIZZBANG (IRE) 6 b g Getaway (GER) – Lakil Princess (IRE)
A cracking horse who won a point-to-point in Ireland before we bought him. He surprised us last season because, having won first time out over hurdles at Hereford, he improved so much and then won under a penalty at Exeter in March. Built for fences, he will go novice chasing over three miles plus on soft ground. I hope he will make a smart staying novice chaser.

DANSE IDOL (IRE) 6 b m Dansant – Screen Idol (IRE)
A nice mare who did well over hurdles winning at Wincanton and Fontwell and was runner-up in a Grade 2 mares' hurdle at Sandown and two Listed hurdles. She will run in a mares' handicap hurdle at Wincanton (9th November) and then we will decide whether to keep her over hurdles or go chasing.

DARLING MALTAIX (FR) 6 b g Voix Du Nord (FR) – Rosalie Malta (FR)
He won a handicap hurdle at Ascot before Christmas and was fifth in the Listed Lanzarote Handicap Hurdle at Kempton next time. A bit keen over hurdles, he will go chasing and I am hoping he will settle better over fences. Two and a half miles is his trip.

DIAMOND GUY (FR) 6 b g Konig Turf (GER) – Unique Chance (FR)
Missed the whole of last season, he is back now and is a nice horse. A bumper winner, he won twice over hurdles the previous year and I think he will make a lovely novice chaser this time around. He likes good ground but, now that he is much stronger, I am expecting him to cope with slower surfaces.

DIEGO DU CHARMIL (FR) 7 b g Ballingarry (IRE) – Daramour (FR)
He has had a wind operation because his breathing was an issue last season. A Grade 1 winning novice chaser the previous season, he was in no man's land last year. The handicapper has dropped him a few pounds and I want to try him over two and a half miles this season because I have always thought he would stay further. He is good fresh.

DOGON 4 b g Intello (GER) – Poppets Sweetlove
A winner over fences in France, he has only raced three times for us and remains a novice over hurdles. Runner-up at Wincanton in February, he pulled up in the Fred Winter Juvenile Hurdle at Cheltenham and the handicapper has dropped him four pounds since. We have operated on his wind and I don't think we have seen the best of him.

DOIN'WHATSHELIKES (IRE) 4 b f Presenting – Karkiyla (IRE)
We acquired her at the Cheltenham April Sale having run in two Irish points for Denis Murphy. Runner-up on her second start, she looks a very nice filly who will run in a mares' bumper in the Autumn.

DOLOS (FR) 6 b g Kapgarde (FR) – Redowa (FR)
Enjoyed a very good season winning twice over fences at Sandown and Kempton. Life won't be easy for him off his mark of 157, but we will start him off in the Grade 2 Haldon Gold up at Exeter (5th November).

DR SANDERSON (IRE) 5 b g Jeremy (USA) – Guydus (IRE)
He won three out of five over hurdles scoring at Worcester, Ffos Las and Ludlow. Sold as part of the Million In Mind dispersal at the Doncaster May Sales, he was subsequently bought by J.P.McManus to stay in the yard. He will go novice chasing over two and a half miles.

DYNAMITE DOLLARS (FR) 6 bb g Buck's Boum (FR) – Macadoun (FR)
Developed into a top-class novice chaser last season winning four of his five starts, including the Grade 1 Henry VIII Novices' Chase at Sandown followed by two Grade 2 victories at Kempton and Doncaster. We were training him for the Arkle Trophy at Cheltenham but he suffered an injury and hasn't run since January. The plan is to bring him back later on and aim him at the Game Spirit Chase at Newbury in February followed by the Queen Mother Champion Chase in March.

EASON (FR) 5 b g Coastal Path – Maitresse de Maison (FR)
A nice big horse who won a bumper first time out at Chepstow in October before running respectably in Listed events at Ascot and Newbury. He will appreciate stepping up in trip over hurdles this season.

ECCO 4 b g Maxios – Enjoy The Life
A smart horse on the Flat in Germany, he ran well in both his runs over hurdles for us last season. We threw him in at the deep end but he acquitted himself well in both the Grade 2 Adonis Hurdle at Kempton and Grade 1 Triumph Hurdle at Cheltenham. Sixth on each occasion, he will continue novice hurdling over two miles and is a nice horse.

ENRILO (FR) 5 bl g Buck's Boum (FR) – Rock Treasure (FR)
He is a very nice horse who we like a lot. A winner of two of his three runs in bumpers last season, he won on his debut at Worcester in the Autumn before finishing a running on fourth in a Listed race at Ascot before Christmas. He then won under a penalty at Kempton in February and is one to look forward to over hurdles this winter. He will start off over two miles but will stay further.

ERITAGE (FR) 5 b g Martaline – Sauves La Reine (FR)
A French bumper winner in the summer of last year, we didn't make enough use of him on his first run for us in another bumper at Exeter when finishing third. He then made all to win at Wincanton in April. He goes novice hurdling and will appreciate a trip.

FIDELIO VALLIS (FR) 4 b g Saint Des Saints (FR) – Quora Vallis (FR)
He is a nice horse who arrived from France in the spring. Runner-up on his only start on the Flat last August, he was then second on his jumping debut at Auteuil in April. Bought by John Hales, he will go novice hurdling.

FLASH COLLONGES (FR) 4 b g Saddler Maker (IRE) – Prouesse Collonges (FR)
We have some very nice unraced four year old bumper horses and he is one of them. Bought at the Derby Sales in Ireland last year, he will run in a bumper in the Autumn.

FLASH DE TOUZAINE (FR) 4 b g Kapgarde (FR) – Narcisse De Touzaine (FR)
Purchased at the Cheltenham May Sale, he finished third in a bumper on his only start for Liz Doyle at Killarney earlier the same month. Still backward, I like him and we could run him in another bumper before deciding whether to go hurdling this season.

FLEMENSTIDE (IRE) 4 b g Flemensfirth (USA) – Keep Face (FR)
He is another lovely unraced four year old who will start off in a bumper this season. He is a very good looking horse who I like.

FLIC OU VOYOU (FR) 5 b g Kapgarde (FR) – Hillflower (FR)
Another promising youngster, he is a nice horse who won two of his three starts in bumpers last season. Twice a winner at Wincanton, we ran him in the Cheltenham Festival bumper and I hope the experience will have done him good. He will go straight over hurdles now and start over two miles.

FRIEND OR FOE (FR) 4 b g Walk In The Park (IRE) – Mandchou (FR)
Ex-French, he won two of his three starts for us at Taunton and Chepstow. His only disappointing run came at Newbury in between when we fitted him with a tongue tie. We had been training him for the Fred Winter Juvenile Hurdle but he missed the cut and didn't get in. He looks to be on a good mark and we will run him in a handicap hurdle and then decide whether to go chasing or not. He has had a wind operation since his last run.

FRODON (FR) 7 b g Nickname (FR) – Miss Country (FR)

An amazing horse who had a remarkable season winning four of his five races. He produced a brilliant performance to win the Grade 1 Ryanair Chase at the Cheltenham Festival. The plan is to run him in the Grade 2 Old Roan Chase at Aintree (27th October) once again, which he won last year. Then, all being well, he will go for the *Betfair* Chase at Haydock (23rd November). He proved last season when winning the Cotswold Chase at Cheltenham in January that he stays three miles plus, and hopefully the ground won't be too bad.

GETAWAY TRUMP (IRE) 6 b g Getaway (GER) – Acinorev (IRE)

A very progressive horse over hurdles last season winning four times and earning a rating of 155. I can't believe we didn't manage to win a bumper with him, but I think the Getaway's need a bit of time and get better with age. Runner-up in the Grade 1 Challow Hurdle at Newbury, he was fourth in the rescheduled *Betfair* Hurdle at Ascot before ending the season with impressive wins at Ayr and Sandown. We toyed with the idea of going down the Champion Hurdle route but we are going to school him over fences and go novice chasing. He is an exciting prospect.

GET THE APPEAL (IRE) 5 b m Getaway (GER) – Lady Appeal (IRE)

A half-sister to Grade 2 winner Fox Appeal, she ran in two Irish points in March finishing second on her debut before going one better next time. She will either run in a mares' bumper or go straight over hurdles.

GIVE ME A COPPER (IRE) 9 ch g Presenting – Copper Supreme (IRE)

There is still a lot more to come from him because I don't think we have seen the best of him yet. He only raced three times last season running well on his return at Sandown before falling at the last in the Ultima Handicap Chase at Cheltenham in March. Fourth in the Bet365 Gold Cup at Sandown last time, we are aiming him at the Badger Ales Chase at Wincanton (9th November). He could be ideal for something like the three miles chase at Kempton in February (formerly known as the *Racing Post* Chase) and we will give him an entry in the Grand National. I think he wants a flat track to show his best.

GLENLIVET (IRE) 4 b g Flemensfirth (USA) – Gleaming Spire

He is a very nice unraced horse who is owned by Thomas Barr. A half-brother to Knockgraffon, we will start him off in a bumper in the Autumn.

GOLDEN GIFT (IRE) 5 b g Gold Well – Five Star Present (IRE)

Runner-up in both his bumpers at Wincanton and Chepstow, he will go jumping and I hope he will develop into a nice staying novice hurdler.

GRAND SANCY (FR) 5 b g Diamond Boy (FR) – La Courtille (FR)

Benefited from a wind operation and had a very good season over hurdles winning four times, including the Grade 2 Kingwell Hurdle at Wincanton and a Listed novice hurdle at Haydock. Runner-up in the Grade 1 Tolworth Hurdle at Sandown in between, he could run in the Grade 2 Elite Hurdle at Wincanton (9th November) off his mark of 152, and then we will decide whether to stay hurdling or go novice chasing.

GREANETEEN (FR) 5 b g Great Pretender (IRE) – Manson Teene (FR)

He is a nice horse who came from France and showed progressive form last season. A dual winner at Exeter and Fontwell, he suffered a minor injury after his last win hence he didn't run again. Back in work, I think he is on a fair mark and looks capable of winning a decent handicap hurdle this year.

GREAT BEYOND 4 b g Dansili – Solar Pursuit
Bought at the Newmarket Horses in Training Sale last Autumn, he won over twelve furlongs on the Flat for Roger Charlton, but has yet to run for us. We have operated on his wind and given him plenty of time. He will go novice hurdling.

GREY GETAWAY (IRE) 5 gr g Getaway (GER) – Miss Greylands
Runner-up in his only Irish point-to-point for Denis Murphy last November, we bought him shortly afterwards at the Cheltenham Sales. He was disappointing in a bumper at Kempton but is much better than he showed that day and, rather like Getaway Trump, he might have needed time to acclimatise having come over from Ireland. I think there is a lot of improvement in him and he will go novice hurdling.

HIGHLAND HUNTER (IRE) 6 gr g Subtle Power (IRE) – Loughine Sparkle (IRE)
He is a nice horse who joined us during the summer having won a bumper and twice over hurdles for Lucinda Russell. A former Irish point winner, too, he is rated 131 and is likely to reappear in a handicap hurdle.

HUGOS OTHER HORSE 5 b g Gold Well – Wicked Crack (IRE)
A half-brother to Cue Card, he had two runs in bumpers last season finishing fourth on his debut behind Flic Ou Voyou at Wincanton on Boxing Day before winning at Fontwell a couple of months later. He will make a nice novice hurdler over two and a half miles.

IF YOU SAY RUN (IRE) 7 b m Mahler – De Lissa (IRE)
She had some very good form last year winning at Wincanton on her reappearance before finishing second a couple of times in Listed mares' events at Kempton and Haydock. Third in a Grade 2 mares' hurdle at Ascot, we have the option of going novice chasing or continuing down the mares' hurdle route. She stays well.

IS A REAL CHAMP (IRE) 5 ch g Getaway (GER) – Siobhans Charm (IRE)
Runner-up in an Irish point for Sean Doyle, he ran well on his only start in a bumper at Chepstow in the spring. He looks a stayer in the making and will go novice hurdling over two and a half miles plus.

JEREMY PASS (IRE) 4 b g Jeremy (USA) – Toulon Pass (IRE)
A faller at the last in his only point-to-point in Ireland, we bought him at the Cheltenham Festival Sale less than a fortnight later. A big strong chasing type, he will probably start in a bumper.

LIEUTENANT ROCCO (IRE) 4 ch g Shirocco (GER) – Five Star Present (IRE)
A half-brother to Golden Gift, he ran in two Irish points finishing third behind Skatman and Barbados Buck's (we subsequently bought the pair) last time. He is a nice type who could start in a bumper.

MAGIC SAINT (FR) 5 b g Saint Des Saints (FR) – Magic Poline (FR)
A winner over fences at Wincanton in February, he is still a young horse having done well in France before joining us. We have operated on his wind, which will hopefully make a difference, and, while he is effective over two miles, I think he will stay further.

MAGOO (IRE) 7 gr g Martaline – Noche (IRE)
He will go back over fences having fallen on his chasing debut at Sandown last season. We decided to revert back to hurdles thereafter and he ran some good races in defeat, including when runner-up at Sandown in March. He wants soft ground.

MALAYA (FR) 5 b m Martaline – Clarte D'Or (FR)
We were delighted with her victory in the Imperial Cup at Sandown in March because it had been the plan for a while. Rated 142, she loves soft ground and we will aim her at mares' novice chases this winter.

MASTER TOMMYTUCKER 8 b g Kayf Tara – No Need For Alarm
A promising and unbeaten novice hurdler a couple of seasons ago, we sent him chasing last year and he was going well when falling at the third last at Chepstow in October. Unfortunately, he sustained an injury which has kept him off the track since. He is due to be x-rayed again and then, all being well, he will come back into training to resume his novice chase career. He didn't start racing until he was seven years old and has plenty of ability.

MCFABULOUS (IRE) 5 b g Milan – Rossavon (IRE)
A half-brother to Grade 1 winning chaser Waiting Patiently, he is an exciting prospect for novice hurdles this season. He did very well in bumpers last year winning three of his four races, including the Grade 2 championship event at Aintree's Grand National meeting. We will start off low key with two or two and a half miles being his trip.

MERCY MERCY ME 7 b g Shirocco (GER) – Monsignorita (IRE)
Owner Malcolm Denmark sent him to us during the summer and he is an interesting horse. A useful bumper horse who ran well in both the Cheltenham and Aintree championship events a couple of seasons ago, he was second twice over hurdles but remains a novice with an official mark of 127. He will continue over hurdles.

MICK PASTOR (FR) 3 b g Meshaheer (USA) – Mick Oceane (FR)
An exciting prospect for juvenile hurdles who won his only start at Auteuil by six lengths in May. Bought by J.P.McManus, he arrived in August and is one to look forward to.

MIRANDA (IRE) 4 b f Camelot – Great Artist (FR)
She won three times on the Flat in France before we bought her at the Arqana Sale in November. A winner of her first two starts over hurdles at Ludlow and Wincanton, she pulled up last time but looks capable of doing well in mares' handicap hurdles off her mark of 127.

MONT DES AVALOIRS (FR) 6 b g Blue Bresil (FR) – Abu Dhabi (FR)
Despite winning a bumper and a couple of hurdle races the previous season, he has been a big backward horse who struggled a bit last season. He was runner-up on his chasing debut at Newton Abbot in October last year, but we decided to go back over hurdles with him. A close third in the Listed Gerry Feilden Hurdle at Newbury, I think he wants two and a half miles nowadays. He will go back over fences.

MY WAY (FR) 5 ch g Martaline – Royale Majesty (FR)
Runner-up twice in Grade 3 chases at Auteuil in France, he joined us last season but was disappointing. He finished second a couple of times over hurdles at Taunton and Kempton, but I am hoping he is better than that. We have operated on his wind and he will go back novice handicap chase off a mark of 122. On the pick of his French form, he is well handicapped.

NIMIX DE JUILLEY (FR) 5 b g Al Namix (FR) – Halbina De Juilley (FR)
Another new French recruit, he won his only start over hurdles at Strasbourg in September last year. Owned by J.P.McManus, he joined us in August and he will stay over hurdles, although he isn't a novice. He is a lovely horse.

NOT A NAIL (IRE) 5 b g Flemensfirth (USA) – Mandys Gold (IRE)
I have always liked him and he ran well on his debut in a bumper at Exeter finishing third in December. Disappointing next time at Ffos Las, he is much better than he showed that day. He will go novice hurdling.

OLEG (GER) 4 gr g Kamsin (GER) – Dramraire Mist
Runner-up over hurdles in France, he won at Kelso on his first run for us in March before finishing second at Chepstow. He has been given a mark of 120 but is still a novice until the end of October. Still lightly raced, he is open to further improvement and could go chasing later on.

PIC D'ORHY (FR) 4 b g Turgeon (USA) – Rose Candy (FR)
He is a lovely horse and I adore him. He arrived from France last winter with some very smart form winning three times over hurdles and finishing runner-up in Grade 2 and Grade 1 three year old hurdles at Auteuil. I shouldn't have run him in the Triumph Hurdle at Cheltenham, but he has had a good break since and I am very pleased with him. He is a big strong horse who is rated 146 over hurdles. We haven't decided whether to stay hurdling or go chasing. It is possible he will run in the Grade 1 four year old hurdle at Auteuil in November, but the day he goes chasing is the one I am looking forward to. He is a proper horse.

POLITOLOGUE (FR) 8 gr g Poliglote – Scarlet Row (FR)
He had another good season winning a Grade 2 chase at Ascot and running a blinder in the Queen Mother Champion Chase finishing second. I thought he was going to win at the last. He has had a wind operation during the summer and, while he is very effective over two and a half miles, I think two miles is his trip. We won't be trying him over three miles again because he didn't stay in the King George on Boxing Day. The intention is for him to reappear in the Grade 2 Shloer Chase at Cheltenham (17th November) before going for the Grade 1 Tingle Creek at Sandown (7th December), a race he won a couple of years ago.

POSH TRISH (IRE) 6 b m Stowaway – Moscow Demon (IRE)
I can't wait to send her over fences. A former winning Irish pointer, she did well in bumpers winning a Listed event and had an even better season over hurdles last term. A four times winner, she won Listed mares' hurdles at Newbury and Taunton before performing well at the Cheltenham Festival. She is likely to make her chasing debut in a Listed novice chase at Chepstow (12th October) before going for the Grade 2 Rising Stars Novice Chase at Wincanton (9th November). I think she will be very competitive against the geldings receiving an allowance. Indeed, she looks more like a gelding than a mare. She is an exciting prospect.

QUEL DESTIN (FR) 4 ch g Muhtathir – High Destiny (FR)
A tough horse, he thrived on his racing last year and developed into a high-class juvenile hurdler. He won five times for us, including the Grade 1 Finale Hurdle at Chepstow over Christmas and two Grade 2 events at Cheltenham and Doncaster. Fifth in the Triumph Hurdle, he is rated 142 and I am not sure what we are going to do with this season. It can be a difficult second season for the previous year's juveniles. We may give him another run over hurdles and then decide whether to go chasing. I think he will appreciate a step up to two and a half miles this year.

RHYTHM IS A DANCER 6 b g Norse Dancer (IRE) – Fascinatin Rhythm
Did well last season winning a bumper at Exeter before scoring three times over hurdles at Wincanton (twice) and Ludlow. He will go over fences and I think he will develop into a lovely novice chaser on good ground.

SAINT XAVIER (FR) 7 b g Saint Des Saints (FR) – Princesse Lucie (FR)
Another recruit from France who has been bought by David Maxwell. He won twice over fences, including a Grade 3 chase at Auteuil in October last year. He is still a maiden over hurdles though and the plan is for him to go novice hurdling over three miles.

SCARAMANGA (IRE) 4 b g Mastercraftsman (IRE) – Herboriste
I like him a lot and he has been running well both on the Flat and over hurdles since joining us. An easy winner at Taunton in March, he was unlucky not to follow up at Ascot next time. Runner-up in a fourteen furlongs handicap at Salisbury in the spring, he is likely to go to Chepstow for a four year old handicap hurdle (11th October).

SECRET INVESTOR 7 b g Kayf Tara – Silver Charmer
Had a very good year winning the Grade 2 Persian War Novice Hurdle at Chepstow before going novice chasing. He won twice over fences, including a Grade 2 event at Ayr's Scottish National meeting. Still a novice until the end of October, he could run at Chepstow (12th October) or go to Newton Abbot (13th October) the following day for an intermediate chase over two miles five. Decent ground is ideal.

SENDING LOVE (IRE) 6 b g Scorpion (IRE) – Dato Vic (IRE)
A new arrival, he is owned by Sullivan Bloodstock. He won his only Irish point-to-point before joining Willie Mullins a couple of seasons ago but didn't run for him due to injury. We haven't done anything with him yet but I would imagine he will go straight over hurdles.

SILVER FOREVER (IRE) 5 gr m Jeremy (USA) – Silver Prayer (IRE)
She is a lovely mare who won an Irish point before joining us last season. Progressive in mares' bumpers, she won twice at Chepstow and Ascot and was placed in her other two races in Listed events at Huntingdon and Sandown. I think she will do well in mares' novice hurdles this season and we may start her at Chepstow (11th October), in a race we have won for the last two years with If You Say Run and Posh Trish. I can't wait to send her jumping.

SIR PSYCHO (IRE) 3 b g Zoffany (IRE) – Open Book
He had two runs on the Flat for Eddie Harty in Ireland finishing third over ten furlongs at Leopardstown in April. The winner (Tinandali) is now rated 102 so the form looks strong. Bought to go juvenile hurdling, he could start off at Chepstow (12th October).

SKATMAN (IRE) 4 br g Mustameet (USA) – Maid For Action (IRE)
A very nice four year old who beat the aforementioned Barbados Buck's in his only point-to-point in Ireland in April. Bought the following month at the Goffs UK Spring Sale at Doncaster, he will run in a bumper in the Autumn and then we will make a decision whether to go hurdling or leave that until next season.

SOLDIER OF LOVE 6 b g Yeats (IRE) – Monsignorita (IRE)
A half-brother to the aforementioned Mercy Mercy Me, he has also been sent to us during the summer by Malcolm Denmark. Lightly raced, he won over hurdles at Taunton in February on his latest start and is rated 113. We might go over fences and run him in a novices' handicap chase off that mark.

SOUTHFIELD HARVEST 5 b g Kayf Tara – Chamoss Royale (FR)
From a very good family we know well, he is a half-brother to Southfield Theatre and Southfield Vic. Third on his debut in a bumper at Exeter in late March, he confirmed that promise by winning next time at Chepstow. Bred to stay well, he will appreciate running over two and a half miles plus over hurdles. I hope he will develop into a nice staying novice.

SOUTHFIELD STONE 6 gr g Fair Mix (IRE) – Laureldean Belle (IRE)
He had an excellent season and is a horse I like. Having won his bumper at Taunton, he went on to win three times over hurdles including the Grade 2 Dovecote Novices' Hurdle at Kempton in February. Rated 142 over hurdles, he will go novice chasing.

STORM ARISING (IRE) 5 b g Yeats (IRE) – Ceol Rua (IRE)
Placed in an Irish point, he had a handful of runs over hurdles last season winning at Wincanton in March. He is therefore still a novice until the end of October and we will probably give him a few more runs over hurdles before going chasing. I think he will appreciate a step up in trip and stay three miles eventually.

SWITCH HITTER (IRE) 4 b g Scorpion (IRE) – Country Time (IRE)
He is a lovely four year old who we acquired at the Cheltenham April Sale. A four and a half lengths winner of his only English point-to-point for Charlie Poste and Francesca Nimmo, he is likely to make his Rules debut in a bumper.

TAMAROC DU MATHAN (FR) 4 b g Poliglote – Thisbee Du Mathan (FR)
A winner of his only start over hurdles in France when trained by Arnaud Chaille-Chaille, he joined us last season but suffered an injury and missed the whole of the campaign. He is back in work now though and will run in a handicap hurdle, but I suspect it won't be long before he goes chasing.

THE GREATER GOOD 4 b g Tiger Groom – Our Kes (IRE)
He was a twenty two lengths winner of his only point-to-point at Little Windsor in April over two and a half miles for Christopher Barber. He could run in a bumper or go straight over hurdles.

THYME WHITE (FR) 3 b g Anodin (IRE) – Jane (GER)
He raced six times on the Flat in France winning over nine furlongs as a two year old and being placed a couple of times over ten furlongs at Toulouse earlier this year. We bought him to go juvenile hurdling.

TOPOFTHEGAME (IRE) 7 ch g Flemensfirth (USA) – Derry Vale (IRE)
A very exciting horse who looks fantastic. Runner-up in the Grade 1 Kauto Star Novice Chase at Kempton on Boxing Day, I thought Harry (Cobden) gave him a brilliant ride when winning the RSA Chase at Cheltenham in March. Not at his best at Aintree last time, he still ran well in second and remains a novice until the end of October. We therefore may give him one more run in a novice chase, possibly at Chepstow in October (11ᵗʰ October) before aiming him at the Ladbrokes Trophy at Newbury (30ᵗʰ November). He will be given entries in the King George at Kempton and the Savills Chase at Leopardstown (28ᵗʰ December) over Christmas before his main target the Cheltenham Gold Cup in March. I have been very pleased with him during the summer and, having only raced five times over fences, I hope he will continue to improve.

TREVELYN'S CORN (IRE) 6 b g Oscar (IRE) – Present Venture (IRE)
A winning Irish pointer, he has only run three times over hurdles scoring at Wincanton in March. He has had a wind operation during the summer and is still eligible for novice hurdles until the end of October. I might therefore run him in the Grade 2 Persian War Novices' Hurdle at Chepstow (11ᵗʰ October) before going chasing later in the Autumn.

TRUCKERS LODGE (IRE) 7 b g Westerner – Galeacord (IRE)
Joined us last season and had a productive year winning twice over hurdles at Chepstow and Exeter. We gave him one run over fences at Newton Abbot in May and he ran well finishing a close second. I think he will do well over fences and, given the fact he likes Chepstow and handles heavy ground, I could envisage us entering him in the Welsh National (27ᵗʰ December) and running well off a low weight. He stays well.

WILD MAX (GER) 4 bb g Maxios – Wildfahrte (GER)
Trained on the Flat in Germany by Andreas Wohler, he won two of his six races before we bought him at the Arqana Sale in February. He will go novice hurdling.

WORTHY FARM (IRE) 6 b g Beneficial – Muckle Flugga (IRE)
He won an English point for Jack Barber before joining us. A strong stayer, he won over hurdles at Taunton and Ascot, but is the sort to improve over fences. He will go three miles plus novice chasing.

YOUNG BUCK (IRE) 5 b g Yeats (IRE) – Pepsi Starlet (IRE)
A five lengths winner of his only Irish point for Shark Hanlon, we purchased him at the Cheltenham Festival Sale in March. We haven't done much with him yet, but he looks a nice horse who could go straight over hurdles.

ZYON 5 gr g Martaline – Temptation (FR)
He is a lovely horse who ran very well on his second start in a bumper at Ascot finishing third behind Emitom. Still immature, we decided to put him away and give him time. He will go novice hurdling and is open to a lot of improvement.

The following are set to go **HUNTER CHASING**:
ALCALA, ART MAURESQUE, BRAQUEUR D'OR, LOUGH DERG SPIRIT, SOUTHFIELD VIC, WONDERFUL CHARM.

TRAINER'S HORSE TO FOLLOW: GETAWAY TRUMP
TRAINER'S ASSISTANT'S (HARRY DERHAM) HORSE TO FOLLOW: ENRILO

Jonjo O'NEILL
Stables: Jackdaws Castle, Temple Guiting, Cheltenham, Gloucestershire.
2018/2019: 56 Winners / 472 Runners 12% Prize-Money £639,239
www.jonjooneillracing.com

ADDICI (IRE) 4 b g Shirocco (GER) – Lughnasa (IRE)
Not over big, he is a nice compact horse who ran well on his debut in a bumper at Warwick during the spring. He finished well and we will try and win a bumper with him before going hurdling. I have been pleased with him during the summer and, while he will stay further, we will start him off over two miles once he goes hurdling.

ANNIE MC (IRE) 5 b m Mahler – Classic Mari (IRE)
She is a lovely mare who did very well for us last season winning twice, including the mares' final at Newbury in March. Rated 140 over hurdles, the plan is to send her over fences. We haven't schooled her yet but she jumps hurdles well, plus she was runner-up in a couple of Irish points before we bought her. Two and a half miles on good ground is probably ideal. She wouldn't want extremes of ground and we will aim her at mares' novice chases.

ARRIVEDERCI (FR) 4 gr g Martaline – Etoile D'Ainay (FR)
A big weak baby last year, he is a nice horse who won on his debut at Hereford in December. Fourth next time under a penalty at Exeter, the race has worked out well and the form is strong. Quite a busy horse at home, he comes to hand quickly and, having schooled well, we will send him novice hurdling in the Autumn. I have been pleased with him during the summer because he has strengthened.

ASHFIELD PADDY (IRE) 5 b g Publisher (USA) – Thats Grace (IRE)
One of our new arrivals, I don't know much about him yet because we haven't done a lot with him. He is a grand type of horse though and I would imagine he will start off in a two miles novice hurdle. He ran in a couple of Irish points and the form of his debut has worked out particularly well. Third on that occasion, the first four home have all won since, including him next time.

CARYS' COMMODITY 4 b g Fame And Glory – Native Sunrise (IRE)
He is a nice horse who ran well on his debut in a bumper at Newton Abbot in May finishing second. A horse with a very good attitude, I am keen to win a bumper with him before sending him hurdling. He is another who will start off over two miles over jumps but will stay further in time. It was lovely ground at Newton Abbot and he wouldn't want extremes.

CLOTH CAP (IRE) 7 b g Beneficial – Cloth Fair (IRE)
His long-term target is the Grand National but he needs to rise in the weights to get in because he is currently rated 137. Not the biggest, he took well to chasing last season winning twice at Stratford and Catterick before finishing third in the Scottish National at Ayr last time. I was delighted with his run because he lacked experience, but I thought he travelled and jumped very well. Good ground is important to him and that will dictate his programme. His first target could be the Grade 3 Sodexo Gold Cup Handicap Chase at Ascot (2nd November), a race we won a couple of years ago with Go Conquer. We are likely to give him an entry in the Ladbrokes Trophy at Newbury (30th November), too.

COBOLOBO (FR) 7 br g Maresca Sorrento (FR) – Nanou Des Brosses (FR)
A dual winner over hurdles, he raced three times over fences last season finishing a short head second behind Kilbricken Storm at Ffos Las on his chasing debut. Still in contention when unseating his rider in the Devon National at Exeter last time, he wants soft/heavy ground. A thorough stayer, he is still a novice over fences and there are plenty of options for him.

COSTANTE VIA (IRE) 8 b m Milan – Spirit Rock (IRE)
Placed three times over hurdles last season for Nigel Twiston-Davies, she has joined us during the summer. We have schooled her over fences since arriving and the plan is to send her chasing. I think she will appreciate decent ground.

DARSI IN THE PARK (IRE) 6 b g Darsi (FR) – Rock In The Park (IRE)
A winning Irish pointer for Donnchadh Doyle, the form of his victory has worked out OK with runner-up Captain Drake winning twice over hurdles for Harry Fry. We bought him at the Cheltenham December Sale 2017, but he has only raced twice for us. Disappointing on his hurdles debut at Uttoxeter last Autumn, he has been off since but I hope he will make his mark in novice hurdles this season.

DHOWIN (IRE) 5 b g Yeats (IRE) – On The Way Home (IRE)
From the family of Get Me Out of Here, he ran in a couple of bumpers last season. Fifth on his debut at Exeter, they went no pace early on, which didn't suit him. He then ran well at Wetherby finishing second. Only five, he will go hurdling this season and strikes me as a staying type of horse.

DJANGO DJANGO (FR) 6 gr g Voix Du Nord (FR) – Lady Jannina
Enjoyed a good season over hurdles winning twice, including the stayers hurdle series final at Haydock on Easter Saturday. That had been his target for a while, so it was nice to see it pay off. Rated 131, he will reappear in another handicap hurdle and then we will decide whether to send him chasing or not. We haven't schooled him over fences yet. Effective over two and a half to three miles, he doesn't seem to mind the state of the ground.

DREAM BERRY (FR) 8 gr g Dream Well (FR) – Kalberry (FR)
He has been a grand horse for us over the years being placed at Aintree and Punchestown, and he has also run well at the Cheltenham Festival in the past. Rated 140 over hurdles, he is in the grip of the handicapper at the moment. We tried him over fences at Ffos Las in October last year but he fell early on, so we switched him back to hurdles. I would imagine we will mix and match between the two this season. Two and a half miles is probably his trip.

EY UP ROCKY 6 b g Dylan Thomas (IRE) – Polo
A nice consistent horse, he won well at Newbury in March. Unfortunately, he knocked himself at Newbury hence he hasn't raced since. Raised ten pounds since his last win, he is back in now and we may give him another run over hurdles before going chasing. Two or two and half miles is ideal.

FLEMINPORT (IRE) 6 b g Flemensfirth (USA) – Geek Chic (IRE)
Twice a winner over hurdles the previous season, he didn't manage to win over fences last winter but ran some nice races. Runner-up at Bangor in December, he was fourth at Chepstow last time. Suited by some cut in the ground, he stays well and has strengthened up since last season.

FLIGHT DECK (IRE) 5 b g Getaway (GER) – Rate of Knots (IRE)
We trained his mother who finished runner-up in the mares' novice chase final at Newbury. He had three runs over hurdles last season over two miles but was still on the weak side. I have been pleased with him during the summer because he looks stronger and is bred to stay further.

FOLKS ON THE HILL (IRE) 4 b g Black Sam Bellamy (IRE) – Any Pearl
A grand big horse, we bought as a three year old at the Derby Sales in Ireland last year. From the family of Pearlyman, he measures 17hh and has a good pedigree. We will take our time with him but, all being well, he will be running in a bumper around Christmas time.

FRISCO BAY (IRE) 4 b g Yeats (IRE) – Heath Heaven
Bought on behalf of Bassaire Cleanrooms Limited at the Cheltenham May Sale, he is a full-brother to Pileon, who won a bumper for Philip Hobbs last season. He ran in two Irish points for Sam Curling finishing fourth on his debut and then runner-up last time. A good looking horse, he has plenty of size and is very much a chaser in the making. It is early days but we may give him a run in a bumper before going hurdling.

GARRY CLERMONT (FR) 4 b g Maresca Sorrento (FR) – Kalidria Beauchene (FR)
A big tall horse, he won his only point-to-point in the UK before we bought him at the Cheltenham February Sale. It is the first horse Mrs Mary Walsh has had with us and we were therefore delighted when he won the point-to-point bumper at Aintree in the spring on his first run for us. A good jumper, he will go straight over hurdles over two and a half miles plus.

HEY JOE (IRE) 4 b g Oscar (IRE) – Joddrell (IRE)
Another nice unraced four year old we bought at the Derby Sales in Ireland last year. Not the biggest, he is from the family of Crocodiles Rock who we used to train. Owned by the Hitchins family, he has worked nicely at home and will make his debut in a bumper.

KILBROOK (IRE) 4 b g Watar (IRE) – Daly Lady (IRE)
A half-brother to Huntsman Son, he was bought at the Aintree April Sale for Dominic Burke and Delancey. He is a nice big chasing type who finished runner-up in his only Irish point a few days before the sale. A good looking type, he jumped well in his point-to-point but we may give him a run in a bumper.

LITHIC (IRE) 8 b g Westerner – Acoola (IRE)
Still a novice over fences, he is capable of winning a decent race. Runner-up on three occasions last season, he travels well in his races but has been unlucky. Consistent, he jumps and stays well and likes some cut in the ground. He is for sale.

LUNAR BABY (IRE) 4 b f Fame And Glory – Fiddlededee (IRE)
We trained her mother, who was talented but frustrating, and this filly is similar. Successful on her debut in a bumper at Warwick in November, she had two more runs and I was disappointed she didn't win again. I think she has got more ability than she has shown so far. If things fall her way, I think she could be very good and it wouldn't surprise me if she ended up in the mares' final at Newbury in the spring. She jumps well.

MEYER LANSKY (IRE) 4 b g Mahler – Sea Breeze Lady (IRE)
From the family of Grand National runner-up Oscar Time, he is a nice horse who finished third in his only Irish point behind Papa Tango Charly, who we also subsequently purchased. Bought at the Aintree April Sale for Michael O'Flynn and Delancey, he is a tough, likeable horse who kept on well in his point-to-point. He got in close to the second last but I liked the way he rallied and stayed on afterwards. Cantering at the moment, he could run in a bumper.

MINELLA ROCCO (IRE) 9 b g Shirocco (GER) – Petralona (USA)
A previous Cheltenham Festival winner and Gold Cup runner-up, he has been struggling with his wind and isn't the easiest to get right nowadays. He will run in handicap chases during the first half of the season and then there is a possibility he will go hunter chasing in the New Year. I have yet to finalise a plan with Frank (Berry) but it could well suit the horse.

MONDESCA (FR) 3 b g Maresca Sorrento (FR) – Mondovi (FR)
He is a gorgeous looking unraced three year old we bought at the Derby Sales in Ireland this summer. Related to Saint Calvados, he is for a sale and is a lovely horse. We have given him a break since arriving, but he will be running in a bumper later in the season.

ON THE BANGWAGON (IRE) 4 b g Oscar (IRE) – Deep Supreme (IRE)
A half-brother to Heath Hunter and from the family of Ned Kelly and Nick Dundee, I love him. Runner-up in his only Irish point-to-point in late March when trained by Denis Murphy, we bought him a few days later at the Aintree Sale. Measuring 17hh, he is owned by Andrew Nolan and we may give him a run in a bumper for experience purposes. He is a fine big horse and I like him a lot.

ORRISDALE (IRE) 5 b g Oscar (IRE) – Back To Loughadera (IRE)
He is a nice type of horse and typical of one of Trevor Hemmings. Very much a chaser in the making, he was sixth on his debut in a bumper at Chepstow before winning at Bangor next time. He was the second leg of Jonjo's (O'Neill jnr) first ever treble that day and there were a few fancied in the race, which is always a good sign. He will go novice hurdling and I am expecting him to stay well.

PAPA TANGO CHARLY (FR) 4 ch g No Risk At All (FR) – Chere Elenn (FR)
A lovely big horse who was purchased on behalf of Martin Tedham at the Goffs UK Aintree Sale in April. Previously trained by Colin Bowe, he won his only Irish point by four lengths and has always had a big reputation. We went to see him after his win and then bought him at the sale. He is a smashing horse and I love him. We haven't made any plans but there is every chance he will start off in a bumper. We probably won't see the best of him for another couple of years.

PENS MAN (IRE) 4 ch g Sholokhov (IRE) – Dudeen (IRE)
A two lengths winner of his Irish point-to-point when trained by Sam Curling, he now belongs to Castle Racing having been bought at the Goffs UK Aintree Sale. He is a lovely horse who I really like and the form of his win has worked out well with the third scoring next time.

PERFECT CITY (IRE) 4 b g Elusive City (USA) – Tall Perfection (USA)
He won three times on the Flat in France for Jean-Claude Rouget before we bought him at the Arqana Sale at Deauville in February. Following a run on the Flat at York in May, he was in the process of running OK on his hurdles debut at Southwell when falling at the second last. The form of the race is good but I have a suspicion his stamina is going to be stretched over jumps. His wins on the Flat were gained over seven furlongs to a mile and one, so we will be keeping him to sharp tracks over hurdles.

PIGGY WINKLE (IRE) 5 b g Fame And Glory – Ar Muin Na Muice (IRE)
He is out of a very good mare who we used to train. I hope he is growing up because he hasn't been the easiest horse to train hence he didn't make his debut until May this year. Third at Uttoxeter over two miles, he finished well and it was an encouraging start. His mother won the mares' final at Newbury and he is therefore bred to stay further.

POP ROCKSTAR (IRE) 7 bb g Flemensfirth (USA) – Special Ballot (IRE)
We were delighted when he won on his final start at Chepstow in April because his owner Laura Day had a box that day and it couldn't have worked out better. The handicapper has raised him twelve pounds since, which is going to make life tougher. However, he stays well and handles soft ground and we will campaign him in long distance handicap chases at the likes of Chepstow and Ffos Las.

PREFONTAINE (IRE) 3 gr g Mastercraftsman (IRE) – Cochabamba (IRE)
Owner Paul Smith kindly sent him to us during the summer and he is the first horse we have trained for him. Rated 87 on the Flat for Roger Varian, he won over ten furlongs as a juvenile and has run three good races this year. We have schooled him with a view to sending him juvenile hurdling on nice ground.

PRESENT CHIEF (IRE) 5 b g Presenting – Daizinni
Fifth on his debut in a bumper at Bangor last Autumn when trained by Ronnie O'Leary, he had his first run for us at Worcester in late July. Beaten a short head, the first two pulled nine lengths clear of the third and then he went one better at the same track in early September. He will now go novice hurdling.

QUARENTA (FR) 7 bb g Voix Du Nord (FR) – Negresse De Cuta (FR)
Had a good season winning two staying handicap chases at Warwick. A three times winner at the track during his career, he ran well last time at Haydock finishing a close second in one of those series finals on Easter Saturday. Raised seven pounds, he is now rated 134 and will follow a similar programme. He likes good ground.

READY AND ABLE (IRE) 6 b g Flemensfirth (USA) – Gypsy Mo Chara (IRE)
Progressive over hurdles last season, he won three times but went up a lot in the ratings as a result. He then suffered a fall at Newbury and failed to recapture his best form on his next two races. Switched to fences, he won narrowly at Southwell during the summer. We have given him a break since but he will resume in staying novice chases in the Autumn.

RUSSIAN INVASION (IRE) 4 b g Aizavoski (IRE) – Kerso (IRE)
Owned by Trevor Hemmings, he was runner-up in an Irish point for Michael Goff towards the end of May. Bought four days later, he is a chaser in the making but will spend this season over hurdles.

SEATON CAREW (IRE) 5 b m Getaway (GER) – Millys Gesture (IRE)
From a very good family including Rhinestone Cowboy and Wichita Lineman, she is a half-sister to Coney Island. She is a grand mare who finished fifth on her debut at Warwick before winning a mares' bumper at Wetherby next time. She will start off in a two miles mares' novice hurdle and we will go from there. She is a lovely mare who looks more like a gelding.

SKY PIRATE 6 b g Midnight Legend – Dancingwithbubbles (IRE)
Despite the fact he remains a novice, he ran some very good races over fences last season. Runner-up at Uttoxeter and Carlisle, he was still going well when falling at the second last at Cheltenham's November meeting. Seventh in the Kim Muir at the Festival, he jumps well and likes good ground. We are going to drop him back to two and a half miles and he could start off at either Chepstow (12th October) or in a Listed handicap chase at Wetherby (1st November). We are hoping to win on his reappearance with a view to aiming him at the BetVictor Gold Cup at Cheltenham (16th November).

SKYLANNA BREEZE (IRE) 4 b g Primary (USA) – Waist Deep (IRE)
Bought at the Cheltenham May Sale, he was placed in two of his three Irish points and is from the family of Keen Leader. Not over big (16.2hh), he is a grand horse who will start off in a bumper and is for sale.

SOARING GLORY (IRE) 4 b g Fame And Glory – Hapeney (IRE)
A nice unraced four year old who is a half-brother to dual Grade 3 winner Three Stars. Bought at the Derby Sales in Ireland last year, he has a very good pedigree being related to the likes of Direct Route and Joe Mac. A fine big horse, he will run in a bumper before Christmas.

TEDHAM 5 b g Shirocco (GER) – Alegralil
I think he is a grand horse who will make a very nice chaser one day but we are going to keep him over hurdles this season. He ran well on his first three runs over hurdles, including at Carlisle and Exeter, before winning next time at Wincanton. Seventh at Aintree's Grand National meeting, I was disappointed at the time but it was a tough race against twenty opponents on a sharp track, which wouldn't have played to his strengths. Plus, the race came on the back of a long season for such a young horse. Only five, he is growing up all the time and I like him a lot.

TEGEREK (FR) 5 b g Mount Nelson – Takaniya (IRE)
A winner on the Flat in France when trained by Alain De Royer-Dupre, he has yet to win for us over hurdles but has got plenty of ability. Third at Leicester in December and runner-up at Chepstow last time, he works well at home but hasn't reproduced it on the track yet. Quite a keen horse, he will continue over hurdles for the time being, but we may switch him to fences later on. He is capable of winning races.

TERRY THE FISH (IRE) 7 b g Milan – Have More
A maiden over fences, he was runner-up a couple of times at Market Rasen and Uttoxeter. I always thought he wanted good ground but as he gets older and stronger, I think he will cope with some ease underfoot. A strong stayer, there are plenty of options for him in long distance handicap chases at the likes of Chepstow and Warwick.

THATS THE TRUTH (IRE) 5 b m Darsi (FR) – Lucy Walters (IRE)
Previously trained in Ireland by Sean Doyle, we bought her at the Goffs UK Spring Sale at Doncaster in May. A full-sister to Spiritofthegames, who was placed at the Cheltenham Festival in March, she finished runner-up in two of her three point-to-points. The form of her debut run has worked out well with the race producing five subsequent winners. Not over big, she looks gutsy and is a grand honest mare who goes nicely at home.

THE COMPOSEUR (IRE) 4 b g Mahler – Oscar's Reprieve (IRE)
Related to Keepitsecret who we used to train, he was acquired at the Aintree April Sale having run in two English point-to-points for Philip Rowley. Runner-up on his debut, he won by four lengths next time and is a grand horse who has settled in well. A chaser in the making, we will run him in a bumper for experience purposes before going hurdling. He is a nice big horse.

TIDAL WATCH (IRE) 5 b g Harbour Watch (IRE) – Najmati
Did well over hurdles winning five times, including at Kempton (twice) during the spring. Switched to fences during the summer, I thought he ran well on his chasing debut finishing third at Market Rasen in July and was then very unlucky at Newton Abbot the following month when falling at the last when clear. He likes good ground and I think he will develop into a nice chaser over two and two and a half miles.

WASDELL DUNDALK (FR) 4 ch g Spirit One (FR) – Linda Queen (FR)
Fourth on his debut in a bumper at Huntingdon in the spring, I was a bit disappointed afterwards because I thought he would run better than he did. However, it transpired he had fractured his pelvis. He is OK now and we are going to try and win a bumper with him before going hurdling. A more galloping track will suit him.

WHEN YOU'RE READY (IRE) 5 gr g Malinas (GER) – Royale Wheeler (FR)
Jumped very well, prior to finishing second in his only Irish point before we bought him at the Cheltenham February Sale. I thought he ran a cracker on his first run for us in a hotly contested bumper at Warwick in May. Beaten a length in third, he is a lovely mover and I think the better ground suited him. He shows a lot of speed at home and we will try and win a bumper with him before going novice hurdling. Two miles over hurdles will suit him.

YOUNG WOLF (IRE) 6 b g Vinnie Roe (IRE) – Missy O'Brien (IRE)
Twice a winner over hurdles at Ludlow and Stratford, he is rated 132 and I suspect the handicapper has got him at the moment. Disappointing at Southwell last time, he ran flat and I think he was still feeling the effects of his win at Stratford on his previous start. We have schooled him over fences with a view to sending him chasing. He isn't over big but jumps well and we will probably run him until the end of October and then give him a winter break before bringing him back in the spring.

Unnamed 4 b g Fame And Glory – Supreme Melody (IRE)
A gorgeous looking horse belonging to Trevor Hemmings who only arrived in August. Bought as a three year old at the Goffs Landrover Sale, he is from the family of Supreme Prince and Supreme Serenade. He will start off in a bumper.

Unnamed 3 b g Shantou (USA) – Glens Melody (IRE)
The first foal of dual Grade 1 and Cheltenham Festival winning mare Glens Melody, he was bought at the Goffs Landrover Sale in June. He has been broken in and will run in a bumper later in the season. He has a great pedigree and is for sale.

TRAINER'S HORSE TO FOLLOW: ARRIVEDERCI

David PIPE

Stables: Pond House, Nicholashayne, Wellington, Somerset.
2018/2019: 44 Winners / 364 Runners 12% Prize-Money £583,292
www.davidpipe.com

BARRANCO VALLEY 8 b g Midnight Legend – Shali San (FR)
Plagued with problems, he was previously trained by Nick Williams and has only raced twice for us. Returning from a long absence (1256 days), he ran well over hurdles at Exeter in March finishing fourth. Stepping up to two and a half miles for the first time on his next start at Ffos Las in June, he made all and did it nicely. Still a novice over hurdles, I think he will stay three miles and we will hopefully get a clear run with him.

BUSTER EDWARDS (IRE) 6 b g Kalanisi (IRE) – Hot Oscar (IRE)
A good fun horse who won over hurdles at Fontwell in May before finishing third on his next couple of starts. We have operated on his wind since and given him a break. A former Irish pointer, he will continue over hurdles for the time being but it won't be long before we send him chasing. He jumps and stays well and hopefully the wind operation will bring about more improvement.

CATCH THE SWALLOWS (IRE) 5 b g Masterofthehorse (IRE) – Nafrah (USA)
Runner-up in his only Irish point, he produced a good performance to win on his first run for us in a bumper at Bangor in January. His work beforehand had been good and we thought he would run well. Unfortunately, he picked up an injury shortly afterwards, which forced him to miss the rest of the season. Back from his summer break, he may have another run in a bumper before going hurdling. Despite the fact he stays further, two miles on a galloping track over hurdles ought to be OK.

COLLNGWOOD COURT (IRE) 5 b g Court Cave (IRE) – West Hill Rose (IRE)
A half-brother to Grand Vision, he ran in three Irish points for Colin Bowe winning his latest start by six lengths in May. He looks a nice stayer in the making.

DAKLONDIKE (IRE) 7 b g Gold Well – Strong Irish (IRE)
Talented but quirky, he showed what he is capable of last season winning the Tommy Whittle Chase at Haydock before Christmas. He went back to the same track the following month for the Peter Marsh Chase and, having lost his rider early on, he got loose. It affected him mentally hence he refused to race in the Eider Chase at Newcastle last time. It is a case of going back to basics with him. Still a young horse, he stays well and enjoys soft ground.

DUC DE BEAUCHENE (FR) 6 b Saddler Maker (IRE) – Quatia D'Angron (FR)
He won nicely over hurdles at Plumpton before finishing runner-up at Sandown. Very much a three mile chaser in the making, he will start off in a handicap hurdle. He likes soft ground and wants a trip.

EAMON AN CNOIC (IRE) 8 b g Westerner – Nutmeg Tune (IRE)
We have always felt he is capable of winning a big prize and, having operated on his wind mid season, he won at Chepstow in February and then ran very well in the Brown Advisory & Merriebelle Stable Plate Handicap Chase at the Cheltenham Festival finishing fourth. Below par on his final two starts at Aintree and Punchestown, he is a talented horse who will hopefully improve again this season. Effective over two and two and a half miles, his owners The Angove Family come over from America for the Cheltenham November meeting (15th – 17th) and he is likely to be given entries at that meeting.

EDEN DU HOUX (FR) 5 b g Irish Wells (FR) – Maralypha (FR)
An exciting horse, who won his only Irish point-to-point before joining us. He had a racecourse gallop prior to winning a bumper at Plumpton in December. We then stepped him up in class and he won a Listed bumper at Ascot less than three weeks later. The form has worked out well and he is a horse with a good attitude and a big engine. We tried to have him ready for the spring Festivals but he had done a lot during the first half of the season, so we decided to give him time to mature. He has strengthened up and looks well. Even though he has only raced on soft or heavy ground, I don't see any reason why he won't handle better ground and we will probably start him off over two miles over hurdles.

EUR GONE WEST (IRE) 6 b g Westerner – Floating Euro (IRE)
He has always promised to do well and enjoyed a good season winning handicap hurdles at Exeter and Taunton. We fitted him with a hood halfway through the year and it helped him relax. I would put a line through his final run at Perth because he had had enough by that stage of the season. Life will be tougher this year off a mark of 133, but we have the option of going chasing later on. Trips around two and a half to three miles are ideal.

EXTRA MAG (FR) 5 b g Kapgarde (FR) – Qrystale Mag (FR)
Ex-French, we were aiming him at the Imperial Cup at Sandown in March but, unfortunately, he picked up an injury and won't be running until the second half of the season. Unlucky not to win on his hurdles debut at Wetherby when stumbling shortly after the last when in front, he then won next time at Exeter. Runner-up at Sandown under a penalty, he has yet to race beyond two miles but stays well and will get further in due course even though he isn't short of speed. Effective on most types of ground, he possesses a lot of ability and will go handicap hurdling when he returns.

FIRST LORD DE CUET (FR) 5 gr g Lord Du Sud (FR) – Alyce (FR)
A winner of his only Irish point for Donnchadh Doyle, we subsequently bought him at the Cheltenham May 2018 sale a few days later. A likeable sort, he ran well on his Rules debut in a bumper at Taunton in February finishing a close second. He improved for the run and bolted up next time in a similar event at Plumpton. I have been pleased with him during the summer because he has strengthened up and ought to make a nice staying novice hurdler. We may start him over two miles on soft ground but he wants a trip. He jumps well and has a good attitude.

FORT SUMMER (IRE) 4 b g Kalanisi (IRE) – Glen Ellie (IRE)
We purchased him at the Goffs UK Spring Sale at Doncaster in May having shown promise in three point-to-points for Warren Ewing. Third on his debut, he had reportedly worked well beforehand, but disappointed on his final start. I would imagine he will run in a bumper before going novice hurdling.

GLEN VINE 5 ch g Robin Des Champs (FR) – Gaspara (FR)
Out of our Imperial Cup/Cheltenham Festival winning mare Gaspara, he finished a good second on his debut in a bumper at Worcester. A bit disappointing on his next two outings, he is a three miles chaser in the making and will benefit from stepping up in trip over hurdles this season.

INDUNO (IRE) 5 b g Flemensfirth (USA) – Vast Consumption (IRE)
A nice prospect and the first horse we have trained for Ronnie Bartlett. We have always liked him and therefore it was no surprise to see him run well on his debut in a bumper at Warwick in late April. While it was disappointing that he didn't win, he ran a very good race in second behind a well regarded winner. A stayer in the making, we may run him in another bumper before going hurdling.

INTO THE WOODS (IRE) 5 b g Milan – Wall of Silence (IRE)
Acquired at the Ascot July Sale, he ran in five Irish points for Sam Curling finishing second a couple of times in May. He will spend this season over hurdles but is a long distance chaser in the making.

ISRAEL CHAMP (IRE) 4 b g Milan – La Dariska (FR)
A big strong four year old who was visually very impressive in his only point-to-point in Ireland winning by a dozen lengths. Bought privately soon afterwards on behalf of John White and Anne Underhill, we have given him time to strengthen up since arriving. Quite free going, he is likely to run in a bumper in the Autumn and, depending on how he performs, we will then decide whether to stay in bumpers or go novice hurdling.

JASMIN DES BORDES (FR) 5 b g Great Pretender (IRE) – Queen Des Bordes (FR)
Runner-up in an Irish point, he ran well in a bumper at Exeter finishing second before filling third position on his hurdles debut at Chepstow over Christmas. Disappointing at Taunton next time, he wasn't right afterwards and missed the remainder of the season. We have given him plenty of time off and operated on his wind in the meantime. He will continue over hurdles and will come into his own over three miles eventually.

KEPAGGE (IRE) 5 b g Getaway (GER) – Miracle Lady
He is a big horse who fell in his only Irish point when upsides the winner at the last. The form has been boosted (winner has scored twice since) and, while he has yet to run for us, we did a bit with him when he arrived and we liked what we saw. He was recommended to us and is another who will run in a bumper in the Autumn.

KING'S SOCKS (FR) 7 b g King's Best (USA) – Alexandrina (GER)
He was in the process of running well in the BetVictor Gold Cup Handicap Chase at Cheltenham in November when losing his rider at the third last. Unfortunately, he picked up an injury in the process and missed the rest of the campaign. All being well, he will be back in the second half of the season. It has been frustrating because he is a very talented horse but has only raced four times for us since arriving from France. Still only seven, we are hoping we can get him back to his best later in the season.

KNOW THE SCORE (IRE) 6 b g Flemensfirth (USA) – Prairie Bell (IRE)
A winner over hurdles at Hexham in December, he found the ground too quick and track too tight when finishing third at Bangor next time. A relentless galloper who enjoys soft ground, I am hoping there is a lot more to come from him. We may run him in another handicap hurdle but he will come into his own over fences and I would like to think he is on a fair mark (124). Quite laid back nowadays, it wouldn't surprise me if he ended up in something like the National Hunt Chase at the Cheltenham Festival next spring.

LEGAL HISTORY (IRE) 4 b g Lawman (FR) – Nina Celebre (IRE)
Purchased at the Newmarket Horses in Training Sale in October last year, he has proved a great buy. Twice a winner at Ascot and Exeter, he was runner-up in the Sussex Champion Hurdle at Plumpton in the spring and also second in the Listed Summer Handicap Hurdle at Market Rasen in July. He was then third at Newton Abbot in August. Despite a five pounds rise, I think he has more to offer with two miles on good or faster ground being ideal. He does stay further though having finished second over two miles three at Newbury in March.

LITTLE RED LION (IRE) 5 b g Sans Frontieres (IRE) – Rever Up (IRE)
A big backward gelding who finished second in a bumper at Ffos Las on his debut. However, he was disappointing in three races over hurdles. A three miles chaser in the long-term, he is crying out for a step up in trip and we will look for a suitable novices' handicap hurdle to begin with.

MAKE ME A BELIEVER (IRE) 4 br g Presenting – Kiltiernan Robin (IRE)
Previously trained in Ireland by Colin Bowe, he was still going well when falling three out in his only Irish point in March. He was recommended to us and is a good looking horse. Despite being a big horse, he was quite light framed when arriving and therefore has benefited from a summer break and has strengthened up. He is likely to contest a bumper before going hurdling.

MEEP MEEP MAG (IRE) 5 b m Getaway (GER) – Deadly Pursuit (IRE)
She is not the biggest of mares but appears to have a good attitude. A winner of her second Irish point, we bought her at the Cheltenham May Sale. We gave her a break soon afterwards and I am hoping she will prove good value. She jumps well but may have a run in a mares' bumper before going hurdling.

MR CLARKSON (IRE) 7 b g Jeremy (USA) – Wynsleydale (USA)
A typical son of Jeremy being tough, he has done well during the summer winning over hurdles at Worcester and Cartmel. Suited by soft ground, he is only small but finished runner-up in an Irish point behind the ill-fated Finian's Oscar and will go novice chasing at some stage this season.

NEW AGE DAWNING (IRE) 5 ch g Stowaway – Captain Supreme (IRE)
Runner-up in a point-to-point, he battled on well to win a bumper at Exeter on New Year's Day on his first run for us. Having finished second on his hurdles debut at Lingfield, he made all when winning at Chepstow next time. Not the quickest, he likes soft ground and has a likeable attitude. Rated 133, he could run in a staying handicap hurdle before going chasing later on. I am hoping he will develop into a decent long distance staying chaser one day.

NORDIC COMBINED (IRE) 5 b g Haafhd – Chilly Filly (IRE)
Still a maiden over hurdles, he ran some good races in defeat, including when finishing second at Lingfield, Newbury and Ffos Las. Soft ground helps him because it slows his opponents down and he can handle it. His best runs have been over two miles but I think he will stay all day. Indeed, the only time we stepped him up in trip at Sandown, he fell and it was too early to say where he would have finished.

POKER PLAY (FR) 6 ch g Martaline – Becquarette (FR)
Produced a good performance to win a valuable handicap hurdle at Uttoxeter in March. Well held at Aintree last time, he found the ground too quick. He must have soft ground. He jumped fences well at home but didn't take to it on the track when we ran him at Worcester last Autumn. However, we will try him again over fences and see how he gets on. There is also a possibility we might take him to France in October. Two and a half miles plus is his trip.

QUEENS CAVE (IRE) 6 b m Court Cave (IRE) – Shuilan (IRE)
A smart mare in bumpers a couple of seasons ago winning at Uttoxeter before finishing a neck second in a Listed contest at Sandown. She made her hurdles debut at Ayr last winter but pulled up. We found she was suffering with a fibrillating heart and she therefore missed the rest of the season. Back in work, she will hopefully have a full season this time around and show what she is capable of in mares' novice hurdles. She has a lot of ability.

RAMSES DE TEILLEE (FR) 7 gr g Martaline – Princesse D'Orton (FR)
He has been a superstar and enjoyed a very good season winning at Chepstow before finishing runner-up in both the Welsh National and Grand National Trial at Haydock. He was in the process of running well, too, in the Grand National when the rein broke after a mistake at the Canal Turn and David Noonan rode him with one rein thereafter. We have always thought he wanted soft ground, but it was good ground at Haydock in February. Still only a seven year old, I am hoping there is more improvement to come. His first target is the Becher Chase at Aintree (7th December) and we will more than likely give him an entry in the Welsh National at Chepstow (27th December) once again. We also have the option of running him over hurdles because he is still a novice, which is handy.

REMASTERED 6 ch g Network (GER) – Cathodine Cayras (FR)
An impressive winner on his hurdles debut at Ffos Las in November, he wasn't at his best at Exeter next time. Runner-up at Newbury in the spring behind a useful horse (Dashel Drasher), the ground that day was good to soft compared to his previous wins on heavy. He has strengthened up and will benefit from stepping up to three miles this season. Rated 133, he could be one for the Grade 3 *Betfair* Exchange Stayers' Handicap Hurdle at Haydock (23rd November) before going over fences. I think he will be an exciting novice chaser.

STORY OF FRIENDS (FR) 5 b g Kingsalsa (USA) – Royale Malinelle (FR)
A winning pointer, he wasn't quite finishing off his races in the spring. We therefore fitted him with a tongue tie and he won a bumper at Exeter and over hurdles at Warwick. Runner-up at Newton Abbot in June, he was beaten by a good horse (Thebannerkingrebel). He will have a wind operation shortly and will be suited by a return to two and a half miles. Still a novice over hurdles, he looks to be on a workable mark of 118.

THINKING (IRE) 4 b g So You Think (NZ) – Laetoli (ITY)
Successful in his only run over hurdles at Vichy in France last season when trained by Guy Cherel, he suffered a tendon injury shortly after joining us. He therefore won't be running until the second half of the campaign when he will continue over hurdles. He is owned by Nick Shutts.

UMBRIGADO (IRE) 5 br g Stowaway – Dame O'Neill (IRE)
Second in his only Irish point for Aidan Fitzgerald, he looked good when winning his bumper at Uttoxeter and then over hurdles at Southwell and Exeter. Sixth in Grade 1 company at Aintree last time, I don't think he was at his best that day. We have operated on his wind since and he will start off in a handicap hurdle over two and a half miles plus. He is another who could be aimed at the Grade 3 *Betfair* Exchange Stayers' Handicap Hurdle (23rd November).

VIEUX LION ROUGE (FR) 10 ch g Sabiango (GER) – Indecise (FR)
He has been a super horse for us over the years winning the Becher Chase and Grand National Trial at Haydock, plus contesting the last four Grand Nationals. Rated 142, it won't be easy for him this year but we have the option of taking him to France in October and running him in veterans' chases, culminating in the final at Sandown in early January.

WARTHOG (FR) 7 gr g Martaline – Shekira (FR)
A big horse who measures 17hh, he made a good start to his chasing career when jumping brilliantly and making all to win easily at Sandown in December. Raised twelve pounds, he never jumped as well in his subsequent three starts and failed to recapture his best form. A non stayer in the National Hunt Chase at the Cheltenham Festival, I think front running over two or two and a half miles on soft ground is ideal.

YAA SALAAM (IRE) 5 ch g Helmet (AUS) – Ya Hajar
A five times winner on the Flat in Germany, we bought him at the Newmarket Horses in Training Sale last October. I thought he ran two decent races over hurdles finishing third at Ffos Las in February and then runner-up at Market Rasen the following month. Given a break since, he is a likeable horse who is capable of winning races over hurdles. Two miles is his trip at the moment.

TRAINER'S HORSE TO FOLLOW: FIRST LORD DE CUET

Nicky RICHARDS

Stables: Rectory Farm, Greystoke, Penrith, Cumbria.
2018/2019: 42 Winners / 222 Runners 19% Prize-Money £680,689
www.nickyrichardsracing.com

BETTER GETALONG (IRE) 8 b g Gold Well – Arequipa (IRE)
Having not quite reached the heights his owner David Wesley Yates was hoping for, he was sent to the sales at Doncaster in the spring and we bought him back relatively cheaply. Runner-up over hurdles at Haydock in December, he never really got his ground thereafter because it was such a dry winter. Two and a half miles on soft ground is ideal and I am sure he will find his level this year. We have schooled him over fences and have the option of going chasing or we could stay over hurdles for the time being. There are more races to be won with him.

BIG BAD BEAR (IRE) 5 br g Jeremy (USA) – Our Polly (IRE)
From the family of the ill-fated Thyestes Chase winner Invitation Only, he is a nice horse who was consistent in bumpers last year. Unlucky not to win on his first couple of runs at Sedgefield and Wetherby, he bumped into some above average types. Thankfully, he got the job done at Perth last time running on strongly and winning in good style. He will go straight over hurdles now and will be suited by two and a half miles.

BLAKERIGG (IRE) 8 b g Presenting – Azalea (IRE)
Twice a winner over fences last season, he won nicely at Ayr and Newcastle. It was very testing ground next time at Uttoxeter when finishing third. Two and a half to three miles on good to soft ground on big galloping tracks are his optimum conditions and I would like to think he will be competitive off his mark of 114.

CAIUS MARCIUS (IRE) 8 b g King's Theatre (IRE) – Ain't Misbehavin (IRE)
He is a grand horse who won twice over hurdles last season, including a Listed event at Market Rasen. He has taken well to chasing, too, during the spring/summer winning three times. Successful at Sedgefield, Hexham and Newton Abbot, his jumping has been very good. There is a two miles novice chase at Cheltenham's first meeting (25th October), which I have got my eye on. We will then probably give him a break because he doesn't want soft ground and the race I have in mind for him later on is the Grade 2 Lightning Novices' Chase at Doncaster towards the end of January.

CATHAL'S STAR 6 ch g Malinas (GER) – Hand Inn Glove
Yet to run for us, he is a fine big horse who finished second over hurdles for Ruth Jefferson. He has been off the track since the summer of last year, due to a setback, but is back in work now and will continue in novice hurdles.

CHAPEL STILE (IRE) 7 b g Scorpion (IRE) – Peggy Cullen (IRE)
Did very well during the 2017/2018 season, winning three times over hurdles and appreciating the step up to three miles. From a very good family, he is a half-brother to Rathvinden. Unfortunately, he picked up an injury when winning at the Scottish National meeting at Ayr in April 2018 and therefore missed the whole of last season. Back now, I am hoping he will develop into a nice staying novice chaser. All being well, he will be in action in November/December.

CHIDSWELL (IRE) 10 b g Gold Well – Manacured (IRE)
Had a good season winning twice at Kelso and Doncaster, including the Grimthorpe Handicap Chase at the latter track. He bled next time in the Scottish National at Ayr and then pulled up again at Perth at the end of a long season. Ground on the easy side of good is probably ideal because I don't think he wants it too soft. We will be looking towards the decent staying chases for him again, such as the Rehearsal Chase at Newcastle (30th November). The Grimthorpe and Scottish National are other likely targets, too.

COURT DREAMING (IRE) 6 b g Court Cave (IRE) – Louis's Teffia (IRE)
A consistent horse who won twice over hurdles at Perth and Kelso last season. He ran well at Ayr during the spring with his only disappointing effort at Cartmel in July. We have given him a break since and it is his first proper one since coming into training. There is every chance we will send him chasing and I think he is handicapped to be competitive, although he may not want it too soft.

DUKE OF NAVAN (IRE) 11 bb g Presenting – Greenfieldflyer (IRE)
He has been a grand horse for us over the years and was unlucky not to win a big one last year. I thought he ran two tremendous races at Cheltenham in October and Leopardstown at the Dublin Racing Festival in February finishing second and third respectively. He deserves to win a good prize with a strongly run two miles being ideal.

ELIOS D'OR (FR) 5 b g Puit D'Or (IRE) – Naker Mome (FR)
A speedy type, he made his debut in a bumper on the all-weather at Newcastle in January. Having looked like winning with a couple of furlongs to run, he got tired late on before finishing fifth. I think he will benefit from racing on grass and, having strengthened up during the summer, I hope he is capable of winning a bumper. His owners Langdale Bloodstock like to win a bumper and then sell them on.

GLENDUFF (IRE) 5 b g Gold Well – Last of The Bunch
From a great family and a half-brother to Cheltenham Festival bumper winner Relegate, he is a typical horse owned by Mr Hemmings. A big strapping three mile chaser in the making, he ran well first time out in a bumper at Kelso finishing second. He didn't run quite as well second time out at Newcastle finishing fouth but he isn't a bumper horse. We will send him novice hurdling over two and a half miles plus this season and educate him before going chasing the following season. He is a grand horse.

GLINGER FLAME (IRE) 7 ro g Daylami (IRE) – Titan Flame (IRE)
An interesting horse who we still don't know how good he is. Having shown promise in a couple of bumpers, he was placed twice over hurdles before winning three lowly races at Hexham during the spring. He remains a novice until the end of October and then we have the option of going chasing because he is a good jumper. We have fitted him with cheekpieces on his last three starts but Brian (Hughes) doesn't feel he will need them for the whole of his career.

GLITTERING LOVE (IRE) 7 b g Winged Love (IRE) – Glittering Image (IRE)
Did well in point-to-points for my daughter Joey the previous season winning four out of five. The experience he gained there stood him in good stead and he won all four of his races for us last year with his rating rising from 92 to 125. He improved with every run and I hope he will continue that trend this winter. A thorough stayer, he wants soft ground and could be one for something like the Eider Chase at Newcastle in February. I think he is open to more improvement, especially when encountering testing conditions.

GUITAR PETE (IRE) 9 gr g Dark Angel (IRE) – Innishmore (IRE)
He has been a cracking horse who has been competing at a high level for a long time and is still running in those big Saturday races. Runner-up in a Listed chase at Wetherby last November, he was then third in both the BetVictor Gold Cup and Caspian Caviar Gold Cups at Cheltenham. Unfortunately, he then had a little accident at home which took a long time to heal and was he forced to miss the rest of the season. His owners are keen to try him over three miles once again with races like the *SkyBet* Chase at Doncaster in January and the three miles handicap chase at Kempton, formerly known as the *Racing Post* Chase, in February possible targets. In the meantime, we may even give him another run on the Flat. He never lets us down.

HEADSCARF LIL (IRE) 5 b m Getaway (GER) – Bleu Money (IRE)
A cheap buy, she is a grand mare who ran a nice race on her debut in a bumper at Kelso in the spring. We ran three in the race and she was very green early on but finished well and was only beaten three parts of a length. She has shown enough to suggest she can win a similar event and I am expecting her to stay well once sent jumping.

HIGHLAND GOLD 5 b m Yeats (IRE) – Crevamoy (IRE)
Half-sister to staying chaser Singlefarmpayment, she ran in the same mares' bumper as Headscarf Lil and didn't run badly finishing fifth. She had been buzzy at home, so we feared she may not settle during the race. However, she showed some promise and I would like to think she is good enough to win races. We will give her another run in a bumper.

HOLME ABBEY 6 b g Fair Mix (IRE) – Brockwell Abbey
A big old fashioned chasing type from a staying family. We ran him in three bumpers at Ayr (twice) and Hexham and he looked a stayer in the making. We have schooled him and he is ready to go novice hurdling over two and a half miles plus. His long-term future lies over three miles.

IMADA (IRE) 9 br g Arcadio (GER) – Anck Su Namun (IRE)
He is a useful horse but we need a clear run with him because he has been injury prone and hasn't had a lot of racing. A winner over fences at Perth in the spring, his mark looks workable and I think he is capable of winning a good race. He travels and jumps well in his races and, even though he has been winning over two and a half miles, I think he will stay three miles.

INNISFREE SPIRIT (IRE) 5 br m Yeats (IRE) – Mrs Dempsey (IRE)
She was all set to make her debut in a mares' bumper last season but got cast in her box at home. We thought she would run well, too. She has a very good pedigree and is a nice mare.

KAJAKI (IRE) 6 gr g Mastercraftsman (IRE) – No Quest (IRE)
Previously trained by Kevin Ryan, his owner Frank Gillespie kindly sent him to us during the summer. Twice a winner over hurdles at Sedgefield and Wetherby, he is rated 119 and, while we are still getting to know him, handicap hurdles will be on his agenda.

KARAMOKO (IRE) 7 b g Manduro (GER) – Virevolle (FR)
Still a maiden over hurdles, he has been consistent and will find his own level. Third at Ayr last time, he doesn't want extremes of ground with two and a half miles on good to soft being his optimum conditions. He will continue over hurdles.

KILCOOLEY (IRE) 10 b g Stowaway – Bealaha Essie (IRE)
Charlie Longsdon did a very good job with him because he's a trainer's challenge. A giant of a horse, he is very good but brittle. We have had a few hold ups with him but he showed in the Rendlesham Hurdle at Haydock last season that he retains a lot of ability finishing third. A strong traveller and good jumper, I think we will keep him over hurdles and aim him at the conditions races.

KITTY HALL (IRE) 5 b m Fame And Glory – Set In Her Ways (IRE)
She ran in the same mares' bumper at Kelso as Headscarf Lil and Highland Gold and I thought she would be the pick of trio. I have always liked her and I still do, despite the fact she only finished third. A very well bred mare, she came back from Kelso with an abscess in her foot and that may explain her performance, although she didn't run badly. She will have another run in a mares' bumper.

LANTY SLEA (IRE) 4 b g Beat Hollow – Catleen (IRE)
A grand sort, he is a nice horse we bought in Ireland last winter. Big and weak when he first arrived, he has done well during the summer and will be running in a bumper in the Autumn/ early winter. He belongs to Langdale Bloodstock.

LEGAL BEAGLE 4 b g Rule of Law (USA) – Knockamullen Girl (IRE)
Another lovely unraced four year old with a very good pedigree. We bought him at the Tattersalls Ireland Sale in August last year and he is a half-brother to Carefully Selected, who was runner-up in the Cheltenham Festival bumper, and also dual bumper winner Midnight Run. He is the third one out of the mare so we are hoping he can continue the family tradition. He will start off in a bumper.

LOOKING WELL (IRE) 10 b g Gold Well – Different Level (IRE)
He must be one of the most unlucky horses in training. Two seasons ago, he was all set to win the Edinburgh National at Musselburgh when swerving and unseating his rider going to the last and, then last season, I think he would have won the Borders National at Kelso but fell three out. He won a veterans' chase at Doncaster in February and went back there the following month for the Grimthorpe Handicap Chase and Aidan (Coleman) felt he still had a chance when coming down at the last. He picked up an injury that day and therefore won't be back in action until January. Rated 142, I think he could be a Grand National horse because he travels and stays and prefers nice ground. Good to soft is probably ideal.

MAROWN (IRE) 5 b g Milan – Rosie Suspect (IRE)
From the family of Cannington Brook, he is another one of Mr Hemmings' and is a lovely big strapping horse and typical of one of his. Measuring 17hh, he is not a bumper horse but it didn't stop him from winning one on his debut at Newcastle last March. He lobbed round for most of the race before showing signs of greenness. However, the penny dropped late on and he won going away in the end. Brian (Hughes) loved him and he is one for a National Hunt novice hurdle over two and a half miles. He is a staying type.

MAYO STAR (IRE) 7 b g Stowaway – Western Whisper (IRE)
A full-brother to Outlander, he has yet to run for us having won a bumper and run well over hurdles for the late Malcolm Jefferson. Off the track for nearly two years, he has had a few problems but his form is good and he remains a novice over hurdles.

MISS MILANO (IRE) 4 b f Milan – Dewasentah (IRE)
Unraced, she is a classy looking filly by Milan who we bought in Ireland in August last year. Malcolm Jefferson trained the dam and she is related to the likes of Issaquah and Kings Measure. She is a grand filly and will run in a mares' bumper in the Autumn.

MY OLD GOLD (IRE) 9 b m Gold Well – Tenbo (IRE)
She is a good mare who is very honest and never runs a bad race. A former winning Irish pointer, she jumps well and was progressive over fences last season winning at Wetherby and Perth. The Listed mares' chase at the latter venue in April had been the plan for a while and she is now a black type winner, which makes her valuable. There aren't that many races for her during the first half of the season but we could aim her at mares' chases, including another Listed event over two and a half miles at Carlisle (1st December). Two and a half miles on soft ground is fine but she stays well, too, with three miles on better ground suiting her as well. Very consistent, she is a nine year old but she didn't start racing until she was seven.

NELLS SON 4 b g Trans Island – Miss Nellie (IRE)
An unraced half-brother to Amberose and Rubytwo, who have both won for us, this is the third foal. A nice big strong horse, he has plenty of size and will start off in a bumper.

NO REGRETS (IRE) 5 b g Presenting – E Mac (IRE)
A very nice horse who we bought as a three year old in Ireland. We have purposely given him plenty of time and I thought he would run well on his debut in a bumper at the Scottish National meeting. I told Craig (Nichol) not to give him too hard a race and he stayed on well in fourth. It was the perfect introduction and it did him the world of good because he came out of the race bouncing. There is plenty more to come from him and we will find a suitable two miles novice hurdle to begin with.

ON A PROMISE (IRE) 7 gr g Definite Article – Silvers Promise (IRE)
Did well the previous year winning three times over hurdles. However, he had his problems last season and missed the whole campaign. Back trotting now, he has grown into a fine big horse and we will send him chasing this time around. Rated 120, he will be aimed a novices' handicap chase and I hope he will continue to improve.

REIVERS LAD 8 b g Alflora (IRE) – Reivers Moon
He won on his chasing debut at Newcastle in December but then had a little problem which sidelined him for the rest of the season. I think he is a high-class horse and, while he lacks experience over fences, he is a big hardy horse who will run in handicaps off a mark of 132. Even though he looks like a three miler, he wants two miles on soft ground. I have been pleased with him during the summer and we are looking forward to seeing him back on a racecourse.

RIBBLE VALLEY (IRE) 6 b g Westerner – Miss Greinton (GER)
A very nice horse who bolted up in two of his three bumpers. We thought it would take a good horse to beat him first time out at Ayr and he duly won well. We then took him to Cheltenham for a Listed bumper a fortnight later but it was a messy race and he finished sixth. He had the subsequent Grade 2 Aintree bumper winner McFabulous back in seventh. Back on track at Ayr in January, there was no point going hurdling at that stage of the season so we gave him time to mature. He will go straight over hurdles now and, while I think he will handle soft ground, I would say good to soft is ideal. Quick enough for two miles, he is a lovely horse.

SHE'S A ROCCO (IRE) 4 b f Shirocco (GER) – Hannigan's Lodger (IRE)
Bought in Ireland last year, she is a grand unraced filly who, like all my youngsters, has had a racecourse gallop. A half-sister to Leave At Dawn, she will run in a mares' bumper and is a nice filly.

SIMPLY NED (IRE) 12 ch g Fruits of Love (USA) – Bishops Lass (IRE)
He is in great form at home and, even though we brought him back in two weeks earlier than normal, it has taken a while to get the weight off him. He has been a fantastic horse for us over the years winning the Grade 1 at Leopardstown over Christmas for the second time last winter. He was due to contest another Grade 1 at the same track in February but we think he banged his knee in the stable over there and it came up like a tennis ball. He has always shown his best form during the first half of the season and it will be a similar campaign starting off at Kelso (6th October), a race he has contested for the last five years. He will then go to Cheltenham for the Shloer Chase (17th November), which he has also run in for the last five years, before returning to Leopardstown at Christmas.

SKIDDAW VALLEYS 7 ch g Three Valleys (USA) – Skiddaw Wolf
Very consistent, he won over hurdles at Perth in May and remains a novice for this season. Runner-up on his three previous runs, he was unfortunate not to win more having bumped into some good horses. He stays two and a half miles but Brian (Hughes) feels he is effective over a strongly run two miles.

TAKING FLIGHT (IRE) 5 b g Stowaway – Cailin Vic Mo Cri (IRE)
A proper staying type, he ran well in both his starts in bumpers last season. Green on his debut at Carlisle, he finished well in third and then next time at Perth, he didn't get the clearest of runs before staying on. I thought he showed plenty of encouragement in both races. From a staying family, he will go hurdling and wants a trip.

TAKING RISKS (IRE) 10 b g Golden Tornado (IRE) – Downtown Rosie (IRE)
He has done us proud throughout his career and it was brilliant to see him win the Scottish National at Ayr last spring. He won over hurdles at Ayr in November and then Danny McMenamin had his first ride over fences on him at Haydock but, despite running well in second, we thought he might have lost his confidence a bit. Third in the Rowland Meyrick Chase at Wetherby over Christmas, he was disappointing next time at Newcastle. Ryan Day rode him that day and felt he would benefit from being fitted with cheekpieces and duly won next time at Carlisle in a veterans' chase. The Scottish National was the obvious next target and he was in tremendous form beforehand and it went like clockwork. He jumped and travelled and crept into contention. A four lengths winner, he stays well and has always been a very good jumper. I am keen to aim him at the Grand National but I need to persuade his owner, who hasn't always been a fan of the race. If we go down that route, the plan will be to run him over hurdles beforehand.

UNCLE ALASTAIR 7 b g Midnight Legend – Cyd Charisse
I thought if we had a Graded horse last season it would be him as a novice chaser. I was delighted with his chasing debut at Carlisle finishing runner-up behind Vinndication over two and a half miles, especially as he took a blow. Unfortunately, he had a setback afterwards and hasn't run since. He has spent the summer with Jason Maguire and, all being well, he will be back in action around November/December time. He is 100% and at least he remains a novice for this season, unlike Reivers Lad. Although he is quick enough for two and a half, I think three miles is his trip.

UNIVERSAL FOLLY 4 b g Universal (IRE) – Madam Jolie (IRE)
Bought in Ireland as a three year old, he is another nice unraced horse who will run in a bumper during the Autumn. His work has been good and I like him.

WESTERN RULES (IRE) 9 b g Westerner – Ryehill Lady (IRE)
A good consistent horse who won over fences at Kelso in January. I think he wants two and a half miles on a galloping track in a bog but he rarely got his conditions last season. We have tried him over three miles over fences last season but it stretches him. Two miles six is OK. Still lightly raced over fences, he will hopefully improve again.

WILHELM VONVENSTER (FR) 5 b g Apsis – Princesse Gaelle
Owned by Mr & Mrs Ricci, he was very green on his debut in a bumper at Newcastle but Brian (Hughes) liked him. A few of my horses were affected by the injections we had to give them following the bout of equine flu and he was one of them. Returning over hurdles at Perth in May, he raced with the choke out and didn't get home. He is better than he showed that day and hopefully he will make his mark over hurdles this season.

Unnamed 4 b g Milan – So Proper (IRE)
He is a lovely unraced four year old we bought at the Tattersalls Ireland August Sale last year. From the family of Chomba Womba and Island Chief, he will start off in a bumper and is a nice horse.

Unnamed 4 b g Califet (FR) – Salsaparilla (FR)
Another nice unraced four year old we acquired in Ireland in August last year. Well bred, I like him and he is another who will be going down the bumper route.

TRAINER'S HORSE TO FOLLOW: TAKING FLIGHT

BROMLEY'S BEST BUYS

The *Highflyer Bloodstock* team of Anthony Bromley, David Minton and Tessa Greatrex had another cracking season in 2018/2019 with **12 winners** (including 7 at Grade 1 level) at the three Spring Festivals of Cheltenham, Aintree and Punchestown. Their highlights included the victories of **ALTIOR**, **BUVEUR D'AIR**, **FRODON**, **PENTLAND HILLS** and **TOPOFTHEGAME**. Indeed, probably the pick of their season's achievements was buying the first three home in the Queen Mother Champion Chase – **ALTIOR** coming home in front of **POLITOLOGUE** and **SCEAU ROYAL**.

Bromley's Best Buys produced **22 winners** in last year's *One Jump Ahead* including **DR SANDERSON (3 wins), LAKE VIEW LAD (8/1 & 5/1), MILLARVILLE (7/1)** and **THE GLANCING QUEEN (16/1 & 5/1)**. For the **TWENTIETH** consecutive year, Anthony Bromley has kindly put together a list of names he has bought in France and Ireland, who are set to make an impact in their new surroundings in the UK this winter.

ARCHIE BROWN (IRE) 5 b g Aizavoski (IRE) - Pure Beautiful (IRE)
Trainer: Paul NICHOLLS
Dr Sanderson won three times for Million In Mind and Paul Nicholls last season and he was bought by J.P. McManus to stay in the yard when the Partnership had to sell him in May. We have gone down a similar route for Paul's "Million" horse this time and purchased this grand looking scopey five year old from Stuart Crawford after showing plenty of promise in one of the bumpers at Perth's big Spring Festival. Stuart rated this horse quite highly beforehand and I am excited about what Paul might do with him.

CALVA D'AUGE (FR) 4 b g Air Chief Marshal (IRE) - Hill Ou Elle (FR)
Trainer: Paul NICHOLLS
A useful performer on the Flat as a two-year-old (rated 90), he showed some promise in France last winter as a juvenile hurdler. Indeed from a handful of runs he finished second on three occasions on all types of ground at Pau, Bordeaux and Toulouse. He could be a horse to start off in novice handicap hurdles over here at around two miles.

CAP DU MATHAN (FR) 4 b g Kapgarde (FR) Nounjya Du Mathan (FR)
Trainer: Paul NICHOLLS
I bought this son of the top French sire Kapgarde privately on behalf of The Stewart Family in the spring. A good looking youngster by the sire of Clan Des Obeaux, he showed tons of promise to be placed on both his starts at Auteuil before Christmas for Arnaud Chaille-Chaille. A second season Auteuil placed maiden with the scope for fences in time, he ticks all the right boxes and I have high hopes for him. I have had plenty of luck for The Stewart Family over the years with the likes of Big Buck's, Cenkos, My Will, Celestial Halo, Poquelin and Saphir Du Rheu and it would be great to think that this new addition might be a name we all remember in years to come.

DINO BOY (FR) 6 b g Diamond Boy (FR) - Odeline (FR)
Trainer: Nigel TWISTON-DAVIES
The Million In Mind horse at Nigel's this time is this rangy six year old who was purchased off Welsh point-to-point trainer Tom Faulkner at the Cheltenham May Sales. He had shown plenty of talent in his British points, prior to a great run to be a close second to Garry Clermont in the Aintree point-to-point bumper in mid-May. He has form on all types of ground and will start off in novice hurdles and may even go chasing in the spring, if Nigel decides that to be a good plan.

ECLAIR ON LINE (FR) 5 gr g Dream Well (FR) – Odeline (FR)
Trainer Charlie LONGSDON
Interestingly, this is the younger half-brother to the aforementioned Dino Boy, although they

do not look alike. This neat grey is more of a hurdling type in physique but really scooted clear to win his Irish maiden point-to-point on soft ground in mid-April on his second outing (having been seventh to Glynn on his debut). The second won next time and the third, Largy Nights, was also purchased by Tessie on behalf of Charlie Longsdon after he was second in his subsequent point. This £34,000 buy looked to represent value at the sales this spring and he certainly struck me as a likely type to be ready early this Autumn.

FANFARONADE (USA) 3 gr f Exchange Rate (USA) – Fanzine (USA)
Trainer: Charlie LONGSDON
I bought this big grey filly from Kirsten Rausing and John Gosden at the Tattersalls July Sales on behalf of the same owners (The Slater, Stockwood, Nicholson Partnership) who I found the smart but ill-fated Castafiore for at the same sale three years ago. She cost a similar amount too (£22,000) and, whilst she showed a bit of ability and stamina to be placed in three staying Flat maidens this spring, I am hoping she might improve a bit as she develops and strengthens to her rather massive frame.

FIDELIO VALLIS (FR) 4 b g Saint Des Saints (FR) - Quora Vallis (FR)
Trainer: Paul NICHOLLS
I acquired this grand stamp of a horse for long-standing client John Hales to join Paul Nicholls. I think one of the first horses I found for John was Azertyuiop and we have had plenty of success over the years with the likes of Neptune Collonges, the ill-fated but high-class Granit Jack and current Festival scorer Aux Ptits Soins. Realistically we may not see the best of this fellow for another year but he is definitely a horse to keep on the right side of.

FIN DU MATCH (FR) 4 b f Poliglote - Onde De Choc (FR)
Trainer: David COTTIN
Robert Waley-Cohen bought this filly earlier this year after she had won on her Pau hurdles debut in good style. She has won twice this summer in his colours, including impressively in a competitive handicap hurdle at Clairefontaine on her latest start in July. The plan is to now go to Auteuil this Autumn with her to hopefully gain some black type and, the longer-term aim, is to bring her to the UK. I imagine she will be joining a UK trainer once Auteuil closes for the winter in late November.

FRANKEUR (FR) 4 b g Khalkevi (IRE) – Razia (FR)
Trainer: Dan SKELTON
This half-brother to one of the stable's top novice chasers from last season, Destrier, showed plenty of promise to be third in both of his bumpers this spring in France. He was not beaten far by Fighter Allen (subsequently sold to Ireland) in May and also by a subsequent Grade 3 bumper winner on his debut in April.

FRATERNEL (FR) 4 b g Kap Rock (FR) – Valence (FR)
Trainer: Alan KING
This tall French gelding was bought on behalf of Tim Syder after a promising close third in the prestigious Alfred Torrance Hurdle at Pau in January. Alan decided not to run him this spring as the ground had firmed up but is looking forward to having a full season as a novice with him this time around.

GET PREPARED (GB) 4 b g Black Sam Bellamy (IRE) - Star Ar Aghaidh (IRE)
Trainer: Ben PAULING
I think Tessa Greatrex may have done a shrewd bit of buying when securing this easy UK winning pointer for £60,000 at the Aintree Sale. He comfortably beat a useful-looking field (13 ran) in soft ground with the 28 lengths third winning his next two starts.

GLYNN (IRE) 5 b g Winged Love (IRE) - Barnish River (IRE)
Trainer: Nicky HENDERSON
This is a big horse with plenty of quality who was purchased at the sale held on the evening of

Pentland Hills' Grade 1 success at Aintree. He was bought for Owners Group and I understand virtually everyone in the Champion Juvenile Hurdler signed up again for this fellow when it was opened up to the membership. I think they have done the right thing as I felt he was one of my most exciting point-to-point buys this year. I think he would have made more money at the sale if it had been possible to actually watch his easy Northern Irish point victory but, due to a glitch, no one could. The form of the race has worked out wonderfully well with four subsequent pointing winners coming out from behind him.

GRAND ROI (FR) 3 b g Spanish Moon (USA) - Ultra D'Anjou (FR)
Trainer: Nicky HENDERSON
A handsome French jumps-bred juvenile, this athletic type showed a nice bit of ability in two bumpers in April and May at a couple of the leading French bumper tracks of Vichy and Le Lion D'Angers. The form has a solid look to it already and, being by the same sire as Laurina and Dallas Des Pictons, I am very hopeful he will really come into his own once he goes over jumps. He will run in the Million In Mind colours.

GUENA DES MOTTES (FR) 3 b g Soave (GER) - Sara De Flee
Trainer: Ben PAULING
An interesting juvenile hurdler who narrowly won his only hurdles start at Fontainebleu in early April with the first two pulling nicely clear of the field. The well held fourth and fifth have both won a couple of races since. This attractive youngster will run in the Munir/Souede colours and has joined Ben Pauling, who did so well for the owners with his only two horses for them last season, Kildisart and Delire D'Estruval.

HACKSAW RIDGE (IRE) 4 b g Stowaway - Erins Lass (IRE)
Trainer: Alan KING
The Cheltenham point-to-point sales have proved to be a happy hunting ground for Alan (King) and myself in recent years with the likes of Talkischeap, Alsa Mix, The Cull Bank and The Glancing Queen coming from only a small number of buys. The only purchase we made in 2019 is this smashing big youngster and, given the strength of the sales this spring, he did not appear to be too expensive with a price tag of £60,000. He had in fact cost €50,000 as a store and was backed off the boards to make a winning point-to-point debut in early March. He led to three out that day but then weakened out of it. He came back with a nasty abscess behind and his trainer Richard Black faced a race against time to get him back on the track this season. He managed it on the 26th May and, even though he was only workmanlike in victory, we are strongly of the opinion (as was his previous trainer) that he has a lot more talent under the bonnet than has been seen in public so far. We shall have to wait and see if we are correct.

IT SURE IS (IRE) 4 b g Shirocco (GER) - Stay At Home Mum (IRE)
Trainer: Nicky HENDERSON
David Minton bought this gorgeous big son of Shirocco at the Aintree Sale for Al Boum Photo's owner Mrs Joe Donnelly to join Nicky Henderson. He bravely made all to win his only point-to-point at the end of March from the Gigginstown owned Bloodstone with the front pair pulling well clear. His dam is a full-sister to Hennessy and a half-sister to Voler La Vedette, as well as being a half-sister to the dam of the promising Sishkin, who we also bought for the same connections.

LITTLE LIGHT (FR) 5 b m Walk In The Park (IRE) - Luna Rossa (IRE)
Trainer: Lucy WADHAM
We were keen on this mare when she came up for sale at the 2018 Aintree Sale, having been narrowly beaten in a four year old point by Tara West, but she made a lot more than we had her valued at the time. Roll forward a year and she popped up near the end of the Doncaster May Sale, as part of the Exors Dispersal Sale of Peter Magnier, having had a busy campaign under the tutelage of Joseph O'Brien. She had won her maiden hurdle at Sligo and was placed a further four times, including on her last start at Clonmel a week before the sales. A versatile sort

as regards trip and ground, I felt she could be placed to good effect in the UK off her handicap mark, given the amount of mares' races here and she is at the right yard, of Lucy Wadham's, from which to do just that.

LUST FOR GLORY (IRE) 6 b m Getaway (GER) - Maisie Presenting (IRE)
Trainer: Nicky HENDERSON
It was such a shame that Grech and Parkin decided to disperse their horses in May but we were particularly pleased to keep this mare at Seven Barrows for the future. Robert Waley-Cohen bought her at Doncaster and I have a real soft spot for this gorgeous-looking mare, as does Nicky. She looks tailor-made for mares' novice chases and hopefully she can develop into a serious contender for the following season's inaugural Cheltenham Festival mares' chase.

MADIBA PASSION (FR) 5 b g Al Namix (FR) – Birsheba (FR)
Trainer: Alan KING
Whilst this is not strictly a "new buy" he was acquired at the Cheltenham December Sale last year after his second win from three starts in Irish points from the same team who sold us Talkischeap. Whilst he did manage a couple of bumper starts this spring, I don't think we have seen the best of him yet and he is still a bit of a dark horse in my opinion. His staying on third at Kempton on his UK bumper debut was full of promise behind a couple of useful sorts and I don't believe he ran to form in the Listed bumper on his last run.

MISS MONDITO (IRE) 4 ch f Shirocco (GER) - Lillies Bordello (IRE)
Trainer: Tom LACEY
At only £8,000, this filly is the cheapest purchase in this particular selection but she does not know her price tag and I think she can win her share of races this season for her canny new handler, Tom Lacey. From three points starts, she finished fourth twice but that does not tell the whole tale as she was only just beaten on both those occasions. Indeed, on her debut she was only a length behind Pure Bliss who made €100,000 at the Punchestown Sale (to join Harry Fry). She was bought at the recent August Sale at Doncaster and I imagine Tom will try to have her out before the bigger guns start appearing.

SAINT D'OROUX (FR) 3 b g Saint Des Saints (FR) – Benghasi (FR)
Trainer: Gordon ELLIOTT
The form of his only hurdles start when a close second at Dieppe in May has worked out well, so I am hopeful he could prove a decent buy for the double green colours of Simon Munir and Isaac Souede. Seven individual winners came out of the race subsequently and the fourth-placed horse finished runner-up at Auteuil in early July to give some substance to it. However, it is still not top-class French form and he will need to progress from his debut effort. However, given his bloodlines and looks, I am reasonably confident that he will.

SHISHKIN (IRE) 5 b g Sholokhov (IRE) – Labarynth (IRE)
Trainer: Nicky HENDERSON
I am sure this grand type went into most people's notebooks after an impressive bumper win at Kempton at the end of Cheltenham Festival week. He was purchased by David Minton at the Cheltenham December Sale for the Donnelly's for £170,000 after a really impressive point-to-point win and, so far, he is looking worth the money as he does appear to be one of the most exciting youngsters at Seven Barrows. He is due to go novice hurdling.

TIMBERMAN (IRE) 4 b g Califet (FR) - Millrock Lady (IRE)
Trainer: Nicky HENDERSON
The son of Califet was bought on behalf of John Turner at the Cheltenham May Sale after running a race full of promise to be second to another exciting prospect in Kakamora (made £105,000 to join Emma Lavelle) in his only maiden point in mid-May. He was probably given a bit too much to do in the race by the trainers' jockey/brother, Ben Crawford, as they travelled supremely well throughout the race but it appeared that they allowed the leader just a bit too much rope up front as, despite staying on well, he was never closer than at the line.

TOMBEE DU CIEL (FR) 3 b f Zanzibari (USA) - In Caso Di Neve (FR)
Trainer: Nicky HENDERSON
A juvenile filly with plenty of scope, she posted three promising efforts over hurdles at Auteuil in the spring and luckily is still a maiden for the UK. Her best run was probably when she was a close runner-up on her second outing but she also posted another good performance when third in a Listed hurdle at the end of April, too. I suspect her first target will be the Listed juvenile fillies' hurdle at Aintree (7th December).

TRIO FOR RIO (IRE) 6 b g Getaway (GER) - Rio Trio (IRE)
Trainer: Warren GREATREX
Trio For Rio proved a grand buy for the Million In Mind Partnership, winning twice over hurdles last season for Warren (Greatrex). The trainer clearly liked him as his wife Tessa bought him at the Million In Mind Dispersal at Goffs May Sales at Doncaster for Trevor Hemmings, to return to Uplands. He should do well in staying novice chases this time around.

WHEESHT (IRE) 5 b m Scorpion (IRE) - Retain That Magic (IRE)
Trainer: Oliver SHERWOOD
The last four horses trained by Oliver Sherwood for the Million In Mind Partnership have all been sourced from the Crawford Brothers Academy in Northern Ireland and all four have been successful, namely Got The Nac, The Organist, Toberdowney and last season the dual winner Millarville. Wheesht won her only mares' maiden point in decent style in late February in soft ground and subsequently the second, third and fifth placed mares all won a point. I imagine she will be aimed at mares' novice hurdles this winter.

WILD MAX (GER) 4 b g Maxios – Wildfahrte (GER)
Trainer: Paul NICHOLLS
Wild Max is an interesting big, ex-Flat German horse that we picked up at the Arqana February Sales. An expensive yearling, he looked well above-average as a two year old, winning on his debut as well as finishing third in a Group 3 in Germany. He did not manage to cut much ice in the German Classic Trials in the spring of his three year old season and was gelded last summer. He took a while to get over the gelding operation but won again last Autumn over ten furlongs. I am hoping he can win his share of two mile novice hurdles this season.

ZAMBELLA (FR) 4 b g Zambezi Sun – Visby (FR)
Trainer: Nigel TWISTON-DAVIES
A winner of three of her five starts on the Flat and over hurdles in France, she was purchased at the Auteuil Sale held over the Grand Steeplechase weekend in May. She is unbeaten in both her starts over hurdles at Compiegne and Fontainebleau and looks like the sort who will enjoy racing at around two miles in the UK. She remains a novice hurdler until the end of October, and therefore may start off in that company. She has the size to go novice chasing but that may wait until next season once she has got some more racing experience under her belt.

HIGHFLYER BLOODSTOCK'S HORSE TO FOLLOW: CAP DU MATHAN

For all the latest news and how to get involved in the
Million In Mind partnership, please visit
www.millioninmind.co.uk

CHANGING CODES

The following feature highlights a selection of Flat horses set to go jumping for the first time this winter who will, hopefully, prove profitable to follow.

Syndicate **Axom** paid 32,000gns for the former Charlie Fellowes trained **DIVINE GIFT** at the Newmarket July Sales this summer. The gelded son of Nathaniel has joined **Iain Jardine** and it is hoped he will develop into a useful dual purpose horse for his new connections. Rated 81 on the Flat, he won over a mile at Windsor (Soft) last October and has run creditably in three starts in 2019. Fourth behind the progressive Moon King at Haydock (1m 6f : Heavy) in June, he was third behind Calculation (won again since) over the same distance at Doncaster last time. He stays well and handles testing ground and ought to make a useful northern juvenile hurdler.

ELYSIAN FLAME has only raced half a dozen times on Flat but he already has a Lanark Silver Bell on his CV having trounced twelve rivals by upwards of three and a half lengths at Hamilton (1m 4f : Heavy) in late August. **Mick Easterby**'s Champs Elysees gelding won in similar conditions over a mile at Haydock last Autumn as a juvenile and revels in the mud. He stepped up to a mile and six in a valuable three year old handicap at Haydock in September and finished a good third off a mark of 88. Owned by partnership by **Imperial Racing**, of Imperial Commander fame, he is set to go juvenile hurdling this season and ought to be a force to be reckoned with. He could be the best jumper the Sheriff Hutton handler has trained for sometime. The same connections are also responsible for the thrice raced **DREAMS AND VISIONS**. A three year old gelding by Archipenko, he was fourth over a mile at Newcastle in January before catching the eye over ten furlongs at Doncaster in August. Fifth behind the subsequent Melrose Stakes runner-up First In Line (rated 100), the form looks strong with the second (Wise Ruler), fourth (Gabrials Boy) and seventh (Hermosura) winning since. Rated 67, he is capable of winning on the Flat before sent hurdling. Yet to race beyond ten furlongs, he will improve again when tackling further.

GALILEO SILVER is a horse I have followed since he made an eyecatching racecourse debut for Roger Charlton at Windsor (1m 2f : Good) during the summer of last year. Beaten a length and a quarter, the gelded son of Galileo was then absent for 346 days and transferred to **Alan King**. Well held on fast ground on his reappearance at Salisbury in May, he was then fourth at Sandown (1m 2f : Good/Soft) the following month. Stepped up to a mile and three for his handicap debut at Kempton, the four year old stayed on strongly to lead close home by a half a length off a mark of 80. Bought for 155,000gns as a yearling, he is a full-brother to Aidan O'Brien's 115 rated three year old Il Paradiso. Rated 84, he wants cut in the ground and his trainer feels he will develop into a smart novice hurdler this season.

I suspect it won't happen this winter but I sincerely hope **MICRO MANAGE** is sent hurdling. A three year old by Rip Van Winkle who cost €20,000 as a yearling, he beat subsequent Royal Ascot winner South Pacific (rated 109) by four and a quarter lengths at Tipperary (1m 1f : Soft) last October with his rider Rachel Blackmore saying: **"He has plenty of size about him and he has a really nice attitude."** Purchased by **Merriebelle Irish Farm Limited**, Willie Mullins' three year old made a mockery of his opening handicap mark of 91 when annihilating five rivals by upwards of a dozen lengths at the Curragh (1m 4f : Good/Yielding) in early June. Sent off evens favourite, he led over a furlong out before stretching clear. **"The ground was a worry as he's a big, heavy horse who hits the ground hard and he wouldn't have run only for the rain that fell the other day. He's a brilliant jumper. I actually schooled him myself last year, but I'd imagine jumping will be shelved for the time being,"** remarked stable representative David Casey afterwards. Rated 108, he could be top-class over hurdles.

Despite the fact they are reducing their string, I am hoping **Paul and Clare Rooney** elect to send **MIND THE CRACK** over hurdles this winter. Bought for €34,000 as a yearling, the Jukebox Jury gelding has won two of his eight starts on the level for **Mark Johnston** and is rated 91. Following three creditable runs last year, he has improved since stepping up to middle distances as a three year old. A dual winner at Lingfield (1m 3f : Good/Firm) and Haydock (1m 4f : Heavy), he won by an aggregate of eight lengths before being narrowly beaten by stablemate Sir Ron Priestley in a valuable handicap at the latter track (1m 6f) in July. Fifth on his next two outings at Ascot and Goodwood, he handles any ground and has the attributes to make a very useful juvenile hurdler.

Donald McCain is understandably excited about the prospect of unleashing **NAVAJO PASS** over hurdles this season. Bought for 68,000gns as a yearling at the Tattersalls Book 3 sale in 2017, he is by Nathaniel and relishes soft ground. Rated 85, he was third on his sole run last year at Redcar. Stepped up to a mile and a half plus this time around, the **Tim Leslie** owned gelding was runner-up at both Haydock and Ripon in novice events. Beaten a length and a quarter by the 139 rated hurdler Beyond The Clouds at the latter track, he appreciated the step up to a mile and six on his handicap debut at Carlisle (Good/Soft) in August. A short head winner from Celestial Force, he has reportedly schooled well and can develop into a high-class juvenile hurdler. There is a maiden juvenile hurdle at Bangor (13th November), which could be an ideal starting point.

Philip Hobbs has won the Triumph Hurdle on three occasions (Made In Japan (2004), Detroit City (2006) and Defi Du Seuil (2017)) and he will be hoping he has another live candidate in new recruit **RAGNAR**. A gelded son of Toronado, he was purchased for 85,000gns at the Newmarket July Sales having won two of his five races on the Flat. Unraced at two, he won over nine furlongs at Wolverhampton in March when trained by Dominic Ffrench-Davis and was a gutsy winner in testing conditons at Sandown (1m 2f : Soft) in June when under the guidance of Roger Charlton. A nose winner, he beat Rhythmic Intent (won by four lengths at Newbury since and is rated 84) off a mark of 77. Unexposed, he handles slow ground and isn't devoid of speed either, plus he has displayed a willing attitude.

County Tyrone based handler **Andy Oliver** trained Champion Chase winner Dodging Bullets, dual Grade 1 novice hurdler Long Dog and Grade 1 runner-up Bunk Off Early during their Flat racing careers. The last two named were subsequently sold to Willie Mullins and it wouldn't be a surprise to see his impressive Naas winner **THOU ART PETER** jumping hurdles at some stage. A big tall powerful looking three year old by Es Que Love, he didn't make his racecourse debut until August when he ran away with a ten furlongs maiden by six and a half lengths. Sent off 40/1 and ridden by Billy Lee, he led over a furlong out and stretched away. Subsequently given an entry in a Group 3 contest at Leopardstown over a mile and a half, he certainly has the size and scope for jumping.

Another potentially high-class jumper in the making trained by **Alan King**, **TRUESHAN** looks well bought at 31,000gns. A gelded son of Planteur, he finished sixth at Nottingham on his only outing as a two year old last season. Stepped up to a mile and a half this summer, he hasn't looked back since winning twice at Wolverhampton and Ffos Las (Good) and finishing third in a competitive handicap at Haydock (1m 6f) in September off a mark of 91. His trainer excels with his juvenile hurdlers and he may have another very good one on his hands. He appreciates ease in the ground and stays well.

Gary Moore does well with his juvenile hurdlers and it will be no surprise if **WHISTLER BOWL** is sent down that route. A half-sister to former stablemate and dual hurdles winner Whitby Jack, the Mukhadram filly won on her handicap debut at Lingfield (1m 3f : Good/Firm) by nearly four lengths in June off an opening mark of 57. She showed her versatility in terms of ground when failing by three parts of a length to beat four times winner and Melrose Stakes third Land of Oz (rated 84) at Salisbury (1m 6f : Good/Soft) off a seven pounds higher mark in August. Runner-up again over two miles at Goodwood eight days later, she is rated 66 and is a strong stayer.

ENGLISH POINTERS

My *Racing TV* colleague and English point-to-point guru **Jonathan Neesom** has once again kindly put together a list of horses which caught his eye 'between the flags' in the UK last winter/spring. During the last couple of seasons, he has unearthed the likes of **CAPTAIN CATTISTOCK, INTERCONNECTED, KING ROLAND** and **SANTINI**. A number of those discussed feature in the *Talking Trainers* section of *One Jump Ahead*, plus some extra names, and they are set to race under Rules for the first time this season.

BLEUE AWAY (Anthony Honeyball): "Another mare, the five year old Bleue Away ran twice from the Rowley yard, winning a point bumper on soft ground in March and a two and a half miles maiden at Eyton the following month, making all both times. In her point win, she jumped soundly and recorded a similar time to the smart Now Ben on the same card. She has been sold for £60,000 and has joined Anthony Honeyball."

BLOSSOMING FORTH (Ruth Jefferson): "The pointing season of 2018/9 was affected by quick ground and small fields, which makes assessing some of the horses that will graduate to racing under Rules even more tricky than usual. Blossoming Forth beat just two rivals when making her only appearance over two and a half miles at Eyton-on-Severn in May. The ease of the four year old's victory and her breeding (she is a sister to chase winner Beg To Differ) saw her sold to Ruth Jefferson for £130,000 later that month. She should stay well and is the first of four horses in this list who ran in points for Philip Rowley, who trained Hazel Hill to win the Cheltenham Foxhunter in March."

CADZAND (Dan Skelton): "The meeting at Charlton Horethorne in March, run on soft ground, figures prominently in this list. Cadzand made a winning debut over three miles, romping home from nine rivals. The form may be modest but the style was impressive. This four year old from the Lacey academy is related to several winners and has been bought privately to join Dan Skelton to race under Rules."

DINO BOY (Nigel Twiston-Davies): "Beaten at Woodford on his debut in April 2018, the six year old fell on his next appearance in December. Returning to the scene of his initial effort, twelve months later, he scored in ready fashion and then ran very well when runner-up in the Aintree point bumper in May. Sold for £50,000 after that, he will race for Nigel Twiston-Davies under rules."

DOES HE KNOW (Kim Bailey): "The four year old made a winning debut for Cherry Coward at Charm Park in April. In a race run at no great pace (comfortably the slowest time on the card), he quickened best to win narrowly but decisively. Out of a dam that won over hurdles and fences, Does He Know made £38,000 at the Cheltenham Sales later that month and has joined Kim Bailey."

FLAMBOYANT JOYAUX (Sue Smith): "Beaten in a point bumper in March, the four year old gelded son of Crossharbour reappeared seven weeks later to make a successful debut over point fences at Knightwick, beating four rivals easily (tended to jump slightly to the right). Another from the Rowley yard, this half-brother to a winning French hurdler was sold for £30,000 at the Doncaster Spring Sales in May and has joined Sue Smith."

GET PREPARED (Ben Pauling): "So many maidens are won by the major pointing yards that it must seem a thankless task for smaller operators to compete, so it's good to include this four year old gelding by Black Sam Bellamy. Owned and trained by Shropshire-based Michelle Offen, he was sent on the long journey to Charlton Horethorne (near Wincanton) in March and landed a division of the two and a half miles maiden, in the process registering a quicker time than Presence Of Mind (qv). The win was gained in good style and he made £60,000 when sold at the Aintree April Sale the following month and has joined Ben Pauling."

HEREDITARY RULE (Gordon Elliott): "Beaten on his debut at Kimble in April, the four year old made amends the following month at Edgcote, beating five rivals in comfortable fashion. Trained by Francesca Nimmo, he rather disproves the theory that selling pointing winners is a guaranteed way to make money, having cost £19,000 in May 2018 but fetching just £15,000 a year later. While the form of his two runs may not be exceptional, he has joined Gordon Elliott."

NEVILLE'S CROSS (Tom Lacey): "Bought for €52,000 as a three year old, Neville's Cross ran just once in points, at Tabley in April. All went to plan until he slipped up on the sharp bend approaching two out, when he was poised to challenge and looking very likely to win. Compensation awaits under rules with Tom Lacey."

PRESENCE OF MIND (Olly Murphy): "Another winner at Charlton Horethorne in March, this four year old took a division of the two and a half miles maiden (for Francesca Nimmo) in decisive style, beating among others the subsequent smart hunter chase winner Earth Leader. Four days later, he was sold at the Cheltenham Festival sale for £70,000 and has joined Olly Murphy. Out of a half-sister to the high-class Albertas Run, it will be disappointing if he cannot make his mark under rules."

RAMILLIES (Willie Mullins): "Despite looking quite raw on his debut at Bishops Court in March, on soft ground, this Sophie Lacey-trained four year old beat thirteen opponents very comfortably. A half-brother to winning chaser Miss Yeats, the Shantou gelding attracted plenty of interest when sent to the sales eleven days later, fetching £215,000. He has joined Willie Mullins and his future should be followed closely."

RED NIKA (Tom Lacey): "Bought for €50,000 as a three year old, Red Nika took the first step towards justifying that price tag when making a winning debut over three miles at Woodford in April (six ran, left clear at the final fence but was well in command at the time). Another from the Lacey yard, his pedigree suggests that trips short of three miles might suit under rules."

SWITCH HITTER (Paul Nicholls): "The maiden at Maisemore Park in April, despite having a dozen runners, looked short on quality beforehand. Switch Hitter, a four year old gelding by Scorpion from the Nimmo yard, started favourite but had to work fairly hard to reel in the leader in the closing stages and then showed signs of inexperience once hitting the front. For all that, the placed horses subsequently franked the form and the time was the fastest of the day. That, aligned to an attractive pedigree, saw him make £120,000 at the Cheltenham Sale later that month. He has joined Paul Nicholls."

TEA CLIPPER (Tom Lacey): "Early season maidens at Larkhill have proved the setting for some of the prime four year old prospects from the Lacey yard in recent years - but not anymore. The three meetings that took place in January and February at the track excluded four year olds, so when Tea Clipper made his debut in February, he had to tackle more seasoned rivals in the restricted (winners of one). Despite showing inexperience, the Stowaway gelding was eventually well on top at the finish. Related to several winners, including useful chaser Rathlin Rose, his progress should be noted carefully, given the yard's record with horses at the course."

THE COMPOSEUR (Jonjo O'Neill): "Beaten on his debut in February, The Composeur made no mistake over two and a half miles at Brampton Bryan the following month, beating five rivals with a degree of ease. The form is ordinary (the placed horses failed to win subsequently) but this Rowley-trained half-brother to winning hurdler Secret Reprieve fetched £72,000 at the Aintree April Sale and has joined Jonjo O'Neill."

THE GREATER GOOD (Paul Nicholls): "You could be forgiven for having reservations about this four year old son of Tiger Groom. Hooded for his debut at (the now defunct) Littlewindsor in April, he beat nothing of note and ploughed through the final fence. However, the time was good and he was never out of second gear to win by twenty five lengths. How he will fare under rules is a matter of guesswork but no doubt Paul Nicholls will ensure he is given every chance to show his worth."

WHATEVA NEXT (George Bewley): "Just six runners contested the maiden at Guilsborough in April but the race had the distinct feel of being above average. Victory went to the Nimmo-trained four year old newcomer Whateva Next, who showed a good attitude to beat two promising types that chased him home. By Dubai Destination, he is related to several winners, including Idle Talk and useful hurdler Smart Talk, and was bought by Jonathon Bewley later that month for £53,000. With luck, he can confirm the good impression he made when appearing under rules."

JONATHAN'S HORSES TO FOLLOW: RAMILLIES

Please see pages 187-194
for details of the

One Jump Ahead Updates

Don't forget to read my Diary @

www.mhpublications.couk

FRENCH REVOLUTION

Last year's article produced **19 winners** from 90 runners (21%), including Cheltenham Festival winners **A PLUS TARD** and **KLASSICAL DREAM** and Listed/Graded winners **ALLAHO, ELFILE, ELIMAY** and **FRENCH MADE**, plus **AUTHORIZO (4/1), ÉCLAIR DE BEAUFEU (2 wins)** and **EMBRUN MITJA (14/1)**. In previous years, subsequent ill-fated Champion Hurdle winner **ESPOIR D'ALLEN** and five times Grade 1 and dual Festival winner **DEFI DU SEUIL** were unearthed in this feature, too. The following will hopefully prove exciting recruits for their new connections, none of which have yet raced in either Britain or Ireland. Largely unknown, some of them may develop into household names in years to come.

For the first time, a number of the write-ups have been accompanied by comments from former French champion jockey **James Reveley**. Son of former trainer Keith, James has ridden 11 Grade 1 winners in France, including the Grand Steeple-Chase de Paris in three successive years (2016, 2017, 2018), plus the Grande Course de Haies d'Auteuil aboard the David Pipe trained Un Temps Pour Tout in 2015.

ARAMAX (GER) 3 b g Maxios – Aramina (GER)
Bought for €16,000 as a yearling at the BBAG October Sale at Baden Baden, he is a half-brother to Willie Mullins' Grade 1 winning novice hurdler Aramon. Trained in France by Guillaume Macaire, he finished third on his debut at Dieppe (Very Soft) in May behind Resplendour before winning by five lengths at Vittel (Good/Soft). The runner-up finished second again next time. Subsequently bought by **J.P.McManus**, he is set to join a UK yard but the trainer hadn't been decided, at the time of writing (early September).
Reveley's remarks: **"He was very green on his debut but won well next time. It wasn't a great race but we have always liked him and his work has been good. He ought to do well in juvenile hurdles before making a nice chaser one day."**

BURNING VICTORY (FR) 3 b f Nathaniel (IRE) – M'Oubliez Pas (USA)
A daughter of Nathaniel who cost €80,000 as a yearling, she raced five times on the Flat for Stephane Wattel winning by three and a half lengths at Chantilly (1m 4f : Soft) in May. Placed twice prior to that at Fontainebleau (1m 3f : Heavy) and Saint-Cloud (1m 4f : Soft), she was sixth in the Group 3 Prix de Royaumont at Chantilly (1m 4f : Good) in June behind the unbeaten Pelligrina. Owned by **Mrs Audrey Turley**, she has joined **Willie Mullins** and will go juvenile hurdling.

CAT TIGER (FR) 5 b g Diamond Boy (FR) – Miss Canon (FR)
Forty one year old amateur jockey and owner **David Maxwell** paid €180,000 for the Diamond Boy gelding at the Arqana Sale in November and he joined **Paul Nicholls** during the summer. Previously handled by Dominique Bressou, he has won four times over fences, including two Grade 3 chases. Indeed, Maxwell was on board when he won the Grade 3 Prix Morgex at Auteuil (2m 6f : Heavy) in late November. Prior to that, the five year old had finished fourth in a Grade 1 at the same track. Still a novice over hurdles (6275), he will be campaigned over timber this winter, possibly starting off in the Grade 2 Persian War Novices' Hurdle at Chepstow (11th October).

COUPDEBOL (FR) 4 gr g Rajsaman (FR) – Chance Bleue (FR)
A length and three quarters third on his only run over hurdles at Compiegne (2m 2f : Very Soft) in April, he was trained by David Cottin and was subsequently bought by owners **Tim Syder** and **Terry Warner** and has joined **Tom George**.
Reveley's remarks: **"A big strong grey horse, I rode him at Compiegne and he ran well. He came to win his race but made a mistake at the last. His schooling hadn't been great at home but he has ability and the English style hurdles will suit him better. Capable of winning races, he is a chaser in the making."**

EAGLE MOON (FR) 5 b g Spanish Moon (USA) – Perla Des Pres (FR)
Owned by **Robcour** and trained by **Henry De Bromhead**, he raced twice in APQS Flat races last October. Handled by Augustin De Boisbrunet, the Spanish Moon gelding was narrowly denied on his second outing at Saumur (2m). Bought soon afterwards, he has been given time to mature and will go hurdling for his new connections.

ECHOES IN RAIN (FR) 3 bb f Authorized (IRE) – Amarantine (FR)
A €30,000 yearling purchase, she raced five times on the Flat for Ludovic Gadbin winning twice. Both victories were gained over a mile and a quarter at Argentan in September last year and, most recently, at Angers (Very Soft) in May. A two and a half lengths winner from the Aga Khan's Shafia, the runner-up was fifth in a Listed contest next time. Subsequently bought by **Barnane Stud**, she has joined **Willie Mullins** and her sire has already produced the likes of Nichols Canyon and Tiger Roll. Juvenile hurdling will be on her agenda this winter.

FAN FAN LA TULIPE (FR) 4 b g Cokoriko (FR) – Tinapalo (FR)
Owner **John Turner** has the useful mare and Royal Ascot runner-up Buildmeupbuttercup in training with **Willie Mullins** and the pair are responsible for this APQS Flat winner. Trained in France by Pascal Journiac, he was a two lengths winner from Fidelio Vallis at Saint-Malo (1m 4f: Soft) in August last year. The runner-up filled the same position over hurdles at Auteuil in April and was subsequently bought by John Hales to join Paul Nicholls (the third has won over hurdles since, too). This four year old by Cokoriko could be smart and is one to follow in novice hurdles.

FANION D'ESTRUVAL (FR) 4 b g Enrique – Urfe D'Estruval (FR)
James (Reveley) recommended I included this four year old who has been bought to race in the UK but, at the time of writing, I don't know who is training him. Handled in France by Guillaume Macaire, he has won four of his five career starts and is unbeaten over fences. A two lengths winner on his chasing debut at Toulouse (2m 1f : Good/Soft) in June, the Enrique gelding then followed up by seven lengths at Auteuil (2m 1f : Very Soft) in early July. Still a novice over fences, he will be forced to carry a double penalty, so Graded novice chases could be on his agenda.

FEU DU BRESIL (FR) 4 b g Blue Bresil (FR) – Polyfleur (FR)
Leading owners **Susannah and Rich Ricci** have been busy acquiring new talent and this gelded son of Blue Bresil shaped with plenty of promise on his sole outing over hurdles at Auteuil (2m 2f : Very Soft) last October. Trained by Yannick Fouin, he was beaten two and a half lengths by St Romain Du Derby. The third, fifth and seventh have won since and the fourth (Cap Du Mathan) was second next time and has joined Paul Nicholls. He looks a cracking novice hurdle prospect for **Willie Mullins** and is likely to prove Cheltenham Festival material.
Reveley's remarks: **"The form has worked out OK and it looked a decent race on paper."**

FIGAROC (FR) 4 bl g Masterstroke (USA) – Oxyna (FR)
Another **Ricci/Mullins** bound four year old who finished three parts of a length runner-up on his only hurdles run at Compiegne (2m 2f : Very Soft) in May. Handled by Joel Boisnard, he was beaten by the Francois Nicolle trained Fou Delice who had been placed at Auteuil beforehand. Gelded since, he is another for novice hurdles.

FILS SPIRITUEL (FR) 4 b g Presenting – Toque Rouge (FR)
A half-brother to Paul Nicholls' five times winner Copain De Classe, he was a neck winner of his only start at Ligniéres (1m 3f : Soft) in late April when trained by Nicolas De Lageneste (runner-up finished third next time). He was bought the following month on behalf of **Joe Donnelly** and is now at Closutton with **Willie Mullins**.

FONTAINE COLLONGES (FR) 4 b f Saddler Maker (IRE) – Saturne Collonges (FR)
The top lot at the Arqana Grand Steeple Auteuil Sale in May, she joined **Venetia Williams** for €180,000. The Saddler Maker filly raced three times in APQS bumper races for Fabrice Foucher finishing second on her debut at Saint-Brieuc (1m 4f) in October last year. Sixth next time in a Grade 3 event at Durtal the following month, she won by a length on her latest start at Le Lion D'Angers (1m 4f : Soft) in May. From the family of Grand National winner Neptune Collonges, agent Guy Petit said at the sale: **"She's a very attractive and well-bred filly. She didn't have much luck in her last race, but she won nonetheless. I followed her through her three-year-old career, and I think that she is improving with maturity."** Mares' novice hurdles will be the plan.

FOR LANGY (FR) 4 b g Day Flight – Jubilee II (FR)
David Maxwell also purchased this gelded son of Day Flight for €150,000 at the Arqana Sale in early July. Bought originally for €32,000 by Guy Cherel in November last year, he went into training with Anne-Sophie Pacault and won two out of two. A narrow winner on his debut on the Flat at Orleans (2m 1f : Good) in June, he then won by four and a half lengths on his jumping bow at Les Sables (2m 2f : Good/Soft). The runner-up Fredland won next time at Senonnes. Still a novice for this season, he looks a good addition to **Philip Hobbs'** yard.

FRANCO DE PORT (FR) 4 b g Coastal Path – Ruth (FR)
The Prix De L'Yonne hurdle at Auteuil (2m 1f : Heavy) in March has been won by Aux Ptits Soins (2014) and Blue Dragon (2015) in the past. The Gabriel Leenders trained Franco De Port was a most impressive thirteen lengths winner of the 2019 version. The runner-up Fred has been second again since and subsequently sold to the UK. Bought by **Michael D.Hankin**, he is the CEO of Brown Advisory, and while he is no longer a novice over hurdles, he looks a tremendous prospect.
Reveley's remarks: **"He sluiced up at Auteuil and I liked him a lot. He comes from a shrewd operation and looks to have a bright future."**

FRERE TUCK (FR) 4 bl g Secret Singer (FR) – Tete Et Corde (FR)
Bought for €120,000 at the Arqana Summer Sale in July last year, he won his only APQS Flat race by a nose at Argentan (1m 5f : Good/Soft) the previous month for Philippe Chemin. Harold Kirk, who purchased the son of Secret Singer for **Willie Mullins**, commented at Deauville: **"He's only a baby of a horse but he's shown potential. The man that trained him likes him and he knows what good horses are. He'll be a long-term project for us and hopefully he'll make a nice jumping horse."** Given time last year, the form has worked out well with the close second winning next time before finishing runner-up twice in Grade 3 and 2 events at Vichy and Saint-Cloud. He could be a smashing novice hurdler.

FUSAIN (FR) 4 b g Lord Du Sud (FR) – Savigny (FR)
Another smart recruit bought by **Robcour** and now in training with **Henry De Bromhead**. A former stablemate of the aforementioned Eagle Moon, he raced once for Augustin de Boisbrunet finishing third on his hurdles debut at Vichy (2m 1f : Soft) in early May. Beaten two lengths, the winner Flip De Vega finished runner-up at Moulins next time and the fourth has won since. He is one to look forward to in novice hurdles.

GAOT (FR) 3 b f Crillon (FR) – Truffe (FR)
The daughter of Crillon was a five lengths winner on her debut in an APQS Flat race at Corlay (1m 3f) in June. The third and fourth have won since to give the form a boost. Trained by Yannick Fertillet, she was snapped up by **J.P.McManus** soon afterwards and has joined **Harry Fry**. She has the option of going juvenile hurdling or running in bumpers. The Listed four year old bumper at Cheltenham on New Year's Day could be an option.

GASPARD DU SEUIL (FR) 3 br g Fuisse (FR) – Violette Du Seuil (FR)
As discussed, owner **Sean Mulryan** has some terrific young horses at present, including Cheltenham Festival winner City Island and Punchestown Festival winner Longhouse Poet. He has purchased this unbeaten son of Fuisse who created a big impression on his debut at Nancy (1m 4f : Good/Soft) in June. I watched a replay of his win and the Mickael Seror trained gelding powered clear to win by eight lengths (third and fourth have won since). **Martin Brassil** may have another future star on his hands and his jumping bow is eagerly anticipated.
Reveley's remarks: **"He comes from a good source and was very impressive. Nancy is a decent provincial track and he sluiced up."**

GAULOISE (FR) 3 br f Samum (GER) – Sans Histoire (FR)
Owner **Kenny Alexander** has assembled a strong team of mares, including Grade 1 winner Honeysuckle, and he has been busy during the summer adding to his already burgeoning squad. This daughter of Samum was trained by Nicolas De Lageneste when winning a twelve furlongs maiden at Lignieres (Soft) in late April by two and a half lengths. The runner-up Gamin Original won next time before being sold to Willie Mullins for €100,000 at the Arqana Sale in May. The form therefore looks solid and she is an interesting proposition for juvenile hurdles in Ireland. Trained by **Willie Mullins**, she could be another very useful mare for her new owner.
Reveley's remarks: **"She did well to beat the geldings on her debut and comes from a good yard and is nicely bred."**

GELBOE DE CHANAY (FR) 3 b f Rail Link – Rose Celebre (FR)
Half-sister to Gary Moore's 137 rated hurdler Eragon De Chanay (wears a visor), he only cost €18,000 as a two year old and looked a bargain buy when hacking up on his hurdling debut at Auteuil (1m 7f : Very Soft). Contesting a five runner Listed event and trained by David Cottin, he beat Gipsy De L'Aunay (sixth next time) by fourteen lengths. The Rail Link filly was subsequently bought by **J.P.McManus** and has joined **Philip Hobbs**.
Reveley's remarks: **"She won very easily at Auteuil and there is no doubt she was impressive. However, she did show signs of temperament when flashing her tail late on but that may be her manner."**

GJOUMI (FR) 3 br f Maresca Sorrento (FR) – Onvavoir (FR)
Grade 2 winner French Made carries the green and gold silks of the **Exors of the late Margaret McManus** and this daughter of Maresca Sorrento will do likewise this winter. Handled by Adrien Fouassier in France, she was a three parts of a length winner of her only APQS Flat race at Lyon (1m 4f : Good/Soft) in April. The third and fourth have won since and she is another useful looking juvenile hurdle prospect for **Willie Mullins**.

GUENA DES MOTTES (FR) 3 b g Soave (GER) – Sara De Flee (FR)
Purchased on behalf of **Simon Munir and Isaac Souede** and sent into training with **Ben Pauling**, this three year old won on his only start over hurdles at Fontainebleau (1m 7f : Very Soft) in early April. A narrow winner from Dandy King, the front pair were twelve lengths clear of the third.
Reveley's remarks: **"He looks a decent prospect and the form has received a significant boost with the fourth (L'Ouragan) winning twice at Auteuil since."**

HOOK UP (FR) 3 b f No Risk At All (FR) – Mission Accomplie (FR)
Trained by Ludovic Rovisse, this filly didn't race as a two year old but won on her third start at Compiegne (1m 4f : Heavy) in March by three lengths. The runner-up Lyons has won three times since giving the form some real substance. She then finished a length and three quarters runner-up on her handicap debut at Saint-Cloud (1m 2f : Soft) in April. Acquired by **Willie Mullins** since, she will carry the pink and green silks of **Susannah and Rich Ricci** in juvenile hurdles this season.

LUCKY ONE (FR) 4 bl g Authorized (IRE) – Lady Anouchka (IRE)
Runner-up in both his starts over hurdles for Guillaume Macaire, he is an exciting prospect for **Jared Sullivan** and **Willie Mullins**. Beaten a length on his debut at Fontainebleau (2m 2f : Very Soft) in late October, he was denied by a length and a half over the same course and distance thirteen days later (Very Soft). The third has won twice since.
Reveley's remarks: **"He is a big strong horse with loads of scope. Runner-up in both his starts, he is a nice type of horse who will have improved with another summer on his back. I think he will improve as he gets older."**

MELAY (FR) 4 b g Lord Du Sud (FR) – Elsamoon (FR)
Ninth on his only start on the Flat at Moulins (1m 3f) in August last year for Guy Cherel, the Lord Du Sud gelding then finished third on his hurdling bow at Auteuil (2m 2f : Very Soft) in mid September. Beaten thirteen lengths by stablemate Fraca De Thaix, the runner-up Protektorat is now rated 132 for Dan Skelton, while the fourth Fine Brunello (runner-up in a Grade 2 at Cheltenham in January) is rated 131 for Joseph O'Brien. Gelded since, he, too, has joined **Joseph O'Brien** and is one to look out for in a maiden hurdle in the Autumn.

PURE GENIUS 4 bl g Authorized (IRE) – Finest Cape
Anne-Sophie Pacault trained and Walters Connors (of Espoir D'Allen fame) owned when he won by four lengths at Sable-Sur-Sarthe (1m 6f : Soft) in September last year. **J.P.McManus** bought both him and the runner-up and stablemate Morosini, who has won over hurdles at Ballinrobe for Jessica Harrington since. A big backward four year old, he has been given time to mature since and that kindness is likely to be rewarded over timber this season. He is in training with **Ted Walsh** and is potentially very useful.

ROCHESTON (FR) 4 b g Kapgarde (FR) – Ravna (FR)
A half-brother to the dual Listed hurdle winner Rasango, he was bought for €55,000 as a yearling and trained by Guillaume Macaire. A length third on his only hurdles start at Bordeaux (2m : Good/Soft) in September last year, the winner (Blue Blue Eyes) has won four times since and the fifth has won twice over fences subsequently. Bought by **Jared Sullivan** since, he is another tremendous prospect for **Willie Mullins**.
Reveley's remarks: **"I remember him at (Guillaume) Macaire's and he finished third in a decent race at Bordeaux. I finished fourth on Shaktal and it rode like a good race. He will improve with time and is a nice horse in the making."**

SAINT ROI (FR) 4 b g Coastal Path – Sainte Vigne (FR)
Raced twice for Guy Cherel before being snapped up by **J.P.McManus**. Seven lengths runner-up on his sole Flat outing at Clairefontaine (1m 4f : Soft) in August last year, the Coastal Path gelding switched to hurdles and shaped with loads of promise on his jumping debut. Three and a half lengths third in Listed Prix Finot at Auteuil in mid September, the winner Flying Start has won again over fences since, the runner-up Fandango has won twice over fences subsequently and the fourth Quartz du Rheu won by seven and a half lengths at Tramore next time for Willie Mullins. Unraced since, he has joined **Willie Mullins** and will be hard to beat in a maiden hurdle in Ireland this Autumn.

TOMBEE DU CIEL (FR) 3 b f Zanzibari (USA) – In Caso Di Neve (FR)
A maiden over hurdles, she raced three times at Auteuil for Anne-Sophie Pacault and was placed on her latest two outings. Beaten a length and a half by Aterisk in April (1m 7f : Very Soft), the winner has subsequently won a Listed race and finished third in a Grade 3 hurdle at the same track. The Zanzibari filly was then seven lengths third in the Listed Prix Girofla at the Parisian track (1m 7f : Very Soft) behind Invincible Dina. The Francois Nicolle trained winner was runner-up in a Grade 3 next time. Therefore the form looks strong and she has joined **Nicky Henderson** and ought to be a potent force in juvenile hurdles.
Reveley's remarks: **"She has some good form at Auteuil and is the sort Nicky Henderson excels with. I think she will do very well for him."**

VALAJANI (GER) 4 rg c Jukebox Jury (IRE) – Ventiane (GER)

While he doesn't fit the French criteria because he was trained in Germany, the four year old looks interesting nevertheless. Bought for €265,000 at the Arqana Sale last November by **J.P.McManus**, he has joined **Harry Fry** with a view to going novice hurdling. Previously trained by Gabor Maronka and Markus Klug, he raced eight times on the Flat winning twice at Cologne (1m) as a two year old and Dortmund (1m 2f) in October last year. Fifth in Group 2 company at Cologne (1m 3f : Good) in June 2018, he was runner-up in the Group 3 Italian St Leger at San Siro (1m 6f : Good).

ZARKAREVA (FR) 3 b f Authorized (IRE) – Zarkiyna (FR)

Another exciting three year old bought by **Robcour** who has joined **Henry De Bromhead**. She was trained by Augustin De Boisbrunet when winning by a length and a quarter on her hurdles debut at Clairefontaine (2m 1f : Soft) in June. Bought afterwards, the form hasn't worked out particularly well but she is a well bred filly who should do well for her new connections.

Value Racing Club

"Winning Together"

Our aim at Value Racing Club is to introduce new people into the world of horse racing. We provide a cost effective and simple way of becoming a racehorse owner. There are never any hidden extras such as vet bills. Once the initial purchase has been paid, no further monies are required during the entire racing season.

What we offer and benefits:

- An opportunity to become involved in racehorse ownership.
- What we pay for a horse is what you pay, no added fees of any kind.
- A one-off cost covers the entire racing season.
- Stable visits arranged to watch your horse work on the gallops.
- Free owners badge every time your horse runs.
- Each syndicate keeps 100% of all prize money won.
- 62% overall strike rate of our runners finishing in the first three places.
- Horses in training with Dr Richard Newland, David Pipe, Mick Appleby, Alastair Ralph, Jamie Snowden & Philip Kirby.
- Racing TV pundit Mark Howard is our Club Ambassador.
- We are members of the ROA "Racehorse Owners Association" & RSA "Racehorse Syndicates Association" to ensure good practice.

Big race wins include the £70,000 Imperial Cup, £30,000 Betfred Summer Hurdle, £30,000 Durham National. Big Race placed efforts, 3rd in the £300,000 Galway Hurdle, 2nd in the Eider Chase.

Over £490,000 of prize money won for owners in the last 4 years.

Website: www.valueracingclub.co.uk email: contact@valueracingclub.co.uk Twitter: @valueracingclub

HANDICAP SNIPS

Colin Tizzard has the option of running **BEAUFORT WEST** in novice hurdles having failed to win any of his four races over timber last season. However, his rating of 129 looks tempting and it will be a surprise if the Getaway gelding doesn't end up considerably higher by the spring. From the family of Gold Cup winner Bobs Worth, he was runner-up in a point-to-point for Colin Bowe before joining his current connections. Fourth and sixth behind Bright Forecast and Rathhill respectively in maiden hurdles at Newbury last winter, he was then treated for ulcers. Returning to action at Sandown in early February, he was a length and three quarters runner-up behind Winston C (rated 141), who has subsequently won two Grade 1 hurdles in the US. Outclassed and pulled up in the *Skybet* Supreme Novices' Hurdle at Cheltenham last time, he could even go straight over fences and be aimed at a novices' handicap chase. Yet to race over further than two miles under Rules, he will stay further. Still a maiden, his overall record doesn't reflect his ability.

We may have to wait until the second half of the season but **DANNY KIRWAN**'s reappearance is likely to be worth it, given the fact the six year old has been granted an opening mark of 120. A winning pointer and bumper horse, he only raced twice over hurdles last season. Beaten three parts of a length in a match by the 133 rated Crooks Peak (won again since), in receipt of six pounds at Kempton in late November, the Scorpion gelding was then four and a half lengths runner-up in the Grade 2 Kennel Gate Novices' Hurdle at Ascot behind Angels Breath. He had the 132 rated Seddon and 134 rated Thistle Do Nicely behind him that day. Absent since due to injury, he looks thrown in and will have no trouble staying further. **Paul Nicholls** has won the Martin Pipe Conditional Jockeys' Handicap Hurdle at the Cheltenham Festival on two occasions (Salubrious (2013) & Ibis Du Rheu (2016)) and this former Pat Doyle trained inmate could be tailormade for the 2020 version, although the only time he has raced left-handed, he disappointed in the Grade 2 bumper at Aintree in April 2018.

Owner Terry Warner won the Greatwood Hurdle at Cheltenham (17th November) with Rooster Booster (2002) and Detroit City (2006) and it will be interesting to see if the lightly raced **ELDORADO ALLEN** is targeted at the two miles event. Previously trained in France by Philippe Peltier, the grey was runner-up in an APQS Flat race (1m 4f) before finishing third on his hurdles debut at Auteuil – the Prix De L'Yonne hurdle, which has been won by the likes of Aux Ptits Soins, Blue Dragon and Franco De Port in recent years – in March last year. Subsequently bought on behalf of Warner and John Romans, the Khalkevi gelding made a sparkling UK debut for Colin Tizzard at Sandown in November (2m : Heavy). Leading two out, the five year old powered away for a four and a half lengths victory from subsequent winners Finawn Bawn (twice), Star of Lanka (twice), Oakley, West To The Bridge (twice), Duarigle and Let's Get At It (three times). Reappearing less than a month later at Aintree, he unseated his rider at the first having been hampered. Not seen since, he has yet to race beyond two miles one and anything quicker than soft ground. **"It was frightening how good he was at Sandown that day. He is rated 145 off the back of one run really. We will stay hurdling with him and he could be anything. He could be seriously well handicapped,"** remarked Tizzard in September. Regardless of whether he heads to Cheltenham in November, or steps up in trip, Eldorado Allen can win a big handicap at least this season.

Langholm based **James Ewart** trained 15 winners during the 2018/2019 season and it will be disappointing if he can't exploit a mark of 117 with the lightly raced **ETTILA DE SIVOLA**. A five year old by Noroit, he won his only bumper as a three year old before sent hurdling last term. Following his eleven lengths defeat of Eclat De Star at Sedgefield (2m 1f) in December, his trainer said: **"Ettila De Sivola is a nice horse who we've been very patient with. I don't want to do too much with him this season, we'll have a couple more runs to educate him. My aim is to have a hard season as a novice chaser as I feel that's where we want to be picking the**

fruits." A shade disappointing on his next two outings at Sedgefield and Haydock, he enjoys slow ground and goes well fresh. Unbeaten on his reappearance, he is one to keep on side on his chasing debut in a novices' handicap (0-115, 0-120). Judging by his comments, the French bred is the apple of his trainer's eye.

It was well documented that it was a tough second half of the season for Cheshire handler **Donald McCain** with only 13 winners from the start of Janaury until the final day of the campaign in late April. However, on the flip side, the Grand National winning trainer has some well handicapped inmates, as a result, and none more so than the lightly raced **FIRST ACCOUNT**. A winning pointer for Colin Bowe, the Malinas gelding was beaten less than six lengths by Al Dancer (rated 151) and Windsor Avenue (134) on his hurdles debut at Carlisle (2m 1f) in October. The five year old returned to the Cumbrian venue two months later but didn't look comfortable on the inner track eventually finishing second behind Captain Zebo (rated 130) with the subsequent EBF Final runner-up One For Rosie back in third. Absent since, due to the unhealthy nature of his stable, he is set to go chasing and looks a good thing to win a novices' handicap chase over two or two and a half miles off his opening mark of 114. Look out for him at one of the Autumn meetings at Carlisle (17th or 24th October).

Paul Nicholls has taken charge of the ex-Lucinda Russell trained **HIGHLAND HUNTER** and the Subtle Power gelding looks capable of winning a good staying handicap hurdle before embarking on his chasing career. A point winner for Donnchadh Doyle, the six year old won a bumper at Kelso before sent hurdling last season. Twice a winner at Ayr and Hexham (both 2m 4f on heavy ground), conditional jockey Blair Campbell rode him on the latter occasion saying afterwards: **"He's a nice horse and has done it well. He's got there fairly easily and I was trying to keep hold of him until the last. We have high hopes for him."** Third next time in handicap company at Haydock, he was then fifth in a Grade 2 novice hurdle at the same track in February. Absent since and transferred to the champion trainer, his ideal target may be the £**100,000 Grade 3** *Betfair* **Exchange Stayers' Handicap Hurdle at Haydock Park** (23rd November). His form figures on heavy ground are 111.

A trip to the Carlisle track could also be on the agenda for **HILL SIXTEEN**. Featured in last year's *Irish Pointers*, I have got a lot of time for the Court Cave gelding who still looked green and raw over hurdles. A £100,000 purchase out of Colin Bowe's yard in April 2018, he was placed in his first four races over hurdles, including behind the likes of One For Rosie and Windsor Avenue at Carlisle and Sedgefield respectively. **Sue Smith**'s big strapping six year old then got off the mark at the former venue when beating hurdling debutant Vis A Vis by nearly three lengths (2m 3f). Fourth at Uttoxeter last time in a competitive handicap hurdle in March, he is rated 123 and looks ideal for the 0-135 novices' handicap chase over two and a half miles at Carlisle on Sunday 2nd November. I think he will stay further this year, too. He is a cracking chasing prospect for owner Trevor Hemmings.

The Tim Radford owned and **Mick Channon** trained Glen Forsa was rated 114 when sent chasing last November but following three subsequent wins over the larger obstacles, including a Grade 2 at Sandown, he lined up in the Arkle Trophy at Cheltenham with an official mark of 150. The same combination will be hoping **HOLD THE NOTE** can make similar progress this season. A five year old by Jeremy, he was useful in bumpers winning at Newton Abbot before finishing fourth in a Listed contest at Cheltenham's November meeting. Described as **"a brute, a proper horse who could end up in the Arkle"** by his trainer, he was sent hurdling soon afterwards. He was third at Sandown behind I Can't Explain and Phoenix Way before winning at Doncaster over Christmas. **"Hold The Note is a lovely horse but relatively inexperienced. He's an amazing jumper, though it was still a bit on the sharp side for him around here,"** commented Aidan Coleman afterwards. Runner-up at Huntingdon in mid February over two and a half miles, he has been off since having had five races in four months. Rated 133, he is one to watch out for in a 0-135 novices' handicap chase.

KNOW THE SCORE was an expensive purchase from the Irish pointing field having cost The Angove Family £380,000 following a six lengths win on his only start for Sean Doyle. **David Pipe**'s Flemensfirth gelding was fourteenth in the Cheltenham Festival bumper in March 2018 before sent hurdling last season. Despite winning by eight lengths at Hexham (2m 4f : Soft) in December, he was largely disappointing last winter. Third at Wetherby last time behind Minella Warrior on his handicap debut, he is rated 124 and ought to improve appreciably over fences. It is hoped the six year old will leave his previous form behind, starting in a novices' handicap chase over two and a half miles plus.

I am convinced **Tony Martin** will win a nice handicap hurdle with **NIBIRU** one day. Rated 75 on the Flat and 121 over jumps, the Casamento gelding caught the eye on more than one occasion over hurdles last season. Third behind the ill-fated Sir Erec and Tiger Tap Tap at Leopardstown over Christmas, he filled the same position at Cork and Tipperary before winning by two and a half lengths at Ballinrobe (2m 1f : Good) in July. Yet to be allocated a mark, he is the sort to turn up in the two miles novices' handicap hurdle (0-125) at Cheltenham's November meeting (15th November) – stablemates and subsequent Galway Hurdle winners Quick Jack won the race in 2013 off 113 and Tudor City was runner-up in 2016 off 119. Decent ground appears to bring out the best in him.

PISTOL WHIPPED was acquired for £110,000 at the Goffs Autumn Horses in Training Sale at Doncaster in October last year having run in two Irish points for Colin Bowe. Three and a quarter lengths third behind stablemate Rathhill in a two miles maiden hurdle at Newbury in December on his first start for **Nicky Henderson**, he then appreciated the step up to two and a half miles at Fakenham next time. A length winner, his rider Nico De Boinville said afterwards: **"Pistol Whipped has the class to jump and I can't wait until he gets over fences next year. He was really good as this wouldn't be his track nor his ground."** Pulled up at Sandown last time on his handicap debut, the Beneficial gelding reportedly found the ground too soft. Dropped two pounds since to a mark of 128, expect N.J.Henderson to find a two and a half miles (0-130 or 0-135) novices' handicap chase for him in the Autumn.

The second potentially well handicapped former pointer trained by **Donald McCain** is **POGUE**. Featured in last year's *Top 40 Prospects*, the grey was bought for £100,000 having won the second of his two Irish points for Colin Bowe. The Stowaway gelding shaped well on his first couple of runs over hurdles at Bangor and Kelso finishing third and second respectively. However, with his stable struggling with the equine flu, he ran a lifeless race last time when a distant second behind Captain Zebo at Carlisle (inner track) in March. Off since and rated 117, he ought to be a different proposition over fences this season.

ROCK DE BAUNE has the distinction of beating subsequent *Skybet* Supreme Novices' Hurdle winner Klassical Dream at Auteuil in October 2017. Trained at the time by Bertrand Lefevre, the Saddex gelding was purchased by J.P.McManus soon afterwards and joined **John Kiely** in Ireland. Without a win over hurdles since, he was four lengths fifth in a Pertemps qualifier at Leopardstown over Christmas and has been running well on the Flat since. A nose winner at Ballinrobe (1m 5f) in June, his trainer said afterwards: **"Rock De Baune is a nice horse and he stays. The track was too sharp for him too. He'll be a grand horse in time."** Fourth over ten furlongs at Roscommon in August off a mark of 83, he is rated 121 over hurdles, which looks attractive. Only five, he can win a big handicap hurdle this season.

Jonjo O'Neill has won the **Grade 3 Silver Trophy at Chepstow** (12th October) twice (Hasty Prince (2003) & Don't Push It (2007)) and he reportedly has the two and a half miles event lined up for **TEDHAM**. The five year old gelding has only raced a handful of times over hurdles and is rated 131. The Shirocco gelding ran well in defeat against the likes of Al Dancer, The Big Bite and Getaway Trump before winning on his handicap debut at Wincanton (2m 5f) in January.

A length and three quarters winner off a mark of 125, he was made favourite for a twenty one runner handicap hurdle at Aintree's Grand National meeting. Seventh behind the vastly more experienced Three Musketeers, he remains well treated and unexposed. Bred to stay further, too, he could also be aimed at the £100,000 Grade 3 Betfair Exchange Stayers' Handicap Hurdle at Haydock (23rd November) later on. Former stablemate Holywell finished runner-up in the three miles event when it was run over brush hurdles in 2012.

Finally, it will be a surprise if multiple champion owner **J.P.McManus** doesn't win some big prizes with the following quartet.

APPLE'S SHAKIRA has yet to race beyond two miles five but I think she is crying out for three miles. A full-sister to Apple's Jade (Grade 1 winner over three miles), she was beaten less than three lengths when sixth in the Coral Cup at Cheltenham last March. Rated 141, Nicky Henderson's mare looks tailormade for the **Pertemps Final** at next year's Festival. Her form figures at Prestbury Park are 11146.

CHAMPAGNE PLATINUM looked a smart novice hurdler when winning at Newcastle and Newbury in December but was then absent for 122 days with a foot problem. The former Irish pointer was well held in Grade 1 company at the Punchestown Festival behind Klassical Dream. **"He's very good and will be very good,"** remarked Nicky Henderson after the Stowaway gelding had won an 'introductory' hurdle at Newbury over Christmas. It is possible he will be sent chasing but there is a good handicap hurdle to be won with him off 138 beforehand. He has yet to race beyond two miles under Rules but will stay further.

Another McManus/Henderson filly who looks better than her mark is **EPATANTE** who was sent off 15/8 favourite for the Dawn Run Mares' Novices' Hurdle at Cheltenham. Only ninth, she had previously looked a high-class filly when sluicing home at Kempton and Exeter. A strong traveller with a turn of foot, she may prefer flatter tracks and could be *Betfair* Hurdle material in February (her stable have won it fives times). Dropped six pounds since her last run, she is much better than a 137 rated filly.

The Joseph O'Brien trained **TOWER BRIDGE** was a never nearer second in the novices' handicap chase at the Cheltenham Festival. Beaten sixteen lengths by A Plus Tard, he hasn't race beyond two miles five over fences but will relish racing over further. Still a maiden over the larger obstacles but rated 143, he won a Grade 1 novice hurdle at Leopardstown over two miles six and was also third in the Grade 1 Sefton Novices' Hurdle at Aintree during the same season. His record at Leopardstown is 413 and High Chaparral gelding looks ideal for the valuable **Paddy Power Handicap Chase** (27th December).

Don't forget to read my Diary @
www.mhpublications.couk

IRISH POINTERS

As in previous editions, point-to-point expert **Declan Phelan** has written his invaluable article regarding those horses who caught his eye 'between the flags' in the Emerald Isle last winter/ spring. Last year's feature yielded **40 winners** at an impressive **strike-rate of 29%** and produced a £10 level stakes **PROFIT** of **£462.90**. They included exciting prospects **ANDY DUFRESNE, ASK FOR GLORY, BIRCHDALE, BOLD PLAN, HONEYSUCKLE** (4 out of 4 including Grade 1 success), **LISNAGAR OSCAR** (Grade 2 winner), **MEGA YEATS** (3 wins), **MINELLA INDO** (50/1 & 5/1 – dual Grade 1 winner), **RATHHILL, TRUCKIN AWAY** (14/1) and **UMBRIGADO** (3 wins).

ADRIMEL (FR) 4 bb g Tirwanako (FR) – Irise De Gene (FR)
Trainer: Tom LACEY   **Form Figures: 1**

The point to point track of Ballyarthur, which lies within a mile of the town of Fermoy, is one which places an emphasis on stamina: it can be punishing for younger horses and the two maidens it staged for four year olds in 2019 (one for mares, the other for geldings) clocked the two slowest recorded times for races in the four year old class of 2019: 7.38 and 7.26, the latter for the geldings race, which was won by Adrimel. With the ground riding on the soft to heavy side, the ability to stay the trip was of paramount importance. Adrimel is a tall bay gelding with four white socks around his hooves. He had been brought to Ireland from his native France by bloodstock agent J.D. Moore and purchased for less than ten grand by the Ryans from Clare. Joe Ryan and his son Josh (works as a pilot with Ryanair), have a healthy win strike-rate with their small squad and their charges are inevitably ready to roll on debuts. With James Hannon in the saddle, Adrimel led from the start, jumping fluently: he increased the pace on the climb to the third last and all but one of his rivals had surrendered as he raced towards the final fence, he popped it safely to score by an easy eight lengths. The runner up, Firak, scored on his next start to advertise the form. Adrimel then had a date with Aintree Sales and Tom Lacey had to dig deep into his pockets for the £280,000 to acquire this talented recruit. He is a son of a little-known French sire and there is one familiar name on his page, that of Halcon Genelardais.....he was a proper mudlark who won the 2006 Welsh Grand National. Another link to the same Welsh National, is that the 2018 runner up, Ramses De Teillee happened to win his maiden point at Ballyarthur, the 2016 version. The signs are that Adrimel could be destined one day to play a leading role in a soft/ground staying marathon over fences. This coming season will be mostly about educating him over hurdles. His second season onwards will be the time to take an interest in Adrimel and, if a race like the Welsh National is the long term goal, it will be most entertaining to monitor the journey which will be travelled en route by a canny handler such as Lacey. I rate Adrimel comfortably a 130+ soft/heavy ground chaser in the making.

AIN'T THAT A SHAME (IRE) 5 b g Jeremy (USA) – Castletown Girl
Trainer: Henry DE BROMHEAD   **Form Figures: 2**

Powerfully built bay gelding, raced once for the Johnnie/Shirley Berry yard: at Kilfeacle (Soft) in January, he sat midfield until he steadily picked up places inside the final mile: after jumping the second last, he was kicked into a two lengths lead: a combination of testing ground and perhaps hitting the front too soon, resulted in him idling on the run in and he was caught on the line by the rallying Solo Cargo. Ain't That A Shame moved through this race like the most talented horse on show and circumstances may have contrived against him at the finish. The race has worked out promisingly with the third and fourth recording easy wins. His sibling Catching Shadows was best at two miles and the history of that half-brother could render a vital clue. Robcour bought the horse for £110,000 at Cheltenham in February and he has pleased Henry de Bromhead in his homework: his new trainer feels the horse has speed and will operate on soft and good and not the extremes. He will win a maiden hurdle this winter and the longer term plan is to try and develop him into a 130+ two to two and a half miles chaser: he has the size and scope, making those plans realistic.

ARD ABHAINN (IRE) 5 br m Jeremy (USA) – Sheer Frustration (IRE)
Trainer: Gordon ELLIOTT   **Form Figures: 1 - 1**
An athletic black mare: when she won a slowly run mares' maiden at Lingstown (Yielding/Soft) after a battle with Get The Appeal, the form did not excite. Jamie Codd rated the form more than most and encouraged Gordon Elliott to pay £80,000 for her at Cheltenham Sales in March, a price which at the time looked expensive for a mare with little pedigree. Her first run for Gordon was a revelation, because she faced off against the geldings in a Punchestown Festival bumper and powered home with honesty to defeat nineteen rivals in the style of a Graded class mare. She has now won on soft and good and over two miles and three miles (versatile), and one would imagine she has the ability required to win Graded novice hurdles this coming winter.

BAPTISM OF FIRE (IRE) 4 b g Jeremy (USA) – Julia Glynn (IRE)
Owner: Henry De BROMHEAD   **Form Figures: 1**
Tall black gelding, he looked in trouble as he nestled an eight lengths sixth approaching the second last at Courtown (Sofy) in April. With his jockey, Jamie Codd, getting stuck into him, this debutant responded generously and galloped honestly in the last two furlongs and managed to reel in the leaders and in the final stride he gained the day, scoring by a neck. He had appeared to be tapped for toe when the tempo increased in the final half mile, and this performance may hint that stamina rather than speed is his forte. The race also was timed at over seven minutes, though still some twenty one seconds faster than the other division of the four year old maiden on the day. Denis Murphy had secured this horse for €48,000 at the 2018 Derby Store Sale and Gigginstown House Stud were suitably impressed to fork out £100,000 for him at Cheltenham Pointers Sale in April on foot of the win. His pedigree page is rather slim, and for now a career as a 120+ staying handicap chaser could be his calling. Whilst he may be lacking in gears, he has a willing attitude and that trait should stand to him over time.

BARBADOS BUCK'S (IRE) 4 b g Getaway (GER) – Buck's Blue (FR)
Trainer: Paul NICHOLLS   **Form Figures: 2**
Richard Black an associate of Colin Bowe paid €60,000 for this bay gelding at the 2018 Derby Sale: this gelding belongs to a stout jumps family, his half-brother is More Bucks (8 times winner) and his granny is a half-sister to Big Buck's: hence, if Richard Black could get a performance between the flags, it was almost certain to reward his investment. The maiden in late April at Dromahane (Good) was run on the inside line of the track, hence it was a very sharp three miles (if it was actually three miles at all): jumping crisply, Barbados Bucks leaped to the lead at the fourth last in a competitive race laden with choicely bred opponents. From the third last, the race boiled down to a head to head between Barbados Buck's and Skatman: they were locked together until the run in when Skatman asserted close to the winning post, the duo pulling well clear of the remainder. Barbados Buck's turned up at Goffs Punchestown Sales five days later and I noted that on his vetting inspection sheet it said he had a medial splint on both front legs (not ideal). Given the family heritage, it was no surprise that Paul Nicholls was responsible for the successful bid of €210,000 (a tasty return for Richard Black). Purely based on this second at Dromahane, Barbados Buck's does not look worth that six figure price, as I could merely regard him as a 115 to 125 hurdler/chaser and he will have to make massive strides to threaten to become a Graded class hurdler. He will win track races, perhaps not of the highest standard. He coped with the good ground at Dromahane, when he encounters softer terrain a little more about him will be revealed.

BIG BRESIL 4 b g Blue Bresil (FR) – Cutielilou (FR)
Trainer: Tom GEORGE   **Form Figures: 2**
As his name may suggest this French bred gelding is a monster of a physical unit and cost team Monbeg €40,000 at the 2018 Land Rover Sale. He contested one point to point this spring, at Liscarroll (Yielding/Soft) at the end of March. Jumping cleanly, he was always sited close to the pace: the field was tightly packed as they faced into the third last: the tempo increased racing

towards the second last with two quickening clear, Big Bresil and Papa Tango Charly: this duo opened up a gap of six lengths in the matter of a hundred yards: away from that penultimate fence and tight home bend, the eventual winner Papa Tango Charly found more than Big Bresil and with a second kick, edged four or five lengths clear. At the death, Big Bresil kept on for a clear second best. From a Gallic family jam packed with middle tier French jumps winners and others such as Cheltenham Festival bumper winner Cheltenian, this bay is a big striding galloping type: he tickled the fancy of owner Roger Brookhouse as he stumped up £170,000 at the Aintree Sales in April. The old cliché of "whatever he achieves as a hurdler will be a bonus" applies to this lad, as he will find chasing his preferred vocation. Apart from maybe winning a modest maiden hurdle, I cannot see him making an impact in the premier novice hurdles this coming winter. Long term, he fits the mould of those 125-140 style chasers that tend to contest the "Saturday" feature handicap chases, i.e., a decent chaser but not really star material.

BLOODSTONE (IRE) 4 br g Court Cave (IRE) – Spirit Leader (IRE)
Owner: Henry De BROMHEAD   **Form Figures: 22**

As befits a horse who cost connections €120,000 at the 2018 Derby Store Sale, this youngster is a fine physical specimen: he has size and scope and certainly looks the part condition wise. Gordon Elliott signed the sales docket on behalf of Gigginstown House Stud and ultimately he will have control of the future of this bay gelding. Pat Doyle had the task of tutoring Bloodstone this spring and he raced twice, filling the runner up spot on both occasions. He seemed to find the two and a half miles trip insufficient when a tenderly handled second to Ferny Hollow in a classy renewal of the Knockanard (Soft) in February. With Evan Dwan (inexperienced jockey) retaining the ride at Ballynoe (Good) in March, the punters swerved him and he was friendless in the market for his first try at three miles. He picked his way through the field to challenge on the climb to the second last: from there to the finish he tussled with It Sure Is, only to lose out by half a length. My verdict is that, if assisted by a more senior jockey, Bloodstone would have claimed gold. For now, he may remain a maiden, though a talented one with much potential. His mother, Spirit Leader, was a cracking racemare for Jessica Harrington, a former Cheltenham Festival winning mare in fact and a two mile specialist (she has already bred Prince Of Scars (Grade 1 winner) and Folsom Blue). Bloodstone seemed to function on soft and good terrain, and he has bright prospects of winning a bumper before Christmas and then should be a competitive 120+ novice hurdler, with perhaps 2m4f-2m6f his optimum. A super jumper, he can be entertained as one that can win at Graded level in future years when he embarks on a chasing career.

BOBHOPEORNOHOPE (IRE) 4 b g Westerner – Bandelaro (IRE)
Trainer: Kim BAILEY   **Form Figures: 1**

A medium sized bay gelding, he won an auction maiden at Dromahane (Soft) from Black Gerry: Bob was ridden prominently and pulled clear with Black Gerry from three out: headed at the last, he rallied demonstrating a gutsy attitude to wrestle the verdict in the final fifty yards. Both winner and runner-up were owned by the Monbeg Doyles and, just as Black Gerry accomplished a tasty profit, Bobhopeornohope capped that in the sales ring. With a slim current pedigree (tracing back a few generations to Corbiere, an Aintree Grand National winner), Bob cost a mere €15,000 at the 2018 Derby store sale: with this point win on his C.V., Kim Bailey acquired him for £105,000 via the Cheltenham Sales ring in April. Dromahane staged three fixtures in the spring of 2019, featuring five races for four year olds: with plenty of land, the racing line moves from meeting to meeting, with the broader circuit using thirteen fences and the sharper inner track fifteen fences: hence making time comparisons between individual fixtures at the track can be misleading. Although the auction maiden won by Bobhopeornohope was the slowest of the five races for four year olds staged at Dromahane this spring, it was run on the softest terrain and widest racing line. Bobhopeornohope is unlikely to become a Graded performer: I do like his honesty of effort and he can become a potent force in middle tier hurdle and chase races as he has scope and he is an uncomplicated type in terms of racing style who may be versatile ground wise as well.

BOLD ASSASSIN (IRE) 4 b g Golden Lariat (USA) – Drumnaskea (IRE)
Trainer: Henry De BROMHEAD   Form Figures: 2
Big, tall raw specimen who can grow into a physical monster: plenty of talented ex-chasers mixed in his pedigree, including Shannon Spray, Direct Access and One Knight. Pointed by Ulster handler Warren Ewing, he travelled south to the county Meath venue of Oldtown (Good/ Yielding) to contest the early season two and a half miles maiden in February. A small field of six faced the starter and they raced along at a steady tempo until the inevitable quickening on the downhill journey to the second last. One of four close up at this fence, Bold Assassin was temporarily tapped for toe: under a determined Jamie Codd steer, he conjured up more from the final fence and failed by a short head to justify favouritism, Slip Road edging him out. The form of this Oldtown race remains questionable. De Bromhead secured this youngster a few weeks later at Cheltenham sales at a tariff of £150,000: stock by his sire are in short supply and relatively unknown: as an individual one could expect him to progress with maturity and a true run two and a half miles plus race over hurdles should bring rewards in maiden/novice events this winter. He could be on the cusp of Graded novice hurdle class and he will make his presence felt as a decent chaser in time.

BOLD CONDUCT (IRE) 5 b g Stowaway – Vics Miller (IRE)
Trainer: Colin TIZZARD   Form Figures: 1
One of the more impressive maiden winners in the autumn: a big physical unit with bags of potential, he represented Warren Ewing at Loughanmore (Good/Yielding) in November in the first division of the four year old maiden: indicating a high cruising speed, he moved stylishly in the hands of Richie Deegan, striding to the lead after two out, a spectacular jump at the last capped a memorable debut as he accounted for Sidi Ismael by more than two lengths. He clocked a time twenty four seconds faster than the division which followed. His full brother was an Irish pointer in 2018 Solo Cargo: said horse is an on/off bridle merchant now racing in the UK for Harry Whittington: Bold Conduct has the polar opposite system of racing and is a vastly superior racing individual. Snapped up by Colin Tizzard for £150,000 at Cheltenham November sales: the fact he did not run this five year old in the spring could be a blessing as it may have allowed him time to mature and muscle up his frame. An exciting prospect, one with bright prospects of earning a track rating of 140+ and therefore on the cusp of Cheltenham Festival standard.

BRAVEMANSGAME (FR) 4 b g Brave Mansonnien (FR) – Genifique (FR)
Trainer: Paul NICHOLLS   Form Figures: 1
An imposing full-bodied bay gelding: a French bred with multiple Gallic jumps winners in his family tree. Cost the Monbeg Doyles €48,000 at the 2018 Derby Sale. Debuted at Lingstown (Yielding/ Soft) in March and defied market weakness to notch up an emphatic victory. Tucked away towards mid division for the first mile, he basically ploughed through one fence at the halfway juncture and managed to survive (sole error). Produced to challenge at the third last, his long stride clicked in as they raced downhill to the second last and, once at full pelt, he surged away to score by eight lengths in the fastest time of the afternoon. Horses who get a head of steam and lead in the final half mile at Lingstown (downhill finish) are rarely beaten and, by times, the performances can be flattering. Will that be the case with Bravemansgame? Impossible to predict. He changed hands for £370,000 when purchased by Paul Nicholls on behalf of John Dance and the Drew family at Cheltenham March Sales. He is a fine big galloping customer with some speed and is likely to be capable of mixing it at Graded level as a hurdler: he should be comfortable operating in the two and a half to three miles range and a little juice in the ground could be his ideal conditions for optimum returns. When chasing, he will become a 130+ player.

CALTHOR (IRE) 4 bb g Califet (FR) – Blackthorne Winter (IRE)
Trainer: Ellen HOLDEN   Form Figures: F1
A €42,000 2018 Land Rover sale store: a half-brother to dual UK bumper winner Black Kalanisi: a lanky leggy unfurnished bay gelding. Strongly fancied for his point debut at Ballynoe (Good): he

was poised to mount his challenge when he fell at the fifth last fence. Derek O'Connor retained the ride for the next start at Ballysteen (Yielding), a race won famously in the past by Faugheen. Derek rode with supreme confidence: electing to educate his charge out the rear for the first half of the race and then making headway from five out to lead at the third last and emphatically draw away in the manner of a talented horse to post a ten lengths win. Certainly an above average youngster, he has a touch of class and should win a bumper and can be competitive at Graded level over hurdles and has aspirations of a life as a 140+ chaser and enjoy some chunky pay days during his track career. Handles good and soft ground and could prove effective from 2m 2f to 3 miles plus.

CILL ANNA (IRE) 4 b f Imperial Monarch (IRE) – Technohead (IRE)
Trainer: Paul NICHOLLS   **Form Figures: 1**

In previous years, Paul Nicholls has purchased talented four year old winning mares from the Irish pointing ranks: Posh Trish in 2017 and Silver Forever in 2018, both very much up to Listed grade on the track. In 2019, his acquisition which may follow that trend is the stout bay mare Cill Anna. Handled by Colin Bowe, she prevailed on her debut at Monksgrange (Good/Yielding) on the last day of March. She was responsible for an honest pace in the thirteen runner field as Barry O'Neill allowed her to share the lead throughout. Travelling smoothly, along with Whos The Boss, the pair accelerated away from the pack at the second last. Surviving a clumsy leap at the final fence, Cill Anna dug deep to fend off Whos The Boss by a head in a tight finish. The time was decent (5.44) and some of those in behind have advertised the form, and therefore this Monksgrange contest was arguably one of the top four races for four year old mares in 2019. Cill Anna cost Bowe €38,000 as a store, hailing from mostly Flat stock, though her dam has already bred two jumps winners, Distime and Half The Odds. Cill Anna went under the hammer at Aintree April Sales and cost new connections £115,000. She can win a mares' bumper and be a player in the upper class mares' winners/Graded/Listed bumpers in 2019/20, and will more than hold her own further down the line as a quality participant in mares' novice hurdles and chases. She floated over the cushioned ground at Monksgrange and should handle good or soft terrain and a trip of two and a half miles is possibly her optimum, three miles may not necessarily be her cup of tea.

CLONDAW CAITLIN (IRE) 4 b f Court Cave (IRE) – Kilmessan (IRE)
Trainer: Ruth JEFFERSON   **Form Figures: P – F2**

Thrice raced compact bay mare: Ran for the Mick Goff yard (most of his horses who carry the "Clondaw" prefix): first time at Ballycahane (Soft) she suffered on the testing conditions and dropped out from the third last and pulled up. Her second start was inconclusive as she fell at halfway in a Necarne (Yielding/Soft) race before the taps had been turned on. Her true worth was unveiled at Bartlemy in May. Enjoying good ground for the first time, she can be adjudged to have been an unfortunate loser as she was forced to settle for second, defeated half a length by Fantasia Roque: she was positioned a six lengths fifth jumping the fourth last: on the long four furlongs trek to the next fence, she moved to challenge for the lead: in front but pressed approaching the final fence, she got in too deep to this obstacle, lost vital momentum, surrendering her advantage to the winner. To her credit Clondaw Caitlin fought and responded to pressure and was closing the gap only for the post to come too soon for her. Judged on her three point outings, I believe she requires good ground and a well run race to bring the best out in her. Purchased for £40,000 by Ruth Jefferson at Doncaster May Sales, her jumping needs some correcting. Far from star quality, her game spirit will yield victories on the northern circuit, and she could pick up a minor mares' bumper and a couple of mares' novice hurdles this winter if cannily placed.

COCONUT SPLASH (IRE) 4 ch g Stowaway – Presenting Chaos (IRE)
Trainer: Evan WILLIAMS   **Form Figures: 1**

Supplied his dam with her first winner when scoring on his debut at Castletown (Yielding) for the Monbeg team in the first weekend of April. This compact deep liver chestnut gelding bided his time in mid pack until moving to share the lead on the climb to the third last. From there along with Diamond Grove, they dropped the remainder. Asserting on the downhill approach to the final fence, Coconut Splash pinged the last and was more value than the four lengths winning verdict. He has tactical speed which will serve him well: the Monbeg lads secured a price of £180,000 for this youngster at Cheltenham Sales. He will not be top class, but his new handler Williams has a fair record with 125-140 rated handicappers and Coconut Splash in a season or two will slot into that nest and with his qualities could capture either a valuable weekend handicap hurdle or chase from two and a half miles and upwards. The coming season could be about preparing the ground for an assault on future premier handicaps, so winning a modest maiden/novice hurdle may be the aim in 2019/20 in the hope of attaining an exploitable handicap rating.

DEPLOY THE GETAWAY (IRE) 4 b g Getaway (GER) – Gaelic River (IRE)
Trainer: Willie MULLINS   **Form Figures: 1**
Stout chunky bay gelding who cost Monbeg €25,000 as a 2018 Derby Sale store: ridden positively at Tallow (Soft) in February, he maintained a solid gallop from the start and burned off his rivals one by one. Entering the last half mile, the rest had thrown in the towel: there was one heart stopping moment as this four year old seemed to lose concentration and ploughed through the final fence: jockey Jimmy Walsh sat tight and maintained the partnership and Deploy The Getaway waltzed home an eased down twenty lengths winner. In hindsight, none of the vanquished have franked the form and one could reason that he beat a poor cast of rivals: a counter argument is that in what was a solo run from the front, he clocked the fastest time of the day. He does have a very light plain pedigree, an aspect which failed to deter Willie Mullins as he paid £200,000 on behalf of Cheveley Park to recruit this four year old. Mullins has a fine record with strong travelling gallopers and Deploy The Getaway can win a bumper without much bother: further down the line he will be a Graded class 2m 4f+ novice hurdler. He may prefer some cut in the ground to produce his best and may be in his pomp on soft or heavy ground.

DON DIABLO (IRE) 4 b g Flemensfirth (USA) – Tonaphuca Girl (IRE)
Trainer: Gordon ELLIOTT   **Form Figures: 2**
Picked up for €40,000 by Colin Bowe at the 2018 Derby Sale, this rangy bay gelding hails from an equine dam line associated with Charlie Swan and his father (grand-dam Atteses). He made a late season debut at Stowlin (Good) in one of two divisions of the geldings maiden hosted by this Galway course in May. Jumping economically from the front, he engaged in a head to head with Minella Tara away from the second last: he just had the better of that battle when his rival fell at the last and the race seemed in the bag for Don Diablo: however, he was blindsided as Geraldo swept through in the last fifty yards to rob the race by a neck. In fairness to Don Diablo, he did precious little wrong, succumbing to a masterful piece of riding by Derek O'Connor on Geraldo. Gordon Elliott bought Don Diablo for £70,000 at Cheltenham May sales and this could turn out to be a fair piece of business. He will be competitive in a bumper and can figure in two and a half miles and upwards maiden/novice hurdles this winter and may be capable of competing at Graded level as a novice hurdler. Later in his career, he can become a 125+ chaser and may be versatile trip wise.

ÉCLAIR SURF (FR) 5 b g Califet (FR) – Matasurf (FR)
Trainer: Emma LAVELLE   **Form Figures: 31**
In 2017 Monbeg paid €44,000 at the Land Rover sale for this lengthy French bred bay gelding. He debuted at Lisronagh (Good) in November, and having led to two out, he folded quickly and dropped back to finish third: that sharp track may have left him vulnerable. Next time at Bandon (Heavy) in March, he took no prisoners: he helped set a relentless gallop and burned off his rivals and came home to win by more than a furlong. He appreciated the testing terrain and such conditions may be critical to his advancement as a racehorse. Bought for £140,000 at Cheltenham March sales on behalf of Tim Syder and Dominic Burke, he could be a long term project for a Welsh or Midlands National, races suited to mudlarks.

FADO DES BROSSES (FR) 4 b g Balko (FR) – Nanou Des Brosses (FR)
Trainer: Evan WILLIAMS   **Form Figures: 1**

He won the first three mile four year old maiden of 2019 at Belharbour (Good/Yielding) in February. The race contained five runners, but three of them had a bit of a reputation to live up to. In a steadily run affair, jockey John Barry produced Fado Des Brosses to contest for the lead on the run to the final fence: it was a 50-50 call between him and danger Goaheadwiththeplan, with that threat falling, it allowed Fado Des Brosses to lift the prize (on balance he may have won in any case). He is a sturdy French bred with a rather mundane bloodline. Pat Doyle trained him for this point and in winning the race, Doyle won this particular maiden for the third time in five years. With small fields, it can be tricky to put an accurate value on form: Fado Des Brosses clocked a time of 5:56 in winning, which in fact was the fastest running of this maiden over the last five years: comparatively, 6m (2015), 6:23 (2016), 6:19 (2017) and 6:12 (2018), means the clock gives a very good impression on the 2019 version. It must be taken into account, that the winter of 2019 was drier than normal, hence the good/yielding terrain may have played a role in the sub six minutes of Fado Des Brosses. Evan Williams stepped up to the plate and his bid of £200,000 at Cheltenham February Sales resulted in a new Welsh home for Fado. For now, with limited evidence, I would say he has talent and can compete as comfortably at two and a half miles as three miles and can win a maiden/novice hurdle this winter and he would be one to review after a first season of track racing in terms of potential.

FAKIR D'ALENE (FR) 4 b g Cokoriko (FR) – Serbanne (FR)
Trainer: Gordon ELLIOTT   **Form Figures: 1**

The Monbeg lads like French bred stores and this is another four year old they managed to get a first time win out of. An athletic, light on his feet, bay gelding with a white strip on his forehead, he triumphed at Broughshane (Good/Yielding) in May. Close to the leaders from the start, he moved to lead on the climb to the second last: he was in control when his nearest rival fell at the last and a wide margin win materialised. A €30,000 store purchase, there is little to excite in his French bloodlines: Gordon Elliott found favour in the Broughshane win as his bid of £160,000 at Doncaster May Sales was enough to land the youngster. Judging the win alone, my impression was that he was a summer jumper and would need to unlock significant improvement to compete at the higher levels. He should win a bumper in the late autumn as he enjoyed the fast ground at the Ulster venue.

FRENCH DYNAMITE (FR) 4 b g Kentucky Dynamite (USA) – Matnie (FR)
Trainer: Mouse MORRIS   **Form Figures: 1**

Team Monbeg picked this tall gelding up as a two year old store at the Arqana Sale in 2017 for €32,000, he has a sprinkling of French Graded winners in his pedigree. He made his only point appearance late in the season at Tralee (Good/Yielding), where he won the slower of the two four year old maidens staged that day. Well punted in the ring, he launched his bid from midfield as the field entered the last mile: in front rounding the hometurn with two to jump, he looked in complete control landing away from the penultimate fence. He then either idled or hung from the last and had to be driven out to score by a length and a half. The climax was either a case of a green inexperienced horse or one that will hang/idle if in front too long. The following week, he was in the sales ring at Cheltenham and made £165,000 and will sport the Robcour colours and is one of a few horses that owner has for the first time dispatched to Mouse Morris. French Dynamite has a fine long stride on him and, depending on how his ball bounces, he may develop into either a Graded chaser (140+) or a 120-135 handicapper. On pedigree, he ought to function even better on rain softened conditions.

FRONTAL ASSAULT (IRE) 4 b g Presenting – The Folkes Choice
Trainer: Gordon ELLIOTT   **Form Figures: P4**

The owners purchased this eye filling bay gelding for €50,000 at the 2018 Derby Store Sale: his dam won over hurdles and fences for Henry de Bromhead (good ground), and others in his direct family include Special Tiara: in essence, the evidence might say that two miles to two and a half miles may be his forte. He was farmed to Mouse Morris for pointing experience, racing twice. First time, at Turtulla (Good/Yielding), he was hunted round for two and a half miles and pulled up, a tender non taxing introduction. Then he travelled to north Cork for the Liscarroll (Yielding/Soft) four year old maiden: jumping neatly, he was within six lengths of the leader leaving the third last. Then the pace lifted and he was caught flat footed: from the second last, he was not pressurised and allowed to amble home a fifteen lengths fourth. In time, the kindness dispensed to him in these two points may be repaid on the track proper. The formbook will relate figures of P4 from his two runs, they mask a horse with potential. Switched to Gordon Elliott for track racing, I anticipate much progression in the next twelve months.

GERALDO (IRE) 4 b g Jeremy (USA) – Jim's Article (IRE)
Trainer: Gordon ELLIOTT　　　　　　　**Form Figures: 1**
Ann Marie Holden and her father have changed their approach to racing from the track to focus upon developing pointers: last season Derek O'Connor came onside with the family in the preparation of the Holden pointing stock and frequently rode them. Geraldo was a €27,000 purchase by the Holden family at the 2018 Land Rover Sale: a compact bay gelding with nothing to note in his family tree. He debuted at Stowlin (Good) in May and Derek was aboard and elected to hunt him around at the back for two miles: then be persuaded Geraldo to take closer order: by the second last he had closed to within six lengths of the leaders. In a dramatic conclusion, one of the leaders, Minella Tara fell, leaving Don Diablo with a healthy lead. Derek somehow conjured a super turn of foot out of Geraldo and they flew home in the last hundred yards of the run-in to scalp Don Diablo at the winning post and record a win against the head. The speed Geraldo offered at the finish will serve him to effect in track races and his style of racing will lend itself to winning handicaps over hurdles and fences. He enjoyed the good ground and for now one can mark him down as a 125+ track horse with the promise of upward movement on the ratings ladder.

GETAWAY PAT (IRE) 5 ch g Getaway (GER) – Sunset Gold (IRE)
Trainer: Henry De BROMHEAD　　　　　　**Form Figures: 1**
Rangy chestnut with white face and socks: on his one start at Dungarvan (Yielding) in January in a seventeen runner five year old maiden, he moved in style from the start: coasting to lead at the second last, for minimum persuasion he drew away from the pack and his jockey, John Barry, was easing him down with two hundred yards to race, his margin of victory, three lengths, no guide to his superiority. An impressive galloper and a fine chaser in the making, he was sold out of Pat Doyle's following this win, bought by owner Philip Reynolds and now a new addition to the de Bromhead squad. In 2019, said stable won the Albert Bartlett at the Cheltenham Festival and Getaway Pat could progress as a novice hurdler this winter and become the yard's representative in the 2020 version of that Grade 1 race: he has the class and talent to compete as an above average hurdler/chaser.

GET IN ROBIN (IRE) 4 ch f Robin Des Champs (FR) – Get In There (IRE)
Trainer: Donald McCAIN　　　　　　　**Form Figures: F1**
Tall liver chestnut mare, her dam was a three-time winner over hurdles and she can count Harbour Pilot and River Wylde amongst her relations. Another to represent Monbeg, she fell at the last on her debut at Ballyarthur (Soft/Heavy), where she struggled with the testing ground and was floundering and beaten when taking the tumble. Encountering a livelier surface at Fairyhouse (Good/Yielding) in April, she set out her stall to make all in a thirteen runner mares' race: in control of the pace, she asserted at the second last and won by a cosy four lengths, in a rather slow time. Picked up by Donald McCain for £55,000 at Doncaster May Sales, she will be one of a talented band of pointing mares her trainer has at his disposal this winter and I expect plenty of them to win maiden/novice hurdles, including this madam. She may not enjoy testing conditions or races when she gets serious competition, and she is likely to be a mare shy of Graded/Listed class amongst her own sex.

GOLD DES BOIS (FR) 5 ch g Full of Gold (FR) – Equatoriale (FR)
Trainer: Jessica HARRINGTON   **Form Figures: F1 - 0**

Big raw chestnut: pointed twice for Kildare trainer Peter Fahey. At Templenacarriga (Yielding) in January, he travelled best of all, and moved towards the final fence upsides Dolphin Square, he unfortunately fell at this obstacle. The next month he travelled north to Kirkistown (Yielding/Soft), he was ridden close to the leaders from the start: he merely had to be nudged out from the final fence to win convincingly: the runner-up Lowtown Charlie has two track wins to his name since then, suggesting the form is to be respected. Robcour purchased this French bred for £100,000 at Cheltenham in February and Jessie Harrington took the levers of control. He worked like a class horse on the gallops up The Curragh, prior to his bumper debut at the Punchestown Festival and started favourite for the contest. Alas, he found the ground too lively and was left alone once it was obvious he could not compete and finished tailed off in mid pack. The key to this five year old will be the ground...he wants soft or heavy and when he encounters such suitable conditions, then he will be in his element and has bright aspirations of winning at Graded level as a hurdler and chaser. He may become more of a two and a half miles chasing specialist rather than a dour stayer.

GRANDADS COTTAGE (IRE) 4 ch g Shantou (USA) – Sarah's Cottage (IRE)
Trainer: Olly MURPHY   **Form Figures: 1**

Full brother to the former 140 rated chaser Super Duty: chunky chestnut with big feet. Team Monbeg made the long trek to the northern coastal venue of Portrush (Good/Yielding) in April with this fellow and it proved a worthwhile journey. The four year old race was divided and the Monbeg representatives won both divisions, Grandads Cottage the more impressive in the fastest time of the day. Driven to the lead three out, he pinged the last two fences to win with plenty up his sleeve. Most effective on the sound surface, this €58,000 Derby Sale store found favour at the Aintree Goffs Sale and Olly Murphy triumphed in the bidding exchanges, £200,000 the tariff. The one minor issue with Grandads Cottage is that he is the produce of an old mare, normally a negative: apart from Super Duty, this four year old has other winning siblings, a feature of the family is that two and a half miles reads as their optimum distance. He should enjoy speed biased circuits in the two miles two to three miles range, the likes of Kempton, and he would have realistic aspirations of achieving a chase rating of 130+.

GRANGECLARE NATIVE (IRE) 4 ch g Shantou (USA) – Navaro (IRE)
Trainer: Gordon ELLIOTT   **Form Figures: 1**

Athletic likeable chestnut related to Mighty Mogul and Ballynagour, a €45,000 2018 Derby Sale store. Denis Murphy trained him for one point race, the four year old maiden at Curraghmore (Good) on Easter Sunday: Jamie Codd arrived for this specific mount and the top amateur enjoyed an almost armchair spin: Grangeclare relaxed for two miles, eased closer three out and then swept to the lead nearing the last and went clear on the run in without Codd having to resort to the whip. He floated on the good ground, which may suggest that will be his preferred surface. Then bought by Gordon Elliott for a reasonable £125,000 at Cheltenham April Sales, he should win a bumper and build into a better than average novice hurdler in 2019/20. He can be more than competitive at distances from two and a half to three miles over jumps.

HEARTBREAK KID (IRE) 4 b g Getaway (GER) – Bella's Bury
Trainer: Donald McCAIN   **Form Figures: 1**

With an older sibling (Sonic) in his yard, Donald McCain elected to purchase this lanky unfurnished bay gelding for a paltry €6,000 at the 2018 Land Rover Sale. It now looks like an inspired piece of business. With the Auction related series of four year old maidens commencing in Ireland during 2019, McCain decided to send Heartbreak Kid to Colin Bowe and try and win one of these limited maidens. The plan worked a treat: he debuted at Kirkistown (Soft/Heavy) in an auction maiden and relishing the testing conditions, he turned the race into a procession to win by a distance from a fair benchmark in Kearneys Hill. This four year old is made for three miles in muck around Carlisle and other stamina testing tracks. Suffice to say he will be handled by McCain forthwith and had the horse come under the hammer after this success, he certainly would have secured many multiples of his store price. He will develop into a middle of the road hurdler/chaser (120ish) and win a few hurdle races in the novice division this winter when testing elements are in play.

HOLD THAT TAUGHT 4 b g Kayf Tara – Belle Magello (FR)
Trainer: Venetia WILLIAMS   **Form Figures: 1**

A big boned bay gelding sporting a white face with notably huge feet: a €70,000 2018 Derby Sale purchase by Denis Murphy: his dam has produced eight winners, including Banjaxed Girl, and most of that family look to prefer two and a half miles. Murphy debuted this lad at Turtulla (Good/ Yielding) in March and one can take mixed messages from his winning effort. The field moved along at a decent lick throughout (ultimately ten seconds faster than the preceding four year old mares' maiden): Hold That Taught raced at the rear of midfield and was clumsy at fences: when improving his position he bulldozed his way through the fourth last: to his credit, he instantly got back into rhythm: sweeping to the lead on the climb to the second last, he again misjudged this fence and survived a dive: gathered up again, he then galloped powerfully to the win to register a ten lengths success over Battle Of Actium (subsequent winner). The negative, his disrespect for the fences, the positive, a long powerful galloper when at full tilt. His family record would recommend the two and a half miles suits the kin: this gelding will buck that trend as he was most forceful in the final half mile and three miles and upwards will be to his taste. Venetia Williams paid a personal record for a pointer of £220,000 at Cheltenham March Sales: I would fancy that this coming season will concentrate on gaining experience in minor novice hurdles (probably winning a low key race): the long term goal will be to develop him into a project for the premier staying handicaps such as the Welsh National.

IT SURE IS (IRE) 4 b g Shirocco (GER) – Stay At Home Mum (IRE)
Trainer: Nicky HENDERSON   **Form Figures: 1**

When Annie Power won the 2016 Champion Hurdle at around the time the stallion Shirocco moved to Rathbarry Stud, it looked like Shirocco was going to become a leading National Hunt sire. Alas, whilst he has much stock on the ground, most have been at best middle rankers and he requires a new headline act to come along to maintain the value of his currency. It Sure Is could be argued to be his best four year old pointer from the spring of 2019. Colin Bowe bought him as a €48,000 store and he appealed on pedigree, numbering the likes of Voler La Vedette and Hennessy (Graded winners) in his family. A sturdy bay gelding, he commenced his career in a point at Ballynoe (Good) in March. He contributed to a decent clip: racing towards the second last he was troubled by Bloodstone: he showed the greater resolution under Michael O'Sullivan to triumph by half a length, in a race where there was no hiding place: on a competitive days racing, it was significantly the fastest race on the card. He jumped crisply and stays the stiff three miles stoutly: Nicky Henderson paid £150,000 at Aintree sales in April and he now has a 125+ prospect in his care. I like his attitude, the Shirocco factor would worry me that he may not bridge the gap to Graded level (140+) as a novice hurdler.

JANUARY JETS (IRE) 5 b g Presenting – Poetics Girl (IRE)
Trainer: Jessica HARRINGTON   **Form Figures: F1**

Medium bay with a white face and white front socks: well connected, he is a half-brother to Runfordave and current Grade 1 bumper winning mare Colreevy. Raced twice for owner Walter Connors and trainer Pat Doyle in 2018/19. He debuted at Tattersalls (Yielding) in December: he shaped nicely but was held in third when falling two out in the race won by Chantry House. He did some damage to his facial area in that tumble as he had breathing difficulties for some weeks after: he had X-rays but no broken bones were detected in his skull. So he had a minor holiday and nature was allowed to do the healing process. He returned to action at Ballysteen (Yielding) in April: under a tender ride from Derek O'Connor, he won this maiden without receiving any rough treatment: he looked in control when his main threat fell at the last fence, resulting in a ten lengths winning margin (albeit a modest affair). Bought by Robcour for €115,000 at Punchestown Goffs Sale and Jessica

Harrington will train. If January Jets enjoys a clean run health-wise, he can win his maiden hurdle and hopefully improve into an above average (125+) novice hurdler: he has a nice cruising speed and can be potent from 2m 2f to 2m 6f....staying a stiff three miles may be doubtful.

JEREMY PASS (IRE) 4 b g Jeremy (USA) – Toulon Pass (IRE)
Trainer: Paul NICHOLLS   Form Figures: F
An unfurnished bay gelding, his grand dam produced Aintree Grand National winner Montys Pass: he was fancied for his sole start at Ballycahane (Soft) in March: he was shaping nicely in the inclement conditions and booked for an honourable second when he fell at the final fence in the race won by Giants Table. Handler Mick Goff was prepared to offer him for sale based on this performance and he secured a price of £100,000 at Cheltenham March Sales. He should win a race or two as a novice hurdler this winter (2m4f and upwards) and, if he could unearth a bit of improvement, earn a place at one of the spring Festivals. One with genuine aspirations to become a 130-140 chaser over time.

KAKAMORA 4 b g Great Pretender (IRE) – Roche D'Or
Trainer: Tom GEORGE   Form Figures: 1
Another late season first time out winner for the Monbeg Doyles: he made all the running as he landed the slower of the two divisions of the maiden staged at Loughanmore (Good) in May. He was in control and sealed the win with a slick jump at the final fence. A compact bay gelding with a white star on his forehead, he is the first produce of his unraced dam, he is related to seven times winner Bitofapuzzle. He has scope and could be versatile enough to compete between two miles and three miles: following his three lengths success he changed hands for £105,000 at Cheltenham Sales in May.

KEARNEY HILL (IRE) 4 b g Dylan Thomas (IRE) – Sunny Glen (IRE)
Trainer: Brian ELLISON   Form Figures: 2F
Some years ago, Brian Ellison bought his number one jumps horse, Definitly Red, from Brian Hamilton and he was happy to buy another offering from that source at Doncaster Sales in May, paying £44,000 for this compact bay gelding. He has a light pedigree and that contributed to his low €14,000 store price, and that same low price qualified him for auction races. On his debut at Kirkistown (Soft/Heavy), in an auction race, he found Heartbreak Kid an opponent outside his class, yet finished a distance second, best of the also rans. His next start was in a division of the maiden hosted by Taylorstown (Good): he coped with the tight contours of this track and was one of two who had drawn clear moving to the final fence: he fell when about half a length down and simplified the task of winner, Dancewiththewind: whether it was the previous experience or better ground, this performance represented progression and he sold on the back of this run. He may develop into a handy middle tier horse for northern racing (115-125) and will win minor races as a novice hurdler and chaser, and depending on how he is campaigned, there may be a valuable northern handicap in him some day.

KEEP WONDERING (IRE) 5 b g Scorpion (IRE) – Supreme Touch (IRE)
Trainer: Philip HOBBS   Form Figures: 2S1
Powerful bay gelding, his slate shows three point runs for team Monbeg. He commenced his career at Oldcastle (Good) in May 2018, hampered at a key moment, he posted a creditable second in the circumstances, defeated by Cenotice. Fortune again deserted him when he reappeared in 2019 at Ballycahane (Soft) as he was sitting pretty getting ready to pounce when he slipped up on the flat after the third last. Three weeks later, at Liscarroll (Yielding/Soft), he served notice that he is a racehorse of merit. This time coming to lead at the third last, in a few strides he left his rivals for dead, extending away for an eight lengths win from Barrowlands (a good benchmark opponent). Carrying 12st 2lbs he clocked a time two seconds faster than the four year old Papa Tango Charly (carried 11st 11lbs), and that to me signifies a highly commendable win. Progeny by the sire Scorpion do have a reputation for their moods by times: this gelding could

be a very decent handicap chaser in the making (135+) and he can succeed as a staying novice hurdler this winter.

KILLER CLOWN (IRE) 5 b g Getaway (GER) – Our Soiree (IRE)
Trainer: Emma LAVELLE   **Form Figures: 1 - 2**
Rangy bay gelding with a white face: cost Colin Bowe €40,000 Euros as a store. Made a winning point debut at Corbeagh (Soft) in December when emerging on top of a fine late tussle with Carry On The Magic. Sold for £135,000 at Cheltenham December Sales to Emma Lavelle, he ran a commendable second on his track debut in May: in a hot bumper at Warwick for the time of year, he hung in the closing hundred yards and this action may have caused his three parts of a length defeat as he placed second. It is conceivable he hung due to the ground being faster than he may like. He relished the soft/heavy at Corbeagh and may well be a proper winter horse: I would hold out a positive view on his future prospects: a 130+ hurdler/chaser and one liable to scale further heights, if he progresses with maturity.

LARGY FIX (IRE) 4 ch g Notnowcato – Fix It Lady (IRE)
Trainer: Mouse MORRIS   **Form Figures: F1**
Largy Fix was trained for his two points by Stuart Crawford and he had paid €28,000 for him at the 2018 Land Rover Sale. By a recently deceased sire, there is nothing whatsoever in his pedigree to set the pulses racing. A tall, unfurnished chestnut with white features, he has a long stride and I suspect the tight bends of Taylorstown (Good) were alien to his nature on his debut: he fell two out when sixth and trying to make some ground. His other point start was at Loughanmore in May, also on good ground: the four year old maiden was divided and both splits attracted runners from the top yards. In his division, Largy Fix sat at the rear of midfield: he clicked into gear as they raced to the third last and made a number of places, and landed a close third at the second last: on the long run to the final fence, he picked off the leaders and clearing the final fence at speed, he pulled away for a four lengths win without the jockey having to pressurise him. As it was a late season maiden, the form has not had the opportunity to be franked: by the end of the upcoming Autumn Point campaign, I would fancy three or four of the also rans will have gained a maiden pointing win under their belts. He has a likeable nature and evidently an engine. One extra piece of evidence in his favour was that he clocked a time seven seconds faster than the preceding first division. In the past three years, Malone Road, The Very Man and Battleoverodoyen have won four year old maidens at this Loughanmore circuit and the time posted by Largy Fix was faster than any of those talented trio when they won over the same venue. I hope Mouse Morris can translate his potential into track success and I think this youngster will perform at trips from two and a half miles and above on good or soft ground.

LETS GO CHAMP (IRE) 4 b g Jeremy (USA) – Dark Mimosa (IRE)
Trainer: Tom GEORGE   **Form Figures: 1**
A big powerful elegant bay gelding: given his physique and the fact that he is a close relative of Triumph Hurdle winner Our Conor, he commanded €90,000 when Monbeg purchased him as 2018 Derby sale. His debut was delayed until Bartlemy (Good) in May and he was punted with confidence into favouritism. Tucked away in the pack until produced on the long run to three out to share the lead: he ran a little wide off the home bend and winged the second last to land three lengths clear: with Full Back finishing nicely, he was challenged at the last, where he got in a little deep: he was forced to find inside the last fifty yards, and did so to score by a length and a half. Given that he arrived at the meeting with a tall reputation, in reviewing the victory, it has an aspect of either the glass half full or half empty about it. On the plus side, he possesses bags of scope and potential and he has a big stride and an engine. The race time was twelve seconds faster than the mares' four year old contest half an hour earlier. On the debit side, he was clumsy and rather guessy at his fences and did not look to be a natural at locating a take off stride (the jumping department needs attention) and he also ran a bit green. He sold then at Doncaster Spring Sales as the top Irish pointer, making a price of £375,000. I remember Stellar Notion finishing second in

the corresponding Bartlemy maiden for the late Willie Codd in 2013: he was the physical match of Lets Go Champ and, in his career, he peaked as a mid 140s horse who never won the highbrow race that looked in his grasp: Lets Go Champ could develop in the same mould as a 130-145 handicapper, but not quite classy enough for the top of the ladder Graded races.

MACKENBERG (GER) 4 b g Jukebox Jury (IRE) – Mountain Melody (GER)
Trainer: Donald McCAIN   **Form Figures: UF**
Monbeg paid £56,000 for the four year old as a store and he hails from a German family with black type Flat winners peppered through it. A bay gelding with size and scope, he ran twice in the spring: his debut at Monksgrange was short lived as he unseated his rider at the third fence. Then he ran in a division of the maiden at Courtown (Soft): held up out the back, as they entered the home run with three to jump, he was still sixth about twelve lengths down: with the tacky ground putting an emphasis on stamina, he began to click into gear at the finish and was coming home best of all and looked to be set to lead when he fell at the last in the race won by Crack Du Ninian. He failed to sell through the ring at Cheltenham April sales, with Don McCain buying him privately outside for £90,000 on behalf of Tim Leslie. With form figures of UF: punters may ignore this lad when he first surfaces for track races. I think he could be an above average novice type for northern racing and becoming a 130+ handicapper is within his grasp: so there may be betting value in his early track races. If the Courtown race is a fair indicator, then two and a half miles plus and soft/heavy may be his favoured ingredients.

MINELLA MELODY (IRE) 5 b m Flemensfirth (USA) – Cottage Theatre (IRE)
Trainer: Henry De BROMHEAD   **Form Figures: 112 - 3**
Arguably the top pointing mare of 2018/19: she delivered on a lofty home reputation when she scooted clear from three out to triumph by ten lengths at Boulta (Soft) in December. A chucky six figure private sale resulted in Kenny Alexander purchasing her and moving her to Henry de Bromhead. She made an instant track impact, turning the point to point limited bumper at Gowran (Soft) into a procession under Patrick Mullins. She lost no honour in defeat when placed in mares' Graded bumpers at the Aintree and Punchestown Festivals. I sensed she may have been over the top for the season at Punchestown. A candidate for major honours in the mares' novice hurdle division in 2019/20, her ground and trip versatility a big plus.

MINELLA TARA (IRE) 4 b g Kayf Tara – Jolie Landaise (FR)
Trainer: Fergal O'BRIEN   **Form Figures: F**
Another John Nallen acquired as a foal: his grand dam bred Grade 1 winner Bilboa: we encountered him in one point race, at Stowlin (Good) in May: sited fourth/fifth for the majority of the contest, he then made a move to kick and try and win the race at the second last: prospects of victory looked bright temporarily, then re-pressed in sight of the last, he began to curl up and he fell at this fence when possibly losing the battle. On this evidence, he may be a bridle merchant who needs holding up for one late surge, and he may not find as desired when under pressure. Fergal O Brien takes charge following a £90,000 purchase from Doncaster May Sales. Conceivably, two and a half miles rather than three miles may suit him best.

MOSSY FEN (IRE) 4 b g Milan – Inch Native (IRE)
Trainer: Nigel TWISTON-DAVIES   **Form Figures: F1**
The son of a winning pointer from a family containing Sound Man and Pairofbrowneyes: a Monbeg €30,000 2018 Derby buy. Appeared twice in point to points: falling at the first fence on his initial run at Castletown, he then won second time out at Loughbrickland (Yielding/Soft). Jumping cautiously for the first half of the race, sited in rear, he gradually improved his position inside the last mile and arrived up a close second at the second last fence. The leader Somptueux seemed to have his measure as they ascended to the final fence: upon jumping the last, the greater stamina reserves of Mossy Fen kicked in and he conquered his rival by two lengths. A medium sized bay gelding, Nigel Twiston Davies bought him for £60,000 at Cheltenham April

Sales on behalf of owner Carl Hinchy and he is the type of tough hardy equine which said handler can get a successful tune out of. Staying races in testing conditions is when he will be likely to figure at the business end of track races.

MUCKAMORE (IRE) 5 b g Sholokhov (IRE) – Gales Return (IRE)
Trainer: Paul NICHOLLS   **Form Figures: 2**

Tall bay gelding: a light immediate pedigree page, four generations back you find the Jezki line. Ran at then owner Wilson Dennison's track at Loughanmore (Good/Yielding) in November: disputing the running from halfway, he made minor mistakes and, in the final two furlongs, he was no match for easy winner Beyond Redemption. When he appeared at Cheltenham November sales the buzz word relating to this horse was scope, and it encouraged Paul Nicholls to pay £190,000 for him. With Beyond Redemption devaluing his currency in the interim, the form does now look suspect. Allowed time to physically mature, he may prove a different proposition with reconditioning, the balance of probabilities relate that his grade may be as a 110-125 handicapper.

NOREEN BAWN (IRE) 4 b f Jeremy (USA) – Rose N Alice (IRE)
Trainer: Alan FLEMING   **Form Figures: 2**

A strong bay mare with size and stature, her half-sister is the 120 rated jumper Cotton Jenny, and her dam won a two miles novice chase on good ground. In what was a competitive field featuring runners from the top yards, she debuted at Dromahane (Good) in April in a mares' maiden. To the fore from the start: she poured on the pace on the entrance to the home straight with three to jump and soon pulled away in company with Tucanae: neither would yield over the last quarter mile: close to the final fence, Noreen jinked to her right (her eye possibly caught by the horse boxes nearby) and caused a minor check on Tucanae. Together on landing, it was nip and tuck to the line with Noreen Bawn poking her head down at the line to prevail by a slim margin. There was an inevitable stewards' enquiry, and in what was a 50-50 call, the stipes elected to alter the placings in favour of Tucanae. Connections of Noreen Bawn may have gone home slightly irked, within a few days they had joy as this mare proved very attractive at the Punchestown Sales and fetched a price of €220,000 with owner Barry Connell securing him. Noreen Bawn is an above average (120+) lady, family custom would relate that good/fast ground are ingredients required for optimum results.

OFFTHESHOULDER (IRE) 5 b g Gold Well – Zafilly
Trainer: Lucinda RUSSELL   **Form Figures: 1**

Tall bay gelding from a modest family of Flat racers: won on his only outing for Monbeg: at Cragmore (Yielding/Soft) in February having engaged in combat with Oscar Robertson from three out, he gained the upperhand in the last fifty yards to record a narrow win. Sold for a steep £110,000 at Cheltenham February sales, I view him as a winning pointer likely to prefer dropping in trip to either two miles or two and a half miles as he has raw speed. One likely to score on the speed biased Scottish/northern racecourses such as Kelso or Musselburgh.

OSCAR ROBERTSON (IRE) 5 b g Oscar (IRE) – Beaus Polly (IRE)
Trainer: Tom GEORGE   **Form Figures: B2**

Chunky bay gelding with three prominent white socks: represented the David Fitzgerald yard for two point races: he was green on his Boulta (Yielding) debut and in the process of being nursed home to finish fifth/sixth when he was brought down at the final fence. His next engagement was at his local track, Cragmore (Yielding/Soft) in February. Weight of money in the ring forced him into favouritism: ridden to oblige, he was in the van from four out, pestered from three out by Offtheshoulder, he succumbed and was beaten a length. Of the two involved in that finish, I see more potential in Oscar Robertson: bought privately by Tom George, still a maiden, he could be a surprise packet as a track horse and could emerge as a 125+ mid distance handicap chaser of some merit.

PAPA TANGO CHARLY (FR) 4 ch g No Risk At All (FR) – Chere Elenn (FR)
Trainer: Jonjo O'NEILL   **Form Figures: 1**

In 2018 two of the most expensive Irish pointers bought in public auction were Envoi Allen (£400,000) and Malone Road (£325,000): both had looked special in their respective points and by any scale their track performances in 2018/19 reflected that they were indeed Grade 1 standard and justified the exalted price tags. From the 2019 crop of four year old Irish pointers, the most expensive sold in public was Papa Tango Charly: Akin to Envoi Allen, he was sourced in France as a yearling by Walter Connors. He was trained for his point by Colin Bowe, his date with destiny the Liscarroll (Yielding/Soft) maiden in March. I went to the horseboxes to study the stock before the race and Papa Tango Charly was instantly forgettable, a plain jane medium sized angular chestnut, a French bred from a limited racing family. Leaving aside pre-race impression: in the race, he quickened the tempo along with Big Bresil running to the second last, and then moved away from his threat rounding the home turn: far from fluent at the last, he still posted a four lengths win. Yes, he absolutely proved he had gears and that appealed to agents. The scope factor is lacking in my view. Jonjo O Neill will train him after Michael Tedham paid the season high fee of £440,000 for him at Aintree April Sales. Light on his feet, he should cope with good and soft ground and anything tripwise from two miles two to two miles six will suit him. My fear is that he will ultimately become one of those Grade 3 (130-140) horses who falls through the cracks and never wins anything of note.

POWER OF PAUSE (IRE) 4 ch g Doyen (IRE) – Shady Pines (IRE)
Trainer: Willie MULLINS   **Form Figures: 1**

Mark O'Hare is another amateur jockey, who in recent times has been dabbling in the pointing version of pinhooking: buying store horses, preparing them for points and then attempting to sell on for a profit after a good performance between the flags: in 2018 he was responsible for the talented mare Honeysuckle when she won her maiden at Dromahane and she enjoyed an excellent first season on the track which culminated with a Grade1 win at Fairyhouse in Easter. Mark restocked last summer at the store sales and one of his investments was Power Of Pause, costing him €28,000 at the Land Rover sale. In truth, his page made little appeal, his dam won a minor two miles maiden hurdle at Sligo and nothing of note pops up in the family. A compact chestnut with white markings: he debuted in an early season two and a half miles maiden at Punchestown (Good) in February. Pre-race, it gave the impression of a decent contest with the leading yards all represented, in action, it turned out to be an easy assignment for Power Of Pause, as he readily mastered his rivals and surged away from two out to win by six lengths. Since then, none of the others have advertised the form. One cannot take away from the success of Power Of Pause because he could only beat what was in front of him: at Cheltenham Sales in March he fetched a price of £180,000 for Mark O'Hare, a handsome profit. I have found that the sire Doyen has yielded four year old point winners who one could post under the umbrella term of "exciting". They tend to do fine in bumpers but they are not really training on to a higher class as hurdlers/chasers. It is possible that Power Of Pause can win one or two bumpers for Willie Mullins and his currency may not rise to a level beyond Grade 3 when he heads over jumps on the track.

PURE BLISS 4 ch f Mount Nelson – Burton Ash
Trainer: Harry FRY   **Form Figures: 1**

A light framed athletic chestnut mare with a Flat biased pedigree, her half-brother Secret Edge was a 130 rated hurdler for Alan King. In a slowly run race, she delivered a sustained run to win on her debut at Rathcannon (Good) in April (form not franked) for Denis Murphy. I noted there were a selection of minor issues with her vetting prior to Punchestown Sales, an event at which Harry Fry risked €100,000 to nab her. She strikes me as a winning pointer who could score over the shorter trips when hurdling: Fry has a fine record with previous ex- Irish pointers and it is feasible he may eek more out of this lady than one would currently expect.

RIVER TYNE 4 b f Geordieland (FR) – Not Now Nellie
Trainer: Dan SKELTON   **Form Figures: 1**
Tall British bred bay mare: a half-sister to the 140 rated Close House. Contested one point for
Sam Curling at Turtulla (Good/Yielding) in March: one of four mares to drive clear from four out,
she engaged in a ding dong battle with Lady Tremaine (subsequent winner) from two out and
showed guts and determination to win the race by a couple of lengths. Bought by team Skelton
for £50,000 at Cheltenham March sales, they have a mare with scope on their hands and she will
be potent in true run races and can win a few mares' hurdle races in 2019/20 as a novice and she
is a mare likely to figure further down the line as a 120+ novice chaser.

ROYAL CROWN (FR) 4 ch g Creachadoir (IRE) – Royal Army (GER)
Trainer: Colin TIZZARD   **Form Figures: 2**
Colin Bowe picked up this muscular bay gelding for €55,000 as a store: his dam was a four times
Flat winner and there are several continental black type Flat winners on his page. He ran in the
Lisronagh (Good) maiden in March: handy for most of the journey: he pressed Pens Man from
two out, never getting past and ultimately beaten two lengths into second. He was not subjected
to the same punishment meated out to the winner. He may not stay three miles, but he may
comfortably slot in as a two to two and a half miles hurdler/chaser. Colin Tizzard may unlock the
potential in this youngster, he changed hands for £110,000 at Aintree Sales: he is one of the more
interesting maiden pointers set to head to the track proper and one who could prove a surprise
package.

SILVER HALLMARK 5 b g Shirocco (GER) – Gaye Sophie
Trainer: Fergal O'BRIEN   **Form Figures: 13**
Big robust grey gelding: made a successful point debut for Pat Doyle at Tattersalls (Yielding) in
December: overwhelming his rivals from three out and driving clear to win by an eased down
three lengths: it is noteworthy that he won a division of the four year old geldings maiden, and
he clocked a time three seconds faster than the other division won by Chantry House. From the
family of Champion hurdler Gaye Brief, he is a half-brother to 148 rated Gayebury and I think his
price of £115,000 when sold to Fergal O'Brien at Cheltenham December Sales was warranted.
He was introduced to track racing in a bumper Newbury in the spring: in a race run at a stop-start
gallop, it culminated with a three furlongs dash to the line, and Silver Hallmark was compromised:
initially tapped for toe, he cranked into full tilt about a furlong out and finished with purpose, a
closing third to winner McFabulous. I like his attitude: now owned by the Ruckers, they may have
another long term Grand National prospect in Silver Hallmark, as his career may climax at the age
of eight or nine when he is functioning as a 130-145 staying handicap chaser. This winter he will
be gaining experience in novice hurdles and can be competitive to a 125 level, without making
Festival championship standard.

SKATMAN (IRE) 4 br g Mustameet (USA) – Maid For Action (IRE)
Trainer: Paul NICHOLLS   **Form Figures: 1**
Medium bay gelding with little to excite in his pedigree: he left his calling card by taking a fast
run maiden at Dromahane (Good) at the end of April. Moving to lead four out, he slipped clear in
company with Barbados Buck's from three out: he was the sharper of the pair on the day, taking
the spoils by two lengths. Paul Nicholls paid £170,000 for him at Doncaster May Sales, and he
also incidentally bought the runner up: my hunch is the latter has more scope. Skatman is what
I would regard as a "ready to go" four year old: more forward than many of the age group, he
can win a novice hurdle before Christmas and then test his mettle in the better winners' races.
He reminds me of another recent Nicholls pointing recruit, Getaway Trump, and he is a horse
who may stand plenty of racing and pay his way without becoming anything special. With natural
speed, he will operate comfortably at two miles or two and a half miles, and he enjoys a sound
surface.

SOMPTUEUX (FR) 4 b g Spirit One (FR) – Best Day (FR)
Trainer: Henry De Bromhead   **Form Figures: 2**
Middle sized bay French bred: his dam was a dual jumps winner and Theinval (150 rated chaser)
is a product of his grand dam. Bought in France as a store for €18,000 in Arqana sales. He ran
once for Stuart Crawford in the Loughbrickland (Yielding/Soft) maiden in April. Despite market
weakness, he travelled like the best horse in that eleven-runner race. Striking the front after three
out, he looked all over a winner climbing to the final fence: either stamina or the tacky terrain
found him out as Mossy Fen scalped him inside the final fifty yards, a two lengths second his
return. Examining the family, one can reason two to two and a half miles tends to be their favoured
distance. A few years ago Henry de Bromhead purchased Plan Of Attack from the same source
after he won the corresponding race in 2017: he was happy to receive Somptueux when a bid
of £70,000 proved successful at Cheltenham April Sales. This four year old will now carry the
Robcour silks and he could become a decent chaser over shorter trips and on a sound surface.

SPRINGFIELD FOX 6 gr g Sagamix (FR) – Marlbrook Fox
Trainer: Tom GEORGE   **Form Figures: 111**
Former English permit holder John Needham, bred this stout grey gelding and sent him as
an unraced five year old to Declan Queally to point in Ireland last autumn. A horse with a long
stride, he managed to complete a hat trick of wins inside two months: starting his sequence
with an eight lengths win at Boulta (Soft) in December, then adding to his haul in winners grade
at Aghabullogue (Good/Yielding) and Kilfeacle (Soft) in January: he can front run or take a lead
and is an accurate jumper. In terms of form, although unbeaten, he has not defeated any horse of
merit and therefore he has not faced a serious test. Bought by the George yard for a sum reported
to be circa £130,000: he will win chases from two and a half miles and upwards, probably in the
middle grades rather than those in the upper echelons. I don't envisage him making much of an
impact as a novice hurdler.

TAKE IT AWAY (IRE) 5 b m Yeats (IRE) – Claudia's Pearl
Trainer: Nicky HENDERSON   **Form Figures: 3 - 1**
Well-proportioned bay mare from a Flat biased family: a €22,000 store from the 2017 Derby sale.
Her debut run during the spring of 2018 was disappointing, as she folded from four out and was
fortunate to place a remote third. A different lady on her reappearance at Dromahane (Good/
Yielding) in November: handled with confidence by Jamie Codd, she was always moving in style
and once shaken up from the second last fence, she quickened to post a twelve lengths win:
although just a seven runner mares maiden, the second, third and fifth all went on to win their
points, recommending the form as reliable. J.P. McManus added her to his large team with a
£105,000 purchase at Cheltenham December sales and she has joined Nicky Henderson. Should
win her mares' maiden hurdle and then sit on the fringes of Graded mares' company. A mare who
may peak as a chaser.

TELMESOMETHINGGIRL (IRE) 4 b f Stowaway – Wahiba Hall (IRE)
Trainer: Henry De BROMHEAD   **Form Figures: 1**
Medium sized bay mare, a €39,000 store purchase: Colin Bowe made the unusual decision to
pitch her into an open four year old maiden (geldings & mares) at Ballinaboola (Good/Yielding)
and the decision came up trumps as she won the early season two and a half miles race and
was the solitary four year old mare to beat the other sex of her age group in 2019's Irish pointing
spring. In the race at Ballinaboola, Barry O'Neill got into in a nice rhythm from the beginning:
jumping with elan and close up throughout: with rivals blundering, O'Neill kicked for glory and
the mare was full value for her three lengths winning margin. Scottish owner Kenny Alexander
is assembling a talented bunch of racing mares, and he added Telmesomethinggirl to his team
having acquired her for £150,000 at Cheltenham March sales to join Henry De Bromhead.
Hailing from a family including Wahiba Sands and Medaille Militaire and guided by her winning
performance, the likelihood is that this mare can win hurdle races from two miles to two and a half

miles, and she will make a fair fist of adding black type to her name, as she has the capacity to figure in Graded/Listed mares' novice hurdles or chases: my hunch is that she has more natural speed than stamina.

WALK AWAY (IRE) 6 b g Black Sam Bellamy (IRE) – Pegus Love (IRE)
Trainer: Henry De BROMHEAD Form Figures: 114 - 7
This bay gelding is a big boned old fashioned chasing model: he races keenly: galloping with purpose and he routed his rivals in his only point outing at Ballindenisk (Yielding/Soft) in December: he made all, and there was a heart stopping moment at the final fence, when well clear, he threw a massive jump but slithered on landing: smart enough not to lose balance and with his jockey sticking to him, the damage was repaired and he won eased down by four lengths. He was then sold to Henry de Bromhead/Robcour for £130,000 at Cheltenham December Sales. He was working on a par with Cheltenham class stablemates, prior to his track debut: a risk was taken running him on good ground at Thurles in a two miles six maiden hurdle: settled in behind, he tanked through to lead racing to the second last and bombed away for a nine lengths win. It was decided to have a crack at Grade 1 level at Aintree: he had a minor blood issue leading up to the meeting, nonetheless he ran a stormer on his second track start to finish twelve lengths fourth to Champ in a top level novice hurdle. That race knocked the edge off him and he was over the top when seventh in another Grade 1 novice hurdle at the Punchestown Festival. He has come a long way very quickly in a short space of time: from winning a five year old maiden in December to finishing the spring with a hurdles rating of 140. With a summer break and a full season with de Bromhead, this lad could be a top class novice chaser in 2019/20 and he is one capable of downing others with big reputations: the major Festivals will be in his sights as a staying novice chaser.

YOUNG BUCK (IRE) 5 b g Yeats (IRE) – Pepsi Starlet (IRE)
Trainer: Paul NICHOLLS Form Figures: 1
Chunky bay gelding: racing for the Shark Hanlon yard, he stepped out for his only start to date at Nenagh (Yielding) in February and made all the running to win a fair maiden in the joint fastest time of the day: along the way he was ignorant when jumping some fences, he got away with a clumsy jump at the final fence. The exercise at Nenagh signalled that he can sustain a proper gallop. Originally a €36,000 store, from the same family as Bradbury Star, he made a price of £150,000 at the Cheltenham March sales. The last ex-pointer Paul Nicholls acquired from the Shark was Posh Trish, a multiple winner, and the Shark rates this gelding as talented as that mare. This gelding can win at a decent level (135+), we must observe if he will be potent on soft/tacky ground or versatile in that aspect. He could become a winter specialist around Chepstow over hurdles, although his jumping technique needs tightening.

DECLAN PHELAN'S
NATIONAL HUNT SERVICE 2019/20

If you would like to join Declan's jumps service for this season, please contact him on mrdeclanphelan@hotmail.com for full details, a limited number of places available.

For Irish (only) clients, if you wish to hear Declan's nightly views on the next day's racing, they are available nightly from 10pm on 1560 111 112.

STABLE GOSSIP

BRIAN ELLISON feels he has more quality in his team this season and one of his principal hopes is **WINDSOR AVENUE** who starts his chasing career this Autumn. A half-brother to former stablemate Ravenhill Road and the unbeaten Malone Road, the winning pointer developed into a 134 rated novice hurdler last winter. A dual winner at Hexham and Sedgefield, he was four lengths runner-up in the Grade 2 Premier Novices' Hurdle at Kelso in March over a trip shy of his best. The Winged Love gelding should make an above average northern novice chaser over two and a half miles.

Don't be surprised if Brian has his eye on a **junior bumper** for the unraced three year old **FAIR STAR**. A well bred son of Sea The Stars, he is a half-brother to dual Group 3 winner Majestic Queen and was unraced for William Haggas. Bought for 30,000gns at the Newmarket July Sales this summer, he is now owned by Dan Gilbert and could be a shrewd acquisition. I contacted William in early September and he described him as **"a nice horse just backward."**

* *

As discussed, **DAN SKELTON** had a magnificent season with 205 winners last term and there is a feeling at Lodge Hill that the yard has even more quality this year. **ANYTIME WILL DO**, who is rated 135, will be aimed at the Silver Trophy at Chepstow (12th October) and is considered fairly handicapped. **ARDLETHEN** is a novice chaser to watch out for having won twice over hurdles (rated 139) last season. He has reportedly done very well during the summer. Grade 2 winning novice hurdler **BEAKSTOWN** is another who will go over fences but may have one more run over hurdles beforehand. Rated 140 over timber, he is a winning Irish pointer and ought to take high rank. **BOSS MAN FRED** was purchased for £70,000 at the Aintree Sale in April having won his only point-to-point in Ireland. He has pleased in his work since arriving and the Dubai Destination gelding may start off in a bumper. Dan bought the ill-fated North Hill Harvey from Tom Lacey having won a point-to-point and he returned to the same source to acquire the exciting **CADZAND**. The four year old by Stowaway was an impressive winner of his sole outing and is now owned by Chelsea. A big imposing type who shows a lot of speed at home, he is considered one of the stable's leading novice hurdle prospects for this winter. The yard won the mares' final at Newbury in March a couple of seasons ago with Roksana and the same event could be **GETARIVER**'s main target this time around. The unbeaten six year old won both her bumpers at Ludlow and Newbury. **GETAWAY MAG** is another nice mare to keep an eye on. Bought for 45,000gns at the Cheltenham April Sale on behalf of Mrs Sarah Faulks, she won the second of her two Irish points having been carried out on her debut. **INTERCONNECTED** arrived with a lofty reputation and an even bigger price tag having been purchased for £620,000 by owner Darren Yates at the Doncaster Spring Sale. The Network gelding won an English point for Tom Lacey before finishing second over hurdles behind Emitom at Newbury in March when trained by Nicky Henderson. Described as a big strong horse, he was still weak when joining the yard but has reportedly put weight on and strengthened during the summer. Grade 1 and Cheltenham Festival winner **ROKSANA** has thrived during the summer and is in tremendous form at home. Rated 151, she will continue over hurdles with a return to the Festival next March very much her principal aim. **SHAN BLUE** is a name for the notebook. Successful in his only Irish point, he was third in a hotly contested bumper at Warwick in March. Described as a smart prospect, he was too keen last season but is much more relaxed and is viewed as a potential Grade 2 Leamington Novice Hurdle horse at Warwick next January. Skelton has won the two and a half miles event twice in the last five years (Three Musketeers (2015) & Beakstown (2018)). Dan has done well with horses he has purchased from Timmy Hyde in Ireland, namely Brewin'upastorm and Robin Roe and he has taken charge of the unbeaten **WEST CORK**. A four lengths winner of his only point-to-point, he is a five year old by Midnight Legend and a half-brother to Alan King's William H Bonney. He has pleased in his work at home and could run in a bumper before sent hurdling. He belongs to Mike and Eileen Newbould. **VISION DU PUY** is the first horse owner J.P.McManus sent to Skelton and the four year old filly won by nearly three lengths on her British debut at Perth in late April. Unbeaten in two starts over hurdles, she is rated 134 and has thrived during the summer. Previously trained in France by Domininque Bressou, the Vision D'Etat filly is considered very well handicapped and is one to follow. Finally, my contact in the yard has given me a couple of unraced bumper horses owned by John Magnier to look out for. **ACROSS THE LINE** is a four year old by Fame And Glory who goes very nicely at home, while the other is an **unnamed four year old by Martaline**. He is described as a lovely horse who has shown all the right signs in his work.

* *

NIGEL TWISTON-DAVIES has a formidable team of novice chasers for the winter ahead and he has a few other names to bear in mind this season. The Naunton handler has won the BetVictor Gold Cup at Cheltenham (16th November) on four occasions (Tipping Tim (1992), Imperial Commander (2008), Little Josh (2010) & Splash of Ginge (2017)) and he has got the two and a half miles event very much in mind for **COUNT MERIBEL**. Rated 146 over fences, the Three Valleys gelding has won two of his four races and his form figures at the track are 217. Plagued by sore shins last season, they have been pinfired and the seven year old is open to further improvement.

GUY is a novice hurdler to follow having shaped with plenty of promise on his sole run in a bumper last spring. A four year old by Getaway, he was two and a half lengths runner-up behind the more experienced Big Bad Bear at Perth's spring Festival and is considered a smart prospect.

The stable invariably unearths a promising bumper horse or two and it will pay to follow the Paul and Clare Rooney owned **ONE FINE MAN**. A four year old gelding by Jeremy, he worked well last spring and has pleased his trainer since. He has a lot of class about him, according to my source in the yard, and shouldn't be missed on his racecourse bow.

Please see page 195
for details of the
Ahead on the Flat 2020

Don't forget to read my Diary @
www.mhpublications.couk

Don't forget to check out my Racing *Diary* @

www.mhpublications.co.uk

Wednesday 8th May 2019

In the same race, the fourth **NONCHALANCE** made a very encouraging start to her career. A daughter of Dubawi and trained by John Gosden, she was towards the rear with a couple of furlongs to run before staying on strongly under Robert Havlin. Beaten five and a half lengths, she will stay further and is a winner waiting to happen. **NONCHALANCE won her next two starts @ 6/4 & 4/5**

Friday 24th May 2019

I thought stablemate **WHIMBREL** shaped with plenty of encouragement in third. A filly by Dark Angel, she too had made her racecourse bow at Wolverhampton (in November) finishing seventh. Partnered by Nicky Mackay, she wasn't unfancied being sent off 5/1 and finished with real purpose. She is out of a twelve furlongs winner and will appreciate an extra couple of furlongs. **WHIMBREL won next time over 1m 2f at Chelmsford (6th June) @ 9/2**

Saturday 8th July 2019

Regular purchasers of *AOTF* will recall that **Night of Thunder** featured in the *Top 40 Prospects* in 2014 when the Richard Hannon trained colt won the 2000 Guineas under Kieren Fallon from Kingman and Australia belying odds of 40/1 in the process. The son of Dubawi has made a tremendous start to his stallion career in 2019 with 10 individual winners already. These include the Hannon trained pair **Man of The Night** and **Wild Thunder**, plus **Under The Stars** who made a winning start to her career on her debut for James Tate on Monday evening at Ripon. The trio look above average and Night of Thunder's progeny are well worth a second look. **UNDER THE STARS won the Group 3 Princess Margaret Stakes at Ascot (27th July) @ 25/1**

Sunday 21st July 2019

At a lesser level, I think it is only a matter of time before Tim Easterby places the five year old **Regal Mirage** to advantage. The Aqlaam gelding contested a ten furlongs handicap at Haydock on Saturday evening and he caught the eye finishing well in fourth under Rachel Richardson. A six times winner, he is rated 70 and two pounds lower than his last success at Beverley last August. Five of his six wins have been gained at Hamilton (3 times), Beverley and Pontefract with trips around a mile and three or a mile and a half being ideal. Look out for him stepping up in trip, especially on a stiff track. **REGAL MIRAGE won next time at Pontefract (28th July) @ 6/1**

APPENDIX

As in previous years, I have attempted to highlight a number of horses, in various categories, who are expected to contest the major prizes during the 2019/2020 campaign.

Ladies First:

There have been some outstanding mares over the years but it appears to be a golden era for the fairer sex at present with the likes of Grade 1 winners **Apple's Jade** (became the first mare to win the Irish Champion Hurdle last season since Like-A-Butterfly in 2003), **Benie Des Dieux** (French Champion Hurdle winner), **La Bague Au Roi** and **Laurina** currently operating. Indeed, Ireland is blessed with some tremendous mares, including **HONEYSUCKLE**, who is unbeaten in five careers starts and is rated 150 over hurdles. A fifteen lengths winner of her only point-to-point (left-handed), she beat subsequent mares' final winner Annie Mc and was recommended to Henry De Bromhead by her rider Mark O'Hare. The daughter of Sulamani was snapped up for €110,000 on behalf of owner Kenny Alexander. Four wins over hurdles followed, including a Listed success at Thurles (2m) in December, a Grade 3 victory at Fairyhouse (2m 2f) in late January and a five and a half lengths win in a Grade 1 mares' novices' hurdle at the Punchestown Festival (2m 4f). In doing so, she provided Rachel Blackmore (4 from 4) with her first Grade 1 victory in Ireland (following her first Grade 1 winner at the Cheltenham Festival aboard Minella Indo). Her winning rider said afterwards: **"This mare is a bit special. She's got a very exciting future. She didn't put a foot wrong."** Henry De Bromhead commented: **"She's a super mare. It was very frustrating at the time when she missed Cheltenham. She just went a bit flat and we weren't happy with her. She's some five year old and has achieved so much already. She's won over two miles, two and a half miles, and looks like she could go further again. She jumped really well bar one, and is a really exciting mare."** It will be interesting to see if Honeysuckle remains over hurdles or goes chasing. Either way, she looks an exceptional mare.

Compatriot **GYPSY ISLAND** looks out of the top drawer, too. A five year old mare who only cost €6,000, she was beaten on her hurdles debut at Navan in November but was four from four in bumpers last term. Successful at Ballinrobe in August and Naas in March, Peter Fahey's charge then destroyed eleven rivals in a Listed mares' bumper at Fairyhouse's Easter Festival. Ridden by Derek O'Connor, she beat Yukon Lil by eleven lengths. **"Gypsy Island is a lovely filly and is improving with every run. She travelled into it well and they went a nice gallop so Derek (O'Connor) was able to switch her off. She's a filly to look forward to next year, and she goes on soft equally as well,"** remarked her trainer. The Jeremy filly then followed up in similar fashion in a Grade 3 mares' bumper at the Punchestown Festival (Yielding). A five lengths winner, Fahey enthused: **"Derek (O'Connor) was beaming after Fairyhouse, so he clearly liked her. The plan going out was to settle her in as she got very keen with Mark Walsh the first day over hurdles. Derek said that once she picked off one or two, she came alive. To find another gear and sprint away from them was a very good performance. I'm really looking forward to seeing what she can do next year over hurdles as well, and I think she'll be better with a bit of ease."** Owned by J.P.McManus, the Dawn Run Mares' Novices' Hurdle at Cheltenham in March is likely to be her ultimate target this season.

THE GETAWAY STAR is another potentially high-class bumper mare from last spring. A four year old trained by Declan Queally, she beat eighteen rivals by upwards of eight and a half lengths in a bumper at the Fairyhouse Easter Festival (2m 4f : Good/Yielding). Bought for €4,500 as a foal, her owner Michael O'Callagham commented afterwards: **"She looks a real good mare and Declan (Queally had been telling me all year that she was good. For a four year old filly to win like that is impressive and she's been in seven or eight months, so I'd say she will be left off now before coming back in the Autumn. Maybe for some of those**

good mares' bumpers, she looks that sort of mare." In receipt of eighteen pounds from runner-up Larquebuse, she was well supported beforehand. The Listed ITBA Mares bumper at Navan (24th November) could be an option.

Alan King has handled some smart mares over the years, including L'Unique and Senorita Rumbalita, but he believes **THE GLANCING QUEEN** could be the best of the lot and it is difficult to argue, judged on her performances in bumpers last season. Another daughter of Jeremy, she won a Listed event at Cheltenham's November meeting before running well against the geldings at both Ascot (3rd) and in the Festival bumper at Cheltenham in March (5th). She crowned her season though with a smooth two and a quarter lengths win in a Grade 2 bumper against her own sex at Aintree. **"We've always adored her. She was a bit unlucky not to finish closer at Cheltenham – she got stopped coming down the hill. She's won a point, she jumps great and she's exciting,"** commented the head of Barbury Castle.

LUST FOR GLORY and **POSH TRISH** met three times last season and, having beaten each other at Newbury during November and December, the pair finished fifteenth and eighth respectively in the Dawn Run Mares' Novices' Hurdle at Cheltenham in March. Expect more clashes this season with the duo going chasing for the first time. Lust For Glory was sold as part of the Grech & Parkin dispersal at the Doncaster Spring Sales. Bought by Robert Waley-Cohen for £235,000, she remains with Nicky Henderson. The Getaway mare was rated 132 over hurdles, while Posh Trish had an official mark of 142. A four times winner over hurdles, Paul Nicholls has already earmarked the Grade 2 Rising Stars Novices' Chase at Wincanton (9th November) as a possible early season target. The champion trainer has won the two and a half miles event ten times. The pair should be two cracking novice chasers.

At the time of writing, the best juvenile hurdler seen out so far is the Emmet Mullins trained **FUJIMOTO FLYER**. A daughter of Japanese stallion Admire Moon, she failed to win in seven races on the Flat with a rating of 71. However, since sent hurdling she has improved enormously. A half-sister to the Mick Channon trained Very Good Day, she won by eighteen lengths on her jumping debut at Killarney (Yielding/Soft) in August and then followed up by nine lengths in a Listed hurdle at Auteuil (2m 2f : Very Soft) thirteen days later – she was Emmet's first runner at the track. I asked James Reveley about the form because he has ridden the runner-up Want Of A Nail in the past and he said: **"She looked very good because she pulled for a lot of the race and still won going away. The runner-up is a fair yardstick and she beat some of the best three year old fillies in France."**

Two Mile Chasers:

On the assumption reigning dual Champion Chaser **ALTIOR** tackles longer trips this season, the two mile crown looks up for grabs. Willie Mullins has yet to capture the Queen Mother Champion Chase but he will be hoping the fragile **CHACUN POUR SOI** remains in one piece. The ex-French gelding, who featured in the *Top 40 Prospects* in 2017/2018, had been absent for 1089 days, prior to winning by 31 lengths on his chasing debut at Naas in March. Having his first run for Mullins, the Policy Maker gelding was previously trained in France by Emmanuel Clayeux. **"He is very likeable, it's like riding a handicapper. He's very exciting,"** commented Paul Townend afterwards. The seven year old then produced another thrilling performance in the Grade 1 Ryanair Novice Chase at the Punchestown Festival when beating Cheltenham Festival winners Defi Du Seuil and Duc Des Genievres by upwards of four and a quarter lengths under Robbie Power. **"I told Robbie (Power) we think he's a star and that, if he's as good as we think he is, God knows what would happen. To turn in with an Arkle winner on one side of him, a JLT winner on the other side and to still be cantering marks him out as a special horse. He looks spectacular,"** enthused his trainer afterwards. Rated 167, he is a hugely talented horse and still has time on his side.

Stablemate **DUC DE GENIEVRES** provided Ireland's champion trainer with his fourth win in the Arkle Trophy at Cheltenham in the last five years. A thirteen lengths winner, Mullins said afterwards: **"He held his position at the top of the hill, jumped impeccably and motored home – it looked like a schooling session for him. We thought he might have wanted a little further but, after that performance, we won't be in a rush to step him up in trip, although he might want further on good ground."** Beaten twenty lengths by his stablemate at Punchestown, he reportedly found the ground too quick. Rated 162, his owner Jared Sullivan is keen for the six year old to have a crack at the Tingle Creek Chase at Sandown (7th December). The softer the ground the better for the grey with the underfoot conditions likely to dictate his target at Cheltenham next March.

Duc De Genievres finished six and a half lengths behind stablemate **CILAOS EMERY** when the pair met at Gowran Park in late January. **"My two jockeys came in and said they went down over the first three fences as fast as they'd go in any Arkle or Champion Chase. It sounded like a really good test so it was good for Cilaos Emery to come out and be able to win like that,"** remarked Mullins. The Califet gelding, who was fifth in the Supreme Novices' Hurdle at Cheltenham in 2017 before winning a Grade 1 at Punchestown, was one of the leading fancies for the Arkle Trophy as a result. Unfortunately, the seven year old pulled a muscle in February and hasn't been seen since. Having only raced once over fences, he lacks experience but is a Grade 1 winner and his form at Gowran is strong.

Another leading Irish novice chaser from last season who was forced to miss the Arkle was Joseph O'Brien's **LE RICHEBOURG**. A four times winner over fences, including twice at Grade 1 level, he is rated 160. Following his seven lengths win in the Grade 1 Frank Ward Solicitors Arkle Novice Chase at Leopardstown in February, his trainer commented: **"Le Richebourg jumped well on the whole and when he had to be clever he was. A bit of nice ground helps him. He needs a strong pace."** Having worked on Saturday 23rd February, his connections weren't happy with the Network gelding and he was found to be injured. Significantly, there were 26 non-runners on the final day of the Dublin Racing Festival, 22 of which were due to the fast ground. It is hoped the six year old returns this season.

Rated 155, stablemate **DARASSO** has a long way to go before he is considered a Champion Chase contender but the former Guy Cherel trained gelding looked progressive when dropped back in trip last season. Purchased by J.P.McManus, the six year old, who beat the useful Janika (now rated 162 over fences) twice over hurdles at Auteuil earlier in his career, joined Joseph O'Brien. Beaten over two and a half and three miles over hurdles, the Konig Turf gelding successfully dropped back to the minimum trip in the Grade 3 Red Mills Trial Hurdle at Gowran Park (Yielding) in February when beating the 144 rated mare Forge Meadow by eleven lengths. His trainer said: **"Darasso ran okay in the Galmoy Hurdle over three miles here last month but dropping back in trip seemed to suit. He also likes soft ground."** A month later, he beat subsequent Topham Chase winner Cadmium by two and a quarter lengths in the Grade 2 Webster Cup at Navan (2m : Soft) back over fences. Leading before the last, he pulled away to win readily with Barry Geraghty (2 from 2) saying: **"Darasso is a good horse and you would have to like him."** Unbeaten in three races over fences and over the minimum trip, he is only six and has time on his side. Don't be surprised if he breaks through into the top division.

At a lesser level, I am looking forward to seeing **CLAIMANTAKINFORGAN** back in action this season. Rated 151 over hurdles, he was an impressive two and a half lengths winner on his chasing debut at Uttoxeter in November, in a race which has been contested by the likes of Bristol De Mai, Charbel, Garde La Victoire, Le Prezien and Top Notch in recent years. Reappearing sixteen days later in a Grade 2 novice chase at Cheltenham, he only finished third behind Lalor. The race almost certainly came too soon and the seven year old missed the rest of the season. Sold for £100,000 at the Goffs UK Spring Sale at Doncaster as part of the Grech & Parkin dispersal, he now belongs to **Lady Dulverton**. He could win a big handicap chase this season for Nicky Henderson.

Two and a half Mile Chasers:

A PLUS TARD was one of the most impressive winners of the Cheltenham Festival in March when trouncing nineteen rivals by upwards of sixteen lengths in the novices' handicap chase. The former French trained gelding provided Rachel Blackmore with her first winner at the Festival as the five year old made a mockery of his mark of 144. The son of Kapgarde had beaten subsequent Arkle winner Duc De Genievres by three and a quarter lengths at Naas (2m 3f) in December. Tried over three miles in Grade 1 company at the Punchestown Festival, he was beaten over fourteen lengths by Delta Work with Henry De Bromhead saying afterwards: **"He ran okay but he does look to be a superior horse going left handed."** Indeed, his record racing left-handed since joining his current yard is 11 compared to 223 on right-handed tracks. His trainer won the Ryanair Chase at the Festival in 2018 with Balko Des Flos and he may have another leading contender for this season's version in the 160 rated chaser.

The Ryanair Chase is very much the long-term target for **KALASHNIKOV**, according to his trainer Amy Murphy. The Kalanisi gelding came within a neck of winning the *Skybet* Supreme Novices' Hurdle at Cheltenham in 2018 and he was still going well when being hampered and unseating his rider at the sixth fence in the Arkle last March. Stepped up to two and a half miles for the first time, the six year old gained ample compensation in the Grade 1 Manifesto Novices' Chase at Aintree when beating La Bague Au Roi by a length and a quarter. Similar to A Plus Tard, his form suggests he is much better racing left-handed (1111211U1). His form figures going right-handed are 222. Rated 155, he is set to return to Liverpool for the Grade 2 Old Roan Chase (27th October).

SIRUH DU LAC provided Nick Williams with his third Cheltenham Festival winner when beating old rival Janika by three parts of a length in the Brown Advisory & Merriebelle Stable Plate in March. Unbeaten in four races last term, the six year old has been raised nine pounds since to a mark of 150 (started the season off 123). **"He's not a horse who takes a lot of racing. He could be a wonderful horse for next season,"** commented his trainer afterwards. Earlier in the season when winning at Newbury in November, Williams remarked: **"Siruh Du Lac is a beautiful jumper. That's his strength. He could be very good and will only get better. Two and a half miles is ideal and we don't need to go three miles as he has got gears."** The BetVictor Gold Cup at Cheltenham (16th November) looks an obvious starting point and, having won first time out last season, the six year old is likely to go straight there. His form figures at Prestbury Park are 411 (all on the New Course).

Staying Chasers:

The staying chase division promises to be stronger than ever this season with **ALTIOR** (rated 175) and **CYRNAME** (176) set to tackle three miles for the first time. The pair may even clash in the Grade 2 Christy 1965 Chase at Ascot (23rd November). The likes of Gold Cup winner **AL BOUM PHOTO,** King George winner **CLAN DES OBEAUX,** Grade 1 winners **KEMBOY** and **LA BAGUE AU ROI** all look sure to play their part in the top staying chases this winter, too. The following five were all novices last season but I feel they will bridge the gap into open company and be more than competitive against the very best chasers.

BURROWS SAINT is rated 156 having won three times over fences last season. A length and three quarters winner of the Irish National at Fairyhouse, it was Willie Mullins first victory in the race (he trained the second and third for good measure). **"It was Burrows Saint's third win in just over six weeks and that says a lot about him and the future he might have. It was only his fourth run over fences for us but he did run in two chases in France,"** commented his trainer afterwards. Twenty two lengths fifth in the Grade 1 Grand Steeple-Chase de Paris at Auteuil in May, Mullins said: **"Burrows Saint travelled too well. He landed in front at the second water jump and he was just doing too much too soon in the race."** At the time of writing, he is available at **66/1** (Bet365) for the Cheltenham Gold Cup, which could look a huge price by next spring. Still only six, he jumps and stays and is improving rapidly.

Old rivals **DEFI DU SEUIL** and **LOSTINTRANSLATION** clashed three times over fences last season with Philip Hobbs' dual Festival winner holding sway 2-1. The former, who is a former Triumph Hurdle winner, is a five times Grade 1 scorer and, despite the fact he has yet to race beyond two and a half miles, I think he is tailormade for the **Ladbrokes King George** at Kempton on Boxing Day. Generally available at **25/1** and **33/1**, Philip Hobbs' gelding is a strong stayer with speed, too. The latter's two wins over fences were gained in the Grade 2 Dipper Novices' Chase at Cheltenham (2m 4f) on New Year's day and the Grade 1 Mildmay Novices' Chase at Aintree (3m 1f) in April. **"Hopefully he'll run in a Gold Cup one day because he's got pace, he stays and he jumps. He's got everything,"** commented Colin Tizzard at Prestbury Park on the 1st January. Following his six lengths defeat of Topofthegame at Liverpool, his regular rider Robbie Power (2217223121) said: **"The most impressive part of the whole thing was when he popped the second last, I picked him up and next thing, boom. He's a very exciting horse and potentially could be anything."** The Flemensfirth gelding's record on the New course at Cheltenham is 12, whereas his record racing right-handed is 42.

KAISER BLACK was included in this feature last year and Pat Doyle's stable star didn't let us down. Despite the fact he only raced twice, the Germany gelding chased home La Bague Au Roi in the Grade 1 Flogas Novice Chase at the Dublin Racing Festival at Leopardstown (2m 5f : Good). Beaten a length and a quarter, he was conceding seven pounds to Warren Greatrex's mare. Last time, the eight year old beat Camelia De Cotte (won a Grade 3 since) by eleven lengths in a Grade 3 novice at Naas (2m 4f : Yielding/Soft) in March. Still lightly raced, he doesn't want testing ground but is capable of winning more Graded chases, possibly at the highest level.

Not much went right for **SANTINI** during his first season over fences but Nicky Henderson's gelding still reached an official mark of 163. An easy four lengths winner on his chasing debut in Grade 2 company at Newbury in December, he was then taken off his feet before staying on to finish third in the Grade 1 Kauto Star Novices' Chase at Kempton on Boxing Day. Denied a run in the Reynoldstown Novices' Chase at Ascot in February, due to the fact the Milan gelding had to undergo an equine flu vaccination, he then lost a shoe whilst working at Newbury in early March, which resulted in him being lame and his near fore foot had to be poulticed. Given his preparation, he therefore ran very well to finish half a length runner-up behind old rival Topofthegame in the RSA Chase with Henderson saying afterwards: **"I wish I had a clear run at it but I'm not making excuses. Fair play to the winner, he's the one I always said would be the hardest to beat. Both horses have a great future."** It is difficult to argue with that and the pair could clash again in the Ladbrokes Trophy at Newbury (30th November). Unbeaten at the Berkshire track (2 from 2), the Seven Barrows team have won the race three times (Trabologan (2005), Bobs Worth (2012) & Triolo D'Alene (2013)). He looks Cheltenham Gold Cup material, although I would always side with Topofthegame because I think he is the quicker of the pair.

Two Mile Hurdlers:

It was announced in August that the current Champion Hurdle Espoir D'Allen had been put down following a freak accident at home. The five year old had provided Gavin Cromwell with his first Festival winner when beating Melon by fifteen lengths in March. The Voix Du Nord gelding was owned by J.P.McManus, who was winning hurdling's Blue Riband for a record eighth time. **BUVEUR D'AIR** provided him with two of those victories in 2017 and 2018 and the eight year old, who fell at the third flight in March, won two more Grade 1 prizes at Newcastle and Punchestown last season. An eight times Grade 1 winner, he will continue to be a force in the top two mile races but, at the same time, looks vulnerable to a younger rival.

Stablemates **FUSIL RAFFLES** and **PENTLAND HILLS** may emerge as Champion Hurdle candidates with Nicky Henderson seeking his eighth win in the race. The former arrived from France last season having won over hurdles for Guillaume Macaire. A nine lengths winner of the Grade 2 Adonis Hurdle at Kempton on his UK debut in February, he picked up an injury in doing so – he banged his off-hind shin bone on the final hurdle and had to have a flap of skin stitched back and then required ten days box rest. Forced to miss the Triumph Hurdle, the Saint Des Saints gelding returned at the Punchestown Festival and provided the Seven Barrows team with their fourth win in the Grade 1 four year old hurdle. A two and three quarters of a length winner from Fakir D'Oudairies, his trainer said: **"He's done very well to get back from that injury he suffered at Kempton. I was nervous whether he'd be quite ready for a battle like that, mentally and fitness wise, because we started training him again only three weeks ago. He's got boots on his hind legs to protect him as the wound is still there. He's a tough horse and a good one."**

PENTLAND HILLS was a dual winner on the Flat for Chris Wall (rated 73) before being bought by Anthony Bromley on behalf of the Owners Group 031. Unbeaten in three races over hurdles and rated 153, he is a dual Grade 1 winner having only made his jumping debut at Plumpton on the 25th February. A three lengths winner of the Triumph Hurdle, Henderson said afterwards: **"Next year's Champion Hurdle is a long time away but we'll see. He's a horse that is going to improve and he strikes me like a Punjabi type."** The Motivator gelding completed the Cheltenham/Aintree double twenty days later when beating Fakir D'Oudairies by a neck. **"We sent him to Henrietta Knight to teach him to jump and, by god, he was slick today – he's like Buveur D'Air,"** commented his trainer. Rated 153, it is debatable how strong last season's juvenile hurdlers were but the pair have earned a crack at the top two mile events.

Willie Mullins has won the Champion Hurdle four times in the last nine years and his *Skybet* Supreme Hurdle winner **KLASSICAL DREAM** looks set to be his chief challenger this season. Featured in the *French Revolution* section of *OJA* in 2018/2019, the ex-French gelding won all four starts for Mullins last season, including three Grade 1 events. **"Klassical Dream has a super attitude and jumps brilliantly. He definitely wants slower ground through,"** commented Ruby Walsh after his head victory in the Grade 1 novice at Leopardstown's Dublin Racing Festival (Good). A four and a half lengths winner of the Festival opener, Mullins remarked: **"We knew he had a fair engine all along. He's a very good horse. He worked last week at the Curragh and we came away thinking here's one who's going to take a lot of beating. He looks a real one, especially in this type of ground. He's a brilliant jumper, I don't think he missed a beat out there."** The Dream Well gelding followed up with a five and a half lengths victory at Punchestown with his trainer saying: **"Ruby (Walsh) felt he was too settled under him and he wasn't as pleased as at Cheltenham, but I thought at Cheltenham he just ran very free. We might look at trying to make a Champion Hurdle horse out of him – he could be good enough."** The head of Closutton confirmed those plans in late August: **"He could start off in the Morgiana Hurdle at Punchestown (17th November), but the race at Down Royal (1st November) is definitely an option, too, and there is the Hatton's Grace at Fairyhouse (1st December) as well. I don't like to pin mine down to one specific target this early, so we'll keep our options open."** Soft ground may be the key to him in the top races over two miles.

Don't forget to read my Diary @

www.mhpublications.couk

INDEX

SELECTED HORSE = BOLD   *Owners' Enclosure & Talking Trainers = Italics*

A Perfect Gift.......................... 99
A PLUS TARD 179
ACROSS THE LINE 174
Acting Lass............................. 63
Addici.................................... 117
Adjourned.............................. 58
Adrien Du Pont....................105
ADRIMEL 89, 155
AIN'T THAT SHAME.......... 155
Air Horse One........................ 63
AL DANCER 10
ALLAHO...............................9
Alpha Carinae 99
Alsa Mix 82
ALTIOR 177
Annamix................................ 50
Annie Mc 117
Another Emotion................... 68
Antey.................................... 50
Any Drama............................ 63
ANYTIME WILL DO 173
APPLE'S SHAKIRA 154
Arab Moon............................ 93
ARAMAX........................... 145
ARCHIE BROWN.............. 135
ARD ABHAINN................. 156
ARDLETHEN..................... 173
Arrivederci 117
Artistic Language.................. 55
As I See It.............................. 63
Ashfield Paddy 118
Ask For Glory........................105
Astrologist 99
At Its Own Expense.............. 74
Awake At Midnight................ 74
Azzerti.................................. 82
Bags Groove......................... 63
Bailarico............................... 69
Ballasalla.............................. 93
Ballotin................................. 75
Ballywood 82
Bapaume 50
BAPTISM OF FIRE 156
BARBADOS BUCK'S .. 105, 156
Barranco Valley......................124
Bathsheba Bay......................105
BEAKSTOWN................... 173
Beau Du Brizais..................... 75
BEAUFORT WEST............. 151
Benie Des Dieux.....................51
Better Getalong....................129
Big Bad Bear........................129
BIG BRESIL 156

Big Shark 75
Bird On The Wire 94
Birds of Prey.........................106
Black Corton.........................106
Black Mischief....................... 63
Blackjack Kentucky...............106
Blakerigg..............................129
Blazer's Mill 99
BLEUE AWAY 142
BLOODSTONE 157
BLOSSOMING FORTH 142
Blueberry High 69
Bob And Co.........................106
Bob Mahler........................... 69
BOBHOPEORNOHOPE..58, 157
BOLD ASSASSIN 158
BOLD CONDUCT 158
Bon Calvados........................ 99
BOSS MAN FRED 173
Brahma Bull...........................51
BRAVEMANSGAME.. 106, 158
Brelan D'As...........................106
Brewers Project....................106
Brewin'upastorm................... 99
Bright Side Oflife.................. 94
Brio Conti.............................106
Broken Halo..........................106
Broughtons Admiral.............. 55
Bubbles of Gold....................100
Bullionaire............................. 63
BURNING VICTORY 145
Burren Walk........................... 82
BURROWS SAINT 51, 179
Buster Edwards.....................124
BUVEUR D'AIR 180
CADZAND.........93, 142, 173
Caius Marcius.......................129
Calipso Collonges................100
CALTHOR 158
CALVA D'AUGE 106, 135
Calvario................................. 69
Canelo................................... 83
CAP DU MATHAN .. 11, 107, 135
Capac.................................... 89
Cape Milano 75
Capeland 107
Capitane 107
Captain Cattistock 107
Captain Drake 64
Caribert................................. 64
Carry On The Magic 107
Carys' Commodity 118
Casko D'Airy 107

CAT TIGER................ 107, 145
Catch Me Not........................ 58
Catch The Swallows 124
Cathal's Star.........................129
CHACUN POUR SOI.....51, 177
CHAMPAGNE PLATINUM .. 154
Champagnesuperover..........100
Chance Finale 107
Chante Neige 55
CHANTRY HOUSE 12
Chapel Stile..........................129
Charbel 58
Chef D'Equipe....................... 75
Chef Des Obeaux.................. 52
Chez Hans 107
Chidswell 129
Christopher Robin................. 89
Christopher Wood.................107
Chti Balko 94
Chuvelo 94
CILAOS EMERY 178
CILL ANNA 108, 159
CLAIMANTAKINFORGAN .. 178
Clan Des Obeaux.................108
CLONDAW CAITLIN 159
Cloth Cap.............................. 118
Cobolobo.............................. 118
COCONUT SPLASH......... 159
Colditz Castle 83
Collingwood Court............... 124
Collooney.............................100
Commodore Barry................ 58
Coninsby 89
Costante Via 118
Cotswold Way....................... 75
COUNT MERIBEL 174
Coup De Pinceau.................108
COUPDEBOL 145
Court Dreaming 130
Cresswell Legend 58
Crooks Peak 75
CYRNAME 108
Daklondike........................... 124
Dalila Du Seuil...................... 64
Dan McGrue.........................108
Dandy Dan............................ 58
DANNY KIRWAN 108, 151
Danny Whizzbang 108
Danse Idol............................109
DARASSO 178
Darling Maltaix 109
Darsi In The Park................... 118
Deadringerforlove 64

Deal D'Estruval........................51
Dear Sire.................................. 94
DEFI DU SEUIL 75, 180
Definitelyanoscar 64
Deise Aba 76
DEPLOY THE GETAWAY ... 160
Deyrann De Carjac................. 83
Dhowin.................................. 118
Diamond Gait 58
Diamond Guy 109
DICKIE DIVER..................... 13
Didonato................................ 83
Diego Du Charmil 109
Diese Des Bieffes.................. 52
Dingo Dollar 83
DINO BOY 135, 142
Diplomate Sivola 76
DIVINE GIFT..................... 140
Django Django 118
DOES HE KNOW........ 59, 142
Dogon 109
Doin'whatshelikes................109
DOLCITA..................... 14, 52
Dolos.....................................109
Dolphin Square 76
DON DIABLO 160
Donnie Brasco 59
Don't Ask................................ 69
Dont Hesitate.......................... 52
Dorking Boy............................ 90
Dorking Cock 90
Dorrells Pierji 52
Dostal Phil...............................76
Double Esprit.......................... 94
Douvan....................................51
Dr Sanderson 109
Dream Berry 119
DREAMS AND VISIONS 140
Drumlee Watar 69
Drumreagh 59
Duc De Beauchene...............124
DUC DES GENIEVRES..53, 178
Duke of Earl 59
Duke of Navan......................130
Dundrum Wood......................100
Dynamite Dollars...................109
EAGLE MOON.................... 146
Eamon An Cnoic...................124
Eason 110
Ebony Gale..............................76
Ecco...................................... 110
ECHOES IN RAIN............... 146
ECLAIR ON LINE 135
ECLAIR SURF 160
Ecu De La Noverie 76
Eden Du Houx 125
Eden Flight 50

Edwardstone 83
Eglantine Du Seuil 53
El Barra 50
El Presente 59
ELDORADO ALLEN 151
Elgin...................................... 83
Elios D'Or.............................130
Elleon 69
Elysees.................................. 83
ELYSIAN FLAME 140
EMITOM....................... 15, 70
Emtara 94
Encore Champs 70
Endlessly...............................100
Enrilo 110
ENVOI ALLEN 16
EPATANTE 154
Equus Amadeus..................... 90
Eritage 110
Escapability 83
Estelle Ma Belle..................... 53
Etoile Rebelle 54
ETTILA DE SIVOLA 151
Eur Gone West 125
Extra Mag 125
Ey Up Rocky 119
Eyes Right 83
Fabulous Saga 53
FADO DES BROSSES 161
Fair Kate................................ 90
FAIR STAR 173
FAKIR D'ALENE 161
FAN FAN LA TULIPE 146
FANFARONADE 136
FANION D'ESTRUVAL....... 146
FAROUK D'ALENE 18
Fast Buck............................... 53
Faugheen................................51
FAUSTINOVICK.................. 19
Fehily 64
FERNY HOLLOW 20
FEU DU BRESIL......... 50, 146
FIDELIOS VALLIS......110, 136
Fidux 84
Fiesole 100
FIGAROC 50, 146
Fighter Casseul 90
Filou Des Issards....................76
FILS SPIRITUEL............... 146
FIN DU MATCH 136
Finawn Bawn.........................100
Fingal D'Arthel....................... 94
Finisk River 94
FIRST ACCOUNT 95, 152
First Flow 59
First Lord De Cuet................125
Fitzroy...................................101

Five O'Clock 50
FLAMBOYANT JOYAUX 142
Flash Collonges 110
Flash De Clerval 56
Flash de Touzaine.................. 11
Flashing Glance 90
Flemenstide...........................110
Fleminport 119
Fletch....................................101
Flic Ou Voyou 110
Flight Deck 119
Flinck......................................76
Floating Rock 90
FLY SMART................... 21, 50
Folks On The Hill................... 119
FONTAINE COLLONGES... 147
FOR LANGY 77, 147
Fort Summer 125
FRANCO DE PORT 147
FRANKEUR....................... 136
Frankie Baby.......................... 70
FRATERNEL 84, 136
FRENCH DYNAMITE......... 161
FRERE TUCK 147
Friend Or Foe 110
Frisco Bay............................ 119
Frodon 111
FRONTAL ASSAULT.......... 161
Fubar...................................... 59
FUJIMOTO FLYER............ 177
FUSAIN 147
Fuseau 84
FUSIL RAFFLES 181
Fusionice 101
Gabriel Oak 95
Gaelik Coast 95
Gala Ball 77
GALILEO SILVER 84, 140
Gangster................................ 70
GAOT 147
Garde La Victoire 77
Garrettstown..........................101
Garry Clermont 119
GASPARD DU SEUIL 148
GAULOISE 148
GELBOE DE CHANAY 148
General Custard.....................101
GENERATION TEXT.......... 21
Gentleman Kap 64
GERALDO 162
Get Back Get Back 64
GET IN ROBIN............. 95, 162
Get In The Queue 65
GET PREPARED 136, 142
Get The Appeal..................... 111
Getabird..................................51
Getareason............................ 53

183

GETARIVER 173
GETAWAY MAG................. 173
GETAWAY PAT 162
Getaway Trump 111
GIANTS TABLE 22
GIN ON LIME 23
Give Me A Copper 111
Giving Glances...................... 84
GJOUMI 148
Glasha's Peak........................ 84
Glen Vine 125
Glenduff................................ 130
Glenlivet................................ 111
Glinger Flame....................... 130
Glittering Love...................... 130
Glory And Fortune 90
GLYNN 136
GOLD DES BOIS 163
Golden Gift............................ 111
Golden Sovereign 77
Goobinator 95
GOOD BOY BOBBY............. 24
Good Man Pat....................... 84
Gosheven............................... 77
Grand Bornand 50
GRAND ROI 137
Grand Sancy......................... 111
GRANDADS COTTAGE .. 101, 163
GRANGECLARE NATIVE .. 163
Greaneteen........................... 111
Great Beyond 112
Green Dolphin....................... 65
Grey Getaway 112
Group Stage.......................... 84
GUENA DES MOTTES.. 137, 148
Guitar Pete............................ 130
Gunsight Ridge..................... 101
GUY 174
GYPSY ISLAND 176
HACKSAW RIDGE....... 84, 137
Happygolucky........................ 59
Harambe 85
Headscarf Lil......................... 131
Heart of A Lion..................... 85
HEARTBREAK KID 95, 163
Hell's Kitchen 65
Here Comes Trouble............ 101
HEREDITARY RULE 143
Hes No Trouble 59
Hey Joe 119
Highate Hill.......................... 101
Highland Gold...................... 131
HIGHLAND HUNTER .. 112, 152
HILL SIXTEEN................... 152
HOLD THAT TAUGHT........ 164
HOLD THE NOTE 152
Holme Abbey........................ 131

HONEYSUCKLE 176
HOOK UP 50, 148
Hostile..................................... 85
Hotter Than Hell.................... 85
Hugo 'N Taz............................ 56
Hugos Other Horse.............. 112
I K Brunel............................. 102
If The Cap Fits 65
If You Say Run 112
Illuminated Beauty 60
I'm A Game Changer............. 77
Imada..................................... 131
Imperial Aura 60
Imperial Esprit 65
Induno................................... 125
Innisfree Spirit 131
INTERCONNECTED.......... 173
Into The Woods.................... 126
Is A Real Champ 112
Ishkara Lady 65
ISRAEL CHAMP......... 25, 126
IT SURE IS 137, 164
Itchy Feet 102
Jammin Masters.................... 70
JANUARY JETS 164
Jasmin Des Bordes.............. 126
Jatiluwih................................. 77
Java Point 60
JEREMY PASS 112, 165
Jerrysback............................. 77
Jetaway Joey 102
Johnbb.................................. 91
Jolly's Cracked It................... 66
JON SNOW 26, 50
Just A Sip................................ 70
Just A Sting 66
KAISER BLACK 180
Kajaki 131
KAKAMORA...................... 165
KALASHNIKOV 179
Kalooki.................................. 77
Karamoko 131
Kateson................................. 91
Kayf Adventure 78
KEARNEY HILL................. 165
Keep Rolling 78
KEEP WONDERING 78, 165
Keeper Hill.............................. 71
Kemble's Cascade................. 71
Kepagge................................ 126
Kerrykenny Gold.................... 102
Khamsin Moor........................ 95
Kilbrook 119
Kilcooley 131
KILLER CLOWN 166
Kimberlite Candy 91
KING ROLAND............27, 66

Kings Royal Hussar............... 85
King's Socks......................... 126
Kitty Hall............................... 131
KLASSICAL DREAM 181
KNOW THE SCORE .. 126, 153
La Bague Au Roi..................... 71
La Hulpe 71
Label Des Obeaux 85
Lady Tremaine....................... 95
L'AIR DU VENT.................. 28
Lamanver Storm..................... 91
Lanty Slea............................. 132
LARGY FIX 166
Larkbarrow Lad..................... 78
Laurina 54
LE CAMELEON 29
LE RICHEBOURG 178
Legal Beagle 132
Legal History 126
Leoncavallo 56
LETS GO CHAMP 166
Lieutenant Rocco................. 112
L'Incorrigible......................... 91
LINELEE KING 30, 102
Lisp 85
Lithic 120
LITTLE LIGHT 137
Little Red Lion...................... 126
LONGHOUSE POET 31
Looking Well......................... 132
Lord Apparelli........................ 60
Lord Springfield 95
LOSSIEMOUTH............ 32, 91
LOSTINTRANSLATION 180
Lough Derg Jewel.................. 96
Lovenormoney 71
LUCKY ONE 54, 149
Lunar Baby 120
LUST FOR GLORY 138, 177
Luxy Lou 54
MACKENBERG 96, 167
MADIBA PASSION 85, 138
Magic Saint 112
Magoo.................................. 112
Mahlervous............................ 71
Maitree Express 72
Major Dundee........................ 86
Make Me A Believer............. 127
Malaya................................. 113
MALONE ROAD 33
Mantovani 66
Marown................................. 132
Martha Brae 72
Master Tommytucker............ 113
Master Work 78
Mayo Star............................. 132
McFabulous.......................... 113

McNamaras Band.................. 78
Meep Meep...........................91
Meep Meep Mag..................127
MELAY.............................. 149
Melekhov............................... 78
Mercy Mercy Me.................. 113
Meyer Lansky.......................120
MICK PASTOR.............34, 113
MICRO MANAGE.............. 140
Midnight Glory........................ 78
MIDNIGHT SHADOW.......... 35
Midnightreferendum.............. 86
Midnights' Gift........................ 86
Mighty Meg.........................102
Millbank Flyer........................ 66
Mille Sussurri........................ 66
Millstone............................... 86
Min....................................... 52
MIND THE CRACK............. 140
MINELLA MELODY........... 167
Minella Rocco......................120
MINELLA TARA................ 167
Minella Trump........................ 96
Minella Warrior...................... 60
Miranda............................... 113
Miss Honey Ryder................. 72
Miss Milano.........................132
MISS MONDITO................ 138
Missed Approach................... 72
Misty Whisky.......................... 66
Momella................................ 66
Monbeg Zena................ 55, 102
Mondesca............................120
Monkfish................................ 50
Mont Des Avaloirs................ 113
MOSSY FEN...................... 167
Mount Mews.......................... 96
Mr Clarkson.........................127
MR GREY SKY............. 36, 60
Mr Mcgo................................ 96
Mr One More..........................67
Mr Pumblechook................... 86
MUCKAMORE.................. 168
Mulcahys Hill........................ 72
Musical Slave........................ 78
My Old Gold.........................132
My Way................................ 113
MY WHIRLWIND................ 37
Mystical Clouds..................... 86
NAVAJO PASS............96, 141
Nayati................................... 96
Nebuchadnezzar................... 86
Nells Son.............................132
NEVILLE'S CROSS..... 92, 143
New Age Dawning................127
Newtide................................ 60
N'Golo.................................. 50

NIBIRU.............................. 153
Nickolson............................103
Nimix De Juilley.................... 113
No Comment.......................... 79
NO REGRETS............. 38, 133
Noah And The Ark................ 96
Nordic Command................127
NOREEN BAWN................ 168
Not A Nail........................... 114
Notachance........................... 86
Notre Pari............................103
Oakley.................................. 79
Off The Planet...................... 79
OFFTHESHOULDER......... 168
O'Hanrahan Bridge................97
Oleg................................... 114
On A Promise......................133
On The Bandwagon..............120
ONE FINE MAN..................174
ONE FOR ROSIE................ 39
One For You......................... 79
Onefortheroadtom.................67
Onthefrontfoot.......................97
Orrisdale.............................120
OSCAR ROBERTSON....... 168
Ottonian................................97
Our Power............................. 86
Outofthisworld......................67
Outonpatrol..........................87
Over To Sam..........................67
Overthetop...........................103
PAPA TANGO CHARLIE..120, 169
Party Fuzz............................ 60
Peachey...............................103
Pens Man............................120
PENTLAND HILLS............ 181
Perfect City.........................121
Perfect Predator....................87
PHOENIX WAY............. 40, 67
Pic D'Orhy........................... 114
Pichelot.................................97
Piggy Winkle........................121
Pileon.................................. 79
Pisgah Pike...........................57
PISTOL WHIPPED............. 153
POGUE.....................97, 153
Poker Play............................127
Pol Crocan............................ 79
Politologue........................... 114
Polydora.............................. 92
Pop Rockstar........................121
Portrush Ted.......................... 72
POSH TRISH............. 114, 177
Potterman..............................87
Potters Venture..................... 79
Pougne Bobbi.......................97
POWER OF PAUSE........... 169

Praeceps...............................87
Prefontaine..........................121
PRESENCE OF MIND...103, 143
Present Chief.......................121
Presentandcounting.............97
Prince Llywelyn..................... 60
Printing Dollars...................... 72
Production..............................87
Pull Green..............................97
PURE BLISS................67, 169
PURE GENIUS................ 149
Quarenta.............................121
Queens Cave........................127
Quel Destin.......................... 114
Quiet Penny.......................... 56
RAGNAR.....................79, 141
RAMILLIES................ 93, 143
Ramses De Teillee................127
RATHHILL........................... 41
Raven Court......................... 79
Ready And Able....................121
Real Steel............................. 54
Rebellito................................ 50
RED NIKA.................... 92, 143
Red River................................61
Reikers Island....................... 80
Reivers Lad..........................133
Remastered.........................128
Rhosneigr..............................61
Rhythm Is A Dancer.......... .. 114
Ribble Valley.........................133
Rio Vivas.............................. 54
RIVER TYNE..................... 170
Roccowithlove........................ 73
ROCHESTON........... 54, 149
ROCK DE BAUNE........... 153
Rock The Kasbah.................. 80
Rocky's Treasure....................61
ROKSANA......................... 173
Rolling Dylan........................ 80
Roque It...............................103
ROYAL CROWN.............. 170
Rufio......................................67
Russian Invasion.................121
Sadlermor..............................61
Saint Arvans......................... 92
SAINT D'OROUX.............. 138
SAINT ROI....................... 149
Saint Xavier......................... 114
Saldier...................................51
Salsaretta..............................51
Samarquand..........................67
Samburu Shujaa.................. 80
San Rumoldo..........................87
Sangha River........................103
Santa Adelia........................: 73
SANTINI............................ 180

Sarim 73
Scaramanga 115
Scarlet Dragon 87
Sceau Royal 87
Seaton Carew 122
Sebastopol 92
Secret Investor 115
Seemingly So 103
Sending Love 55, 115
Senior Citizen 88
SHAN BLUE 173
Shantaluze 97
Shantou Express 61
Sharjah 51
She's A Rocco 133
Sheshoon Sonny 88
SHISHKIN 42, 138
Silver Forever 115
SILVER HALLMARK 170
Simply Ned 133
Singapore Saga 80
Sir Psycho 115
SIRUH DU LAC 179
Skandiburg 104
SKATMAN 115, 170
Skiddaw Valleys 133
Sky Pirate 122
Skylanna Breeze 122
Smackwater Jack 104
Smarty Wild 80
Snapdragon Fire 92
Soaring Glory 122
Soldier of Love 115
SOMPTUEUX 171
Son of Camas 52
Sound Wall 67
Southfield Harvest 115
Southfield Stone 115
Speedy Cargo 73
SPORTING JOHN 43, 80
SPRINGFIELD FOX 171
Springtown Lake 80
St Gallen 104
Star of Lanka 73
Station Master 61
Steely Addition 80
Steinkraus 97
Sternrubin 81
Storm Arising 116
Stormy Ireland 54
Story of Friends 128
Subway Surf 61
Sunny Express 73
SWITCH HITTER 116, 143
Symphony Hall 73
TAKE IT AWAY 171
Taking Flight 134

Taking Risks 134
Talk of Fame 61
Talkischeap 88
Talktomenow 73
Tamaroc Du Mathan 116
TEA CLIPPER 92, 143
TEDHAM 122, 153
Tegerek 122
TELMESOMETHINGGIRL .. 171
Terry The Fish 122
Testify 98
Thais Toir 92
Thats The Truth 122
THE BIG BREAKAWAY 44
The Bull McCabe 61
The Butcher Said 104
THE COMPOSEUR 123, 143
The Con Man 98
The Cull Bank 88
The Edgar Wallace 61
THE GETAWAY STAR 176
THE GLANCING QUEEN .. 88, 177
THE GREATER GOOD ... 116, 144
The Milan Girl 62
THE OLYMPIAN 45, 88
The Some Dance Kid 98
Thinking 128
Thomas Darby 104
Thomas Patrick 92
THOU ART PETER 141
Thyme Hill 81
Thyme White 116
Tidal Flow 81
Tidal Watch 123
Tiger Tap Tap 50
TIMBERMAN 138
Timeforaspin 104
Timoteo 88
TOMBEE DU CIEL 139, 149
TOPOFTHEGAME 46, 116
Totally Rejected 98
TOWER BRIDGE 154
Trevelyn's Corn 116
TRIO FOR RIO 74, 139
Truckers Lodge 116
TRUCKERS PASS 48, 81
Truckin Away 81
TRUESHAN 89, 141
Two For Gold 62
Umbrigado 128
Umndeni 81
Uncle Alastair 134
Universal Folly 134
Unowhatimeanharry 68
Vado Forte 93
VALAJANI 68, 150
Valdez 89

Velvet Revolution 57
Vieux Lion Rouge 128
Vinndication 62
Vinnies Getaway 104
VISION DU PUY 174
WALK AWAY 172
Walter White 89
Wandrin Star 62
Warthog 128
Wasdell Dundalk 123
WEST CORK 173
Westend Story 81
Western Rules 134
Western Ryder 74
What A Baloo 62
WHATEVA NEXT 144
WHEESHT 139
When You're Ready 123
Whiskey In The Jar 105
WHISTLER BOWL 141
White Hart Lady 68
Whitehotchillifilli 68
Whiteoak Fleur 98
Whiteoak Molly 98
Who's My Jockey 81
WIDE RECEIVER 48
WILD MAX 116, 139
Wilhelm Vonvenster 134
WINDSOR AVENUE 173
Winningseverything 68
Winter Getaway 81
Winter Glory 62
Word Has It 98
Worthy Farm 117
Wynn House 89
Yaa Salaam 128
Yeavering Belle 62
Yes No Maybe So 98
Younevercall 62
YOUNG BUCK 117, 172
Young Lieutenant 74
Young Wolf 123
Zafar 82
ZAMBELLA 139
Zanza 82
ZARKAREVA 150
Zizaneur 82
Zyon 117

ONE JUMP AHEAD UPDATES

I shall be producing **5 One Jump Ahead** *Updates* throughout the 2019/20 National Hunt season. Each *Update* comprises information about the horses in **One Jump Ahead**, **Ante-Post Advice** (recommendations for the major races), **Big-Race Previews**, **News from Ireland** from one of the most informed Irish experts Declan Phelan and **Significant Sales**. <u>Please note, the *Updates* are</u> <u>ONLY AVAILABLE VIA EMAIL (Not Post).</u>

It is £6 per *Update* (except £10 for the Cheltenham Festival version) or £34 for ALL 5 via **EMAIL**.

Summary of the 2018/2019 *Updates*:

What The Clients Said:
"Cheers Mark re info on Sopat from February *Update*. Had 9/1 this morning." **N.P.**

"What a great tip. Well worth getting the Cheltenham *Update* just for that." **D.**

"February *Update* strikes again!! Get in, Boom!!!.. Great info, cheers Mark, looking forward to Cheltenham preview - The Mecca." **D.W.**

"Thanks Mark for that nice start for the best racing week of the year keep it up thanks again." **R.B.**

"I got 11/4 with William Hill at 9.00am and it never really looked in doubt, thanks Mark." **A.R.**

"Good Evening Mark, what valuable information in your great book from Bloodstock Supremo Mr Bromley! Glowing summary and also his horse to follow, golden information - especially at 16's sp - many thanks!" **S.B.**

"Great results today, managed to include Jerrysback and Lake View Lad in amongst a small stakes Yankee but with a very good return! Fantastic day, appreciate the advice!!" **R.J.**

The PADDY POWER MEETING 2018

WINNERS: ROCK THE KASBAH (Advised @ 10/1), FIRST ASSIGNMENT (Advised @ 11/4 – WON @ 6/4), SCEAU ROYAL (Advised @ 13/8)

Quote: *"**ROCK THE KASBAH** could only finish sixth in the same handicap chase at Chepstow last month which he had won twelve months earlier (five pounds higher now). A three times winner over fences, Philip Hobbs' gelding will be suited by this longer trip having finished sixth and runner-up in the last two renewals of the Bet365 Gold Cup at Sandown. Rated 147, he stays well and has been placed at Cheltenham in the past. His stable have won this with Gold Cap (1994) and Sausalito Sunrise (2015). The ground ought to suit and his trainer is in very good form (11 winners in the last 14 days). **Best Price: 10/1 (Bet365, BetVictor, Boylesports, William Hill)."** Advised @ 10/1, WON @ 9/1.*

Quote: *"**FIRST ASSIGNMENT** was trained to win his only Irish point by Cormac Doyle and he beat Red River (rated 145 over hurdles for Kim Bailey) by a length and a half. Bought for £40,000, he has won two of his five races over hurdles for Ian Williams and still looks attractively handicapped off a mark of 130. The Vinnie Roe gelding won at Huntingdon (2m 4f) before finishing third in the EBF Final at Sandown in March. Returning to action at Cheltenham last month, he landed a gamble when scoring by a short head (2m 5f) off a mark of 125. Yet to race beyond two miles five,*

*Tom Scudamore (2131) said afterwards: **"He's more about stamina."** He is therefore expected to improve over this longer distance and can defy a five pounds rise in the weights."* **Advised @ 11/4, WON by 9 lengths @ 6/4.**

Quote: *"**PALMERS HILL** has other entries at the meeting but would be of definite interest if running here. A winning pointer for Denis Murphy who was subsequently bought by J.P.McManus for £310,000, the Gold Well gelding looked a smart prospect when winning by a length and a half on his Rules debut at Uttoxeter (2m) in October last year. Disappointing in his subsequent two outings at Ascot (2m 5f) and Sandown (handicap debut), he has had a long break since (287 days). First time out could be the time to catch him and, if in the same form as he was at Uttoxeter over a year ago, Jonjo O'Neill's lightly raced five year old could be well in off a mark of 124."* **WON @ 7/1**

FRENCH REVOLUTION – Part II: WINNERS: **EXTRA MAG (11/10), FUSIL RAFFLES (4/1, 13/8), STYLE DE VOLE (2/5)**

Quote: **FUSIL RAFFLES**: *"Another three year old by Saint Des Saints who has joined the champion trainer, he was purchased on behalf of **Simon Munir** and **Isaac Souede** having raced twice over hurdles for Guillaume Macaire. A four and a half lengths winner on his debut at Senonnes (2m 2f : Soft) in July, he was then beaten a neck a fortnight later at Les Sables (2m 1f : Good). The third has won since. He is another for juvenile hurdles."* **WON the Grade 2 Adonis Hurdle at Kempton (23/2/19) @ 4/1 & the Grade 1 juvenile Hurdle at Punchestown (4/5/19) @ 13/8.**

Plus: **BEAKSTOWN (5/4 & 6/1), CHRISTOPHER WOOD (10/11, 6/5), GLITTERING LOVE (4 out of 4: 9/5, 6/5, 2/1, 11/4) (PISTOL WHIPPED (13/8), PRAECEPS (5/2, 8/11)**

Quote: *"My contact at the Dan Skelton keeps telling me **BEAKSTOWN** is a proper horse. Featured on page 132 of One Jump Ahead as one of Declan Phelan's Irish Pointers, the Stowaway gelding held an entry in Graded company at Cheltenham on Friday but he bypasses that engagement. He does, however, hold entries at Uttoxeter (12.50) and Wetherby (12.30) on Saturday, plus another at Hereford on Monday (2.45) and Chepstow on Wednesday (1.40). Runner-up in a Kempton bumper last February, I was sent a video of him schooling on Thursday morning and he worked beautifully. He is one to look forward to."* **WON @ 5/4 & 6/1 (Grade 2 Leamington NH at Warwick (12/1/19))**

Quote: *"Nicky Richards has his team in good order at present with four winners this month already. The lightly raced **GLITTERING LOVE** could prove a well handicapped six year old once stepped up to three miles for the first time under Rules. Owned by Paul and Clare Rooney, the Winged Love gelding is a half-brother to nine times winner Riptide and has shown little in five runs under Rules (yet to race beyond two and a half miles). Rated 92 over hurdles as a result, he fared much better in point-to-points for Nicky's daughter Joey Richards winning four out of five. Successful at Friars Haugh (twice), Corbridge and Overton (all over three miles) between January and March this year, he was well held in a novices' handicap hurdle at Sedgefield in April over an inadequate two and a half miles. He could be a different proposition over three miles this winter, especially if sent novice handicap chasing."* **WON 4 out of 4 – SP's of 9/5, 6/5, 2/1 & 11/4 – with his official rating rising from 92 to 125.**

TALKING TRAINERS: **KEITH DALGLEISH**: WINNERS: **ALRIGHT SUNSHINE (30/100, 8/11), BEAST OF BELSTANE (11/4), BORN FOR WAR (11/4), CHICA BUENA (4/1), GLORIOUS LADY (13/2), I'M TO BLAME (5/6, 2/5), MIXBOY (100/30), ONE NIGHT IN MILAN (100/30), SPORTING PRESS (11/1, 11/4)**.

Quote: **BORN FOR WAR**: *"Had his first run for us at Musselburgh last week finishing fourth over hurdles. I thought he looked a bit ring rusty and I am inclined to stick some headgear on him next time. Still a maiden, we might try him over fences sooner rather than later."* **WON by 13 lengths at Musselburgh (26/11/18) over fences and wearing a visor for the first time @ 11/4**

CHRISTMAS SPECIAL 2018

WINNERS: BIRCHDALE (2/1), HUMBLE HERO (5/2), LADY BUTTONS (Evens, Evens), SIR EREC (11/8, 13/8), TEDHAM (4/1)

Quote: *"McManus is also the new owner of the 109 rated Flat racer **SIR EREC**. A son of Camelot and from the family of Queens Vase winner Mahler, he only raced a handful of times on the level improving with each start. A half length winner of a ten furlongs maiden at the Curragh in late August, he then beat The King by four lengths in a Listed contest at Limerick (1m 4f : Heavy) in October. Joseph O'Brien's charge produced a career best on his most recent start when two and a half lengths third behind Stradivarius and Thomas Hobson in the Group 2 Qipco British Champions Long Distance Cup at Ascot (2m : Soft) a week later. Significantly, he holds an entry in the three year old maiden hurdle at Leopardstown on Thursday (**12.10**) in which subsequent Triumph Hurdle winner Ivanovich Gorbatov made a winning start to his jumping career. If he shows an aptitude for his vocation, he possesses the talent to be a top-class hurdler and the **20/1** (Bet365, Skybet & William Hill) for Festival glory next March is tempting."* **WON twice at Leopardstown, including the Grade 1 Spring Juvenile Hurdle (3/2/19) @ 13/8**

Quote: *"Despite the fact **TEDHAM** has failed to win any of his three races over hurdles this Autumn/Winter, the Jonjo O'Neill trained could prove a well handicapped novice off an opening mark of 125. A well bred four year old by Shirocco out of Donald McCain's dual Listed winner Alegralil, he shaped with plenty of promise in his bumper at Warwick last spring finishing third behind Umndeni. Switched to hurdling this season, he finished fourth behind Al Dancer (won twice since and now rated 141) at Carlisle and then third to The Big Bite at Chepstow. On both occasions, he impressed with the way he travelled during his races before finding two potentially top notch novices too strong late on. Runner-up behind Getaway Trump in desperate ground at Exeter last time, he had previous winners Remastered and Samarquand (rated 135) behind him. Yet to race beyond two miles one, he is bred to appreciate further."* **WON @ 4/1 at Wincanton on his handicap debut over 2m 5f (5/1/19)**

***HUNTER CHASERS*:** WINNERS: **SAUSALITO SUNRISE (11/10), SHANTOU FLYER (8/15, 10/11), UCELLO CONTI (4/6, 4/7, 7/2)**

FEBRUARY 2019

***BETFAIR HURDLE*: AL DANCER WON @ 5/2**

Quote: *"**AL DANCER** bids to become the eighth novice to win the race in the last ten years and provide Nigel Twiston-Davies with his third victory (Splash of Ginge (2014) & Ballyandy (2017) – both six year old novices). The Al Namix gelding started his career with Christian Williams before being transferred to Naunton. Successful in a bumper at Bangor last spring, he then finished a creditable fourth in the Grade 2 championship event at Aintree. The six year old is unbeaten in three starts over hurdles, including when beating subsequent winners Windsor Avenue (twice) and Tedham at Carlisle in October. A comfortable winner at Ffos Las under a penalty, he then made a mockery of an opening handicap mark of 129 at Cheltenham in December. An eleven lengths scorer from Not That Fuisse (won since), he has been raised twelve pounds but it may not be enough to halt his progress. Already towards the forefront of the ante-post market for the Sky Bet Supreme NH at Cheltenham, he ought to go very close off 141, if he is to make an impact in the Festival opener. Unbeaten with Sam Twiston-Davies on his back, he handles good and soft ground but may not want bottomless conditions."* **WON the *Betfair* Hurdle by three and three quarters of a length @ 5/2.**

WINNERS: EMITOM (6/4), L'AIR DU VENT (10/11), MISTY WHISKY (5/1)

Quote: *"Harry Fry has his eye on another Listed bumper for his potentially exciting mare **MISTY WHISKY**. The **EBF Stallions/TBA Mares' Standard Open National Hunt race at Sandown (9th March)** has been earmarked for the progressive daughter of Stowaway. A half-sister to four times winning stablemate Air Horse One and Nigel Twiston-Davies' One For Rosie, she was pitched in against the geldings on her debut at Aintree in November. In receipt of seven pounds, she was sent off 11/10 favourite in a small but select field. The steady early gallop didn't play to her strengths with the front running and more experienced Sojourn dictating matters. Denied by a length and three quarters, she stayed on well to fill the runners-up berth (fifth has won since). Reappearing less than a month later at Ludlow, Sean Bowen's mount made no mistake next time when beating List One by three lengths pulling clear in the home straight. His rider was impressed saying: **"Misty Whisky is very nice. She was very green at Aintree and I was probably there too soon today, but all she does is gallop. She'd come on massively and learned a lot from Aintree and went through that soft ground fine, but went on better ground at Aintree, so I'm sure she's fairly versatile."** Reported to be improving all the time by her trainer, her ultimate target this term is the Grade 2 mares' bumper at Aintree (4th April). It may take a good one to stop her winning at the Esher venue en route."* **WON the Listed mares' bumper at Sandown @ 5/1**

AUTUMN POINTERS: WINNERS: **CHANTRY HOUSE** (8/13), **MINELLA MELODY** (9/10), **MOUNT IDA** (13/8), **SOPAT** (4/1), **WALK AWAY** (13/8)

Quote: *"The headline mare from the autumn, in terms of price was **MINELLA MELODY** (by Flemensfirth): she arrived at Boulta in December with a tall reputation and made light work of making a winning debut: the substance of that race is questionable but her style was pleasing on the eye. She has apparently changed hands for a sum in the region on £300,000 (private deal) and will be in the future care of **Henry De Bromhead**."* **WON by 12 lengths at Gowran Park (9/3/19) on her Rules debut @ 9/10.**

Quote: *"Out of the geldings, I will pick one six year old: **WALK AWAY**, a relentless galloper, he survived a final fence scare to win on his debut at Ballindenisk: another bought by **Henry De Bromhead**, this big unit by Black Sam Bellamy will be a fine 130+ staying handicap chaser."* **WON by 9 lengths at Thurles (7/3/19) on his hurdling debut @ 13/8.**

CHELTENHAM FESTIVAL HANDICAPS PREVIEW: SIRE DU BERLAIS (Advised @ 10/1 – WON the Pertemps Final @ 4/1), DALLAS DES PICTONS (WON @ 7/2 at Leopardstown, plus advised @ 16/1 for the Martin Pipe Conditional Jockeys' HH at Cheltenham finished 2nd @ 7/2 favourite.

Quote: *"J.P.McManus has won the **Pertemps Final** (Thursday 14th March) twice this century (Creon (2004) & Kadoun (2006)) and the legendary owner is responsible for both **SIRE DU BERLAIS** and **THE ORGANIST**. The former is trained by Gordon Elliott and has only raced nine times over hurdles and is unexposed over three miles. Beaten seven and a half lengths in fourth in the Martin Pipe Conditional Jockeys' Hurdle at the Festival last March, the seven year old is now rated two pounds lower off a mark of 142. The Poliglote gelding has only raced twice this season finishing eighth in a two and a half miles handicap hurdle at Naas in November. Stepped up to three miles for the first time in a Pertemps qualifier at Leopardstown's Christmas fixture, Davy Russell's mount kept on in the closing stages to finish sixth and was only around ten lengths behind the winner Cuneo. From the family of Howard Johnson's Becher Chase runner-up and Grade 2 winning novice hurdler Royal Rosa, the ex-French gelding handles most types of ground and is guaranteed a place in the line-up with his rating. Elliott won the race last season with Delta Work and this has probably been the plan all season **(10/1 generally)**."* **SIRE DU BERLAIS (Advised @ 10/1) WON the Pertemps Final at the Cheltenham Festival @ 4/1**

The CHELTENHAM FESTIVAL 2019

5 WINNERS: A PLUS TARD (Advised @ 8/1), TOPOFTHEGAME (4/1). ENVOI ALLEN (Advised @ 4/1), SIRE DU BERLAIS (Advised @ 6/1), SIRUH DU LAC (9/2)

Plus: COKO BEACH (Advised @ 25/1 – 2nd @ 14/1), ANIBALE FLY (Advised @ 25/1 – 2nd @ 22/1)

Quote: *"A PLUS TARD (featured on page 128 of OJA) had alternative entries at the Festival in the RSA and JLT Novice Chases suggesting he may be fairly treated here off 144. Twice a winner over hurdles in France, including a Listed contest at Auteuil, when trained by Dominique Bressou, he was subsequently bought by Cheveley Park Stud and has run three good races over fences for Henry De Bromhead. Runner-up at Gowran in October, he then beat subsequent 15 lengths winner Duc De Genievres (runs in the Arkle) by three and a quarter lengths at Naas in December. Beaten around two lengths by Winter Escape (fifth in a Grade 1 next time) in Graded company at Punchestown last time in receipt of a stone, he is lightly raced and is a superb jumper. Chapoturgeon won this as a five year old and there have been two Irish trained winners (Finger Onthe Pulse (2008) & Tully East (2017))."* **WON the Close Brothers Novices' Handicap Chase by 16 lengths @ 5/1 (Advised @ 8/1)**

Quote: *"TOPOFTHEGAME (Top 40) won a point-to-point for Donnchadh Doyle before being bought for £120,000. A dual winning hurdler who was rated 154, he won a Grade 3 handicap at Sandown before finishing a neck second in the Coral Cup twelve months ago. Returning to chasing (fell at Newbury on his fencing bow last season) this time around, he was runner-up behind Defi Du Seuil at Exeter (2m 3f) having forfeited over twenty lengths at the start. The giant seven year old then looked certain to win the Grade 1 Kauto Star NC at Kempton when jumping to the front at the third last, only to get run out of it after the final fence by the high-class mare La Bague Au Roi (won another Grade 1 since). Paul Nicholls has purposely kept him fresh since and the Flemensfirth gelding is reportedly in tip-top shape. The former champion trainer has won this twice (Star De Mohaison (2006) & Denman (2007))."* **WON the RSA Chase @ 4/1**

Quote: *"ENVOI ALLEN (Top 40) was purchased for £400,000 in February last year having won his only point by ten lengths for Colin Bowe. Unbeaten in three races under Rules for Cheveley Park Stud and Gordon Elliott, he won at Fairyhouse and Navan (Listed) in the space of a fortnight in December before returning at Leopardstown last month. Taken wide by Jamie Codd, the Muhtathir gelding stayed on strongly to beat a host of promising types by upwards of a length and a quarter from Meticulous in the Grade 2 event. He sets the standard but this will be his stiffest test to date."* **WON the Grade 1 Festival bumper @ 2/1 (Advised @ 4/1)**

Quote: *"SIRE DU BERLAIS is another leading fancy from the Elliott yard. Seven and a half lengths fourth in the Martin Pipe Conditional Jockey HH last year off 144, he is only a pound higher now and qualifies for this having finished sixth at Leopardstown last time. It was the first time he had tackled three miles and was staying on under Davy Russell. The Poliglote gelding has only raced twice this term and this has obviously been the plan all year. From the family of Becher Chase runner-up Royal Rosa, he is unexposed over the trip and is very much shortlist material."* **WON the Pertemps Final @ 4/1 (Advised @ 6/1)**

Quote: *"SIRUH DU LAC has been in terrific form this season winning all three of his starts. The progressive six year old has scored at Newbury, Exeter and Cheltenham off marks of 123, 129 and 134. A head winner from the aforementioned Janika at the last named venue, he has been raised a further seven pounds since. Nick Williams' charge handles most types of ground and has won five of his seven races over fences. A tremendous jumper, he looks capable of defying that rise in the weights."* **WON the Brown Advisory & Merriebelle Stable Plate Handicap Chase @ 9/2**

Quote: "**COKO BEACH** is one of five entries Gordon Elliott (Flaxen Flare (2013) & Veneer of Charm (2018)) has left in at the five day stage. A four and a half lengths winner at Nantes (Very soft) when trained by Francois Nicolle, he was bought soon afterwards and plunged straight into Grade 2 company at Leopardstown over Christmas. Sent off 6/1 and backed on the day, he was beaten twenty one lengths in ninth on much quicker ground. Last time, he performed a lot better (again on good ground) in a slowly run juvenile hurdle at Naas last month. Beaten eight lengths by the aforementioned Band of Outlaws, he is now five pounds better off with the ex-Flat racer and a combination of a stiffer track and more testing conditions ought to see the pair finish closer here. I think he is an interesting outsider who could be a different proposition on slower ground." **Advised @ 25/1 – 2ⁿᵈ in the Boodles Juvenile Handicap Hurdle @ 14/1**

Quote: "**ANIBALE FLY** was a running on third in the race last year, eight and a half lengths behind Native River. Tony Martin's stable star has only raced twice this term – withdrawn twice at Leopardstown due to drying ground. Beaten nearly twenty five lengths in the Grade 2 Hilly Way Chase at Cork (2m) in December, he was a good second behind Monalee in the Grade 2 Red Mills Chase at Gowran Park last month. Keeping on in the closing stages, he was fourth in the Grand National last season and will relish the return to this longer trip. His record at Grade 1 level is 32P2F3. The softer the ground the better, he arrives fresh and has definite each-way claims, granted suitable conditions." **Advised @ 25/1 – 2ⁿᵈ in the Cheltenham Gold Cup @ 22/1**

FESTIVAL PREVIEW ROUND-UPS:
ANTHONY BROMLEY: Quote: **PENTLAND HILLS** (Triumph Hurdle): *"An inexpensive buy out of Chris Wall's yard, he won twice on the Flat. He then had ringworm when he first joined Nicky (Henderson). It was therefore a rushed preparation prior to winning very easily at Plumpton on his hurdles debut last month. He beat a useful horse and is an interesting contender for the Triumph Hurdle."* **WON the Triumph Hurdle @ 20/1**

TALKING TRAINERS: **PAUL NICHOLLS: WINNERS: FRODON (9/2), TOPOFTHEGAME (4/1)**

Quote: **FRODON:** *"He has had an amazing season winning three out of four, including the Cotswold Chase at Cheltenham last time over a trip which was only eight yards short of the Gold Cup distance, according to Simon Claisse. He is in seriously good order at home, too, and he looks great. Entered in both the Ryanair and Gold Cup, it will be a last minute call but I suspect he will end up running in the former."* **WON the Ryanair Chase @ 9/2**

Quote: **TOPOFTHEGAME:** *"A huge horse who has been a big baby but has a big engine. He won a Graded handicap hurdle at Sandown last season before being narrowly beaten in the Coral Cup at Cheltenham. Unlucky on his reappearance over fences at Exeter, he missed the start and must have forfeited over twenty five lengths. He just spooked at something but still ran a lovely race behind Defi Du Seuil. Then, last time in the Kauto Star Novices' Chase at Kempton, he hit the front too soon and was run out of it late on. Harry (Cobden) learned his lesson because he held on to Clan Des Obeaux a bit longer and won the King George later the same day. I think he will develop into a Gold Cup contender next season. The plan is to run him in the RSA Chase."* **WON the RSA Chase @ 4/1**

TALKING TRAINERS: **GORDON ELLIOTT: WINNERS: ENVOI ALLEN (2/1), SIRE DU BERLAIS (4/1), TIGER ROLL (5/4)**

Quote: **ENVOI ALLEN:** *"He is a three mile chaser in the making and has looked good in all three of his bumpers this season. His preparation has gone well and I couldn't be happier with him."* **WON the Grade 1 Festival bumper @ 2/1**

Quote: **SIRE DU BERLAIS:** *"He worked very well on Friday morning. Fourth in the Martin Pipe HH last year, the longer trip here will suit him."* **WON the Pertemps Final @ 4/1**

Quote: **TIGER ROLL**: *"Keith Donoghue rides him in the Cross Country chase on Wednesday. He worked well on Tuesday morning and has had a brilliant preparation."* **WON the Cross Country chase by 22 lengths @ 5/4**

DATES FOR THE DIARY:
Quote: *"This is one for Flat racing fans. I interviewed Karl Burke last month (he was en route to watch Liverpool play Bayern Munich at Anfield) and he is very keen on an unraced filly called* **ROBOTIQUE DANSEUR**. *By the same sire as stable star Laurens, namely Siyouni, she is entered in the French 1000 Guineas and the Middleham trainer believes she is very good."* **WON at Newcastle (29/3/19) @ 9/2**

Saturday 23rd March – NEWBURY – 5.00 Goffs UK Spring Sale Bumper
"Harry Fry has won the last two renewals of this £50,000 event courtesy of Bullionaire and Caribert and Paul Nicholls' former assistant can land the hat-trick. **GET IN THE QUEUE** *looks well bought at £40,000 as a three year old having won both his starts. A gelding by Mount Nelson, he won at Uttoxeter in December by nine lengths in the same event the ill-fated stablemate Neon Wolf won two years earlier. The five year old then bolted up under a penalty at Exeter last month by sixteen lengths conceding sixteen pounds to the runner-up. Held in the highest regard, he runs here in preference to the Festival bumper."* **WON by four and a half lengths @ 1/3.**

The AINTREE GRAND MEETING 2019

WINNERS: FELIX DESJY (Advised @ 8/1), MIN (Advised @ 5/1)

Quote: *"**FELIX DESJY** was a useful bumper horse finishing sixth in the championship event at the Cheltenham Festival last season having raced too keenly. The six year old has been in and out over hurdles this campaign winning impressively at Galway on his reappearance in October. Below par on his next three outings, Gordon Elliott's gelding was back to form in January when winning the Grade 2 Sky Bet Moscow Flyer NH at Punchestown (Good) by five lengths. Given a break, he was a creditable fifth in the Supreme NH at Cheltenham last month, holding every chance turning for home. Beaten eleven lengths, he looks a better horse on a flatter track and Aintree ought to suit him."* **Advised @ 8/1 WON the Grade 1 Top Novices' Hurdle @ 7/2**

Quote: *"**MIN** was beaten a neck by Poltilogue in the race last year having raced keenly early on. The eight year old had looked better than ever during the first half of this season winning the Grade 1 John Durkan Chase at Punchestown in December by a length and a half before winning another Grade 1 over two miles at Leopardstown (for the second consecutive year) in February by six lengths. However, Willie Mullins' Walk In The Park gelding produced a lacklustre performance in the Queen Mother Champion Chase at Cheltenham finishing a well beaten fifth behind Altior. His record over 2m 4f is 121 and he is a triple Grade 1 winner. Ireland's champion trainer won this with Boston Bob five years ago and he has a major contender again. Ruby Walsh (11211115) is expected to take the ride."* **Advised @ 5/1 WON the Grade 1 Melling Chase by 20 lengths @ 2/1**

It is £6 per Update (except £10 for the Cheltenham Festival version) or £34 for ALL 5 via EMAIL.

ONE JUMP AHEAD UPDATES 2019/2020 ORDER FORM (EMAIL ONLY)

AVAILABLE AT £6.00 EACH (£10 Cheltenham) OR £34 FOR ALL 5

- **CHELTENHAM PADDY POWER MEETING 2019**
  (Will be emailed on Thursday 14th November 2019)

- **CHRISTMAS SPECIAL 2019**
  (Will be emailed on Friday 20th December 2019)

- **FEBRUARY 2020**

- **MARCH 2020 - CHELTENHAM FESTIVAL PREVIEW**
  (Will be emailed on the Sunday before the Festival)

- **APRIL 2020 – AINTREE PREVIEW**
  (Will be emailed on the Tuesday before the Meeting)

Total Cheque / Postal Order value £............. made payable to MARK HOWARD PUBLICATIONS Ltd. Post your order to: MARK HOWARD PUBLICATIONS. 69 FAIRGARTH DRIVE, KIRKBY LONSDALE, CARNFORTH, LANCASHIRE. LA6 2FB.

NAME: ....

ADDRESS: ....

....

.... POST CODE: ....

Email Address: ....

If you have not received your *UPDATE* via email 24 hours before the meeting starts, please contact us immediately.

Available to order via **www.mhpublications.co.uk**

AHEAD ON THE FLAT 2020

The 20th edition of *Ahead On The Flat* will be published in early April for the 2020 Flat season. It will be formulated along the same lines as previous years with a Top 40 Prospects (the 2019 edition included **DEJA (5/1)**, **JUBILOSO, SPANISH ARCHER (10/1), UAE JEWEL)**, *Ballydoyle Juveniles* (**ARIZONA, ARMORY, PISTOLETTO** included in 2019**)**, *Handicap Snips* (**SEA BATTLE (12/1)**, *Maidens In Waiting* (**DURSTON, MAQSAD, TEMPUS)**)**, *Significant* Sales, *Unraced Three Year Olds* (**DESERT ICON, FIRST IN LINE, LOGICIAN**) & *What's The Craic In Ireland* (**BARBADOS, MICRO MANAGE, NEWCROSS**). In addition, there will be the usual stable interviews with some of the top trainers in Great Britain (this year's included **Andrew Balding, Ralph Beckett, Karl Burke, Roger Charlton, William Haggas, Roger Varian, Ed Walker & Ian Williams**). *Ahead On The Flat* will contain 152 pages and the price is £10.99.

I shall also be producing three ***Ahead On The Flat Updates*** (EMAIL ONLY). There will be a **Royal Ascot Preview** (6 winners in 2019 including **CAPE BYRON (Advised @ 14/1)**, **CLEONTE (7/2)** and **CRYSTAL OCEAN (4/1)**), a **York Ebor Preview** (8 winners in 2019 including **HAMISH (Advised @ 16/1) & QUE AMORO (9/1))** and an **Autumn** *Update*. The Royal Ascot version is £10 with the other two £6 or £19 for the ALL THREE.

ORDER FORM

* **AHEAD ON THE FLAT 2020 (Book ONLY)** — £10.99

AHEAD ON THE FLAT UPDATES 2020 (can be ordered individually at £6.00 EACH (£10 ROYAL ASCOT) or ALL 3 updates for £19.00):

• **ROYAL ASCOT PREVIEW 2020**	£10.00
• **YORK EBOR MEETING PREVIEW 2020**	£6.00
• **AUTUMN PREVIEW 2020**	£6.00
• **ALL 3 UPDATES (EMAIL ONLY)**	£19.00
• **AHEAD ON THE FLAT + 3 UPDATES**	£28.99

Total Cheque / Postal Order value £............ Made payable to **MARK HOWARD PUBLICATIONS Ltd**. Please send to: **MARK HOWARD PUBLICATIONS Ltd. 69 FAIRGARTH DRIVE, KIRKBY LONSDALE, CARNFORTH, LANCASHIRE. LA6 2FB.**

NAME: ....

ADDRESS: ....

....

.... POST CODE: ....

Email Address: ....

Value Racing Club

"Winning Together"

Our aim at Value Racing Club is to introduce new people into the world of horse racing. We provide a cost effective and simple way of becoming a racehorse owner. There are never any hidden extras such as vet bills. Once the initial purchase has been paid, no further monies are required during the entire racing season.

What we offer and benefits:

- An opportunity to become involved in racehorse ownership.
- What we pay for a horse is what you pay, no added fees of any kind.
- A one-off cost covers the entire racing season.
- Stable visits arranged to watch your horse work on the gallops.
- Free owners badge every time your horse runs.
- Each syndicate keeps 100% of all prize money won.
- 62% overall strike rate of our runners finishing in the first three places.
- Horses in training with Dr Richard Newland, David Pipe, Mick Appleby, Alastair Ralph, Jamie Snowden & Philip Kirby.
- Racing TV pundit Mark Howard is our Club Ambassador.
- We are members of the ROA "Racehorse Owners Association" & RSA "Racehorse Syndicates Association" to ensure good practice.

Big race wins include the £70,000 Imperial Cup, £30,000 Betfred Summer Hurdle, £30,000 Durham National. Big Race placed efforts, 3rd in the £300,000 Galway Hurdle, 2nd in the Eider Chase.

Over £490,000 of prize money won for owners in the last 4 years.

Website: www.valueracingclub.co.uk email: contact@valueracingclub.co.uk Twitter: @valueracingclub